Life and Death in the Korean Bronze Age (*c*. 1500–400 BC)

An analysis of settlements and monuments in the mid-Korean peninsula

Sunwoo Kim

BAR International Series 2700
2015

Published in 2016 by
BAR Publishing, Oxford

BAR International Series 2700

Life and Death in the Korean Bronze Age (c. 1500–400 BC)

ISBN 978 1 4073 1351 1

BAR Publishing is the trading name of British Archaeological Reports (Oxford) Ltd. British Archaeological Reports was first incorporated in 1974 to publish the BAR Series, International and British. In 1992 Hadrian Books Ltd became part of the BAR group. This volume was originally published by Archaeopress in conjunction with British Archaeological Reports (Oxford) Ltd / Hadrian Books Ltd, the Series principal publisher, in 2015. This present volume is published by BAR Publishing, 2016.

Printed in England

BAR
PUBLISHING

BAR titles are available from:

BAR Publishing
122 Banbury Rd, Oxford, OX2 7BP, UK
EMAIL info@barpublishing.com
PHONE +44 (0)1865 310431
FAX +44 (0)1865 316916
www.barpublishing.com

Contents

List of Figures and Tables

Abstract

This research focuses on the Bronze Age in selected areas of Korea; Seoul, Incheon, and Gyeonggi province. Two forms of evidence - settlements and monuments - are taken into account to identify their relationship with landscape and the social changes occurring between ca. 1500 to 400 *cal* BC. Life and death in the Bronze Age in Korea has not been synthetically investigated before, due to the lack of evidence from settlements. However, since academic and rescue excavations have increased, it is now possible to examine the relationship between settlements and monuments on a broad scale and over a long-term sequence, although there are still limitations in the archaeological evidence. The results of GIS (Geographical Information System) analysis and Bayesian modelling of the radiocarbon dates from this region can be interpreted as suggesting that Bronze Age people in the mid-Korean peninsula had certain preferences for their habitation and mortuary places. The locations of two archaeological sites were identified and statistical significance was generated for their positioning on soil that was associated with agriculture. It was found that settlements tended to be located at a higher elevation with fine views and that monuments tended to be situated in the border zones between mountains and plains and also within the boundary of a 5km site catchment adjusted for energy expenditure, centring on each settlement. This configuration is reminiscent of the concept of the auspicious location, as set out in the traditional geomantic theory of *Pungsu*. It can be argued that Bronze Age people chose the place for the living and the dead with a holistic perspective and a metaphysical approach that placed human interaction with the natural world at the centre of their decision-making processes. These concepts were formed out of the process of a practical adaptation to the Bronze Age landscape and environment in order to practice agriculture as a subsistence economy, but they also exerted a profound influence upon later Korean peoples and their identities.

Acknowledgements

This research would not have been possible to complete without my two supervisors Prof. Chris Gosden and Dr. Rick Schulting in the Institute of Archaeology at the University of Oxford, who had the patience to instruct and guide me, as I am a foreign student and English is my second language. I will never forget the obligation that I owe to them both. Also, due to the fact that Prof Gary Lock introduced me to Mr. John Pouncett, it has been possible to use GIS in my study: a programme that has underpinned my research. Therefore many thanks to them and I have much appreciated their instruction. I have appreciated too the help given to me by Prof Nick Barton and Dr. Amy Bogaard, who both provided me with very useful comments and encouragement during my transfer and confirmation status meetings. Also, I would like to send my deep gratitude to Dr. Amy Bogaard and Dr. Simon Kaner. They were my examiners and gave their valuable advices to me. In addition, I have appreciated Prof. Christopher Ramsey and Dr. Janet DeLaine's kind consideration when I had to suspend my studies because of a family situation and at the same time, I would like to give my deep thanks to Ms. Lidia Lozano. Thanks to her consideration, I could continue with my studies in the familiar attic of the Institute of Archaeology both before and after my enforced break.

I also would like to say many thanks to the academic and supporting staff in the Institute of Archaeology: Prof. Helena Hamerow, Prof. Andrew Wilson, Dr. Lisa Bendall, Dr. Zena Kamash, Dr. Dan Hicks, Mrs. Liz Strange, Mr. Jeremy Worth, Mrs. Judy East, Mrs. Alison Wilkins, Mrs. Lynda Smithson, Mrs. Barbara Morris, Mrs. Lucy Palmer, Mrs. Carol Neville, Mr. Ian Cartwright, Mr. Steve Hicks and Mrs. Irene Curran. Thanks to their hospitality, I have felt that the Institute has become like a second home. In addition, I would like to send my gratitude to all the academic and supporting staff in the Research Laboratory for Archaeology and the History of Art (RALHA). Many thanks to: Prof. Mark Pollard, Prof. Christopher Ramsey, Mrs. Diane Baker, Mr. Chris Doherty, Dr. Peter Ditchfield, Prof. Tom Higham, Dr. Jean-Luc Schwenninger, Dr. Michael Dee, Dr. Brian Gilmore, Dr. Christine Lane, Prof Michael Petraglia, Dr. Nicole Boivin, Dr. Fiona Brock, Dr. Linda Reynard, Dr Victoria Smith, Dr Rebbeca Fraser, Ms. Julie Hamilton, Dr. Ceiridwen Edwards, Dr. Daniel Miles, Dr. Oliver Pryce, and Miss Hayley Sula due to the fact that they allowed me to sit in on their precious lectures. They have opened my eyes to the scientific archaeology.

In addition, if Wolfson College had not provided accommodation, I could not have completed my research satisfactorily. I have deeply appreciated the kindness of all the staff at the college, especially Ms. Rose Truby. Many thanks to: Prof. Hermione Lee, Dr. Martin Francis, Prof Andrew Neil, Mrs. Caroline Davidson, Mrs. Rina Carvalho, Ms. Rachael Connelly, Ms. Alice Bevan, Ms. Anja Jeczalik, Ms. Margit Kail, Ms. Heather Waring, Ms. Louise Calder, Mr. Barry Coote, Ms. Fiona Wilkes, Ms. Janice Tirda, Mr. John Kirby, Mr. Jerry Ashman, Mr. Karl Davies, Mr. Chris Kitchen, and Late Mr. Barry Long.

It would have been impossible to continue with my studies, without Emeritus Prof. Mong-lyong Choi (Seoul National University)'s guidance and support. Thanks to him, I was able to meet many eminent scholars and was able to receive their academic advices. I would especially like to thank: Prof. Young-moon Lee (Mokpo National University), Prof. Moon-sik Ha (Sejong University), Prof. Jong-chan Kim (Seoul National University National centre for inter-university facilities), Prof. Jong-oh Baek (Korea National University of Transportation), Prof. Dong-hoon Shin, Prof. Soong-deok Lee (Seoul National University College of Medicine), Dr. Hyeong-woo Hong (National Research Institute of Cultural Heritage), Prof. Gyong-taek Kim (Korea National University of Cultural Heritage), Dr. Heon-jae Lee (Gyeonggi Provincial Museum), Dr. Jong-yoon Woo, Dr. So-Young Lee and Mr. Wook-jin Oh (Chungbook National University Museum), Dr. Yeon-woo Jeong, Dr. Jae-yeon Shim (Yeamaek Institute of Cultural Properties), Dr. Jong-mo choi, Dr. Kwon-joong Kim (Gangwon Research Institute of Cultural Properties), Dr. Kyong-sug, Shin (Research Centre of Dolmens in Northeast Asia), Dr. Sung-soo Bae (Incheon Metropolitan City Museum).

In addition, many thanks to Mr Kyoung-Soo Kim, Mr. Seung-Yul Hong, Mr. Jeong-Taek Kim, Mr. Yeong-seo Gwak (The Ministry of Land, Transport and Maritime Affairs, National Land Information Survey Division), Mr. Yi-hyeon Kim (The National Academy of Agricultural Science), Dr. Si-eun Yang (Seoul National University Museum), Prof. Bo-hee Kim, Ms. In-ho Kim, Ms. Jeong-hee Choi, Ms. I-sook Hwang (Ewha Womans University Museum), I could utilise key data. Also, many thanks to Emeritus Prof. Sook-kyoung Choi, Prof. Bae-yong Lee, Prof. Hyeong-sik Shin, and Prof. Yong-mi Kim (Ewha Womans University), Mr. Tim Williams (UCL, University of London), Prof. Roderick Whitfield and Prof. Young-sook Pak (SOAS, University of London), I was able to continue my studies and I have deeply appreciated their supports.

I also have deeply appreciated the offers of and permissions to use photographic materials obtained from The Korea Institute of Heritage, Korea University Museum, The Korean Cristian Museum at Soongsil University, The Research Centre of Dolmens in Northeast Asia, and for the photographic materials sourced from Gyeonggi Institute of Cultural Properties, Konkuk University Museum, The National Museum of Korea, Seoul National University Museum, Prof. C.J.

Choe and Seohae munjip and a drawing from Shinwonbook. The cooperation of these institutions and individuals is most appreciated.

In addition, I would like to send my deep gratitude and love to my friends and family. Especially, Miss Lucy Haines, thanks to her encouragement and proofreading, I can fulfill my work and I will never forget her friendship. Also, many thanks to Mr. William Boot and Ms. Jinyang Kim's supports, I have been overcome my difficult situation and gratefully Ms. Liz Donovan and Dr. Dorothea Martens have encouraged me. Lastly, if there were not Mr. Geuk-yeon Won and Mr. Jo Gook-jae's assists and my family's support, I would not have been able to complete my research.

Finally, I have gratefully appreciated that Mr. Gerald Edward Brisch, Dr. David Davison, Dr. Rajka Makjanic and Mr. Ben Heaney at Archaeopress Limited have allowed me to publish my PhD thesis.

Chapter 1. Aims and research questions

1.1 Introduction

The most significant discussions about the Korean Bronze Age concern how one interprets the monuments of that period and goes about reconstructing Bronze Age society. As Trigger (1990: 29) indicates, monumental architecture is a characteristic shared between all complex societies of the world. Although there are dissimilarities between Europe and the Korean peninsula, such as the different periods of the monument's creation and the variety in monument styles, it is thought that the archaeological theories and methodologies that have been developed in Europe in order to study megalithic monuments could be useful tools to further the understanding of megalithic monuments in the Korean peninsula. In particular, landscape archaeology is relatively new to Korean archaeology, but would appear to be a potentially illuminating approach that would add to our knowledge of the Bronze Age. For these reasons, it is meaningful to study the theory and methodology behind landscape archaeology and then to apply them to the exploration of megalithic monuments in Korea.

Megalithic monuments were influenced by the people who built and interacted with them and the landscape in which they were erected. One type of megalithic monument in the Korean peninsula is the dolmen, which is similar to the shape of portal tombs/dolmens of Western Europe. Although it has been difficult to calculate the accurate dates of dolmens because of the paucity of associated artefacts, it is thought that dolmens were constructed in Korea from around the 15th century BC to the 4th century BC. However their chronology differs from region to region. In addition, it is thought that dolmens appeared at a time when society had become complex through a change in the economic system with an accumulation of surplus products.

On the topic of monuments in Western Europe, there exist several different theoretical approaches and interpretations. For example, regarding megalithic monuments, cultural historians have researched the ethnic identity of their builders, and the consequent diffusion of megalithic cultures (Childe 1957). Processual approaches have been more concerned about the social function and meaning of these archaeological monuments. According to Renfrew (1976), the function of megalithic monuments was as territorial markers. Similarly, Chapman (1981) emphasized that the locations of megalithic monuments were seemingly related to the critical resources in the societies that created them. In the case of Ireland, Cooney (1983) stressed that tombs were constructed on the sites of prior occupation or near settlement areas, on the basis of a series of excavations in the first case, and survey work in the second. He argued that megalithic tombs would have been constructed on the fertile land in Leitrim.

On the other hand, Hodder (1984) applying the post-processual perspective which focuses more upon cultural subjectivity and historical context rather than cultural objectivity and ecology (Trigger 1990: 119; Hodder and Hutson 2003: 4), suggested that long-barrows in western Europe represent modifications to the designs of houses in central Europe in the 5th and 4th millennia. Although he acknowledged processual archaeological interpretations for monuments as territorial markers and the importance of their relationship to critical resources, he also noted that the control of resources and the competition for them varies across different societies. In Atlantic Europe, burial and ritual practices seemed to be linked to the control of productive and reproductive resources through the participation of the lineage and communal efforts. In addition, Bradley (Barrett et al. 1991a; 1991b) pursued studies to understand the long term processes of the shift from the Neolithic to the Middle Bronze Age in Cranborne Chase through landscape perspectives. Darvill (2004) also examined long barrows in the Cotswolds and adjacent areas from the historical perspective of long-term tradition and suggested that the regional cluster of long barrows in the British Isles seemed to express a geographical grouping rather than provide evidence for cultural boundaries. Lastly, Tilley (1994) explored the landscape of three different places, applying a phenomenological approach, and concluded that firstly, monuments in southwest Wales were constructed near to land markers, for example exposed rock; secondly, that the major axis of the chambered cairn in the Black mountains pointed to spurs or routes to the Usk and Wye valleys and finally, that the long barrows at Cranborne Chase seemed to be orientated relative to the positions of earlier barrows. Tilley's phenomenological approach presented new directions for landscape archaeology, but Fleming (1999a; 2005; 2006) pointed out some flaws in the methodology: firstly, the sample size is rather small; secondly, viewpoints can be subjective and it is difficult to evaluate them and lastly, that Tilley failed to consider alternative references such as social contexts or celestial bodies.

1.2 Aims

Although there exist some weaknesses in the practice of landscape archaeology as it is often practiced, as Gosden and Lock (1998: 5) have highlighted in their research: 'the features of the landscape were not just physical things, but the manifestation of social relationships', it is still thought that it is a useful tool by which to explore and reveal the long term processes of prehistory, through the analysis of human traces left in the landscape. In addition, as indicated by Gosden (1994: 79), the research of landscape or place is concentrated upon 'the nature of local experience' and as Tilley (1994: 10-11) pointed out, the particular surroundings of a place plays an important role in understanding its meaning. Together with these aspects, as Whittle (2003: 48-49) and Schulting (2004: 22) have advocated, we have to bear in mind how daily lives were lived in prehistoric society and not concentrate exclusively on the monuments, even though they were enormously important to their associated groups. On the basis of these stances and through applying it to this research topic, this research will examine how the Bronze Age people in the central part of the Korean peninsula chose their placement of the living and the dead and what elements affected their decision-making. In addition, the study will explore what features of long-term changes can be traced in the study area and how we might understand and interpret the results of past actions and interactions between the environmental and the cultural elements that existed within it. The research will argue that a holistic understanding and exploitation of physical landscapes and environmental features in order to adapt seemed to play an important role in Korean Bronze age society. This study will focus both on the effects of environmental elements and cultural factors in determining the location of settlements and monuments. It will also consider how the change to the subsistence economy, especially in the development of agriculture, affected Bronze Age people's planning for their shelters and burials through a process of negotiation between the landscape and the society that inhabited that land. Consequently, this study will show how environmental elements and cultural perspectives were intertwined. Taken together, the social changes of the Bronze Age in the Korean peninsula can be identified through the analyses of long-term changes of settlements and monuments. Based on these data, cultural and group identities can be seen to have emerged through a process of adaptation to and negotiation with their landscape and environments.

1.3 Research questions

Dolmens have been studied for over 100 years and more than six hundred research papers have been published in Korea (refer to Chapter 2. Background information). It is not surprising that they are one of the most significant archaeological aspects of the Korean Bronze Age. A review of the published literature seems to confirm that the role of associated settlements is almost always ignored in the analysis, due to the fact that prior to 1990 in Korea, archaeological sites tended to be excavated on a small scale and not in the full context of the landscape in which they were located. However post 1990 and with a change in the planning laws, like PPG16 in the United Kingdom, it became possible to examine data from excavations that had a broader scope. It has been proposed that there are many possibilities to reconstruct Bronze Age society tentatively through an examination of the relationship between settlements and monuments. Therefore this research will aim to examine the proposition that settlement and monument patterns, analysed using GIS (Geographical Information System) methodology, can be found to be representative of a certain way of thinking apparent in Bronze Age society in the Korean peninsula.

In order to look at Bronze Age people's decision-making processes and their associated social changes through the analysis of their traces in the landscape, the following questions will be raised:

Firstly, what environmental elements affected how settlements and monuments were positioned in the landscape? For example, how near the most fertile soils for rice and dry-field agriculture was the settlements and monuments? How did their positions change through time? What were the relationships between settlements or monuments and water? What were the topographical variables, such as aspect, slope and elevation, which determined the locations of settlements and monuments?

Secondly, which cultural elements affected how settlements and monuments were positioned in the landscape? For instance, which kinds of landform, such as, ridge, inclined plane, and peak, were preferred for settlements and monuments? What was the quality of visibility from them? How did movement affect the location of sites? What were the orientations of houses and dolmens?

Thirdly, how did Bronze Age people perceive and structure their landscape? What were the environmental and cultural motives behind their decisions to select specific locations for the living and the dead? How did site locations change through the Bronze Age, in terms of the Early, Middle, and Late Bronze Age periods? What were the main characteristics of each period? And on that basis, what features of their worldview can we extrapolate from the collected data? Together with these questions, can we identify social change in landscape preference from the end of the Neolithic period to the beginning of the Iron Age in the study area, through analyses of the Bronze Age landscape? What is the import of the Bronze Age in the broader scope of Korean history? To what extent do the results presented in this research support and/or contradict traditional interpretations of Korean Bronze Age archaeology? And what are the new findings and new perspectives expounded in this research?

In order to address these questions, GIS (Geographical Information System) has been used for spatial analysis and Bayesian modelling for chronological analysis; this is due to the fact that GIS does not manage time properly, although there have been attempts to visualize spatial sequences of alteration throughout time (Lock and Daly 1999). A brief outline of the book follows: Bayesian modelling will be discussed in Chapter 3, after background information has been introduced in Chapter 2. GIS methodology will be presented in Chapter 4 and also looks at environmental element analyses and Chapter 5 deals with cultural feature analyses. The discussion will be presented in Chapter 6 and Chapter 7 concludes this research.

Chapter 2. Background information

2.1 Location and geographical description of Korea

Geography

Location

The peninsula of Korea is located at the end of Asia between China and the islands of Japan. The Korean peninsula is bordered by Manchuria and Siberia on the north side, by the East Sea (Sea of Japan) to the east, by the narrow Korean Strait to the south, and by the Yellow Sea to the west (Oh 1958: 35). The Korean peninsula is about 1,000 km long and approximately 300 km wide. The peninsula and its islands are situated between 33°06′40"N and 43°00′39"N (Latitude) and 124°11′00"E and 131°52′42"E (Longitude). Korea is similar to Greece latitudinally and corresponds to the size of state of California (The Korean Overseas Information Service 2003: 8) (henceforth, KOIS) (Figure 2.1)

Territory

The total area of Korea is 222,154 square kilometres. The combined areas of North and South Korea correspond to the size of Guyana (215,000 sq. km) and the United Kingdom (244,100 sq. km). The territory of South Korea covers 99,313 square kilometres, excluding the Demilitarized Zone (DMZ). The size of South Korea by itself is similar to that of Hungary (93,000 sq. km) and Jordan (97,700 sq. km) (KOIS 2003: 9).

Geology

According to Bartz (1972), the base rock of South Korea is the *Granite-Gneiss system*, which is part of the Archaeozoic era, which has been dated to more than 900 million years old. This rock occupies one-third of the country, in particular, in the north and the western parts. This pre-Cambrian bedrock has maintained a stable condition. After the Archaeozoic era, during the late Mesozoic era, faults have developed. For example, 'Young' granite intruded. This granite is differentiated from the Archaeozoic granite, having a more pinkish colour and weathering more rapidly than the old greyish granite. The main mountains of the country, such as the Taebaek, the Sobaek, the Charyong, the Noryong, and the Jiri ranges, are principally made up of this 'young' granite (Bartz 1972: 9-10, Figure 2.2). Due to the fact that most of the bedrock is granite, the soils are acid with the average of 6.0 pH or less (Bartz 1972: 23). That is why bones have been rarely preserved and excavated.

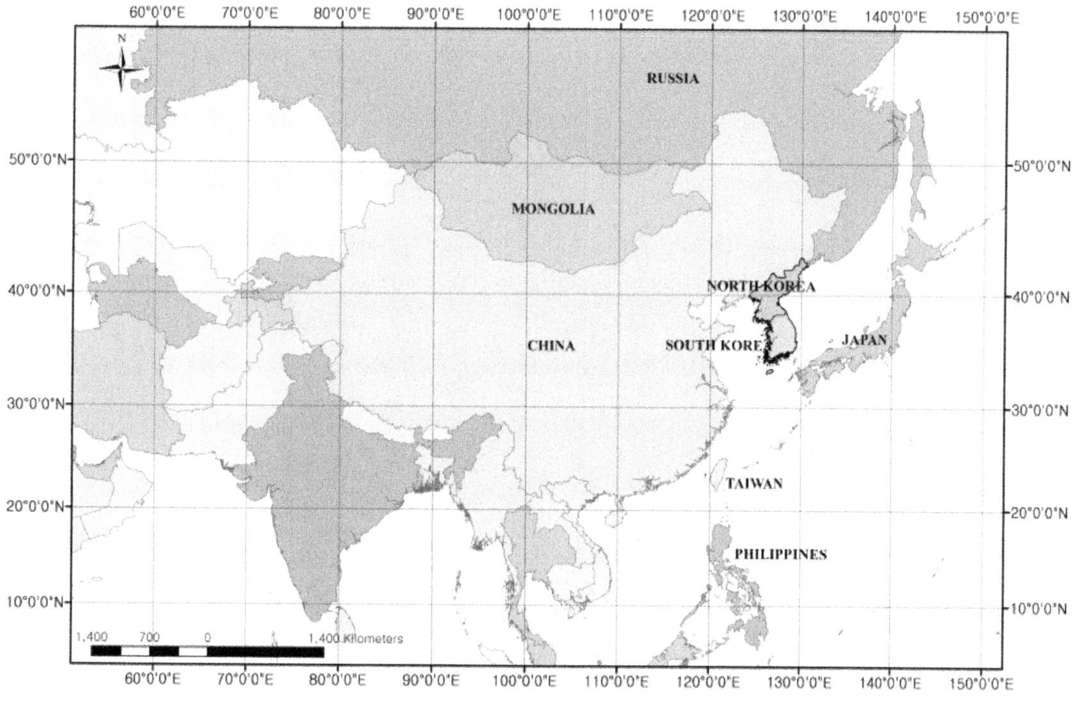

FIGURE 2. 1 THE LOCATION OF KOREA (MODIFIED BY THE AUTHOR FROM THE BASE MAP: WORLD COUNTRIES (ESRI.COM 2011))

The granite and the gneiss are the most prevalent rocks, but sedimentary rocks, such as limestone, argillite, and sandstone, and igneous rocks, including basalt and porphyry, are also plentiful in the Korean peninsula (Yonhap News Agency 1997: 314) (henceforth, YNA). Since a large portion of soil in Korea consists of granite and gneiss, the acid brown forest type is the prevalent soil of the mountain regions, whereas the lateritic or red-yellow types are the most common soils in the lowland agricultural regions (Choi 1984: 26). A high percentage of lowland soils include displaced alluvia or colluvia, which consists of soil that has been separated from the bedrock by natural forces like wind, rain, and streams. In addition, we can find volcanic soils on the Jeju and the Ullung islands (YNA 1997: 314).

The granites of the *Granite-Gneiss system* in Gyeonggi province contain metals, for instance, copper, lead and zinc (Bartz 1972: 11, 86). Copper is located in the south-eastern part of Gyeonggi area. According to a government survey in 1997, 287 minerals are present in Korea. But only limited sets of minerals, such as, gold, silver, copper, iron, lead, zinc, tungsten, kaolinite, barites and molybdenum, are used commercially. Although South Korea contains fundamental metals like copper, iron, and aluminum, they are more abundant in North Korea (YNA 1997:315). Although the distribution map (Figure 2.2) shows basic metal sources, archaeological research about ancient archaeometallurgy needs to be developed in the future.

Topography

Approximately 70 per cent of the total area of the country is composed of mountainous regions (Jo 2000: 30; Kim 2008: 21; Gwon 2011: 82). The slopes of the east coast side are steep, while those of the west coast are moderate. Although the highest mountain, Mt. Baekdu, is 2,744 meters above sea level, the overall height of the majority of mountains on the peninsula is not lofty: for example, mountains which are over 1,000 meters occupy less than 5 present of the country (KOIS 2003: 91; Nelson 1975: 10, Figure 2.3).

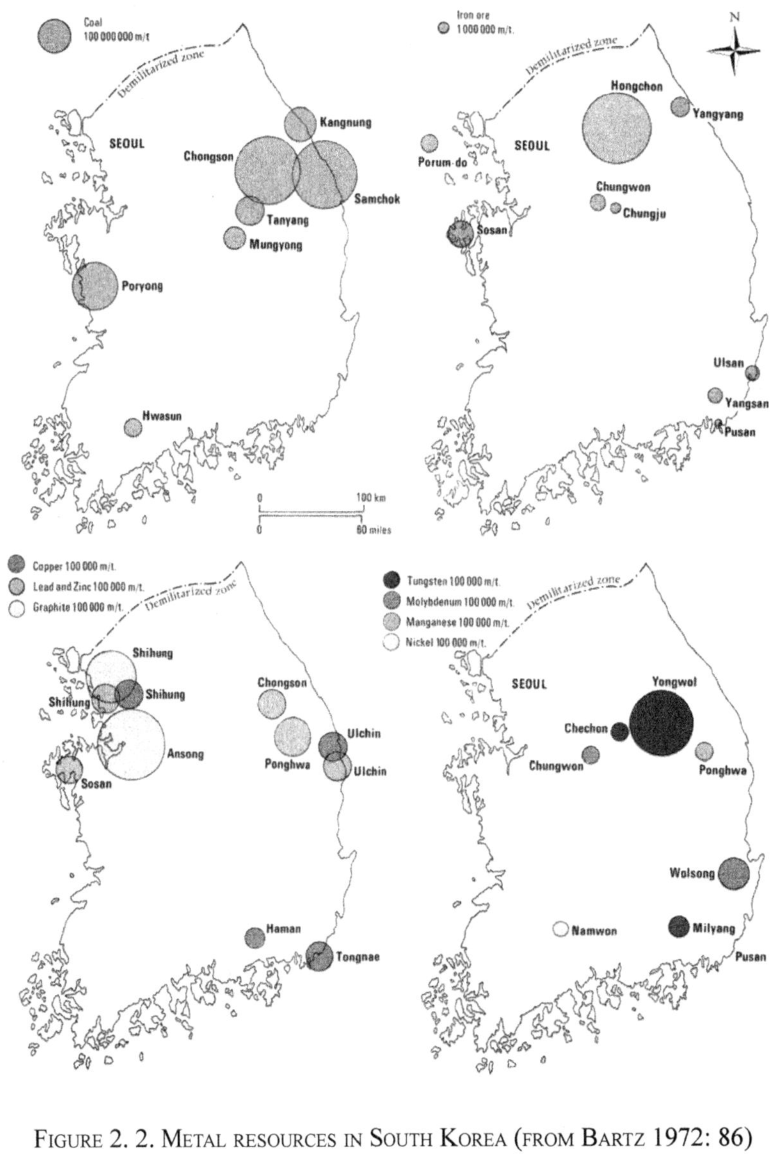

FIGURE 2. 2. METAL RESOURCES IN SOUTH KOREA (FROM BARTZ 1972: 86)

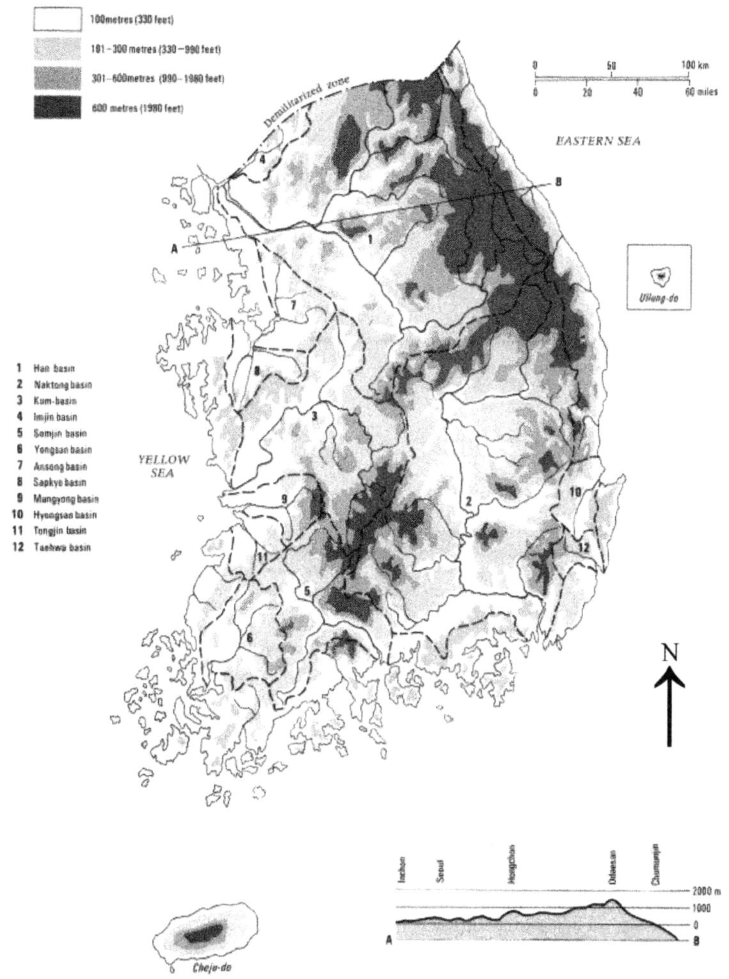

FIGURE 2. 3. A) TOPOGRAPHY OF SOUTH KOREA B) CROSS-SECTION INCHEON-JUMUNJIN (FROM BARTZ 1972: 14)

Ten major rivers run through the Korean peninsula. Eight of them flow westwards into the Yellow Sea: the Amnok (the Yalu) River, which marks the border between China and North Korea; the Cheongcheon and the Daedong rivers in the northwest region, the Yeseong, the Imjin, and the Han rivers in the middle western area; the Gum and the Youngsan river in the southwestern part. One of them, the Nakdong River, runs into the Korean Strait (the southern sea). The last waterway, the Tuman River, which marks the border between Manchuria and North Korea and between Russia and North Korea, runs to the east (Nahm 1996: 18; Nelson 1993: 12, Figure 2.4). Most major archaeological sites and the main cities are situated on the main rivers.

Climate

There are four seasons in Korea. The winters are cold and dry because of the Siberian anticyclone, whereas the summers are hot and humid because of the Pacific Ocean High. However, since the cold winds from Siberia take it in turns with the Pacific warm air currents during the winter, the cyclic pattern, which is expressed in the Korean idiom, 'three days cold and four days warm (삼한사온: 三寒四溫)', appears. The mean air temperature of winter is around 1° Celsius and that of summer is between 22° and 26° Celsius. Spring and autumn are applicable to the seasons of the interchange of two atmospheric pressures. The average temperatures of spring and autumn are between 7° and 19° Celsius (Choi 1984: 25; Nelson 1993: 19; KOIS 2003: 93-95, Table 2.1).

The high temperature and humidity in summer made rice farming possible in this region. In order to cultivate rice, high temperature and abundant water are needed in the growing season. As the yield of rice farming per unit area is high, it is possible to support a considerable population density. On the other hand, rice agriculture requires a significant amount of labour (Gwak 2001: 42-46; Kim 5th, Feb. 2007.; Gyeonggi Provincial Museum 2001: 61).

The range of variation in precipitation is broad. The average annual precipitation differs from region to region: for instance, 500 mm in the northeastern interior and 1,500 mm on the southern coastal region. The mean precipitation of the majority of the country is 800-1,000 mm (YNA 1997: 64, Table 2.2). In particular, 55-65 per

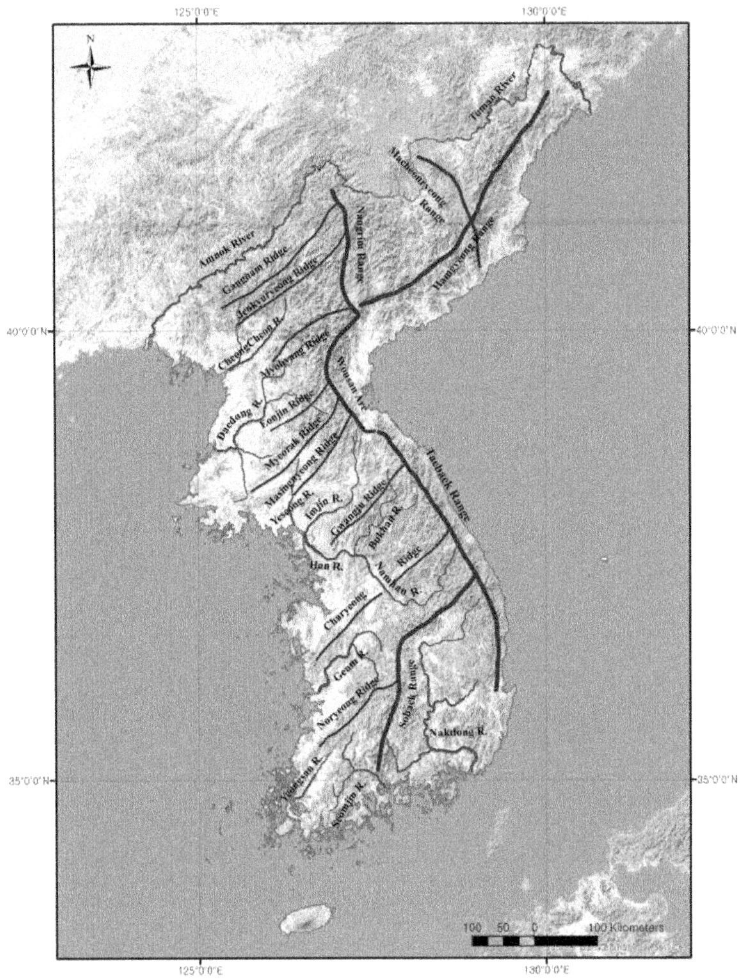

FIGURE 2. 4. MAJOR RIVERS AND MOUNTAIN RANGES IN KOREA (MODIFIED BY THE AUTHOR BASED ON THE MAP FROM KIM 2002A: 6)

TABLE 2. 1. AVERAGE TEMPERATURE BY MAJOR CITY IN 1996 (YNA 1997: 66)

	Seoul	Gangnung	Daejeon	Daegu	Jeonju	Gwangju	Busan
Jan.	-2.2	0.6	-1.6	0.8	-0.4	1.0	3.8
Feb.	-1.6	0.8	1.2	1.5	-0.5	0.4	3.4
Mar.	4.9	4.8	4.8	6.4	5.1	5.7	7.9
Apr.	10.2	12.4	10.2	12.9	9.9	10.4	12.2
May	18.4	16.5	18.0	19.3	17.5	17.9	18.0
Jun.	22.3	19.6	22.1	22.4	22.2	22.0	20.5
Jul.	24.4	23.6	25.2	25.3	25.9	25.6	23.8
Aug.	26.0	23.6	26.1	26.9	26.7	26.6	26.2
Sep.	22.0	20.6	20.5	21.8	21.2	21.8	22.6
Oct.	14.5	15.1	13.7	16.0	14.6	15.8	17.8
Nov.	6.1	8.0	6.7	8.6	7.8	8.8	11.4
Dec.	1.6	4.0	1.1	2.9	2.2	2.9	6.3

(Unit: °C)
Source: Korea Meteorological Administration

cent of the annual precipitation descends from June to August. Moreover, 30 per cent of annual rainfall occurs in July. The pattern of rainfall can be divided into two: a dry season (from October to March) and a rainy season (from April to September) (Choi 1984: 25-26; Oh 1958: 44). In consequence, the river flux varies from season to season. Higher river levels in summer occur regularly. The mean flux of the Han River in winter (January or February) at Seoul is one-twentieth of its mean flux in July. A huge quantity of debris including large stones is carried by the summer rapid streams. Almost 400,000 tons of sediments are carried by rivers and the salinity of the Yellow Sea is diminished remarkably by the quantity of the river water flowing into it (Nelson 1975: 12).

TABLE 2. 2. AVERAGE PRECIPITATION BY MAJOR CITY IN 1996 (YNA 1997: 66)

		Seoul	Kangnung	Taejon	Taegu	Chongju	Kwangju	Pusan	Average
Jan.	(average year)	16.3 (22.9)	37.9 (58.2)	32.7 (33.6)	18.7 (20.5)	36.0 (35.7)	32.9 (38.6)	33.8 (31.8)	29.8 (34.5)
Feb.	(average year)	1.0 (24.6)	92.2 (61.1)	4.4 (40.8)	1.3 (28.8)	5.0 (41.4)	11.8 (46.4)	6.9 (42.9)	17.5 (40.9)
Mar.	(average year)	77.9 (46.7)	107.3 (71.2)	138.0 (58.4)	110.9 (50.7)	120.1 (60.1)	127.4 (62.0)	171.1 (79.2)	121.8 (61.2)
Apr.	(average year)	60.0 (93.7)	58.1 (77.3)	49.8 (96.9)	58.3 (78.0)	40.1 (99.4)	38.4 (110.3)	115.9 (148.4)	60.4 (100.6)
May	(average year)	29.3 (92.0)	17.6 (73.2)	62.9 (95.4)	49.2 (75.2	77.5 (97.2)	37.4 (101.4)	46.8 (147.9)	45.8 (97.5)
Jun.	(average year)	249.7 (133.8)	279.0 (110.7)	411.4 (153.6)	313.2 (128.6)	401.7 (146.7)	302.9 (182.6)	327.1 (224.0)	326.4 (154.3)
Jul.	(average year)	512.8 (369.1)	193.9 (217.4)	257.7 (316.7)	120.1 (233.5)	174.9 (278.5)	186.3 (283.3)	284.8 (256.9)	247.2 (279.3)
Aug.	(average year)	132.4 (293.9)	220.2 (261.7)	114.4 (277.8)	82.5 (193.0)	119.9 (244.5)	261.7 (235.9)	140.0 (203.6)	153.1 (244.3)
Sep.	(average year)	11.0 (168.9)	32.7 (216.4)	11.4 (154.5)	37.6 (122.8)	13.6 (143.8)	66.1 (149.8)	26.7 (186.6)	28.4 (163.3)
Oct.	(average year)	90.3 (49.4)	139.3 (111.9)	90.8 (53.0)	30.2 (48.1)	103.3 (60.2)	60.7 (59.4)	42.3 (62.2)	79.6 (63.4)
Nov.	(average year)	62.9 (53.1)	82.0 (78.1)	77.1 (48.8)	48.4 (37.3)	86.9 (59.0)	112.4 (56.1)	65.4 (64.9)	76.4 (56.8)
Dec.	(average year)	11.0 (21.7)	22.5 (38.6)	28.6 (30.4)	18.1 (14.1)	37.8 (29.7)	30.8 (30.8)	28.4 (24.3)	25.3 (27.1)
TOTAL	(average year)	1256.6 (1369.8)	1282.7 (1375.8)	1279.2 (1359.9)	888.5 (1030.6)	1216.8 (1296.2)	1268.8 (1356.8)	1289.6 (1472.7)	1211.7 (1323.1)

(unit: mm)
Source: Korea Meteorological Administration

Flora

According to botanical studies, there are approximately 190 families, 1,079 genera, 3,130 species, 630 varieties, and 310 forms of vascular plants in the Korean peninsula. In other words, there are more than 4,000 kinds of plants, more than twice the number of species in Britain (Nelson 1993: 20; KOIS 2003: 18). The natural vegetation in Korea is divided into five main types: the montane coniferous forest, such as spruce and fir, in the northeastern part; mixed deciduous pine forest, for example, maple, basswood, and birch, in the north; deciduous oak in the central part; mixed mesophytic forest in the southern area; and finally, evergreen broadleaved forest in the far south (ibid, Figure 2.5).

Fauna

The Palaearctic zoogeographical realm includes the Korean peninsula (Nelson 1993: 22). The faunal distribution of Korea can be divided into two zones: highland and lowland (KOIS 2003: 22). The highland district includes the Gaema Plateau, Myohyangsan mountains, and the Taebaek mountains, which are situated between 800 and 1900 meters above sea level, and they have a similar climate to the Amur River region (*ibid*). Animal species in this district are similar to that of the boreal zone in northern China, Manchuria, and the north part of Japan and representative species are red deer, sika deer, Amur goral, sable, Japanese marten, Asiatic black bear, leopard cat, alpine pika, white-toothed water shrews, hazel grouse, eagle owl, Chinese grosbeak and woodpeckers (*ibid*: 23). The fauna of the lowland district, which has a moderate climate, is similar to that of central China, southern Manchuria, and Japan, comprising Korean hare, roe deer, rat like hamster, white-bellied black woodpecker, fairy pitta and common pheasant (*ibid*). According to the archaeological evidence, dog skeletons and pig bones were found in the Neolithic sites (Nelson 1993: 22; Ahn 1998f: 430).

2.2 Chronology of Korean prehistory and its material culture[1]

On the one hand, Korea is distinct amongst East Asian countries in geographical and geological as well as archaeological terms (Nelson 1993: 12). On the other hand, to come to a balanced understanding of regional development, based on socio-cultural aspects, the task of

[1] The information in this chapter is derived from Choi (1984), Choi and Rhee (2001), Choi (2008), Ha (2007: 646-657), Jo (1992: 169-287), Kang (2002b: 43-64), Kim (2002), Woo (2006: 18-38), and Yu (2003:407-478).

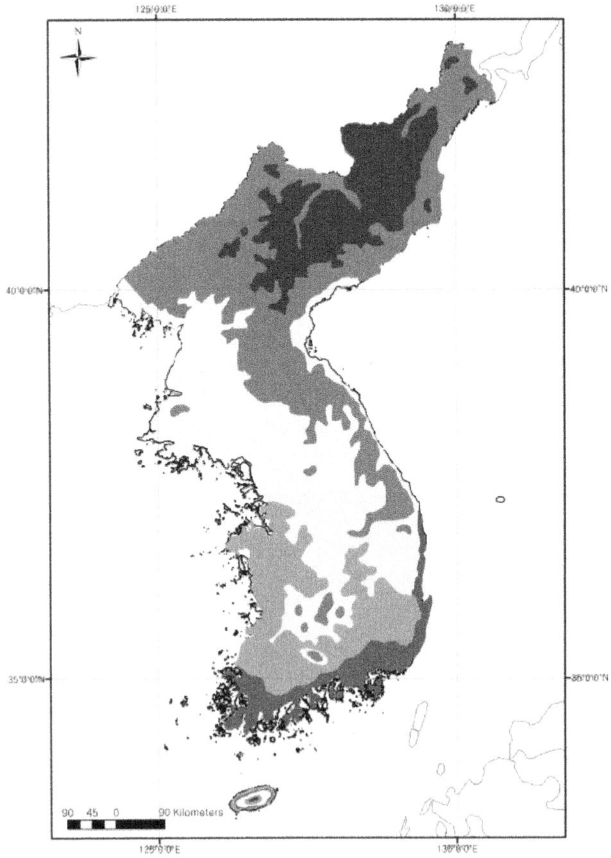

FIGURE 2. 5. NATURAL VEGETATION TYPES IN KOREA. FROM NORTH TO SOUTH: CONIFEROUS FOREST, MIXED HARDWOOD FOREST, DECIDUOUS BROADLEAVED FOREST, MIXED MESOPHYTIC FOREST, EVERGREEN BROADLEAVED FOREST (MODIFIED BY THE AUTHOR BASED ON THE MAP FROM NELSON 1993: 21).

Korean archaeology in the 21st century will be to explore and recognise the complexity of Korean culture (Choi and Rhee 2001: 119).

Christian J. Thomsen (1788-1865) created the three age system as a means of arranging materials when he was the first curator at the National Museum of Denmark (Gräslund 1987). This classification has also been applied in Korean archaeology. M.L. Choi and S.N. Rhee (2001), and M.L. Choi (Choi 2008a) established a revised chronology on the basis of new radiocarbon dating and the division of periods as follows:

2.2.1. Neolithic period

It is estimated that the Neolithic period in the Korean peninsula started around 8000 BC based on the discovery of the Gosan-ri site on Jeju Island. In Choi and Rhee's opinion (2001: 124), this site can be divided into three levels: 1) a late Palaeolithic/Mesolithic level yielding microcores and microliths, 2) a Neolithic level I represented by clay band pottery and triangular arrowheads, and 3) a Neolithic level II in which tanged arrowheads were unearthed. The representative Neolithic material cultures in Korea are pottery and polished stone tools. There were several different ceramic traditions in this area. Firstly, undecorated or clay band design pottery (approx. 6000-4000 BC) was discovered in Osan-ri (Yangyang), Dongsam-dong (Busan), and Seopohang (Unggi). Secondly, comb patterned pottery (around 4000-2000 BC, figure 2.6) with pointed bases[2] was unearthed in the Han River valley, and finally, flat-bottomed pottery represents the type of the northwest part of Korea. We can find Neolithic sites in every part of Korea, for example: Jitop-ri (Bongsan),

TABLE 2. 3. TRADITIONAL AND NEW CHRONOLOGIES OF KOREAN ARCHAEOLOGY (CHOI 2003: 3; CHOI 2008: 20-23, 90-99; KIM 2002: 24)

New Chronology	Calendar Years	Traditional Chronology
Palaeolithic period	700,000 BP - 10,000 BC (New) 500,000 BP - 10,000 BC (Traditional)	Palaeolithic Age
Mesolithic period (or Transitional period)	10,000? BC – 8000 BC (New)	
Neolithic period	8000 BC - 1500-2000 BC (NEW) 6000 BC – 1000 BC (Traditional)	Neolithic Age
Bronze Age	Initial: (Coexistence with Neolithic potteries) 2000 – 1500 BC Early: 1500 – 1000 BC Middle: 1000 – 600 BC Late: 600 – 400 BC (New) 1000 – 300 BC (Traditional)	Bronze Age
Early Iron Age	400 – 1 BC (New) 300 – 1 BC (Traditional)	Early Iron Age
Late Iron Age	AD 1 - 300	Early Three Kingdoms period

*194-108 B.C. Wiman Joseon (위만조선, 衛滿朝鮮)
57 B.C. The establishment of Silla (신라, 新羅)
37 B.C. The establishment of Goguryeo (고구려, 高句麗)
18 B.C. The establishment of Baekje (백제, 百濟)

[2] It was thought that comb patterned pottery in the Korean peninsula may be related to the comb-pit pottery found in Northern Europe and Siberia by Fujida Ryosaku (藤田 亮策) in 1930. But, J.H. Kim (1972), S. Nelson (1973), and L. Sample (1974) have stated that they can find no relationship between the two wares based on their decorative patterns (Kim 2002c: 37-38).

FIGURE 2. 6. COMB-PATTERN POTTERY (NATIONAL MUSEUM OF KOREA 1993: 17) (THE COLLECTION OF THE NATIONAL MUSEUM OF KOREA (HENCEFORTH, NMK), WITH THE PERMISSION OF NMK)

Namgyeong (Pyeongyang), Gungsan-ri (Oncheon), Misa-dong (Hanam), Amsa-dong (Seoul), Dongsam-dong (Busan), Suga-ri (Gimhae), and Osan-ri. They are, by and large, situated on the coast or along rivers (Choi and Rhee 2001: 125-126; Im 2005b) (Figure 2.7, Appendix 1).

It is known that unlike the case of the so-called 'Neolithic Revolution' (Childe 1934) in Europe and the Near East, agriculture in Korea, as in the Far Eastern regions, is likely to have emerged around the middle of the Neolithic period (Ahn 1998c: 383; Im 2005a: 342-343); through the cultivation of dry-field crops and then, step by step to the adoption of rice agriculture (Ahn 1998c; 1998d; Choi 2001; Im 2005a). The background information for agriculture will be presented in Chapter 5. This change in subsistence economy in Korea, from hunting and gathering to agriculture, is comparable in some ways to the transition from the Mesolithic to Neolithic periods in Europe (Bradley 1998; Schulting 1998).

The house types of the Neolithic periods in the study area are mainly pit dwellings, but caves and paved stone-floor houses have also been discovered and these house shapes were circular or round corner square shaped (Ahn 1993: 70-74). According to S.G. Lee's research on house plans

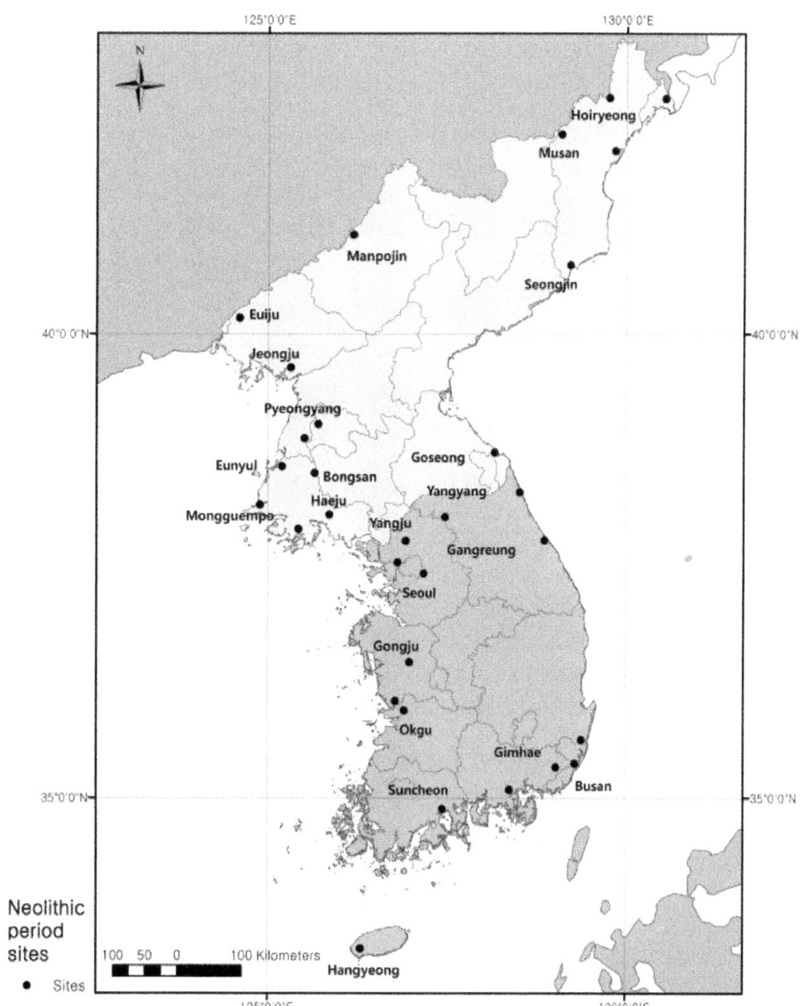

FIGURE 2. 7. NEOLITHIC PERIODS SITES (MODIFIED MAP BASED ON THE MAP FROM THE NATIONAL INSTITUTE OF KOREAN HISTORY 2008: 22)

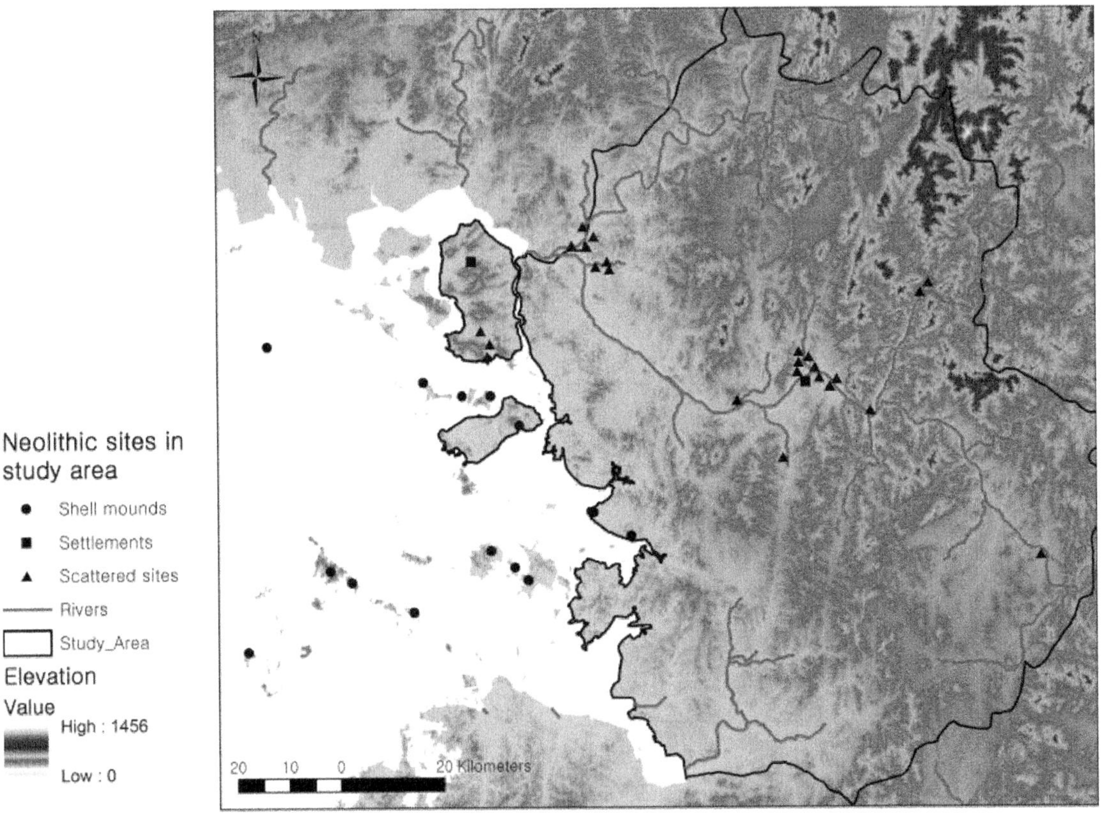

FIGURE 2. 8. NEOLITHIC SITES IN GYEONGGI PROVINCE (MODIFIED BY THE AUTHOR BASED ON THE MAP FROM AHN, 1993: 31)

in the Korean peninsula (2005c: 195), rectangular shaped houses were evident on the whole from the Late Neolithic period, but had not been discovered at that point in the central part of the Korean peninsula, which corresponds to the study area examined in this work. In addition, burials in the Neolithic period were rarely located, except for a cave burial in Gyodong Chunchen and a cairn burial[3] on Sido (Si island). Consequently, it seemed that people in the Neolithic period used pit burials to inter the dead (Ahn 1993: 75).

Although there was evidence of agriculture as mentioned above, due to the fact that most of the sites in the Neolithic period in the Seoul, Incheon and Gyeonggi area were discovered near to the coast and the Han river[4] (refer Figure 2.8) and that shell mounds were located near to the seashore and on islands, fishing appears to have been an important part of the subsistence economy together with hunting, gathering and some farming (Ahn 1993: 75-80).

2.2.2. Bronze Age

It is assumed that the Korean Bronze Age began around the 15th century BC, although this date is still under discussion (refer to Appendix 2). It has been identified that Bronze Age sites hold in common similar material cultures, for example, Bipa-shaped (Liaoning type) bronze daggers, bronze mirrors, polished crescent stone knives, polished stone daggers (Figure 2.9), as well as several kinds of plain pottery. The Bronze Age in Korea may be classified

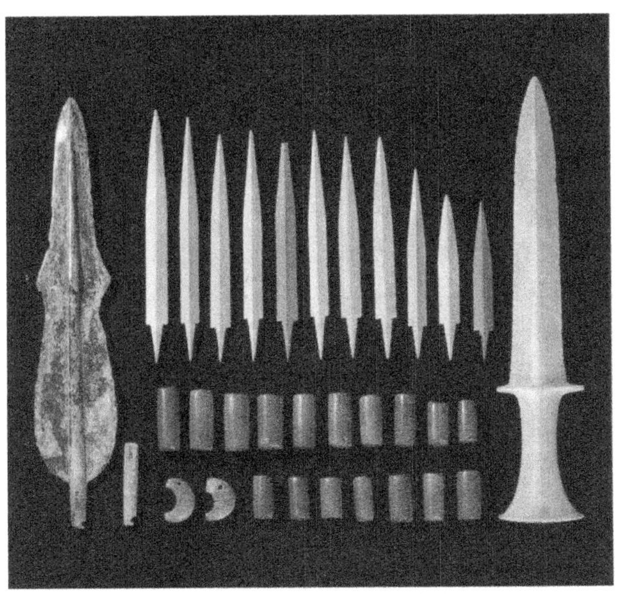

FIGURE 2. 9. A BIPA-SHAPED (LIAONING TYPE) BRONZE DAGGER (FAR LEFT), A POLISHED STONE DAGGER (FAR RIGHT), ARROWHEADS, AND JADES (THE NATIONAL MUSEUM OF KOREA 1992: 10) (THE COLLECTION OF NMK, MODIFIED BY THE AUTHOR, WITH THE PERMISSION OF NMK)

[3] There is an alternative analysis of this site: it is thought that this site might be the outside hearth for cooking similar to that seen at Amsadong (Kim 1986b: 43-44)

[4] Neolithic sites were also discovered inland, through the rescue excavations undertaken before the building of the Chungju, Juam and Hapcheon dams. Therefore, the location of Neolithic sites needs reconsideration (Lee 1992c: 150-151).

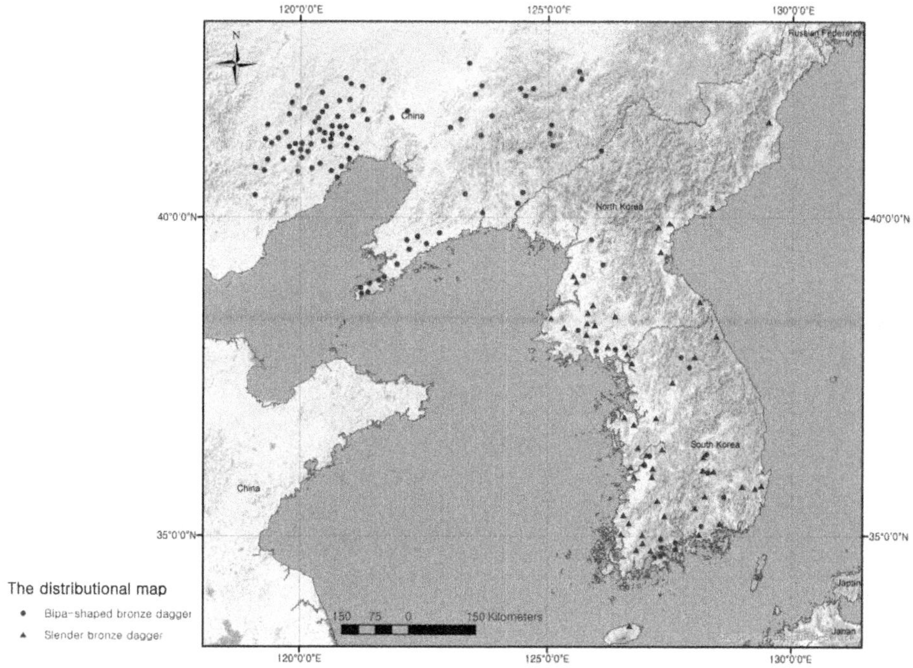

FIGURE 2. 10. THE DISTRIBUTIONAL MAP OF BIPA-SHAPED (LIAONING (요녕, 遼寧) TYPE) AND SLENDER (KOREAN TYPE) BRONZE DAGGERS (MODIFIED BY THE AUTHOR BASED ON THE MAP FROM SONG ET AL. 2004: 21)

FIGURE 2. 11. BOWL WITH ENGRAVED BAND FROM THE INITIAL BRONZE AGE (APPROX. 2000 BC-1500 BC) (GYEONGSANGNAM-DO AND DONG-A UNIVERSITY MUSEUM. 1999: 212) (THE COLLECTION OF KONKUK UNIV. MUSEUM (HENCEFORTH, KUM I), WITH THE PERMISSION OF KUM I)

FIGURE 2. 12. DOUBLED-RIM WITH SLANT LINE POTTERY FROM THE EARLY BRONZE AGE (NATIONAL MUSEUM OF KOREA 1993: 32) (THE COLLECTION OF KOREA UNIVERSITY MUSEUM (HENCEFORTH, KUM II). PHOTOGRAPH WAS PROVIDED BY KUM II)

in terms of different pottery types into four phrases: 1) The Initial Bronze Age (approx. 2000 BC-1500 BC) can be defined as the transitional phase between the Neolithic and Bronze Ages and is represented by plain pottery with an engraved band (Figure 2.11), doubled rim pottery, and plain pottery with comb-patterned designs. 2) The Early Bronze Age (approx. 1500 BC- 1000 BC) yields doubled-rim with slant line pottery (Garak-dong type, Figure 2.12), and pottery with perforated rims (Figure 2.13) or with a notched strip on the rim (Yeoksam-dong type, Figure 2.14-1, 2.14-2). 3) The Middle Bronze Age (approx. 1000 BC-600 BC) is designated by egg-shaped pottery with

FIGURE 2. 13. BOWLS WITH PERFORATED RIM FROM THE MIDDLE BRONZE AGE (NATIONAL MUSEUM OF KOREA 1993: 27) (THE COLLECTION OF NMK, WITH THE PERMISSION OF NMK)

FIGURE 2. 14-1. A BOWL WITH NOTCHED STRIP ON RIM FROM THE MIDDLE BRONZE AGE (NATIONAL MUSEUM OF KOREA 1993: 30) (THE COLLECTION OF SEOUL NATIONAL UNIVERSITY MUSEUM (HENCEFORTH, SNUM), WITH THE PERMISSION OF SNUM)

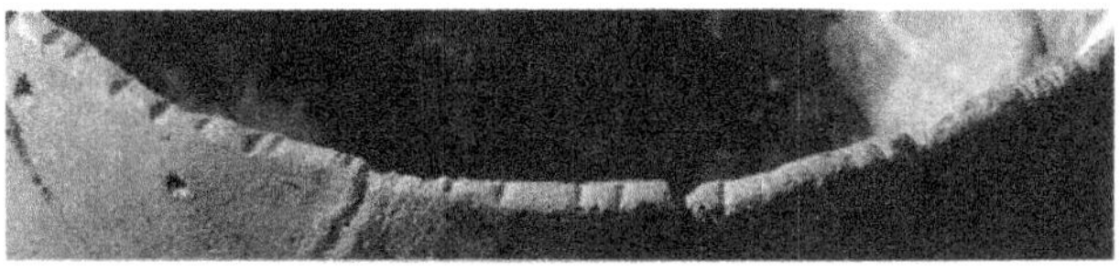

FIGURE 2.14-2. THE MAGNIFIED RIM PART OF A BOWL WITH NOTCHED STRIP AND PERFORATED RIM (NATIONAL MUSEUM OF KOREA 1993: 30) (THE COLLECTION OF SNUM, WITH THE PERMISSION OF SNUM)

FIGURE 2. 15. EGG-SHAPED POTTERY WITH OUTCURVED RIM (SONGGUNG-NI TYPE POTTERY) FROM THE MIDDLE BRONZE AGE (NATIONAL MUSEUM OF KOREA 1993: 39) (THE COLLECTION OF NMK, WITH THE PERMISSION OF NMK)

FIGURE 2. 16. POTTERIES WITH CLAY STRIP ON THE RIM FROM THE LATE BRONZE AGE (NATIONAL MUSEUM OF KOREA 1993: 59) (THE COLLECTION OF NMK, WITH THE PERMISSION OF NMK)

outcurved rims (Songgungni-type pottery, Figure 2.15). 4) The Late Bronze Age (approx. 600 BC-400 BC) is designated by pottery with clay stripes on the rim (Figure 2.16) (Choi 2008b: 21-22). The Bronze Age can be roughly divided into four phases on the basis of pottery types, but we also have to bear in mind regional variations in pottery. In the case of bronze daggers, they are classified into two categories: the bipa-shaped (Liaoning type) bronze dagger and the slender (Korean type) bronze dagger (Figure 2.10). It is suggested that the former were used around the 10th century BC until the 3rd century BC (Lee 1992b) and that the latter were used from the 3rd BC to the beginning of the 1st century AD (Lee 1992a).

It is inferred that there were unparalleled socio-economic and cultural shifts in this period, such as dry and wet rice cultivation, the construction of megalithic monuments, the emergence of social stratification and the development of private ownership, depending on the analysis of material culture (Choi 1984: 156-164).

Figure 2. 17. Table type dolmen in 317 Bugeun-ri Hajeom-myeon Ganghwa Island, Incheon (Photo taken by the author)

Figure 2. 18. Baduk board type dolmen in Gochang, Jeonbuk province (Photo taken by M.L. Choi, modified by the author, with Prof. Choi's permission) (Choi 1999: 236)

2.2.2.1 Dolmens

In the Korean peninsula, it is possible to find two types of megalithic structure, namely, dolmens and menhirs. Although there were two types of megalithic monuments, the relationship between of them has not been explored properly yet. Approximately 29,510 dolmens have been found so far, with more than 12,000 dolmens located in the south-western part of Korea (Choi et al. 1999: 4). Korean dolmens have been traditionally classified into three categories: Northern type (Table type, Figure 2.17), Southern type (Baduk Board type, Figure 2.18), and Capstone type (Figure 2.19), on the basis of the location of the tomb chamber and the existence of supporting stones (Kim 2002c: 92-96; Choi 1999: 21-24). Some scholars (Kim 1981; Lee 2002b: 96-100; Yu 2003: 140-144) have added one more type of dolmen, namely, Circular type (Figure 2.20), which has several flat stones for an upright stone. This form is mainly found on Jeju Island, which is located in the southernmost part of the Korean peninsula.

It has been roughly estimated on the grounds of their affiliated artifacts and some radiocarbon dates that the Korean dolmens were built from ca. 15th century BC to ca. 1st century BC in the area that covers the Korean peninsula and northeast China (Choi 2008a: 139) as well as the north-western part of Kyushu island in Japan (Sim 1999: 155-156, 168).

In order to understand the significance of dolmens in Korea, first it is necessary to examine some of the previous research on the subject.

Before 1945

The earliest recorded interest in dolmens and ancient artifacts can be found in the book '*Donggukisanggukjip* (동국이상국집, 東國李相國集)', written by G.B. Lee (이규보, 李奎報) in 1200 AD during the Goryeo (고려, 高麗) dynasty (918-1392 AD), when he travelled the tributary province of Jeonju, which is located in the south-western part of Korea, as a clerk. He recorded that, according to folklore, dolmens were built by ancient sages and it looked like a miracle had taken place. In the '*Donggukyeojisungram* (동국여지승람, 東國輿地勝覽)', which was published by the government in 1481 AD during the Joseon (조선, 朝鮮) dynasty (1392-1910 AD), there were references to "menhir" as a place

FIGURE 2. 19. CAPSTONE TYPE DOLMEN IN JINSANG-RI, YEONCHEON, GYEONGGI PROVINCE (PHOTO TAKEN BY THE AUTHOR)

FIGURE 2. 20. CIRCULAR TYPE DOLMEN IN YONGDAMDONG, JEJU ISLAND (LEE 2004: 39) (THIS PHOTO WAS PROVIDED BY THE RESEARCH CENTRE OF DOLMENS IN NORTHEAST ASIA, WITH DIRECTOR Y.M. LEE'S PERMISSION)

name. We can also infer the thoughts of these sixteenth century and earlier peoples through the folk beliefs passed down through generations about the stones and the ritual ceremonies for a good harvest and fecundity that were recorded (Choi 1987a: 747-748). In addition, J.T. Son (Son 1934: 19-21) wrote about the legends and folk beliefs held about dolmens: they were regarded as subsequently, an old fairy's house, a commander's tomb, a public cemetery for fallen soldiers, or as the graves of different ethnic groups.

European interest in the dolmens of Korea started with W. R. Carles in 1883, a vice-consul in the British Embassy and Allen, an officer in the British Embassy (Woo 2006: 18). According to the Korean historian J.T. Son (Son 1934: 16-17; Son 1948: 3), Carles was the first person to bring the existence of Korean dolmens to the attention of western academics. It might possibly have been the dolmens in Pocheon, which is located between Seoul and Wonsan, which were the focus of his attention, although it is not easy to identify them exactly because of the brevity of his report. Subsequently, W. Gowland (1895) referred to details about several characteristics of dolmens in Songuri and Pocheon-gun in the journal of the Anthropological Institute of Great Britain and Ireland (Woo 2006: 18; Ha 2007: 612). In 2002, M.S. Ha has ascertained that these dolmens correspond to those in present day Jajakdong, Pocheon. In addition, there exists a record by a Frenchman named Emile Bourdaret who recorded 21 dolmens in Simsanri, Hwanghae-do (Woo 2006: 19; Ha 2007: 612).

For socio-political reasons, that is, the Japanese occupation of Korea from 1910 to 1945, the emergence of modern archaeology in Korea was instigated by Japanese rather than native scholars at the beginning of the 20th century (Choi 1984: 12). Under the patronage of the Japanese Government General in Korea, Japanese scholars, such as Imanishi Ryu (今西 龍), Sekino Tadasi (關野 貞), Fujida Ryosaku (藤田 亮策), and Umehara Sueji (梅原 末治), carried out a number of archaeological schemes as part of Japanese colonial policy (Kim 2002a: 20). During this period, several dolmens were excavated: for example, a dolmen in Hadori, Ganghwa island by Imanishi Ryu at 1916 and dolmens in Gunryangri, Eunyul-gun, in Ipridong and Anak-gun were examined by Tori Ryuzo (鳥居 龍藏) and he published a survey of Korean dolmens in 1926 on the basis of the results of excavations up until that point (Woo 2006: 20-21).

Despite the dominance of Japanaese scholars, Korean archaeologists and historians, such as Nam-seon Choi (최남선, 崔南善), Jin-tae Son (손진태, 孫晉泰), and Hung-su Han (한흥수, 韓興洙), attempted to undertake their own research into dolmens. Namseon Choi (1927) touched upon how the megalithic monuments related to western megaliths, as the central theme of a field survey around the Eunyul, Anak area. It is worth noting that he is the first to use the Korean term 'Goindol', which means 'the big stone which is supported by other stones, as the translated word for 'Dolmen'. In addition, Jin-tae Son (1934; 1948) classified dolmens into two categories on the grounds of the existence of supporting stones. This classification remains in use today. He postulated that dolmens functioned as altars, burials, or residences. He also utilised the research of western missionaries and historical records about Korean dolmens to supplement his own work. Lastly, Hung-su Han illustrated the Table-style and Baduk board-style dolmens through drawings (Woo 2006: 20).

From 1945 to the 1960s

1945 was the year of Korean liberation from Japanese control. However, instead of independence there was a partition along the 38th parallel between south and north. Southern parts were occupied by the American forces until August 1948 and northern parts were held by Soviet military until September 1948. Under Allied control, a provisional government had endeavoured to set up a unified national government, but this had failed. Therefore the division of the country into two separate states in 1948 was agreed (Nahm 1996: 329). The government of the Democratic People's Republic of Korea (DPRK), known as North Korea, chose communism in order to build a socialist state whereas the Republic of Korea, commonly called South Korea, decided on parliamentary democracy. They selected completely different political systems and ideologies but North Korea did attempt to reunify the partitioned country in their own way. As a result, the Korean civil war broke out in 1950. In this research, the primary focus will be on the research history of South Korea and due to complex national security reasons, there have been some restrictions near the Armistice line and DMZ (demilitarised zone), which are close to the northern part of the research area.

After liberation and the Korean civil war (1950-53), it is suggested that there were two distinct characteristics in the archaeological practice of this period. Firstly, the distorted historical and archaeological views of Japanese scholars continued, due to a lack of archaeological evidence and a colonisers' attitude towards Korean cultural heritage (Yi 1988: 226-229). As Won-yong Kim (김원룡, 金元龍) (1981a: 22) has pointed out, Umehara Sueji (梅原 末治) insisted that there were no Palaeolithic and Bronze Age cultures in Korea. According to him, during the third century B.C. bronze and iron were introduced almost simultaneously into Korea from north-eastern China and continued to be used until the end of the fourth century A.D.(Choi 1984: 13). In other words, Japanese scholars insisted that the Palaeolithic period and the Bronze Age did not independently manifest themselves in the Korean peninsula.

Therefore, Korean academics aspired after the liberation from Japan in 1945 to re-examine Japanese scholars' biased points of view on the basis of the results of new excavations. This is the second key characteristic of the practice of archaeology in this period. For instance, the matter of the beginning of the Bronze Age in Korea was raised by W.Y. Kim (1961a). He insisted that the Liaoning type (bipa-shaped) bronze dagger was the prototype for Korean style bronze daggers (Figure 2.11). He estimated that the earliest evidence for the manufacture of this artefact was between the 6th and 5th centuries B.C., based on the examination of a bronze dagger, which was excavated a grave in Shiertaiyingzi (십이대영자묘, 十二台營子墓), Liaoning, northeast China (Jo 1992: 175). Secondly, the most important research result of this period is the publication of 'Studies of Dolmens in Korea' by the National Museum of Korea (Kim and Yun 1967). The reason why this book is important is that they suggested that polished stone daggers did not imitate the slender (Korean) bronze dagger, as Japanese scholars had insisted (Ha 1985: 6). Arimitsu Kyoichi (有光 教一) (1959) concluded that polished stone daggers in the Korean peninsula imitated the shape of slender bronze daggers that had been used from around the 3rd century BC to the beginning of AD 1st century in this area. However, as a polished stone dagger was discovered in the settlement under lying a dolmen in Okseokri, Paju (Deokeunri, present name) and charcoal from the settlement dated 2590±105BP (GX0554. OxCal 4.0: 967- 408 BC (2 sigma)) (Figure 2.21), this meant that polished stone daggers seem to be have been made and used before the period of slender daggers.

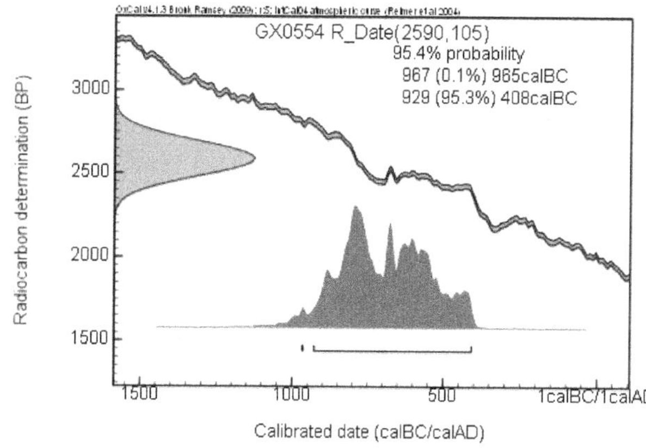

FIGURE 2. 21. PLOT OF THE CALIBRATED DATE OF SETTLEMENT IN OKSEOK-RI, PAJU (CALIBRATED USING OXCAL 4.0. BY THE AUTHOR).

1970s

Moving on to the 1970s, it could be suggested that there were two main trends in this period in the archaeological field and in dolmen research. Firstly, in general Korean archaeology, several scholars tried to study the relationship between north-eastern China/southern Siberia and Korean culture and history. An example of this is the study carried out by J.H. Kim (1978b), which provided an in-depth analysis of the stone compartment burials at Nanshangen (남산근, 南山根) in China. In his study, he assumed that the earliest emergence of Liaoning (요녕, 遼寧) type bronze daggers in Liaoning province was approximately in the 10th century BC. Compared to this region, the discovery of a Liaoning bronze dagger in the Korean peninsula indicated that this type was in use from around the beginning of the 10th century B.C. to the 1st century A.D. Another example of this type of study is that by J.B. Kim (1975). He proposed that the influx of Bronze Age culture in the Korean peninsula occurred after 1300 B.C. based on a comparative study of Korean archaeology with that of the Karasuk culture in southern Siberia. In the meantime, M.L. Choi (1978) focused on the analysis of 109 dolmens in Jeonnam (the contracted form of Jeolla namdo) province. He divided them into three categories, namely, northern, southern and capstone types, on the basis of external forms and suggested that this order might be the same as their chronological order. In addition, he estimated that their period of existence in Jeonnam could be between the 4th ~5th centuries BC to around the first century A.D.

1980s

Turning now to the 1980s, there was a gradual increase in the amount of archaeological research undertaken. The most significant development was that archaeologists broadened their view beyond the Korean peninsula. They attempted to consider the historical context, some of them making attempts through the analysis of pottery to develop a greater understanding of the lives of those who once inhabited the archaeological sites through their material cultures. The trends of this period may be divided into five categories. First of all, we focus on the research of M.L. Choi (1981; 1982; 1984). Following his previous studies, he undertook the analysis of dolmens in Jeonnam province. Through the examination of dolmens in Panchonri, Naju and Chunghyori, Gwangju, by using the evolutionary scheme of Elman Service and bearing in mind the characteristics of the material cultures in Jeonnam province, he argued that wet-rice agriculture and the redistribution of surplus wealth was the propelling force that transformed dolmen society into that of a chiefdom. Other aspects of dolmen society such as labour specialization and class differentiation were seen to be indicated through the analysis of plain pottery and an inner structure located under the capstones. Labour specialisation can be seen in the homogeneous forms and standardised techniques of pottery production: for instance, the use of similar soil (montmorillonite), the porous surface structure, and the low firing temperatures (less than 573°℃). In addition, the study of dolmen construction as a secondary source can give us evidence of the division of labour and of social hierarchy. Choi also suggested that dolmens were constructed for high ranking persons and their families. The existence of chambers for children in the dolmens of Panchonri was argued to indicate that hereditary status existed in these societies. Confirming his earlier position, the time-span of dolmen society in Jeonnam, the southernmost province, was estimated from between the 5-4th centuries B.C. to the inception of the 1st century AD.

Next, the origins of dolmens were the second preoccupation of this period in Korean archaeology. There are three major perspectives about the origin of dolmens respectively: northern origin theory, southern origin theory, and indigenous origin theory (Choi 2000: 20). Based on the northern origin theory, dolmens in the Korean peninsula seem to be influenced by the cist burial tradition of Siberia (Kim 1986a: 92). The southern origin theory was expounded in B.M. Kim's (1981) major study. He argued that the dolmen culture in Korea was related to rice cultivating cultures from Southeast Asia, after the analysis of megalithic cultures in Indonesia. Thirdly, the indigenous theory suggests that dolmens in the Korean peninsula arose independently without external influences. M.S. Ha (1985; 1988) supported the third theory in his research: after the analysis of the dolmens along the Geum and Namhan Rivers, he asserted that Korean dolmens developed autonomously on the basis of the analysis of socio-economic states in those periods. The three positions on the origin of dolmens have been debated. However, according to Y.M. Lee (Lee 2002b: 236-238), each point of view has some problems. For example, with regard to the northern origin theory, no dolmens have thus far been discovered on the periphery of Liaoning province and the northern part of Siberia. Secondly, in the southern origin theory it is noted that there were different forms of dolmens existing between the east coast of China, which is the diffusional route, and Korea. There is also a vast difference in the number of dolmens located in the two areas: only around fifty dolmens in east coast China compared with approx. 30,000 dolmens in the Korean peninsula. Finally, applying indigenous origin theory, it is true that the Korean peninsula contains the densest number of dolmens in the world, although it has been difficult to reveal whether the Korean dolmens originated in terms of form and concept in the Korean peninsula.

In addition, H.H. Park (1984) insisted that the starting point of dolmen construction was the middle of the Neolithic period on the basis of the radiocarbon dating of a dolmen in Yangsu-ri (KAERI-95 3900±200 BP. OxCal 4.0: 2910-1784 BC at 2 sigma) (Figure 2.22) and of chipped stone tools. B.M. Kim (1981) and G.G. Ji (1982; 1987a) suggested that the placement of dolmens was often parallel with the flow of a river or in line with a mountain range. These reflections by Kim and Ji were the first attempts to relate dolmens to their landscape. They inferred respectively that dolmen society was constructed on the basis of agriculture, or that the erection of dolmens might be related to a form of nature worship by prehistoric communities. There is a possibility that dolmens were constructed from the end of the Neolithic period, but, according to the radiocarbon determinations of dolmens in the study area (no. 1-3) and the other regions (no. 4-10) (refer to Appendix 8), and until more supporting evidence can be collected, the basis of this opinion has some weaknesses. That is, there is only one radiocarbon date for a dolmen in Yangsu-ri, Yangpyeong which supports this viewpoint and, the uncertainty is ±200, which is too broad a range for secure dating.

Besides these features, Ji (1987) examined the megalithic monuments in Brittany, France. He identified five different points: 1. Megaliths in France were built on hills or the tops of mounds where there were good views, whereas the dolmens in northeast Asia were located near coasts or riverbanks. 2. By and large, burials in European megaliths were located on the ground while the burials of the one type of dolmen in Korea, the Baduk board type or southern type dolmens, were situated under the ground. 3. The European megaliths were generally used as community cemeteries,

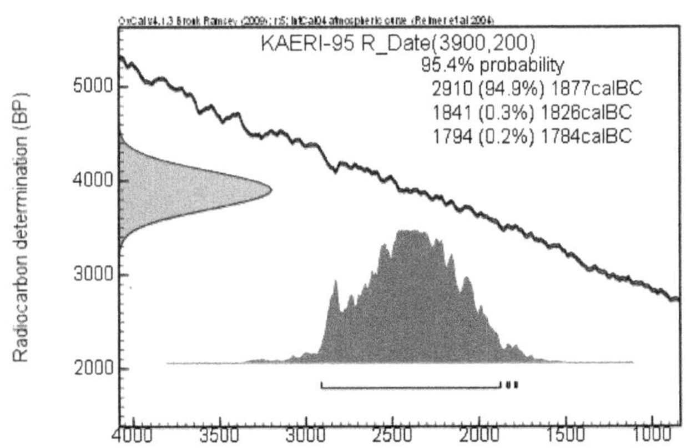

FIGURE 2. 22. PLOT OF THE CALIBRATED DATE OF A DOLMEN IN YANGSU-RI, YANGPYEONG (CALIBRATED USING OXCAL 4.0. BY THE AUTHOR).

whereas overall, dolmens in northeast Asia were used for a single person and as mentioned in the geology section, due to the acid soils, bone preservation has been poor. 4. In Europe, the orientation of the long axis of the megalithic monuments was on an east-west, or northeast-southwest axis. On the other hand, the direction of dolmens was apparently influenced by geographical features, such as the orientation of mountains and river direction. 5. The construction period of megaliths in Europe is estimated to have taken place from approx. 5000 BC to 1800 BC, whereas that of Korean dolmens is dated to around 1000 BC and is considered to have continued for one thousand years in the Korean peninsula on the basis of traditional Korean chronology (refer to Table 2.3). Ji seemed to approach dolmen research from a landscape perspective and above the 4th point, related to axial orientation, will be examined in Chapter 6.

Thirdly, the key trend for this period was that a considerable number of researchers had become interested in the field of archaeology as a useful instrument in solving the question of the origins of Korean culture. This trend is more related to research in the north-eastern part of China. J.B. Kim (1987a) assumed that the bipa (비파, 琵琶)-shaped bronze dagger culture was produced by the so-called 'Yemeak (예맥, 濊貊) tribe', who were a 'tribe' of prehistoric Koreans, with a burial system characterized by stone cist monuments. He concluded that the Bronze Age in Korea began around the 10th century B.C. In his analysis of archaeological sites and bronze artifacts, J.H. Kim (1984; 1987b) suggested that Liaotung (요동, 遼東) province was the formative region of the Korean ethnic group and that the formative period of dry-field farming might have been between 2500 B.C and 1500 B.C.; centering around the Shantung (산동, 山東) peninsula and extending to Manchuria (만주, 滿洲). In addition, he proposed that the 'Gojoseon' (고조선, 古朝鮮) period saw the first chiefdoms develop in the Korean Bronze Age. H.G. Lee (1987b) also concluded that they seem to be of the same lineage as the dolmens in the Korean peninsula, after the exploration of dolmens in the Liaotung peninsula in north-eastern China.

In addition to these studies, research concerning the relationship between Korea and Japan was pursued. For example, B.G. Sim (1981) maintained that the first dolmens in Kyushu province, Japan were disseminated from southern Korea, around the last part of the fourth century BC, after the analysis of dolmens in both areas. The types of dolmens found in Kyushu are the Capstone type and the Go-table type (=Baduk board type). B.H. Son (1987) indicated that dolmen, stone cists, pit burials, and jar-coffins were the burial types in the plain pottery period. According to the chronology of burial types in Korea, pit burials and jar-coffins developed later than dolmens.

The final characteristic of this period is the analysis of plain pottery by a considerable number of scholars. Plain pottery is the representative material culture of the Bronze Age in Korea, compared to the comb-patterned pottery of the Neolithic period. Within the Bronze Age in Korea, several types of plain pottery have been discovered, such as, bowls with perforated rims, bowls with a notched strip on the rim, top-shaped pottery, double-rimmed pottery, Songgungni-type pottery, and red burnished pots. By and large, different types of plain pottery were found in the different regions, and so there are possibilities to present geographical/cultural variation rather than a chronological sequence.

B.G. Lee (1984; 1986) explored the plain pottery assemblages in the Han River valley and then divided the excavated materials into four periods: (1) after the plain pottery from the north-eastern part of the Korean peninsula, including bowls with perforated rim (Figure 2.13) and bowls with notched strip on the rim (Figure 2.14-1, 2-14-2), arrived in the Han River valley, the production of pottery commenced in this region; (2) the pottery from the north-eastern part of Korea and the pottery from the north-western part of Korea, namely, top-shaped pottery (Figure 2.23) that combined and co-existed; (3) the top-shaped pottery and the notched strip type disappeared; (4) bowls with clay strips (Figure 2.16) and slender bronze daggers started to be produced. He also mentioned that dry-field farming was transmitted from the north-eastern part of Korea between the end of the 7th century B.C. and the beginning of 6th century BC and that wet-field farming was disseminated from the north-western part of the Korean peninsula around the middle of the 6th century B.C. His research results were examined and adjusted by J.S. Kim (2001). This point will be referred to in section 2.2.2.2 Settlements.

In his review of plain pottery assemblages and bowls with perforated rims from South Korea, C.G. Lee (1988) divided them into six groups by pottery types: Garak-dong,

FIGURE 2.23. TOP-SHAPED POTTERY FROM HWANGHAE PROVINCE (NATIONAL MUSEUM OF KOREA 1993: 31) (THE COLLECTION OF NMK, WITH THE PERMISSION OF NMK)

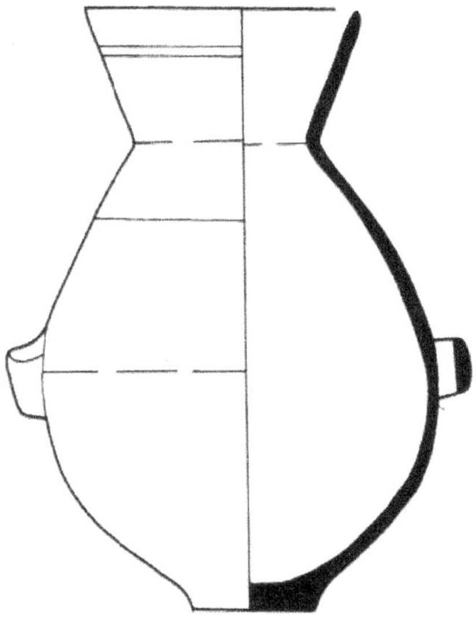

FIGURE 2. 24. MISONGRI TYPE POTTERY (NATIONAL MUSEUM OF KOREA 1993: 26, WITH THE PERMISSION OF NMK)

Yeoksam-dong, Heunam-ri, Songguk-ri, Suseok-ri, and Gungok-ri. In addition, he indicated that the plain pottery culture in South Korea began before the emergence of bronze artifacts and continued to the beginning of the Iron Age. S.R. Choi (1987b) divided the plain pottery culture of Jeonnam province into three periods: (1) plain pottery and stone tools, (2) plain pottery and bronze artifacts, and (3) iron artifacts and plain pottery.

1990s

As for the outcomes of research on dolmens in the 1990s, they can be categorized into the exploration of the relationships between dolmen societies and historical contexts; the reconstruction of dolmen society; synthetic research and study of Korean dolmens as well as dolmens in Gyeonggi province; and finally, the importance of the excavation of dolmens in Gyeonggi province. From this period, I will concentrate mainly on my own research area; namely, Seoul, Incheon, and Gyeonggi province, as a considerable number of important excavations have taken place in these regions as well as all over the country, as archaeological institutes, responsible for local excavations, increased considerably in Korea in this period.

The first trend in archaeological practice is related to a research tendency of the previous period. H.J. Song (1990) explored the identity and location of the Gojoseon (고조선, 古朝鮮) culture. After examining the characteristics of the bipa-shaped bronze dagger culture and the distribution, locality, and cultural characteristics of Misongri-shaped pottery (Figure 2.24), he suggested, firstly, that it seems quite possible that the group using Misongri-type pottery could be identified as the Gojoseon; and secondly, that their field of action could be estimated as the eastern part of the Liao river (요하, 遼河) and the north-western part of the Korean peninsula. Thirdly, due to the cultural influence of the Yan (연, 燕) (which is one among seven states during the Spring and Autumn and Warring states periods

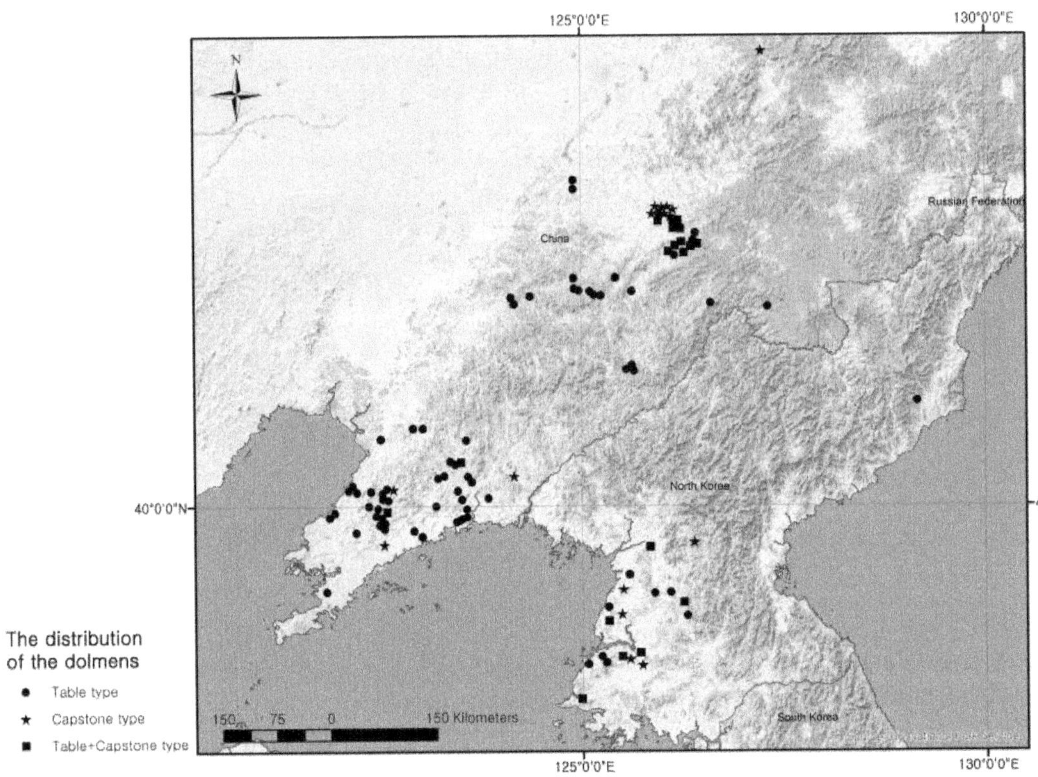

FIGURE 2. 25. DISTRIBUTION OF THE DOLMENS IN THE NORTHEAST OF CHINA AND NORTH KOREA (MODIFIED BY THE AUTHOR BASED ON THE MAP FROM HA 1999: 311-312)

(춘추전국시대, 春秋戰國時代: 770 BC ~ 221 BC in China) the inhabitants of the Liaotung (요동, 遼東) province were moved into the Daedong river (대동강, 大洞江) valley in the northwestern part of the Korean peninsula and because of this situation, subsequently, it is probable that the area of Daedong river became the center of the Gojoseon culture.

Moving on to the second trend, some researchers tried to reconstruct aspects of dolmen society. Y.M. Lee (1993) synthesised the results of Korean dolmens excavated up until that point in his thesis. He scrutinised approximately 16,000 dolmens in Jeonnam province on the basis of three regional divisions: Youngsan River, Boseoung River, and the southern coast. He also suggested three functions for dolmens: burials, altars[5], and territorial markers. Furthermore, he argued that the group which built the dolmens formed one social unit around an area with a 20 km diameter, based on marking 16,369 dolmens on a 1/250,000 map. He noted that the distribution of dolmens could be divided into two scales: small and large clusters. A small cluster denotes a group of dolmens located within approximately a 5 km diametre near coasts, valleys, hills or basins and a large cluster denotes 4-6 small clusters situated within around a 20 km diametre of valleys, mountain ranges, or rivers. Lastly, he drew attention to the fact that the dense dolmen regions were, by and large, coincident with the location of the small states of Mahan (마한, 馬韓, which is estimated to have been formed by 54 small states and located in Gyeonggi, Chungcheong, and Jeolla provinces between approximately 4th century B.C. to A.D. 5th /6th century. Choi 2008: 310), which were designated by G.W. Cheon in 1979 (Lee 2002b: 316-326).

Another doctoral thesis of this period is 'The study of dolmen culture in East Asia' by M.S. Ha (1997), who mainly examined the dolmens in Liaoning (遼寧) and Jilin (吉林) provinces in China, and in North Korea. He investigated the distribution (refer to Figure 2. 25), location, structure, and type of dolmens as well as the grave goods and dating of dolmens. According to the distribution, they were seldom discovered in the western part of the Liao River (요하, 遼河). This geographical distribution of dolmens is the same as that of bipa-shaped (Liaoning type) bronze daggers. Therefore, Ha suggests both material cultures had the same background.

There are some differences in location between Liaoning and North Korea on the one hand, and Jilin, on the other, on the basis of his research. For example, dolmens in Liaoning and the north of Korea are located on hills or flat lands beside rivers, whereas those in Jilin are located on ridges or near the tops of mountains. Although there are differences in dolmen distribution among Liaoning, Jilin, and North Korea, by examining the area near the Yellow Sea (situated between China and the Korean peninsula), he argued that it is possible to postulate 'a Yellow Sea Rim' area of dolmens, basing his theory on the fact that dolmens in East Asia are normally densely distributed in Liaoning (요녕, 遼寧), Shantung (산동, 山東), Zhejiang (절강, 浙江), and on the western coastline of the Korean peninsula. M.S. Ha also divided the geographical locations of dolmens into four categories: plains, hills, mountain skirts, and mountain tops. In the cases of plains and hills, there are water sources near the dolmens, while it is suggested that the view was the major consideration for sites on mountain skirts and tops. In addition, through the analysis of capstone size, the structure of dolmens and the orientation of burial, he tried to reconstruct aspects of society in these areas.

2000s

Tae-yong Yu explored the social hierarchy of dolmen society in the Korean Bronze Age for his doctoral thesis (2001) and his book (2003). First of all, he investigated the geographic distribution of dolmens in Ganghwa Island. There are ten concentrations (refer to Figure 2.27 and Table 2.4).

According to the percentage of the number of dolmens in ten groups, the first group comprises 35% and the other groups comprise 23%, 7%, 19%, 1%, 1%, 8%, 1%, 4%, and 1% respectively (See Table 2.4). The noticeable point is that the location of the first group is central in the distribution on Ganghwa Island. The dolmen groups from No. 3 to No. 10 occur at regular intervals from the No. 1 group and Tae-yong Yu suggested that dolmen society was extended from the area of No. 1 to the area of Nos. 7 to 10 (refer to Figure 2. 26).

In addition, there was a slight difference in the number of dolmen types between the different groups. For example, the number of table type dolmens in area No. 1 and No. 7 exceeded that of the capstone type dolmens. On the other hand, in the remaining small concentrations, the number of capstone dolmens was more than that of table type dolmens. Region No. 1 is located in the plain on the northwest side of Goryeo Mountain. A rectangular Bronze Age settlement was discovered in this area, after sherds of top-shaped pottery were unearthed. Top-shaped pottery originates from the northwest side of the Korean peninsula. Through the existence of this pottery, archaeologists presumed a relationship between the two regions. The second group is located to the east of the first group. Geographically, a round valley existed here, whereas the location area of the first group is a plain. The noticeable thing is that in this location is found the largest dolmen. Tae-yong Yu suggested that this dolmen was built late in the period, because the capstone is finely dressed, and its weight is 108 tonnes. Therefore, he estimated that approximately 1100 people[6] were involved in the construction of this

[5] It is assumed that some dolmens were used as altars because there was no burial evidence found under the capstone, for example, dolmens in Biryong-ri, Suncheon and in Hodong-ri, Haenam (Lee 2002: 264).

[6] Choi, S.R. and S.W. Han. 1989. One example of dolmen reconstruction. *Jeonnam Cultural properties* Vol. 2. pp.11-24. (as quoted in Y.M Lee 2002: 328-329) They attempted the experiment in order to estimate the labour requirements of dolmen construction. As a result, 73 persons were needed to move the 6.8 ton of stone almost 150m by dragging with ropes and logs. They inferred that one person could move 100kg.

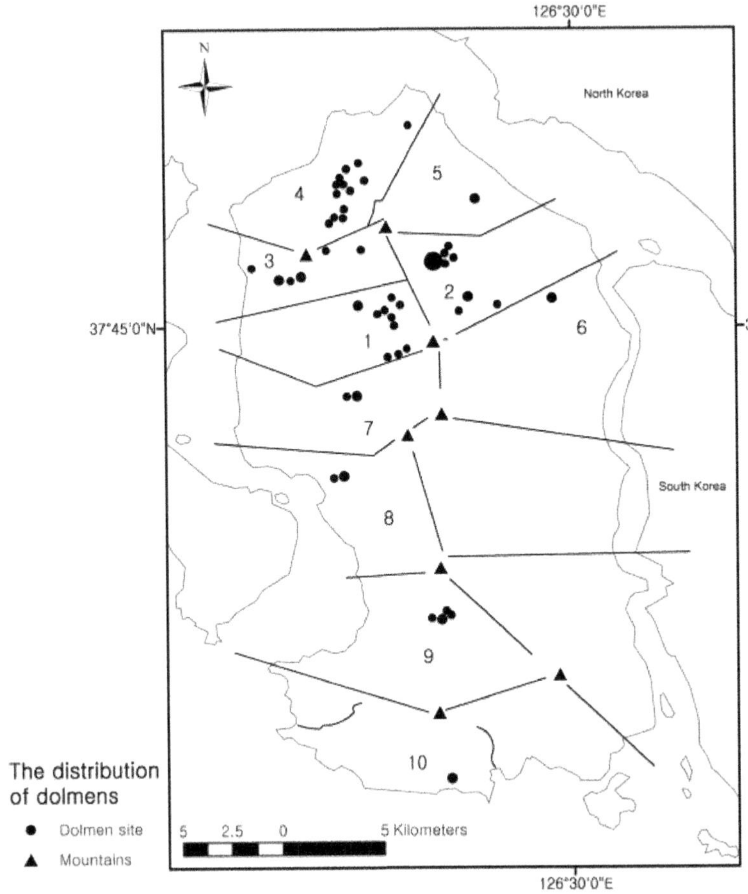

FIGURE 2. 26. THE DISTRIBUTION OF DOLMENS IN GANGHWA ISLAND (MODIFIED BY THE AUTHOR BASED ON THE MAP FROM YU 2003: 411)

TABLE 2. 4. THE GEOGRAPHIC DISTRIBUTION OF DOLMENS IN GANGHWA ISLAND (YU 2003: 413)

Distribution / Group	Distribution (number)	Distribution (percentage)	Dolmen Type		
			Table	Capstone	Others
No. 1	60	36	38	21	1
No. 2	38	23	13	22	3
No. 3	12	7	5	7	
No. 4	32	19	11	21	
No. 5	1	1	1		
No. 6	1	1	1		
No. 7	13	8	10	2	1
No. 8	1	1	1		
No. 9	6	4	1	5	
No. 10	1	1			1
Total	165	100	81	78	6

dolmen, based on Renfrew's approaches. Accordingly, he interpreted that a chiefdom society, where one chief controlled the entire Ganghwa Island, had emerged at that time. The table type dolmen was suggested to show the chief's political and economic power.

T.Y. Yu (2001; 2002) divided locations of the Ganghwa dolmens into five categories: mountain tops, mountain ridges, slopes, plains, and rice fields. They amount to 14%, 19%, 61%, 5%, and 1%, respectively.

TABLE 2. 5. THE LOCATION OF DOLMENS IN GANGHWA ISLAND (YU 2003: 425)

Location	Mountain top	Mountain ridge	Slope	Plain	Rice field
Dolmen (Percentage)	23 (14)	31 (19)	101 (61)	8 (5)	2 (1)

One drawback of this approach is that the criterion is confused as regards the division of the region. For instance, the category of 'rice field' is a modern designation. Yu found slopes to be the most preferred place for dolmen placement. This finding seems to be meaningful, but, it is difficult to accept this conclusion until the natural topography of the area is studied, a key question being to what extent is Ganghwa Island comprised of slopes. This method will be introduced in Chap. 3. He interpreted that the reason why people chose this location is mainly that the slope has a wide view. This approach will be reviewed in Chapter 6. In addition, he examined the relationship between the location and the dolmen types. According to Table 2.6, there are 159 dolmens, which can be confirmed as belonging to one of two types: table type and capstone type, comprising 81 (49%) and 78 (47%) respectively. In the case of mountain tops and ridges, table type dolmens are superior in number. For example, there are 16 table type dolmens (70%) and 7 capstone type dolmens (30%) on mountain tops and there are 17 table type dolmens (55%) and 14 capstone type dolmens (45%) on mountain ridges. In contrast, it can be seen that more capstone type dolmens are found on slope locations, for instance, there are 43 table type dolmens (45%) and 53 capstone type dolmens (55%). It shows promising results, but according to chi-square test[7] results, the two types of dolmens were randomly constructed in relation to these geographical categories.

Yu also explored the presumed chief's political level and the spatial range of his power through the analysis of the weight of capstones and the distribution of dolmens. Table 2.7 is a record of the weight of the largest capstone in each dolmen group.

TABLE 2. 6. THE LOCATION OF TABLE TYPE AND CAPSTONE TYPE DOLMENS IN GANGHWA ISLAND (YU 2003: 427)

Location	Mountain top	Mountain ridge	Slope
Table type dolmen (Percentage)	16 (70)	17 (55)	43 (45)
Capstone type dolmen (Percentage)	7 (30)	14 (45)	53 (55)

[7] Chi-squared test result

	Table	Capstone	Total	Observed	Expected	(Oi-Ei)^2	(Oi-Ei)^2/Ei
Mountain top	16	7	23	16	11.65	18.89	1.62
Mountain ridge	17	14	31	7	11.35	18.89	1.67
Slope	43	53	96	17	15.71	1.67	0.11
	76	74	150	14	15.29	1.67	0.11
				43	48.64	31.81	0.65
				53	47.36	31.81	0.67
	df=2					χ^2 =	4.83
95% confidence level	p = 0.08946						

TABLE 2. 7. THE WEIGHT OF THE LARGEST CAPSTONES OF DOLMENS IN EACH GROUP (YU 2003: 451)

Dolmen group address	Weight (Tonne)
No. 1. Jeomgol 743-4 Bugun-ri Hajeom-myeon	15.2
524-2 Shinsam-ri Hajeom-myeon	17.6
No. 2. 317 Bugun-ri Hajeom-myeon	108.2
A 187-1 Hado-ri Songhae-myeon	15.7
No. 3. A Changhoo San 11 Changhoo-ri Hajeom-myeon	16.8
F Changhoo Sachone Changhoo-ri Hajeom-myeon	17.5
No. 4. H Muckgol San 615 Gyosan-ri Yangsa-myeon	13.3
No. 5. San 11 Yango-ri Songhae-myeon	38.6
No. 6. Cheongsong 1189 Daesan-ri Gangwha-up	12.8
No. 7. Gosanggol 1 San 125 Osang-ri Naegamyeon	16.6
No. 8. Oepo Oepo-ri Naega-myeon	?
No. 9. Eodu 1 Dojang-ri Yangdo-myeon	10.5
No. 10. Dongmack Dongmack-ri Hwado-myeon	?

Based on Table 2.7, Yu mentioned that there is at least one large dolmen in each dolmen group and if the weight of the two heaviest capstones in Bugun-ri and in Yango-ri were excluded, the average weight of a capstone is 15.1 tonnes. According to him, in order to build this kind of dolmen, approximately 150 men would be needed. On the basis of this numerical value, the population of a dolmen group can be estimated at approximately 750 persons (150 persons × 5 persons per household = 750 persons) (diameter 3-5 km, refer to Figure 2.26). The main flaw of this study is the failure to amass sufficient archaeological evidence to support his conjecture, which was that communities comprised up to seven to eight hundred people, which was calculated by him on the basis of the results of experimental archaeology. In addition, perhaps the key problem with this explanation is a statistical mistake; for instance, according to Table 2.8 and Figure 2.27, the average is very skewed by a few very large capstones. Most (approximately 74 %) are 5 tons or less, so fewer people would be required to build them. It is preferable to use the median rather than the mean when a distribution is skewed (refer to Figure 2.28).

TABLE 2. 8. THE WEIGHT OF CAPSTONES OF DOLMENS IN GANGHWA-DO (YU 2003: 452)

Weight (ton)	Number	Percentage (%)
0.1 ~ 1.0	16	13.22
1.1 ~ 5.0	73	60.33
5.1 ~ 10.0	16	13.22
10.1 ~ 15.0	8	6.61
15.1 ~ 20.0	6	4.95
20.1 ~ 40.0	1	0.82
40.1 ~ 110.0	1	0.82
Total	121	100.0

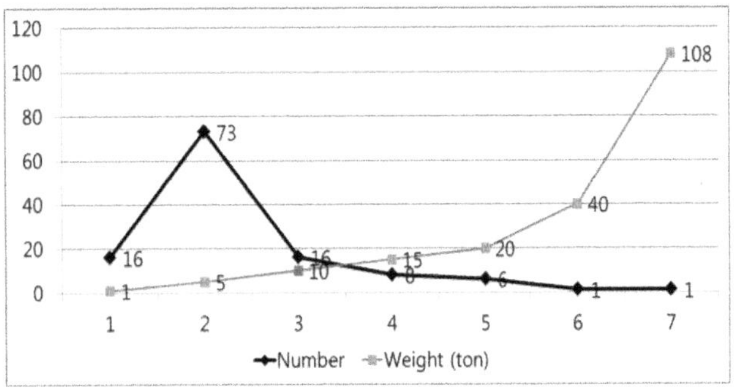

FIGURE 2. 27. THE RELATIONSHIP BETWEEN DOLMEN WEIGHT AND THE NUMBER OF DOLMENS (MODIFIED BY THE AUTHOR FROM YU 2003: 454)

Table 2.8 shows the weight of capstones and the number of dolmens and Figure 2.27 illustrates the relationship between the weight and the number of dolmen, that is, according to in an increase of weight in the capstone, the number of dolmens decreases after the smallest weight category. The dolmen with the heaviest capstone is located on the border between the east and the west of the plain in the north of Goryeo Mountain. Since this location connects the east and the west of island, Tae-yong Yu inferred that the person who was buried in this dolmen had exercised his influence over all the dolmen groups on Ganghwa Island.

Dong-seok Kang examined dolmen society in his MA dissertation (Kang 2002a) and in his article (Kang 2002b). Ganghwa Island has the greatest number of the largest table type dolmens in South Korea and the densest distribution of table type dolmens within a single area. Kang classified 136 dolmens[8], which can be confirmed by type, into 76 table type dolmens and 55 capstone dolmens. On the features of location, table type dolmens tend to be situated singly and to be mainly located on the coast or the ridgeline, while 2~3 capstone dolmens coexisted with the table type dolmens or they have a tendency to maintain independent groups.

As regards the structure of dolmens, according to Kang, the size of capstone shows two things; one is an external grandeur on the aspect of architecture and the other is the reflection of social complexity. If a location and a cluster of dolmens showed variation in the size of capstone, it would become the basic data for the inference of the formation of dolmen society. He analysed 112 dolmens which have been precisely measured, including 52 table and 54 capstone type dolmens respectively. Kang analysed the scale of capstones by dividing them into three classes: small (0-7.5m^3), medium (10.0-15.0m^3), and large (40.0-42.5 m^3). Roughly 75% of dolmens have small capstones, measuring between 0 and 7.5m^3. In addition, he examined the size relationship, between the long and the short axes of the capstones. Not surprisingly, this showed a strong relationship, with a coefficient of correlation of 0.845, significant at the 0.01 level. He undertook various statistical analyses, but he appears not to have interpreted in depth the data that he generated.

[8] There is a difference between the number of dolmens in T.Y. Yu's analysis and here. It is estimated that they might use different data and there might be included the number of unclassified dolmens in previous analysis.

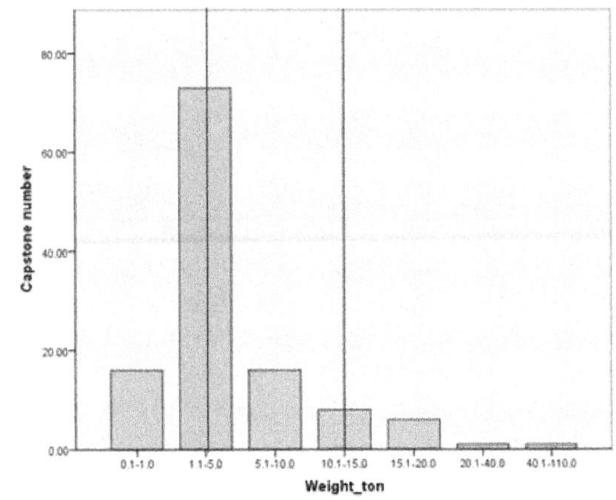

FIGURE 2. 28. THE MEDIAN (LEFT LINE: 1.1-5.0) AND MEAN (RIGHT LINE: 10.1-15.0) OF CAPSTONE WEIGHTS IN GANGHWA ISLAND

He also divided the dolmens into three distributional patterns. The first pattern is small groups of 2~8 capstone type dolmens or table type dolmens located on hills or mountain skirts near to where people built settlements or farmed arable lands. He suggested that this kind of groups seemed to be constructed before the hierarchical society was formed. The second pattern is that most table type dolmens are located in the place with a fine view like the top of a mountain or the top of hill 100 meters or more above sea level. It is supposed that these dolmens represented the political authority of a leader and/or have symbolic meaning such as the indication of territory. The third pattern is that large sized table type dolmens are situated in plains or on the top of hills with set distances to other dolmen groups. As seen in the size and location of dolmens, he assumed that the group which united the northern part of island made this kind of dolmen in order to consolidate the community and establish their identity. Yu and Kang adopting an evolutionary approach assumed that the heaviest dolmen seemed to have been constructed as a result of the development of a dolmen society. These approaches will be compared with the results of this research in Chap.7.

Together with these features, Kang explored the natural and geographical conditions for settlement selection on the basis of the analysis of the Samgeo-ri dolmen site (no. 1 in Figure 2.29), although the main function of dolmen is as a burial monument, because settlements tended to be discovered near to dolmens. He focused mainly on two aspects: the availability of water and of farmland (available cultivated acreage: soil, topography – place between valley and alluvial fan, and gradient - 2~7% or 7~15%), but he also considered fuel, sunshine duration, and trade. Especially, on the element of farmland, he confirmed that the current Samgeo-ri area is suitable to cultivate dry-field products on the basis of a precise soil map made in

1979 by the Agriculture Promotion Office. Although this information does not exactly describe the soil conditions of the prehistoric period, it is thought that by using current data this usage partially compensates for a lack of palaeo-environmental data. In this research, current soil data are also utilised in Chap. 4.

Moon-sik Ha, Ju-yong Kim, and Jin-young Lee (Ha et al. 2004) analysed spatial distribution of dolmens in the Yeoncheon, Gyeonggi province using GIS (Geographical Information System). They investigated the elevation, slope inclination, vertical and horizontal distance of sites from a water sources and main soil and geological features of the sites. The results of their research are as follows: the ranges of elevation are from 12.8 to 80.0 meters above sea level and the average elevation is 41.7 meters. As the average slope of sites is 4.6°, they were gentle slopes and the aspects of site slopes are mostly east and west. However, as with problems noted above with the distributional frequency of dolmens according to landforms, the overall natural slope orientations in Yeoncheon need to be considered, before interpreting the significance of site slope direction and this point will be addressed Chap. 3 and Chap. 5. In addition, they also analysed the average vertical distance from water. It is 5.3 m, whereas the horizontal distance of sites from water sources shows various deviations from the closest at 28.7 m to the farthest at 757 m, with an average of 200 meters. Finally, as for the geological attributes, in the case of hilly areas, sites which are over 60 meters above sea level, for example, Tonghyun-ri, Chatan-ri, and Yangwon-ri, acid volcanic rocks and quartzite are dominant. In contrast, the lower regions, which are between 10 meters and 30 meters above the sea level, for instance, Jeongok-ri, Hakdam-ri, Hakgok-ri, and Eundae-ri, basalt and gneiss are predominant. Through this survey, they attempted to establish the basic information for further study, for example, to set up the standards of geographical classification and to find the quarries of capstones. This research represents the first application of GIS to the study of dolmens in Korea.

Jang-moon Woo examined dolmens in the Gyeonggi area, which includes the areas of Gyeonggi province and the cities of Seoul and Incheon, for his doctoral thesis (Woo 2005), published under the same title in 2006 (Woo). It is estimated that the number of dolmens in this area is at least 611. He explored the distribution of dolmens on the basis of the main three rivers: the Han, Imjin and Ansung Rivers and then on the basis of the streams in the area due to the fact that dolmens tend to be located near to water sources (refer to Figure 2.31). First of all, he investigated the basic characteristics of the dolmens: for example, the size of the capstones and pillar stones, the weight of capstones, orientation, location, existence of cup marks, and the type of dolmen as well as grave goods related to the dolmens.

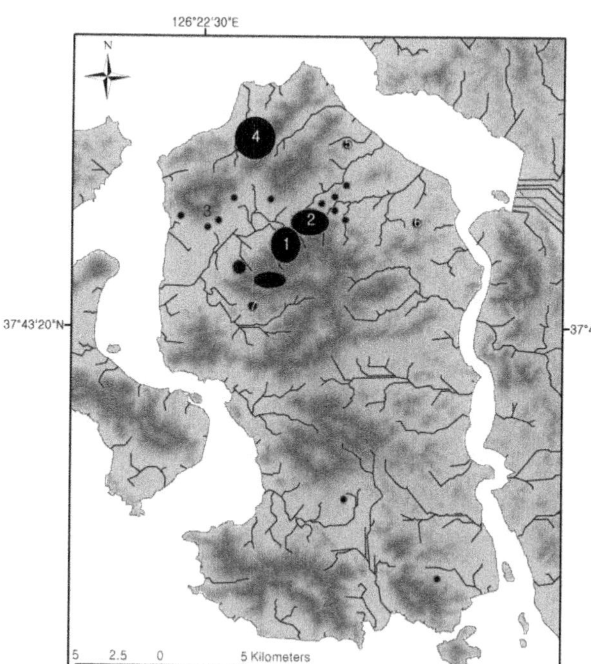

FIGURE 2. 29. SMALL DOLMEN GROUPS AND LOCATIONS ON GANGHWA ISLAND (MODIFIED BY THE AUTHOR BASED ON THE MAP FROM KANG 2007: 659)

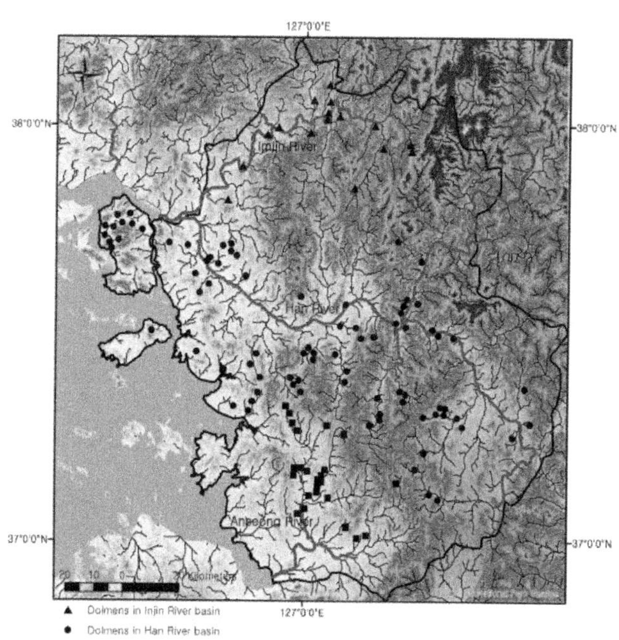

FIGURE 2. 30. THE DISTRIBUTION OF DOLMENS IN GYEONGGI AREA (MODIFIED BY THE AUTHOR BASED ON THE MAP FROM WOO 2006: 394)

J.M. Woo analysed, firstly, the distribution of dolmens according to the branch of the each of the above three rivers and the percentage of each dolmen type. As a result, he found 54 dolmens in 16 locations in the basin of the Imjin River; 506 dolmens in 91 locations in the valley of the Han River, and 51 dolmens in 25 sites near the Ansung River (Figure 2.30). He further divided the location of dolmens into two categories: flatland, and hill and mountain ridges (Table 2.9).

Secondly, he investigated the type of dolmens related to the rivers surveyed (Table 2.10).

TABLE 2. 9. THE LOCATION OF DOLMENS IN THE GYEONGGI AREA (WOO 2006: 397)

Division	Flatland (%)	Hill and Mountain ridge (%)
Ganghwa Island	10 (6)	155 (94)
Namhan River	43 (55)	34 (44)
Bukhan River	42 (78)	12 (22)
Han main stream	27 (14)	172 (86)
Han River total	122 (25)	373 (75)
Imjin River	22 (42)	31 (58)
Ansung River	7 (16)	37 (84)
Gyeonggi area total	151 (26)	441 (74)

TABLE 2. 10. THE TYPES OF DOLMEN LOCATED IN THE BASINS OF THE RIVERS IN THE GYEONGGI AREA (WOO 2006: 401)

Type / Region	Table (%)	Capstone (%)	Baduk board (%)	Unclassified	Total
Ganghwa Island (%)	78 (55)	64 (45)	0	14	156
Namhan River (%)	56 (24)	177 (76)	0	16	249
Bukhan River (%)	3 (5)	53 (93)	1 (2)	20	77
Han main stream (%)	3 (20)	13 (80)	0	8	24
Han River total (%)	140 (31)	307 (68.5)	1 (0.5)	58	506
Imjin River (%)	14 (48)	15 (52)	0 (0)	25	54
Ansung River (%)	1 (2)	44 (86)	5 (12)	1	51
Gyeonggi area total (%)	155 (30)	366 (70.8)	6 (1.2)	84	611

Woo described that in the case of the Imjin River (48%), which is located in the northernmost part of the area surveyed, more table type dolmens were discovered, compared to the basins of the Han (31%) and Ansung (2%) rivers, see Tables 2.10 and 11. The distribution of table type and capstone type dolmens will be reviewed in Chap. 6.

Thirdly, Woo also compared the volume of dolmens from the main rivers and tributaries (Table 2.11).

From this table, he presented that the average volume of dolmens from the tributaries is substantially greater than those located near the riversides. He interpreted this to suggest, on the one hand, as requiring much more labour to move the stones by the main rivers because the local geology is composed of sand. On the other hand, strategically, the areas near the tributaries were easier to protect than the areas alongside the main rivers. This means that the leader of the group, who made the dolmens, controlled his community within the limited area more effectively than in the more open spaces provided along the major rivers. It is difficult to agree with his first opinion, because there is a possibility that the rivers could be used to carry large stones and because quarries have been discovered near dolmen sites in Yeoncheon (Choi et al. 2003a: 290) and in Hwasun (Lee 1999: 305). It is presumed that the closer to the quarry the dolmen site is, the easier it is to transport stones and to build bigger dolmens.

Grave goods were not found to be common: according to Woo's data, among the 143 dolmens in the area which had been excavated at that point, 51 dolmens (36%) contained no grave goods and there were lack of radiocarbon dating information. As with M.S. Ha and H.H. Park, J.M. Woo insisted that dolmens were constructed from the Neolithic period on the basis of the radiocarbon dating at the Yangsu-ri site as mentioned previously (KAERI-95 3900±200 BP. OxCal 4.0: 2910-1784 BC at 2 sigma, refer to Figure 2.22) and on sherds of Neolithic pottery, stone tools and of artefacts excavated at several Neolithic settlements, which were located near dolmens. But, there might be a possibility that long after Neolithic activity dolmens were built near to these places and a ±200 uncertainty is too wide a range for secure dating.

Finally, J.M. Woo considered the cup marks found on dolmens, investigating their presence and the average number at each dolmen. Dolmens having over fifty cup marks were discovered mainly near the Namhan riversides and they are distributed with 6-10 km distance. According to these features, he classified the Gyeonggi area into four regions (Figure 2.31). He proposed that the distribution of

TABLE 2. 11. THE COMPARISON OF THE AVERAGE CAPSTONE SIZE BETWEEN THOSE FROM THE RIVERSIDE AND THOSE FROM THE TRIBUTARY (WOO 2006: 405)

Division	No.	Dolmens on riversides (m)	(m3)	No.	Dolmens on tributaries (m)	(m3)
Namhan River	18	1.98 × 1.19 × 0.51=	1.20	47	2.6 × 1.95 × 0.76=	3.85
Bukhan River	15	1.74 × 1.33 × 0.5=	1.16	3	3.47 × 2.38 × 0.85=	7.02
Imjin River	13	2.46 × 1.86 × 0.47=	2.15	13	3.58 × 2.89 × 0.44=	4.55

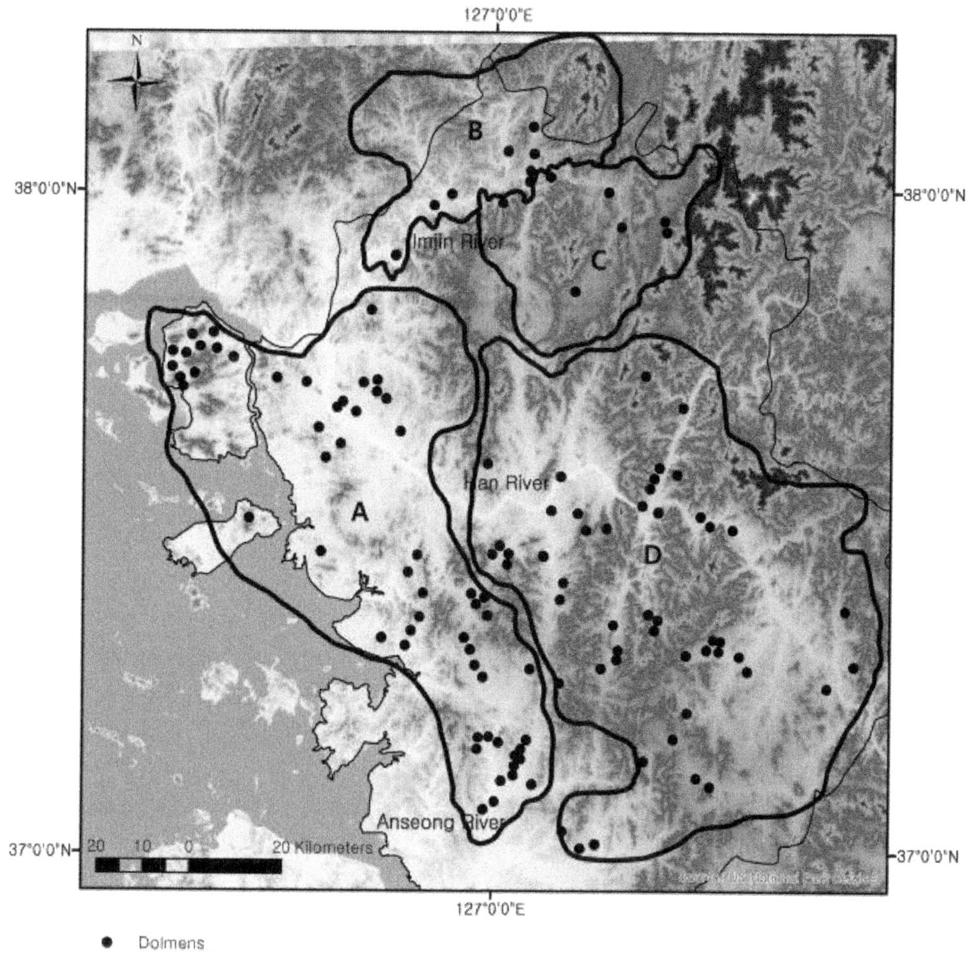

FIGURE 2. 31. THE BOUNDARY OF CUP MARKS IN GYEONGGI AREA (MODIFIED BY THE AUTHOR BASED ON THE MAP FROM WOO 2006: 426)

dolmens with a considerable number of cup marks showed the territories of complex societies, like the distribution of large table dolmens. This perspective is new approach and as such we have to be careful about the interpretation of these data because there is a possibility that these cup marks were made after the construction of the dolmens, as the author has acknowledged (Woo 2006: 432).

So far, previous researches on dolmens have been reviewed. The research gap and the direction of this research will be presented at the end of this chapter after a review of settlement studies and the Iron Age.

2.2.2.2 Settlements

In this section, the study of settlements and related artefacts in the research region so far will be reviewed. According to Baek-gyu Lee (1974b), the Heunam-ri (흔암리, 欣岩里) assemblage[9] (refer to Figure 2.33) was formed in the Han river basin with the fusion of the characteristics of the Yeoksam-dong (역삼동, 驛三洞) assemblage[10] (refer to Figure 2.34 and 2.36) from the northeast region of the Korean peninsula and the Garak-dong (가락동, 可樂洞) assemblage[11] (refer to Figure 2.35) from the northwest region. Since his study, Heunam-ri pottery has been represented as one of the cultural assemblages in the mid-Korean peninsula around the end of the Early Bronze Age. However, Jang-suk Kim (2001) questioned this idea for the following three reasons. Firstly, it is difficult to conclude that a specific group of people, who shared techniques and cultural identity, made and used the Heunam-ri pottery assemblage because it is too diverse to be definitively categorized. Furthermore, there is no difference in the starting point between the Garak-dong and the Heunam-ri assemblages (refer to Appendix 4). Finally, the distribution of Yeoksam-dong and Heunam-ri assemblages deviates from the Garak-dong assemblage (refer to Figure 2.32). Therefore, he suggested alternative notions. Firstly, due

[9] The Heunam-ri pottery has doubled-rims with short diagonal lines and perforated holes in the rim (National Research Institute of Cultural Properties Korea 2001: 1343, Figure 2.34).

[10] The Yeoksam-dong pottery has perforated holes in the rim and/or notched strip on the rim (National Research Institute of Cultural Heritage Korea 2004: 82, Figure 2.35 and 2.37).

[11] The Garak-dong pottery has a doubled rim with short diagonal lines (National Research Institute of Cultural Heritage Korea 2004: 82, figure 2.36).

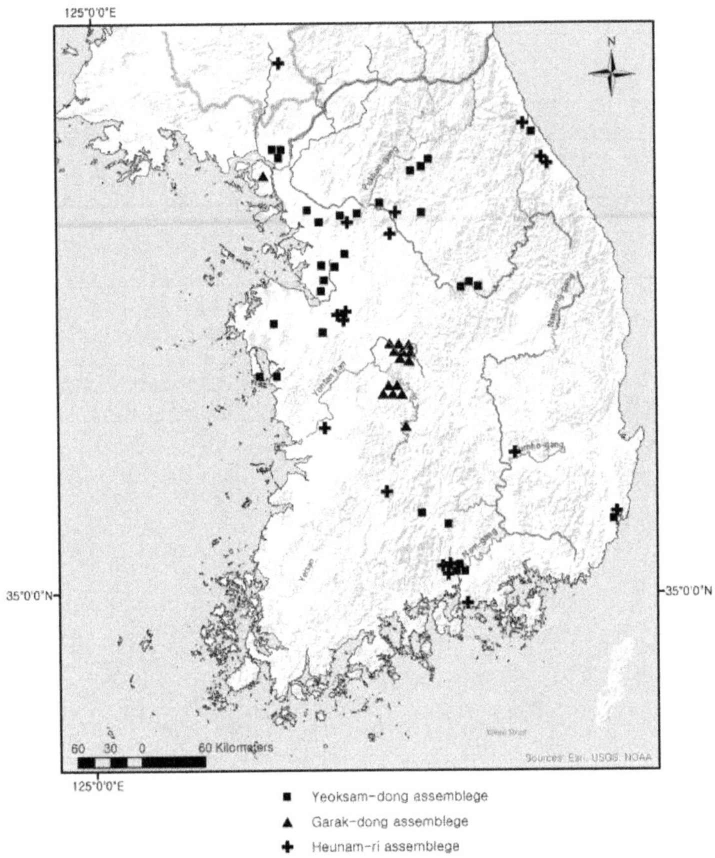

FIGURE 2. 32. THE DISTRIBUTION OF YEOKSAM-DONG, GARAK-DONG, AND HEUNAM-RI ASSEMBLAGES (MODIFIED BY THE AUTHOR BASED ON THE MAP FROM KIM 2001: 42)

to the fact that the group, who possessed the Misong-ri (미송리, 美松里) pottery and bronze artefacts[12] (refer to Figure 2.38), appeared in the Cheongchon River in the northwest of the Korean peninsula, the people, who lived there earlier than the group using Misong-ri pottery and used Gakhyeong (top-shaped, 각형, 角形) pottery[13] (Figure 2.37), migrated to southern Korea. As a result, Garak-dong pottery appeared in this area. Secondly, it is thought that the Heunam-ri pottery was formed concurrently as the consequence of the coexistence and assimilation of these people with groups using the Yeoksam-dong pottery, who had already occupied these areas.

Together with these features, it is useful to look at where the evidence (for example, dry fields and paddies) for Bronze Age agriculture is located in the Korean peninsula. Crawford and Lee (2003) focused their analysis on South Gyeongsang Province (Figure 2.39), from the Middle Chulmun (corresponding to the Neolithic period) to the Middle Mumun (corresponding to the Bronze Age) periods, spanning between ca. 3000 BC and ca. 1000 BC, in order to understand the origins of agricultural in the Korean peninsula. In the Nam River project in Jinju

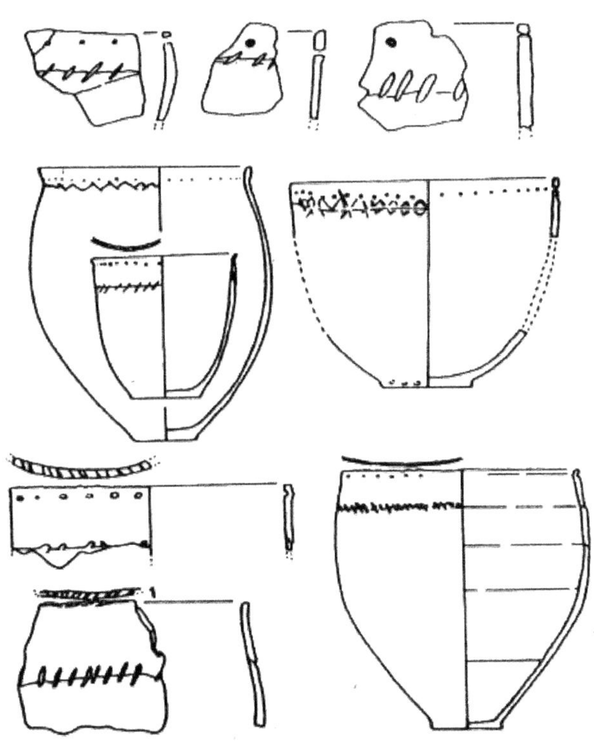

FIGURE 2. 33. THE HEUNAM-RI POTTERY (NATIONAL RESEARCH INSTITUTE OF CULTURAL PROPERTIES KOREA 2001: 1343, WITH THE PERMISSION OF SNUM)

[12] These were discovered in Misong-ri cave, located in the Cheongchon River basin in the Pyeongan Buk-do in 1959 (National Research Institute of Cultural Properties Korea 2001: 434-4; Kim 1978a: 82, Figure 2.39).

[13] This was discovered in the Sinhung-dong site, Bongsan-gun, Hwanghae Buk-do in 1958 (National Research Institute of Cultural Properties Korea 2001: 788-789, 1232-1233; Kim 1978: 69-73, Figure 2.38).

FIGURE 2. 34. THE YEOKSAM-DONG TYPE POTTERY (THE COLLECTION OF THE KOREAN CHRISTIAN MUSEUM (HENCEFORTH, KCH) AT SOONGSIL UNIVERSITY. PHOTOGRAPH PROVIDED BY THE KCH)

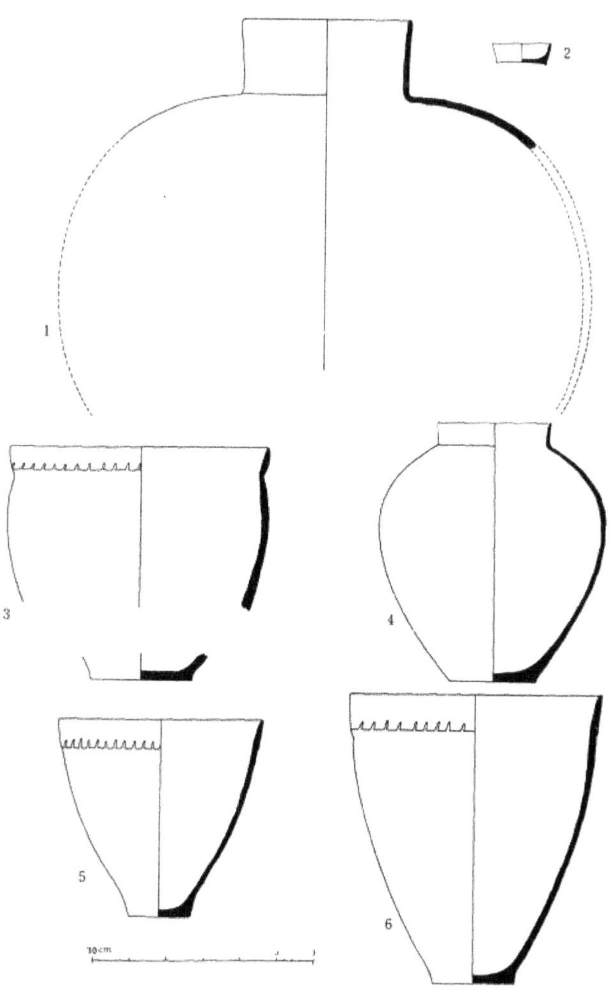

FIGURE 2. 35. THE GARAK-DONG POTTERY (FROM KIM 1963: 17)

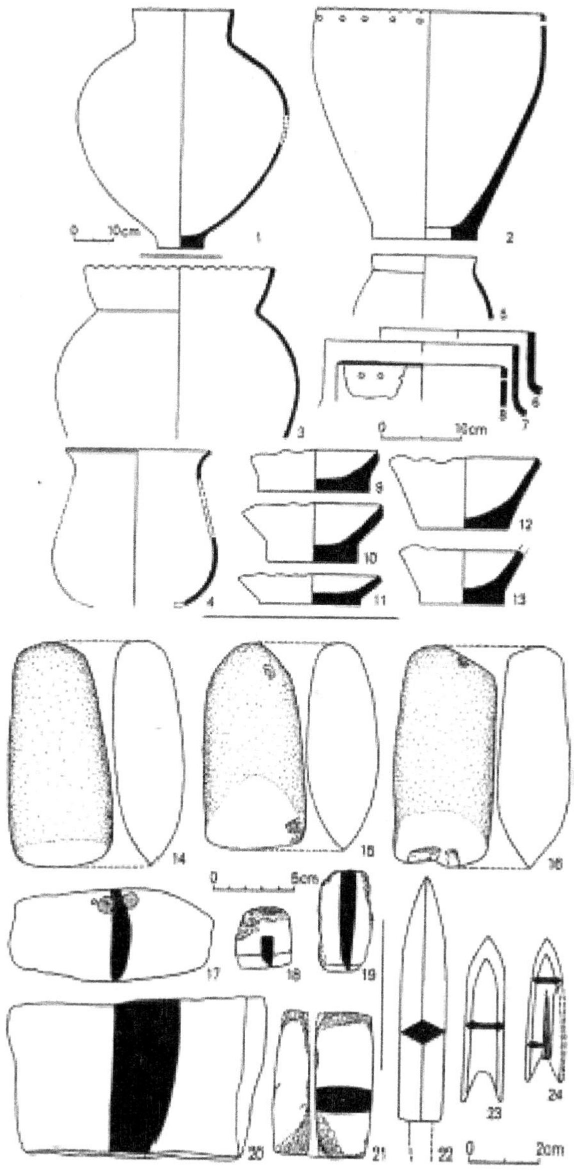

FIGURE 2. 36. YEOKSAM-DONG ASSEMBLAGE (FROM KIM 1978A: 91)

(Oun, Okbang, and Sangcheon sites) 1.8 ha of dry fields were excavated with pit-houses, dolmens, and stone-cist burials in a 400 ha region. Regarding the evidence for dry-field crops, at Okbang site 1, soybean was collected and measured that dated to between 1000 – 900 cal. BC and at Daundong in Ulsan *Vigna* sp. was recovered and the samples were dated to between 760-600 cal. BC. Also, the oldest Korean wheat AMS is dated to ca. 1000 cal. BC (*ibid*: 91). As far as rice agriculture evidence is concerned, the two oldest paddy fields among ten that have been excavated, were found in Okhyun and Yaumdong sites in Ulsan, each dating from the Early Mumun period, supporting the theory that rice seems to have been grown in paddy fields from the Early and Middle Mumun periods (*ibid*: 92). In addition, there are two AMS dates of 1950 and 1000 cal. BC for rice grains from Oun site 1. The latter is related to an Early Mumun context and the former which was recovered from an Early Mumun pit-house, is

FIGURE 2. 37. RESTORED GAKHYEONG (TOP-SHAPED) POTTERY (NATIONAL MUSEUM OF KOREA 1993: 28) (THE COLLECTION OF NMK, WITH THE PERMISSION OF NMK)

dated to the Late Chulmun period. It should be noted that rice has not been recovered from any specific Chulmun period contexts at Oun site 1 (*ibid*). Although this evidence is from a Southern region in the Korean peninsula, when comparing it with that obtained from the research area, the agricultural data provides an understanding of the environment and of the subsistence economy practised in the Bronze Age period.

Sang-gyoon Lee (2003) investigated the plans of dwellings of the Neolithic period in Korea, which have been described as round, square, and rectangular in shape. He presumed that the interior of the structure consisted of a place to sleep, a cooking area, and a work space. In addition, according to the analysis of the arrangement of houses within several settlement sites in the Neolithic period, it is suggested that there were semi-circular spaces for the community in the centre of the settlements (Lee 2003: 29).

Ja-jin Koo (2005) researched the Daecheon-ri Neolithic dwelling site which has well preserved inner facilities and postholes. He used it to extrapolate the structures and the living conditions of the Neolithic period of Korea. The plan shows that there was a living area and an annex. It is conceivable that the living space was divided into two areas: a living place for sleeping and repose and a work place for cooking and heating. Similar dwelling plans have been excavated in inland areas and in southern Korea. It appears that rectangular houses emerged after 3500 BC and continued throughout the Neolithic. Thereafter these structures seem to have been succeeded by the long-

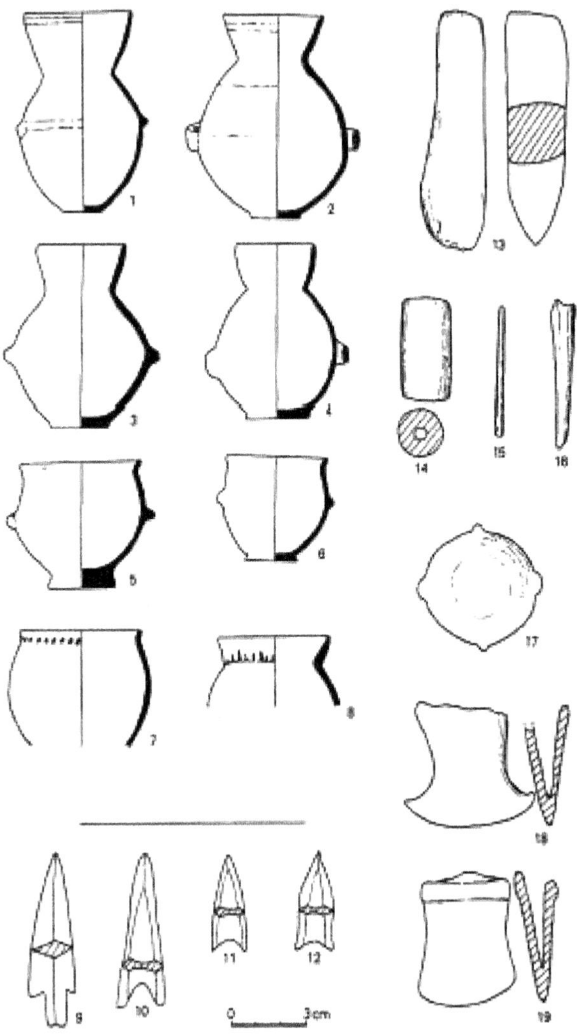

FIGURE 2. 38. SPECIMENS FROM THE UPPER LAYER OF THE MISONG-NI SITE (FROM KIM 1978A: 83)

rectangular house plan in the Bronze Age (Koo 2005: 36). Rectangular-shaped houses seem on the whole to appear in the Late Neolithic period in the Korean peninsula. However Late Neolithic examples of these houses have not yet been discovered in the archaeological record in the study area of the central part of the Korean peninsula (Lee 2005c: 195). This will be discussed further in Chapter 4.

Seong-hee Park (2006) analysed the geographical locations of the Bronze Age settlements in the mid-Western part of the Korean peninsula in order to find the locational pattern of each cultural type, i.e., Garak-dong, Yeoksam-dong, and Songgung-ni (송국리, 松菊里), which were identified on the basis of the shapes of the houses and the assemblages of associated artefacts (refer to Table 2.12). First of all, he divided the settlement location into two categories: 1) hill and 2) riverside and coast. He then sub-divided the hill type into two classifications according to the relative elevation, which is the difference in altitude between the site and its surrounding plain. As a result, the Garak-dong and Songgung-ni types, by and large, were situated in the lowlands (under 40 m), while the Yeoksam-dong types

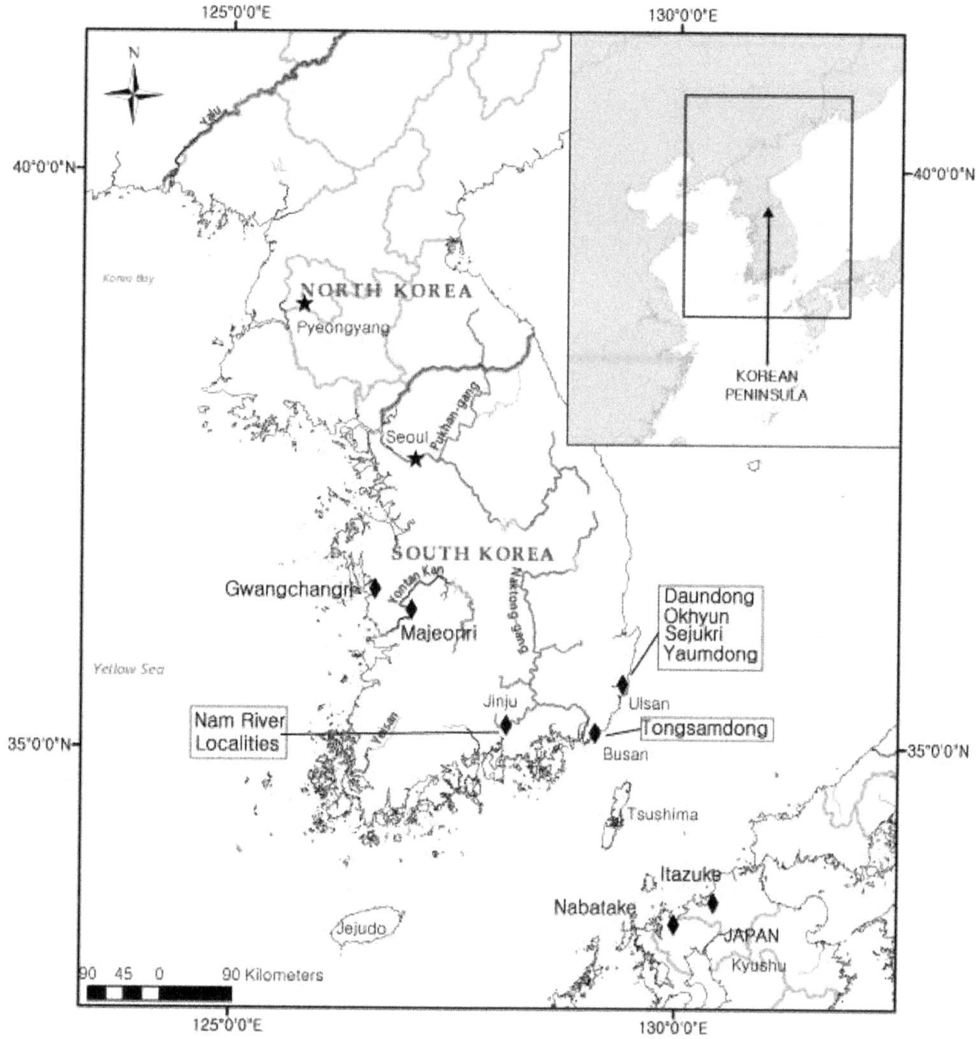

FIGURE 2. 39. SITE LOCATIONS IN THE NAM RIVER PROJECT (MODIFIED BY THE AUTHOR BASED ON THE MAP FROM CRAWFORD AND LEE 2003: 88)

TABLE 2. 12. THE ATTRIBUTE TABLE OF MATERIAL CULTURE ATTRIBUTES IN THE BRONZE AGE KOREA (MODIFIED BY THE AUTHOR BASED ON THE TABLE FROM PARK 2006: 24)

Attribute \ Cultural Pattern		Early Bronze Age			Late Bronze Age
		Misa-ri	Garak-dong	Yeoksam-dong	Songgung-ni
House	Plan	rectangular	rectangular	Thin-rectangular	Circle, Square
	Hearth	Hearth with circular flat stone	Hearth with circular stone	Hearth without stone	Oval-shaped hearth
Pottery		Plain pottery with a band on the rim	Doubled-rim with short slant line	Pottery with perforated rim or pottery with a notched strip on the rim	Egg-shaped pottery with outcurved rim
Stone tools		Polished stone dagger with two- step handle			Polished stone dagger with one step handle Triangular stone knife, stone adze
Bronze artefacts					Bipa-shaped bronze dagger

FIGURE 2. 40. SETTLEMENT NO. 27. HANAM MISARI SITE PLAN (FROM YOON AND LEE 1994: 39)

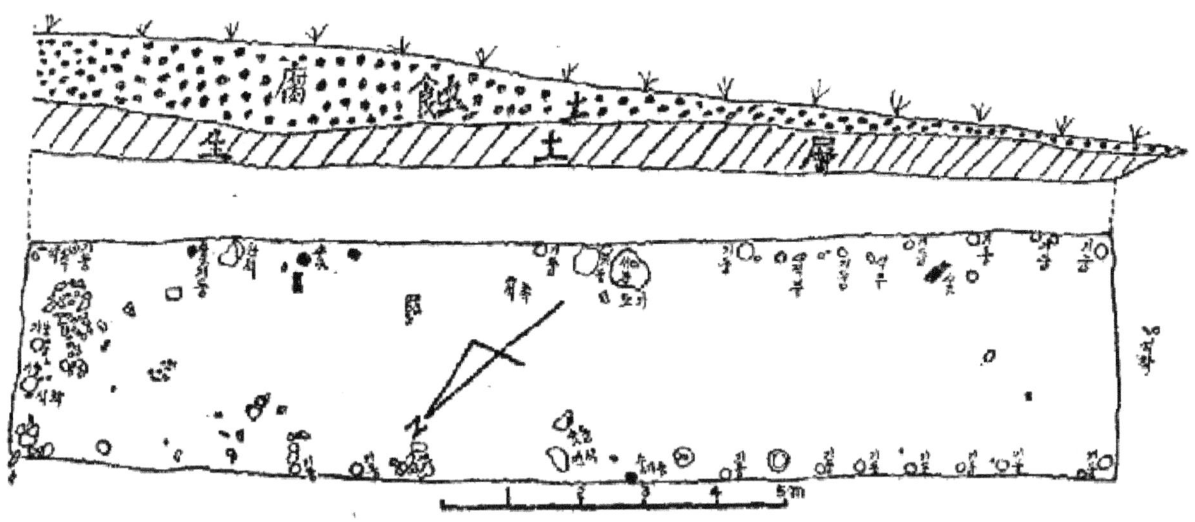

FIGURE 2. 41. SETTLEMENT NO.23. SEOUL YEOKSAMDONG SITE PLAN (FROM KIM AND IM 1968: 25)

tended to be located in the highlands (including and over 40 m). However, some Yeoksam-dong settlements were discovered in the lowlands and their artifactual attributes contained the Garak-dong type, for example, some sherds of double-rimmed pottery and hearths with circular stones. Therefore, it is thought that cultural contact took place between two groups of settlements. According to his interpretation, it has been argued that the highlands held advantages for hunting and gathering, and dry-farming. On the other hand, the lowlands seem to be advantageous for easy access to the flatlands. During the transitional period between the Early and Late stages of the Bronze Age, it is proposed that there was some tension between two groups, namely, the Garak-dong and the Songgung-ni (Park 2006: 47). One question that needs to be asked, however, is whether these complementary sites could have had different functions rather than different peoples.

Although the following researches did not deal with this study area, another feature worth mentioning is that Jong-il Kim (2002b), who introduced landscape archaeology to Korean archaeological circles, investigated the burial placement of the Songgung-ni culture, which is located in the south-western part of the Korean peninsula, dated to between the end of the Middle Bronze Age and the Late Bronze Age. He interpreted the concentric pattern of burials in this culture as a medium of equality within the community and a manifestation of the group's common

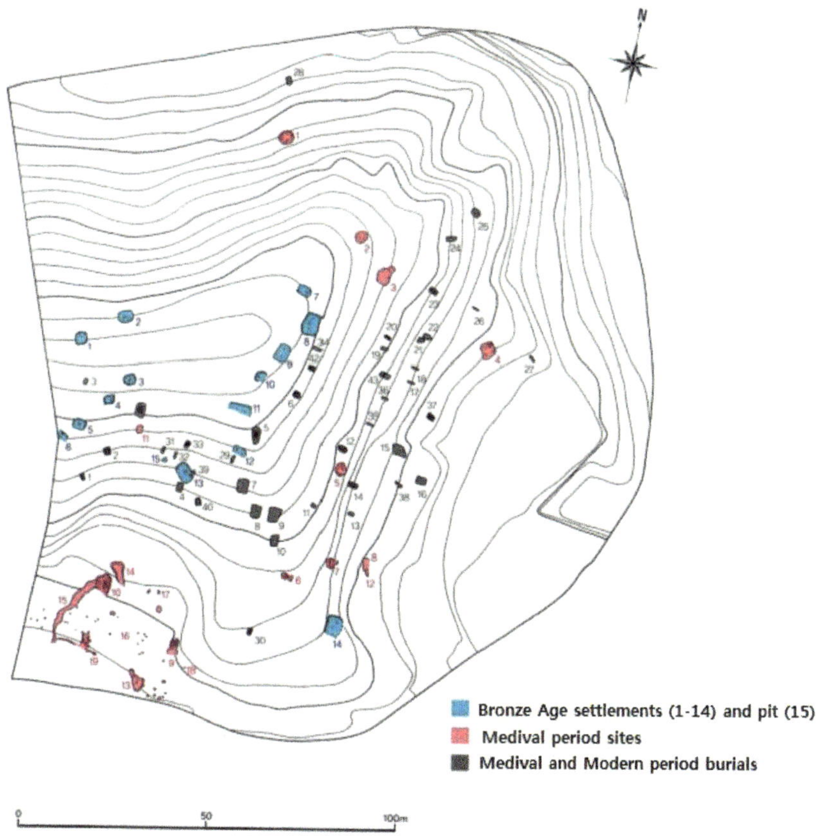

FIGURE 2. 42. SETTLEMENT NO. 39. HWASEONG BANSONGRI SITE PLANS (FROM GWON ET AL. 2007: 33, WITH THE PERMISSION OF HANSHIN UNIVERSITY MUSEUM)

ancestors. On the other hand, he interpreted linear patterns in the burials as demonstrative of gender differentiation (male burials) instead of an expression of hierarchy. In addition, Beum-cheol Kim also examined the relationship between the hierarchical settlement patterns and the intensification of rice agriculture through a series of articles (2005; 2006a; 2006b) about Middle Bronze Age Songgung-ni type settlements situated near the Guem River, which are located in the mid-west of the Korean peninsula.

2.2.3 *Iron Age*

Although the Iron Age is not the main period of focus in this study, in order to examine change and continuity between the Bronze Age and the Iron Age, key characteristics of the latter are briefly discussed here. On the basis of a new chronology for Korean archaeology (Choi 2003: 3; Choi 2008: 20-23, 90-99, 166; Kim 2002: 24, refer to Table 2.3), the Early Iron Age seems to have been established between 400 BC and 1 BC and the Late Iron Age[14] seems to date from AD 1 to AD 300.

According to Seong-rak Choi (1997: 402-403), there are three distinctive features of houses from the Iron Age. Firstly, compared to the Bronze Age, the usage of oval and rectangular shaped houses increased and 凸 (inverted 'T') shaped and a 呂 shaped houses were developed especially in the mid-Korean Peninsula. Secondly, unlike the hearth without a stone and the hearth with circular stones of the Bronze Age, a tunnel type and a stone-paved hearth type have been identified. Choi thought that hearths developed as *Ondol* (Korean floor heater, 온돌, 溫突) as well as a system of kitchen ranges too (부뚜막) during this late period. The latter seemed to be a progression to a space that was recognisable as a kitchen. Thirdly, the depth of the house pit was decreased and a posthole-type building (고상가옥, 高床家屋) emerged as a common form. In addition, enclosures and hill forts had been developed continuously during the period (Min 1997: 444-445). Together with these features, according to Nak-joon Seong (1997: 409-425), various types of burial coexisted in the Iron age, such as dolmens, cists, stacked stone burials, jars used for burials and pit burials. Among these, dolmens seem to have disappeared from around 300 BC in the northern part of the Korean peninsula, but, seem to have been maintained in the southern part of Korea until around the beginning of the first century AD. There were, in addition, three different types of pit burials were practised, such as, a pit burial, a pit burial with a wooden coffin, and a pit burial with a wooden chamber (Seong 1997: 409-425). Finally, Iron artefacts, Bronze slender daggers, bronze mirrors with thin lines, moulds, and pottery with round clay strips on the rim (refer to Figure 2.17) and hard plain pottery,

[14] This Age is applicable to the Three Han (삼한, 三韓: Mahan (마한, 馬韓), Jinhan (진한, 辰韓), Byeonhan (변한, 弁韓) period or Early Three Kingdoms (삼국, 三國: Goguryeo (고구려, 高句麗), Baekjae (백제, 百濟), Silla (신라, 新羅) period) (Choi 2008a: 166).

which was made by firing at 700-850 °C, were the key elements of the material culture relating to the Iron Age (Choi 2008a: 175-179).

During the Early Iron Age, according to the Chinese historical records, *Shiji* (사기, 史記, Records of the Grand Historian) by Sima Qian's (사마천, 司馬遷, 145 BC – 87 BC), Sānguó Zhì (삼국지, 三國志) *Wei Zhi* (위지, 魏志) *Dongyizhuan* (동이전, 東夷傳) by Chen Shou (진수, 陳壽, AD 233–297) and *Hòuhàn Shū* (후한서, 後漢書, Book of the Later Han) *Dongyi liezhuan* (동이열전, 東夷列傳) by Fan Ye (범엽, 范曄, AD 398 -445), there seemed to be several complex societies, such as, Wiman Joseon (위만조선, 衛滿朝鮮), Buyeo (부여, 夫餘), Goguryeo (고구려, 高句麗), Okjeo (옥저, 沃沮), Dongye (동예, 東濊), and Samhan (삼한, 三韓) in the Korean peninsula and Manchuria. Wiman Joseon (위만조선, 衛滿朝鮮, BC 194- BC 108) is assumed to be the first state in Korean history (Choi 2008: 238). That is, it is thought that several states were formed during the Iron Age and were recorded as discreet historical periods at a later date.

2.2.4 Background Summary

As can be seen, on the one hand, previous research on dolmens may be divided into two main debates: firstly, what were the origins of dolmens and when did they start to be built? It is suggested that either their creation dates from the Neolithic period though this is poorly supported or from the Bronze Age. Secondly, it is debated whether the societies who built the dolmens were hierarchical or egalitarian. Traditionally, dolmen societies in the Bronze Age have been defined as chiefdom socio-politically and the scale of society was estimated by the weight or size of capstones. On the other hand, settlement studies have concentrated mainly on material culture, represented by pottery types and house plans. Several researchers have interpreted the similarities of a number of assemblages of pottery styles and house forms as indicative of the migration of different cultural groups.

It has been difficult to synthesise the life and death of Korean Bronze Age peoples by considering the relationship between settlements and monuments, due to the lack of archaeological data concerning the full context of the landscape. However, since excavation data with a broader scope have increasingly been gathered post-1990 and as GIS methodology has been developed, it is possible to reconstruct Bronze Age society tentatively through an examination of the relationship between settlements and monuments. In addition, if traditional research based on a neo-evolutionary stance has tried to reveal or reconstruct Bronze Age society on the basis of its socio-political aspects, this study will set out to explore long-term changes in Bronze Age society in the mid-Korean peninsula on the basis of an analysis of the relationship between settlements and monuments from a combined standpoint of landscape archaeology and phenomenological approaches.

In order to complement the paucity of ^{14}C dating from dolmens, it will be necessary to consider settlements that share similar material cultures with associated monuments. Bayesian modelling is applied to establish the chronology of the five main pottery types of the Bronze Age in this region: pottery with double rims with slanting lines, pottery with perforated rims, pottery with notched rims, Heunamri type pottery, and red-burnished ware, and the specific chronologies of the three different house shapes – thin-rectangular, rectangular, and square – represented in the study area. After that, experimentally, on the basis of dating information from settlements, monuments from 5 km site catchments adjusted for energy expenditure areas and of 5km Euclidean distances (refer to Chap. 6.3) from each settlement will be extracted. Using this information, long-term change in settlements and monuments during the Bronze Age will be examined.

In addition, a change in the subsistence economy might have prompted an alteration of the landscape by people in order to create new settings for agriculture. The traces of this remolding can be read based on the distribution of settlements and monuments and the patterns they form. In order examine what elements affected the positioning of settlements and monuments during the Bronze Age, both physical elements of the landscape – such as pedological, hydrological and topographical analyses – and cultural elements – landform preferences, viewshed, movement and site orientation – will be considered. In order to extract meaningful human decisions, the 'baseline' situation of the study area will be acknowledged using GIS, and the significance of observed patterns will be tested by chi-square tests, in order to resolve another limitation of previous research. That is, in former studies, an objective standard of geographical information for the overall tendency of the research area was not utilised; as a consequence, it was impossible to test the statistical significance of site distributions, and whether or not the patterns observed could be said to be meaningful.

2.3 Research area and data information

Dolmens are distributed across the entire Korean peninsula (Figure 2.43: approximately 29,510 dolmens have been identified so far (Choi et al. 1999: 4)), but for this study the research area was confined to Seoul, Incheon and Gyeonggi provinces, which are the central western parts of the peninsula and are located between a longitude of 126 and 127 degrees, and a latitude of 36 and 38 degrees. The area is approximately 11,800 km^2. There are 76 Bronze Age settlements (Red dots are settlements) and 236 monument sites (Black dots are monument sites) (refer to Figure 2.44 and Figure 2.45: the total number of monument sites in this region is approximately 236[15] (Seoul-8, Incheon-17, and Gyeonggi-211 (Im and Yang 1999; Incheon Metropolitan City and Cultural Heritage

[15] Monument sites include 219 dolmen sites and 17 menhir sites. They may have different fuctions, but, due to the fact that both were made by stone, they were considered as monument in this research.

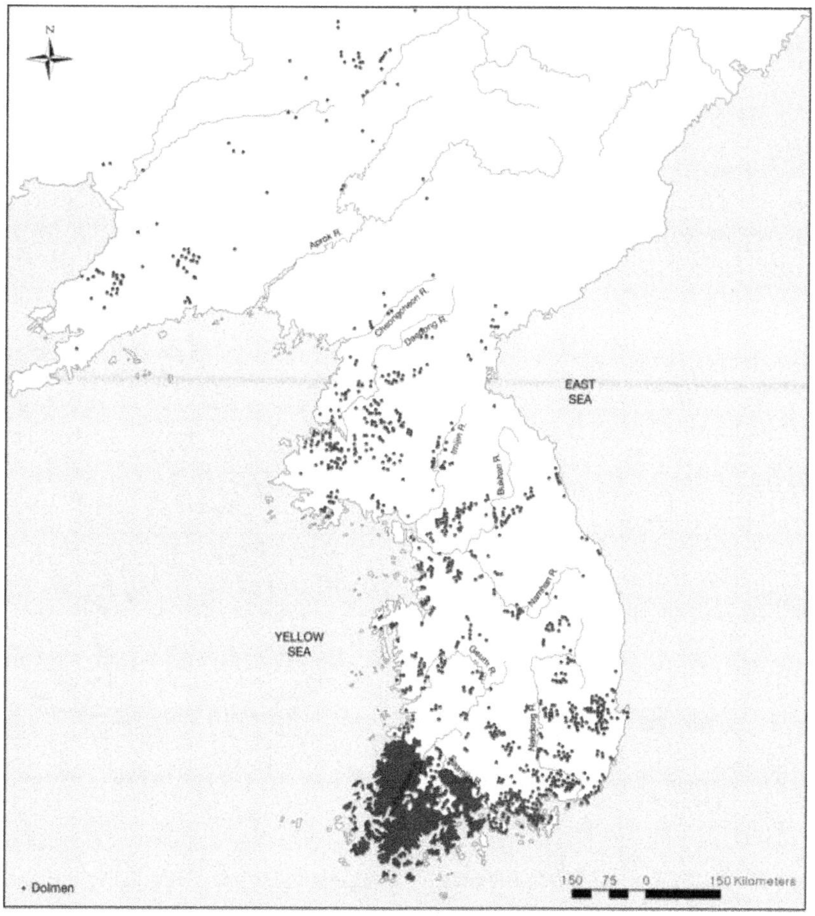

FIGURE 2. 43. THE DISTRIBUTION OF DOLMENS IN THE KOREAN PENINSULA
(CHOI ET AL. 1999: 1207, MODIFIED BY MS. ALISON WILKINS)

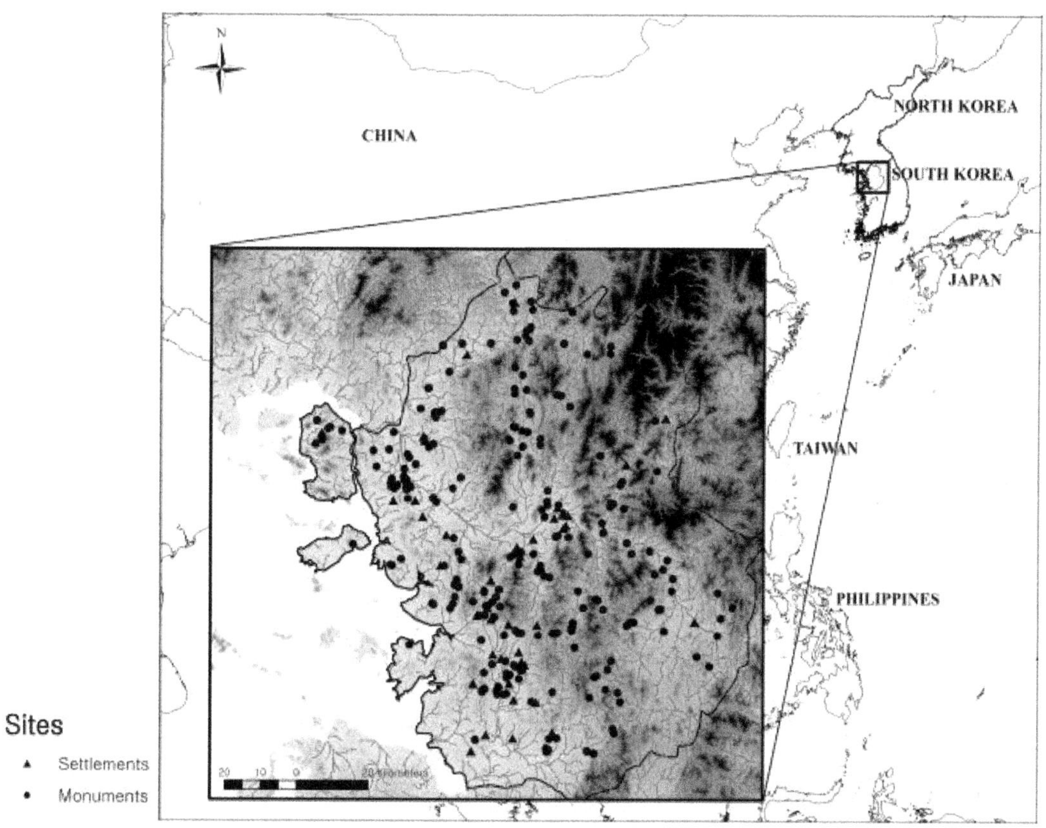

FIGURE 2. 44. MAP OF THE STUDY AREA

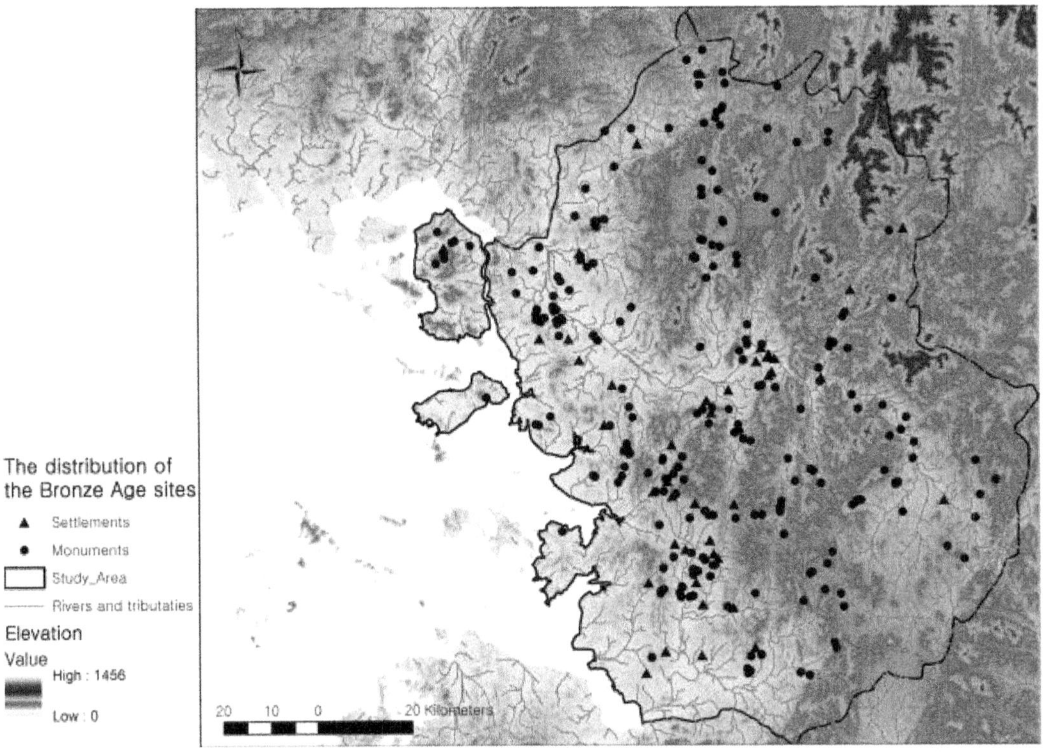

FIGURE 2. 45. THE DISTRIBUTION OF SETTLEMENT AND MONUMENT SITES IN THE CENTRAL REGIONS OF KOREA

Investigation Committee 2002; Choi et al. 2005; Incheon Metropolitan City Council and Inha University Museum 2005; Woo 2006; Gyeonggi provincial museum 2007)) and the number of individual monuments is 730[16] (Seoul-12, Incheon-89, and Gyeonggi-629: among the number of Gyeonggi, 147 has been excavated. Gyeonggi Provincial Museum 2007: 674-687). The reasons why these regions were chosen are that firstly, it has been possible to identify archaeological sites dating from the Palaeolithic to the Iron Age in these areas. In addition, there exist a number of different types of dolmens in this area, for example, table type (northern type), capstone type, and Baduk board type (southern type), although the third type was discovered at only two sites (refer to Appendix 5). Finally, in addition to the dolmen studies, since settlements have been excavated continuously in this region, 76 settlements have been currently identified and a synthesis of all the collected data is required to successfully interpret the evidence. Before presenting the analyses, it is appropriate to consider some potential data limitations for the study area.

Data limitations

Although several different institutes have surveyed the chosen research area up to 2009, they have not cumulatively covered the entire area. Therefore, the present research is based on the currently available data. Secondly, due to agricultural and urban development in the research area, which includes Seoul the capital of the Republic of Korea and its satellite cities, an unknown number of monuments have been destroyed and/or moved from their original location[17]. But due to the sheer weight of the stone monuments, it has been inferred that they may be situated near to their original locations. In contrast, as traces of settlements are now to be found only under the earth, many sites may have been destroyed and so there are taphonomic considerations. If we can consider scattered sites, this may compensate to some extent for the limitations of the settlement data. However, it was rather difficult to identify the X and Y coordinates of scattered sites at this stage, and consequently, only several sites were considered on the basis of paper maps and further work needs to be done to establish this identification.

The major difficulty has been identifying the X and Y coordinates for each site in order to analyse them using GIS (Geographical Information Systems). The reason is that, even though GIS use has pervaded Cultural Heritage studies in South Korea, not all X and Y coordinates for archaeological sites have been recorded. As a result, site locations have been confirmed using a number of methods; first, the dolmen distribution map from the supplement 'Dolmens in Gyeonggido' by Gyeonggi provincial museum was scanned (2007) and geo-referenced with the base DEM (Digital Elevation Models) of the research area. The location of other sites, which were not presented

[16] There are 706 dolmens and 24 menhirs.

[17] Firstly, the project team in Gyeonggi provincial museum researched the number of dolmens on the basis of survey reports by province and county council. They confirmed 556 dolmens in 2000. However, through the results of field investigations, they identified 539 dolmens (382 dolmens remained among 556 dolmens and 157 dolmens have been newly reported by this team) and 24 menhirs. According to the site research, a total 655 dolmens were distributed in Gyeonggi province in 2007 (Baek and Oh, 2007: 17-20).

in the above map, was identified using Google earth. As the base DEM, raster data (30m x 30m grid) was used at the beginning. However, there were some mismatches with the DEM from the Korean National Clearing House. Therefore, it was changed to vector data, SRTM (90m x 90m grid) (CGIAR-CSI (Consultative Group on International Agriculture Research - Consortium for spatial information)) following the suggestion of John Pouncett (pers comm 2011). After that, using the base DEM, contour lines were generated and then, the maps of each site from the excavation reports were compared and thereafter the location points were created. As a result, the locations of 45 settlements (Appendix 6) among 76 and 236 monument sites (Appendix 7) were confirmed.

Chapter 3. Dating

3.1 Aims

Chronology is a critical issue in order to understand the past, especially at specific times and for certain places (Whittle et al. 2007: 124). The consideration of the sequences of archaeological sites has allowed archaeologists to look at long-term patterns of events and processes and to create a sense of history.

The 'burials' in most table type dolmens actually comprise bodies laid out on the ground rather than buried in the earth. Therefore they are poorly preserved and also easily disturbed or plundered from their creation and onwards, so that it has been fairly difficult to identify and clarify the dating results from these sites. Two radiocarbon determinations from monuments and one radiocarbon determination from a settlement under a dolmen in the study area were identified (refer to Appendix 8). In addition, there were seven radiocarbon determinations from monuments situated in regions in the southern part of the Korean peninsula (*ibid*). These data will be informative for our understanding of the time scale of monuments, but, due to the paucity of ^{14}C dating from dolmens, it will be necessary to consider settlements data. There will also be a need to examine the potential multi-period use of settlements themselves. In order to look at long-term change it is preferable to examine the radiocarbon dating from settlements which share similar material cultures, such as pottery sherds with perforated and/or notched rims, red-burnished ware, stone daggers and arrowheads, all recovered from near to and under monuments.

The main questions in this chapter are firstly, what was the duration of active use of the settlements in the study area; and secondly, which temporally sensitive characteristics can be identified, with a focus on pottery types and house shapes. The dating model is applied to establish the chronology of the five main types of Korean Bronze Age pottery (pottery with a doubled rim with slant lines, pottery with a perforated rim, pottery with a notched rim, Heunamri type pottery, and red-burnished ware) and the specific chronologies of the three different house shape types (thin-rectangular, rectangular, and square), represented in the study area.

3.2 Methodology

3.2.1 Bayesian modelling

Following progress in the development of the high precision calibration curves for radiocarbon dating (Pearson and Stuiver 1986; Stuiver and Pearson 1986; Reimer et al. 2009), archaeologists can utilise radiocarbon results with greater confidence and quote calendar scaled dates (Buck et al. 1992: 497).

In order to refine the precision of radiocarbon chronologies, archaeologists and statisticians have applied Bayes' theorem to the process of interpreting calibrated probability distributions (Buck et al. 1991: 809).

Bayes' Theorem:

$$P[\text{parameters}|\text{data}] = \frac{P[\text{data}|\text{parameters}] \times P[\text{parameters}]}{P[\text{data}]}$$

The parameters are the unidentified calendar dates and the data are the radiocarbon determinations, where calendar timescale was calculated from the radiocarbon dates (Buck et al. 1991: 811). P[parameters] are *prior* information or marginal probability of parameters (ibid; Schulting 2009), P[data|parameters] are the *likelihood* of data given parameters and P[parameters|data] is the *posterior* probability of data given parameter (prior information) (Bronk Ramsey 2009: 338).

The distinctions between Bayesian approaches and conventional approaches to the production of calibrated dates are that firstly, Bayesian modelling is applied to more complex situations rather than single radiocarbon determinations (Buck et al. 1991: 809); secondly, a Bayesian application tends to consider uncertainties and focus on estimating duration and therefore, it represents the results of converted calendar dates, as the range of years with a probability of percentage values (Buck et al. 1994: 236); and thirdly, a Bayesian approach considers prior information in order to estimate posterior density functions (Buck et al. 1991: 811; Bronk Ramsey 2009: 338). Unlike simple 'eyeballing' of calibrated dates, Bayes' theorem considers prior information and can utilise prior beliefs for consecutive revisions of new data and as a result, it is possible to learn from experience (Buck et al. 1991: 811, 819).

Bayesian modelling in OxCal

A series of settlements in the study area with recorded stratigraphic information, provide the opportunity for Bayesian modelling employing informative priors (Buck et al. 1991; 1992; 1994; Bronk Ramsey 2009). The models presume a uniform phase of activity. The acceptability of models is evaluated by the agreement of individual datapoints (the dates) and also by the overall index of agreement 'A_{model}' (Bayliss et al. 2007: 6; Bronk Ramsey 2009: 356-357). A value of less than 60% designates that the model is unconvincing and also that the individual data within 'A_{model}' of less than 60% (equivalent to a 5% significant test) indicated poor agreement *(ibid)*. In addition, except some samples, which indicated detailed information or were collected from the hearth area, most samples were acquired from inside house structures, which seemed to have been destroyed by fire and consequently, provided evidence about the size of post holes and wood types. Therefore, in order to avoid the old wood effect and assuming that the timbers had a longer history of use than the structures, the outlier analysis in OxCal 4.1 (Bronk Ramsey 2009b), especially, the 'charcoal outlier model' was applied.

A series of radiocarbon determinations allotted to a phase of activity are presented with modelled 'start' and 'end' dates and use spans. In addition, summed probabilities of determinations were utilised only for visual purposes, as analytical usages could mislead readers because summed probabilities present longer periods than the real continuity of an archaeological event (Bayliss et al. 2007: 9-11).

3.2.2 Data

In an attempt to refine the chronology of Bronze Age settlements in Seoul, Incheon, and Gyeonggi province, a dating model was constructed, consisting of 100 published ^{14}C determinations based on charcoal from 16 settlements (See Appendix 9). Of these 100 determinations, some samples had been divided and sent to different institutes or have been measured twice using the same sample, or else three samples from the same settlement were measured. Therefore, to avoid the duplication of the identical sample they were combined using the R-combine command in OxCal 4.1, before running the Bayesian model. As a result, a total of 75 radiocarbon determinations from settlements in the research area were available (refer to Appendix 10). Among these, three dates with errors of more than 150 years were excluded (GX 22017, 2560 ± 370 BP from Pyeongtaek Hyeonhwari site and KAERI 154-1, 2696 ± 160 BP, KAERI 154-2 2666 ± 160 BP from Yeoju Heunamri). Most of the data were identified from previously published excavation reports (Kim and Yun 1967; Bae and Lee 2002; Jang et al. 2002a; Jang et al. 2002b; Im et al. 2002b; Lee et al. 2006; Jang et al. 2004; Park et al. 1996; Choi et al. 2002a; Department of Archaeology and Anthropology and The University Museum Seoul National University 1974; 1976; 1978; Ha 2004; Choi et al. 2007; Seung et al. 2007; Gwon et al. 2007; Choi et al. 2003b). The species of trees (where available) were reported mainly as (evergreen) oak (*Quercus acutissima*), with alder (*Alnus mandshurica*), cone pine (*Pinus koraiensis*), zelkova (*Zelkova serrate*), mulberry (*Morus*), and chestnut (*Castanaea crenata*) also identified (Park et al. 1996: 237-261; Choi et al. 2007: 365-374). They normally have long life spans and may present an old wood effect. Therefore, unless the reporters recorded in detail the original sampling in their reports, a charcoal outlier model in OxCal 4.1 (Bronk Ramsey 2009b) was applied. Four exceptions were GX-28886-AMS, 3010 ± 40 from the hearth in Hanam Misadong site, SNU00-359, 2880 ± 60, SNU00-360, 2940 ± 60 from Hwaseong Gogeumsan site, and HD-1, 2880 ± 60 from Hanam Deokpungdong. These were identified as branch wood, and therefore they were not treated as charcoal outliers.

In order to construct appropriate chronological models for long-term change, each radiocarbon determination from the settlements was calibrated and modelled using OxCal 4.1. Bayesian modelling was carried out on a total of 72 radiocarbon determinations from settlements in the research area to obtain the 'start' and 'end' boundaries for Bronze Age activity (treated as a single phase of activity). According to previous research (Choi 2008b), period[18] divisions of the Korean Bronze Age are suggested on the basis of different types of pottery. Traditionally, pottery with a doubled rim with slant lines (Garak-dong type pottery) was thought to have originated from the northwest region of the Korean peninsula while pottery with a perforated rim and pottery with a notched strip on the rim (Yeoksam-dong type pottery) seemed to derive from the northeast part of the peninsula (Lee 1974a). Heunamri type pottery, which has a doubled rim with slant lines and perforated and/or a notched rim ware, was likely to combine elements from both the northwest and the northeast parts of the peninsula and to have been developed in the study area (*ibid*). However, as mentioned in Chapter 2.2.2.2, J.S. Kim (2001) thought that Heunamri-type pottery emerged concurrently with the doubled rim with slant line pottery from the northwest. He postulated that Heunamri type pottery was developed when people from the northwest moved to the research region and were acculturated to the pre-existing culture in the area, which used both perforated rim and notched rim pottery. Besides these features, red-burnished ware was also discovered in conjunction with monuments and settlements. But, it has been discovered more frequently in conjunction with burials than at settlements. Bayesian modelling of five types of pottery were conducted in order to look at whether the chronology of the five pottery types can be plotted sequentially, and to assess the level of agreement between traditional and radiocarbon chronologies.

There is also a need to take into account the possible problems of association between pottery and charcoal samples before results can be presented. Most of the dates are obtained from previously published results and

[18] The period divisions in the Korean Bronze Age are based on the different types of pottery (Make a table based on the information from Choi 2008b: 22).

Period	years	Pottery types
Initial Bronze age	2000 BC – 1500 BC	Comb-patterned pottery Pottery with engraved bands
Early Bronze Age	1500 BC- 1000 BC	Pottery with doubled-rims (or with slant lines)
Middle Bronze age	1000 BC – 600 BC	Pottery with perforated rims
Late Bronze Age	600 BC – 400 BC	High temperature fired plain pottery
Late Bronze Age to Iron Age	400 BC – 1 BC	Pottery with clay strips on the rim

many of these comprise charcoal samples deriving from houses. Pottery samples were also discovered within the same houses but it is not recorded whether or not charcoal and pottery samples were identified in precisely the same stratigraphic context. Therefore, it has been assumed that the dates of the charcoal samples represent pottery usage. In addition, some houses might continue to adopt older styles of pottery.

3.3 Results

The results of all settlements in the study area, of pottery types, and of house shapes are presented in order. All dates are described in calibrated calendar years BC at 95.4% probability in the text (abbreviated to 95% in tables and 68.2% probability (abbreviated to 68%) are also presented in tables only).

3.3.1 Modelling activity in the study area

In order to identify the overall span of Bronze Age activity in the study area, radiocarbon determinations from settlements in the research area were taken as a unit. Therefore the Bayesian model treats all of the radiocarbon data from settlements as fitting into a single phase of activity. The modelled distribution is presented in Figure 3.1 and the modelled summed probability distribution is displayed for visual purposes in Figure 3.2. Among the 72 dates, at the first attempt utilising the model, two results (SNU03-212, 3160 ± 60, 58.1% agreement and KAERI No lab no., 2089 ± 60, 36% agreement) were designated as showing poor agreement. But as the first result showed nearly 60% (58.1%), only the second datum was excluded before running the model once again.

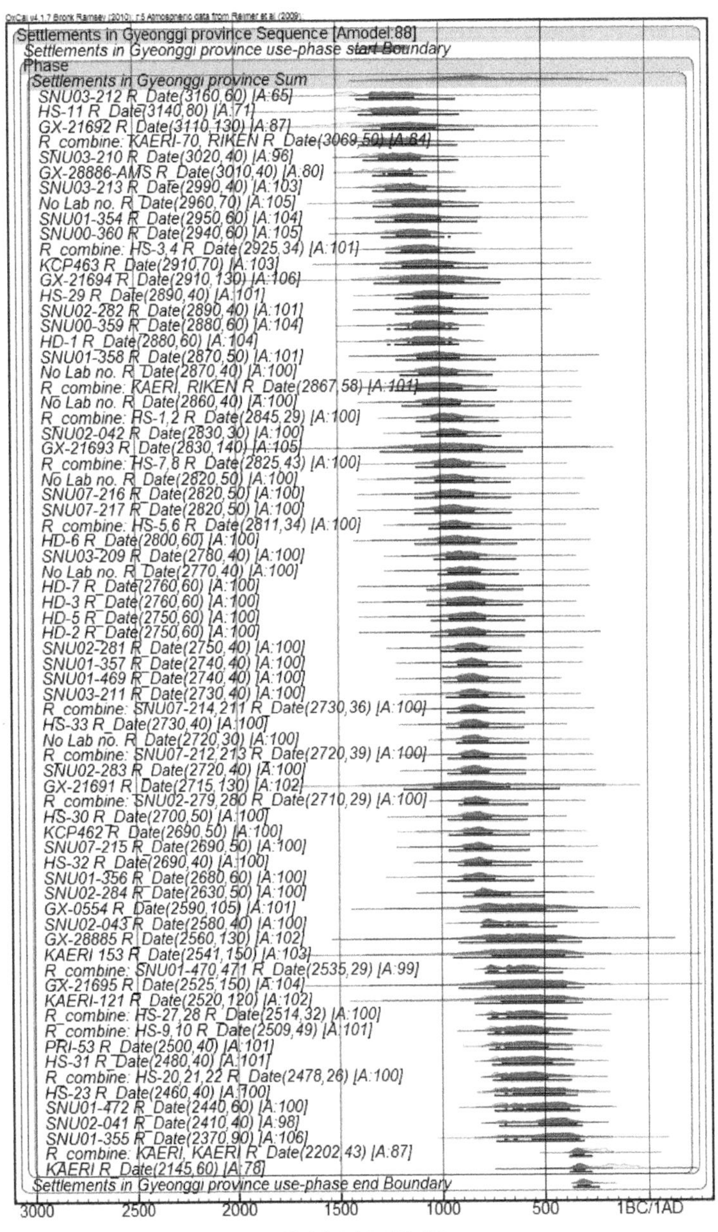

FIGURE 3. 1. MODELLED DISTRIBUTIONS BASED ON AN OUTLIER ANALYSIS (EXCEPT FOUR RESULTS: GX-28886-AMS, 3010 ± 40, SNU00-359, 2880 ± 60, SNU00-360, 2940 ± 60, HD-1, 2880 ± 60) OF 71 RADIOCARBON DETERMINATIONS ON CHARCOALS FROM SETTLEMENTS IN THE STUDY AREA, TREATED AS A SINGLE PHASE OF ACTIVITY (EXCLUDING GX-22017, KAERI 154-1 AND KAERI 154-2).

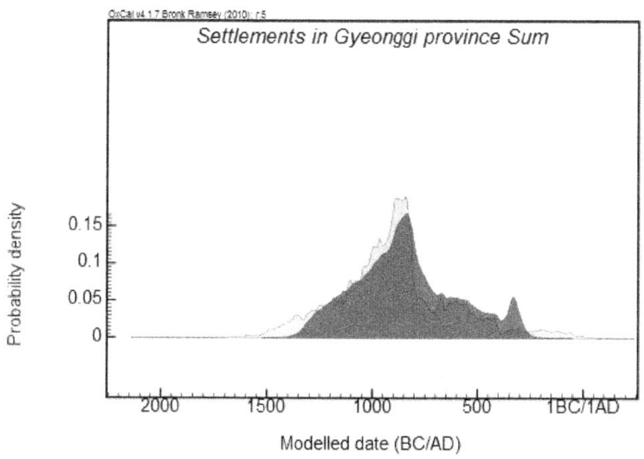

FIGURE 3. 2. MODELLED SUMMED PROBABILITY DISTRIBUTION BASED ON A CHARCOAL OUTLIER ANALYSIS OF 71 RADIOCARBON DETERMINATIONS ON CHARCOAL FROM SETTLEMENTS IN THE STUDY AREA (EXCLUDING GX-22017, KAERI 154-1 AND KAERI 154-2).

In order to identify the difference between simple modelled ranges and the modelled ranges based on the outlier analysis, two analyses were run respectively and the results are presented in Table 3.1. The difference in results between simple and outlier analyses is relatively minor. According to the results of the outlier analysis, the use of Bronze Age settlements in the Gyeonggi area commenced within the period *1390-1127 BC (95.4% probability*, Figure 3.3a), and ended *370-242 BC (95.4% probability*, Figure 3.3b), spanning between *805 and 1093 years (95.4% probability*, Figure 3.4). Comparing the results to the chronology of the Bronze Age in Korea (refer back to Table 2.3), the modelled start date ranges in the study area based on the outlier analysis, were somewhat later than the chronology of the Korean Bronze Age. However, the start date duration practically corresponds with the Early Bronze Age period. In addition, the end date ranges in the study area are somewhat later than the traditional Korean chronology. One reason for these results could be the radiocarbon determinations from the Yeoju Heunamri site. This site is very important among Bronze Age sites in Korea, because rice and agricultural evidence have been discovered at this site and a series of radiocarbon determinations have been produced. However, some dates have large errors (KAERI 154-1, 2696 ± 160 and KAERI 154-2, 2666 ± 160) and there might be a possibility of sample contamination or measurement error[19].

TABLE 3. 1. MODELLED START AND END DATE RANGES (CAL BC, 68% INCLUDED), AND USE-SPAN FOR ACTIVITY IN THE STUDY AREA, TREATING ALL RADIOCARBON DETERMINATIONS FROM SETTLEMENTS AS A SINGLE PHASE OF ACTIVITY. ALL MODELS EXCLUDE GX-22017 (2560 ± 370), KAERI 154-1 (2696 ± 160) AND KAERI 154-2 (2666 ± 160) DUE TO ERRORS OF MORE THAN 150 YEARS (RESULTS OF 'ORIGINAL' DATA INDICATES MODELLED CALIBRATED OUTCOMES BEFORE APPLYING TO THE OUTLIER ANALYSIS (CHARCOAL, 1).

Settlement	n	start	68%	start	95%	end	68%	end	95%	Amodel	span	68%	span	95%
Original	71	1381	1291	1444	1246	363	312	381	275	82.8	949	1060	898	1133
Outlier	71	1330	1170	1390	1127	347	286	370	242	88.7	864	1023	805	1093

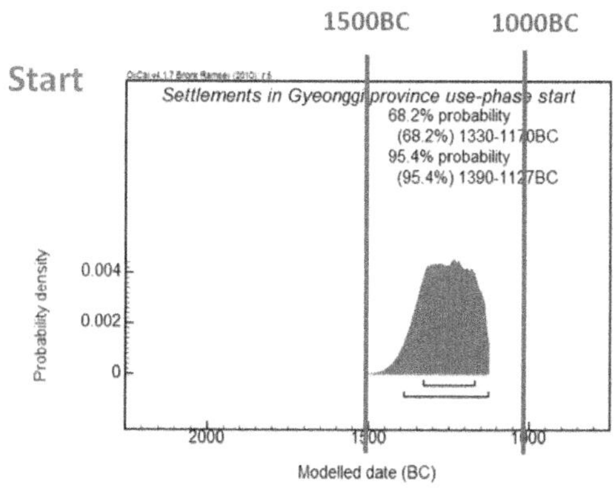

A) MODELLED START DATES

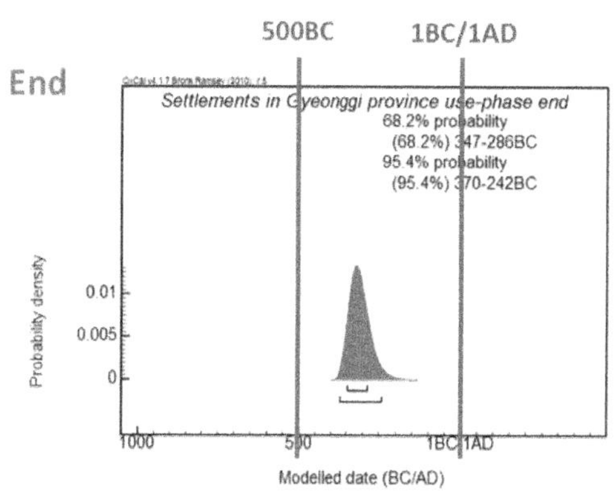

B) MODELLED END DATES

FIGURE 3. 3. MODELLED START AND END DATES BASED ON AN OUTLIER ANALYSIS OF 71 RADIOCARBON DETERMINATIONS ON CHARCOAL FROM SETTLEMENTS IN THE STUDY AREA (EXCLUDING GX-22017, KAERI 154-1 AND KAERI 154-2).

[19] Two charcoal samples from the no.12 settlement were cut in half and were sent to the KAERI (Korea Atomic Energy Research Institute) in Korea and to the RIKEN (Rikagagu Kenkyujo) in Japan respectively. The results of the first sample were 3210 ± 70 B.P. (KAERI) and 2920 ± 70 B.P. (RIKEN) and the results of the second were 2620 ± 100 B.P. and 2980 ± 70 B.P (RIKEN) (Department of Archaeology and Anthropology and The University Museum 1978: 17-18).

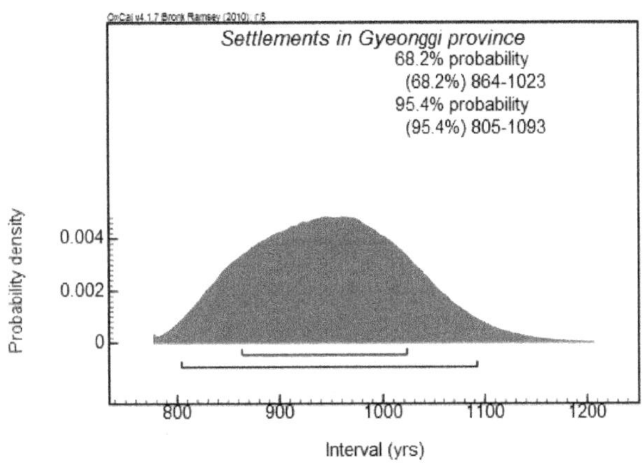

FIGURE 3. 4. MODELLED SPAN OF THE BRONZE AGE IN GYEONGGI PROVINCE BASED ON AN OUTLIER ANALYSIS OF 71 RADIOCARBON DETERMINATIONS ON CHARCOAL FROM SETTLEMENTS IN THE STUDY AREA (EXCLUDING GX-22017, KAERI 154-1 AND KAERI 154-2).

3.3.2 Pottery types

The best currently available estimations for the start and end dates and the usage spans of the five pottery types are presented in Table 3.3: doubled rim with slant lines[20], perforated rim[21], notched rim[22], Heunamri and red-burnished wares (refer to Appendix 11-a to 11-e). In order to compare the start and end ranges, the results presented in graph form were arranged and presented in Figure 3.5 and the modelled summed probability distribution, based on an outlier analysis of the five pottery types was also displayed by using the same scale for comparison, also used in Figures 3.6, 3.7, 3.8, 3.9 and 3.10.

As can be seen Figures 3.5 to 3.10, it is difficult to divide the Bronze Age in terms of pottery types, due to the fact that the five types of pottery seemed to have been used contemporaneously, with the exception that the emergence of red-burnished pottery was to some extent later that the others. With stratigraphic sequences, it might be possible to refine this analysis further.

TABLE 3. 2. MODELLED START AND END DATE RANGES (CAL BC, 68% INCLUDED), AND USE-SPAN FOR POTTERY TYPES IN THE STUDY AREA, TREATING THE RADIOCARBON DETERMINATIONS FROM SETTLEMENTS OF EACH POTTERY TYPE AS A SINGLE PHASE OF ACTIVITY.

Pottery type	n	start	68%	start	95%	end	68%	end	95%	Amodel	span	68%	span	95%
Doubled rim with slant lines	20	1440	1235	1557	1141	305	66	336	*cal*AD 49	88	1030	1351	871	1523
Perforated rim	33	1440	1290	1524	1216	367	292	391	215	82.9	951	1132	868	1253
Notched rim	29	1467	1305	1562	1220	344	226	352	56	78.8	994	1232	908	1426
Heunamri type	10	1503	1231	1771	1132	188	*cal*AD72	315	*cal*AD 338	92.9	1127	1557	951	1954
Red burnished	21	1184	1060	1284	1018	331	128	345	20	90.4	775	1021	715	1194

TABLE 3. 3. MODELLED START AND END DATE RANGES (CAL BC, 68% INCLUDED), AND USE-SPAN BASED ON AN OUTLIER ANALYSIS FOR POTTERY TYPES IN THE STUDY AREA, TREATING THE RADIOCARBON DETERMINATIONS FROM SETTLEMENTS OF EACH POTTERY TYPE AS A SINGLE PHASE OF ACTIVITY.

Pottery type	n	start	68%	Start	95%	end	68%	end	95%	Amodel	span	68%	span	95%
Doubled rim with slant lines	20	1475	1088	1592	682	216	*cal*AD 21	316	*cal*AD 149	92.5	952	1378	611	1575
Perforated rim	33	1333	1016	1455	946	353	236	699	127	88.2	733	1038	676	1217
Notched rim	29	1148	873	1456	822	309	154	331	9	86	645	989	567	1271
Heunamri type	10	1548	1117	1770	700	156	*cal*AD 140	276	*cal*AD 428	95.2	1044	1581	728	1998
Red burnished	21	1181	1047	1289	996	313	117	335	*cal*AD 13	90.3	790	1046	721	1209

[20] This category includes doubled-rim with slant lines, doubled-rim only, and slant lines only on the rim (Lee 2009: 21).

[21] Perforated rim and perforated with notched rim were included in this category.

[22] Notched rim and notched with perforated rim were comprised this group.

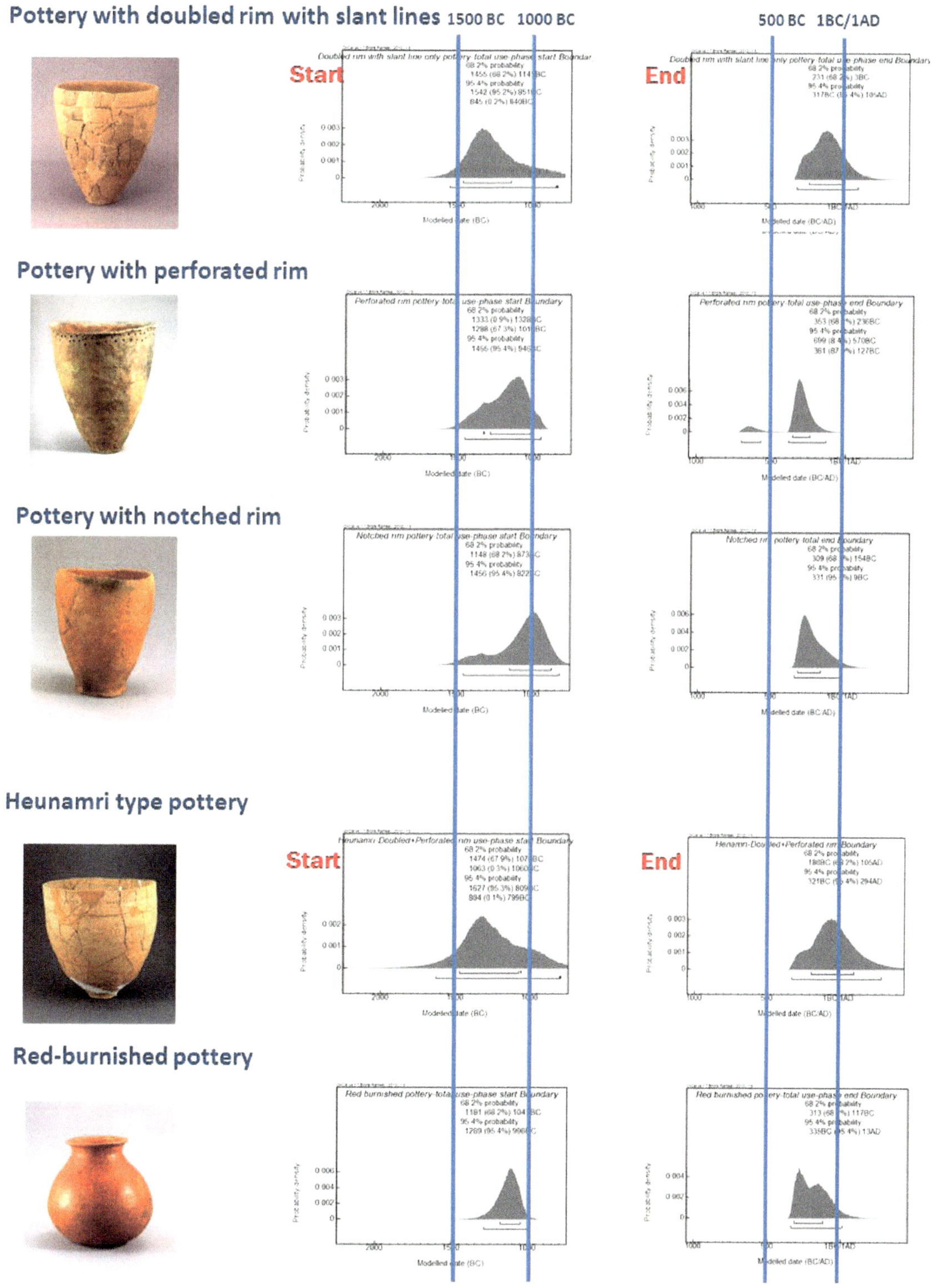

FIGURE 3. 5. MODELLED START AND END DATES BASED ON AN OUTLIER ANALYSIS OF RADIOCARBON DETERMINATIONS ON CHARCOAL FROM SETTLEMENTS WITH FIVE DIFFERENT TYPES OF POTTERY IN THE STUDY AREA (ALL INFORMATION ON EACH GRAPH IS PRESENTED IN TABLE 3.3). (NO. 1 PHOTO WAS PROVIDED BY KOREA UNIVERSITY MUSEUM (KUM II). NO. 2 AND 5 PHOTOS WERE PERMITTED BY NMK AND NO. 3 AND 4 PHOTOS BY SNUM, PLEASE REFER TO CHAP. 2)

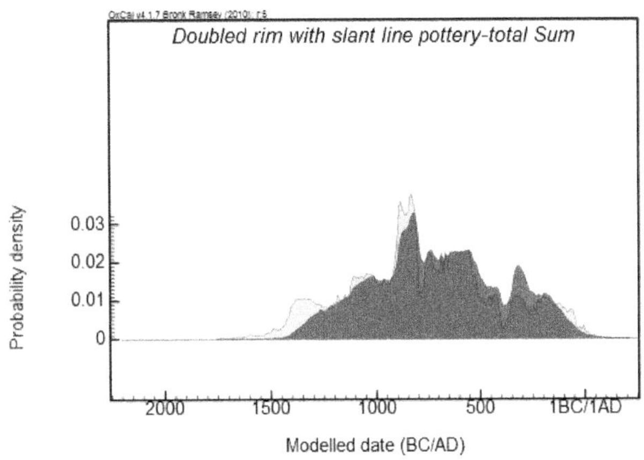

FIGURE 3. 6. MODELLED SUMMED PROBABILITY DISTRIBUTION BASED ON AN OUTLIER ANALYSIS OF 33 RADIOCARBON DETERMINATIONS ON CHARCOAL FROM SETTLEMENTS WITH SHERDS OF DOUBLED RIM WITH SLANT LINES POTTERY IN THE STUDY AREA.

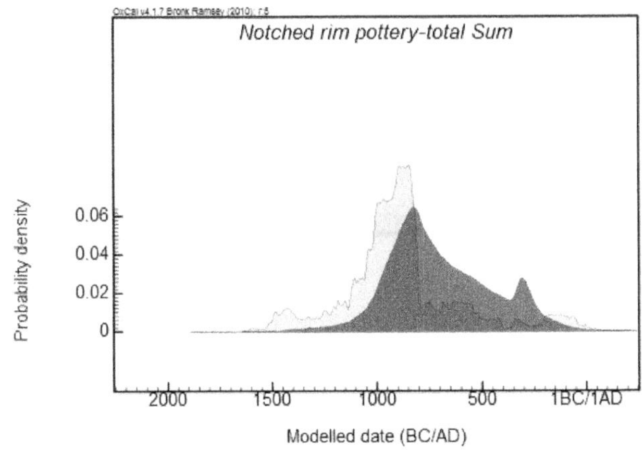

FIGURE 3. 7. MODELLED SUMMED PROBABILITY DISTRIBUTION BASED ON AN OUTLIER ANALYSIS OF 33 RADIOCARBON DETERMINATIONS ON CHARCOAL FROM SETTLEMENTS WITH SHERDS OF PERFORATED RIM POTTERY IN THE STUDY AREA.

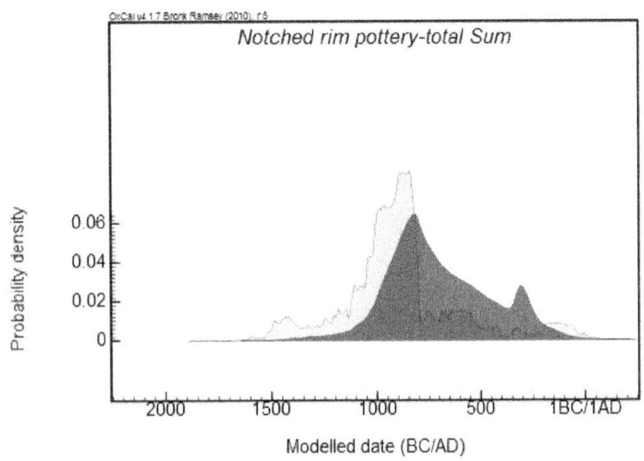

FIGURE 3. 8. MODELLED SUMMED PROBABILITY DISTRIBUTION BASED ON AN OUTLIER ANALYSIS OF 29 RADIOCARBON DETERMINATIONS ON CHARCOAL FROM SETTLEMENTS WITH SHERDS OF NOTCHED RIM POTTERY IN THE STUDY AREA.

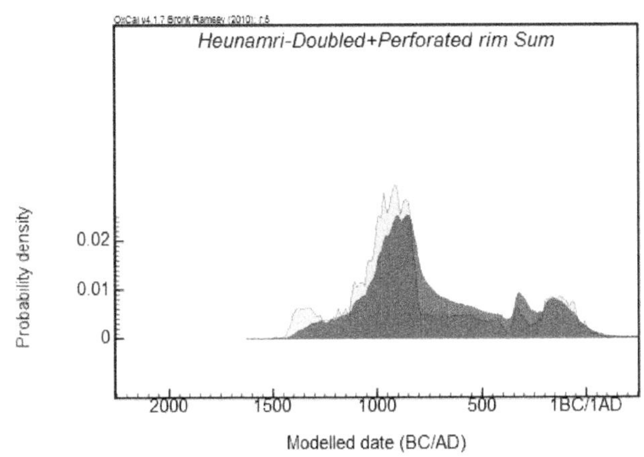

FIGURE 3. 9. MODELLED SUMMED PROBABILITY DISTRIBUTION BASED ON AN OUTLIER ANALYSIS OF 13 RADIOCARBON DETERMINATIONS ON CHARCOAL FROM SETTLEMENTS WITH SHERDS OF HEUNAMRI TYPE POTTERY IN THE STUDY AREA.

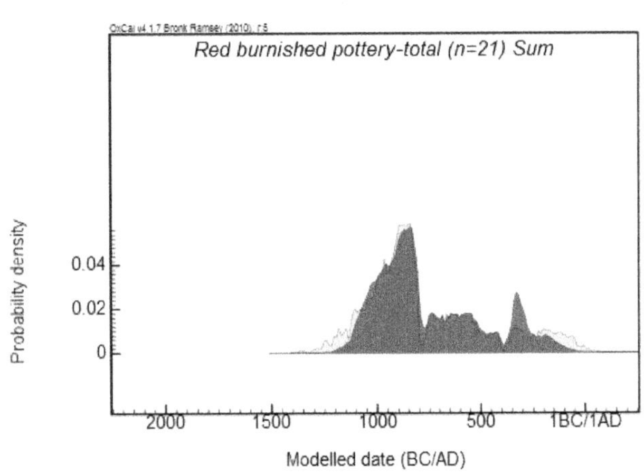

FIGURE 3. 10. MODELLED SUMMED PROBABILITY DISTRIBUTION BASED ON AN OUTLIER ANALYSIS OF 29 RADIOCARBON DETERMINATIONS ON CHARCOAL FROM SETTLEMENTS WITH SHERDS OF RED BURNISHED POTTERY IN THE STUDY AREA.

3.3.3 House shapes

The chronological models of the five pottery types did not provide an appropriate framework for making the divisions of the Early, Middle, and Late Bronze Age. Therefore, another element to aid chronological divisions of the Bronze Age has been explored (Lee 2004: 38-40; Miyazato 2005: 58-59; Kim 2006c: 9-13): thin-rectangular, rectangular and square house shapes were investigated. It should be considered that these categories might have a problem, that is, simplified categories may create a difficulty in the interpretation of developments and trends over periods of pre-historic time (Kim 2011: 32-33). Due to the fact that there is no clear grouping among the 235 houses on the basis of the ratio between house width and length (refer to Figure 3.11), the classification of house plan shapes follows the divisions of the Baekseok-dong site (Lee et al. 1998a: 427). House shapes were divided

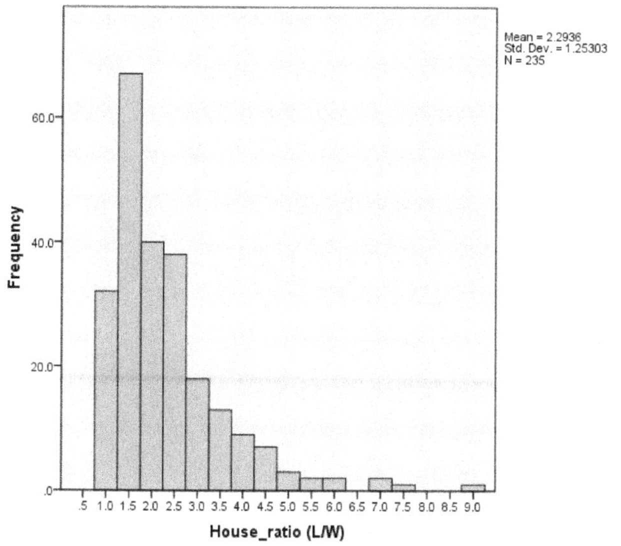

FIGURE 3. 11. THE HISTOGRAM OF THE HOUSE RATIO AMONG 235 HOUSES IN THE STUDY AREA

on the basis of the ratio between their width and length, for example a 1:1 to a 1.5:1 ratio denotes a square shape; between 1.6:1 and 2.5:1 ratio the rectangular shape, and greater than a 2.6:1 ratio the thin-rectangular shape (*ibid*).

Thin-rectangular house shape

A length-breadth ratio of greater than 2.6:1 characterises the thin-rectangular house (Lee et al. 1998b: 427). Round and square houses were in use from the Initial Neolithic period (approx. 8000 BC – 6500 BC), rectangular houses seem to develop from the Late Neolithic period (approx. 3500 BC-2000 BC), with the exception of the central part of the Korean peninsula (Lee 2005c: 195; Koo 2005: 6). Thin-rectangular houses first appear in the Bronze Age (Kim 2006c; Gyeonggi Institute of Cultural Properties and Gyeonggi Provincial Museum 2009: 57). A total of 19 radiocarbon determinations (thirteen houses in seven settlement sites, refer to Appendix 12-a) from thin-rectangular houses were identified and modelled using outlier analysis.

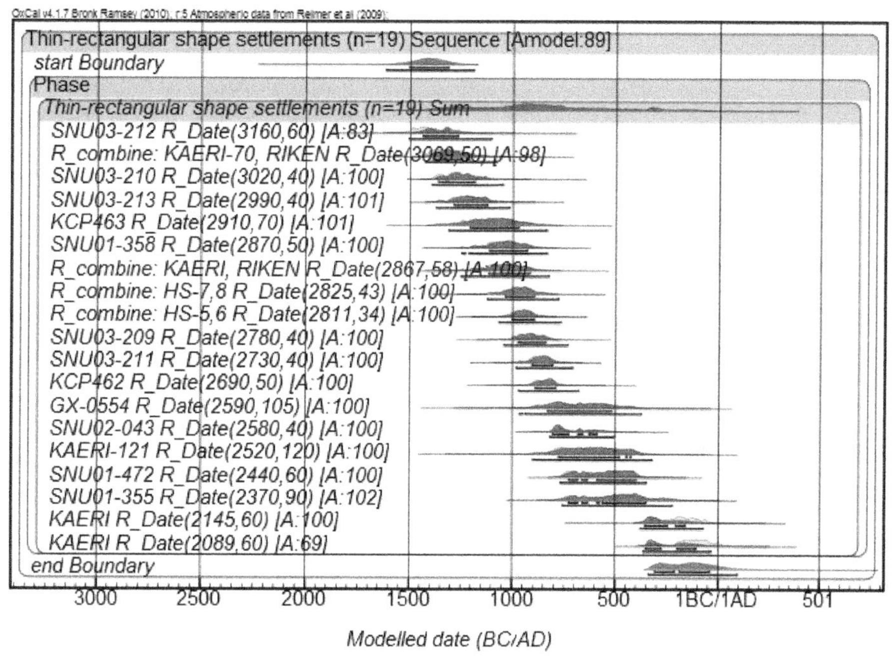

FIGURE 3.12. MODELLED DISTRIBUTIONS BASED ON AN OUTLIER ANALYSIS OF 19 RADIOCARBON DETERMINATIONS ON CHARCOAL FROM SETTLEMENTS WITH THIN-RECTANGULAR SHAPED HOUSES IN THE STUDY AREA, TREATED AS A SINGLE PHASE OF ACTIVITY.

TABLE 3. 4. MODELLED START AND END DATE RANGES (CAL BC, 68% INCLUDED), AND USE-SPAN FOR THIN-RECTANGULAR SHAPED HOUSES IN THE STUDY AREA, TREATING 19 RADIOCARBON DETERMINATIONS FROM SETTLEMENTS AS A SINGLE PHASE OF ACTIVITY (RESULTS OF 'ORIGINAL' DATA INDICATES MODELLED CALIBRATED OUTCOMES BEFORE APPLYING TO THE OUTLIER ANALYSIS (CHARCOAL, 1).

Thin-rectangular	n	start	68%	start	95%	end	68%	end	95%	Amodel	span	68%	span	95%
Original	19	1507	1349	1640	1286	326	61	345	66	87.7	1102	1415	1002	1619
Outlier	19	1504	1318	1616	1193	307	40	338	95	88.8	1096	1413	976	1619

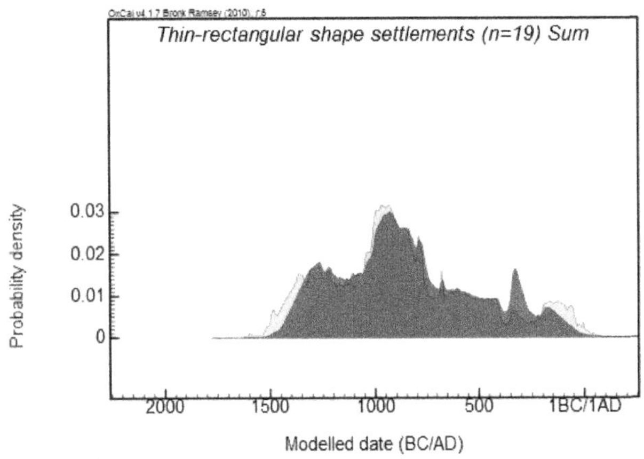

FIGURE 3. 13. MODELLED SUMMED PROBABILITY DISTRIBUTION BASED ON AN OUTLIER ANALYSIS OF 19 RADIOCARBON DETERMINATIONS ON CHARCOAL FROM SETTLEMENTS WITH THIN-RECTANGULAR SHAPED HOUSES IN THE STUDY AREA.

The difference between simple and outlier analyses of the radiocarbon determinations of thin-rectangular houses is also minor, and is similar to the results for the pottery samples (Table 3.4). According to the results, the use of thin-rectangular houses in the study area commenced from between *1616-1193 BC (95.4% probability)*, and ended *338-95 BC (95.4% probability)*, spanning between *976* and *1619* years *(95.4% probability)*. The modelled distribution of 19 determinations is presented in Figure 3.12 and the modelled summed probability distribution is displayed in Figure 3.13.

In order to effectively present the results of the modelled start and end durations, graphs were created using the same scales as in Figure 3.18. As can be seen, the end boundary overlapped with the Earlier Iron Age (refer back to Table 2.3) due to the fact that two results (KAERI No lab no., 2145 ± 60 and KAERI No lab no., 2089 ± 60) from Yeoju Heunamri were considered. The reason is that Bronze Age pottery was discovered in these houses. It is not clear yet, how society transformed from the Late Bronze Age to the early phase of the Iron Age. However, during the Iron Age, the Korean peninsula entered into the historical period of the three kingdoms, namely, Goguryeo (고구려, 高句麗, from BC 37 – 668 AD), Baekje (백제, 百濟, from BC 18 – 660 AD), and Silla (신라, 新羅, from 57 BC -935 AD) were formed (Lee et al. 1984; Choi et al. 2002b: 49; Choi 2008b).

Rectangular house shape

As mentioned in the beginning of this section, from length-breadth ratio of between 1.6:1 and 2.5:1 designates a rectangular shape (Lee et al. 1998b: 427). Rectangular houses seem on the whole to appear in the Late Neolithic period in the Korean peninsula; however, Late Neolithic examples of these houses have not yet been discovered in the archaeological record in the present study area of the central part of the Korean peninsula (Lee 2005b: 176-214; Koo 2005). This pattern has received some confirmation from the present results, as the advent of rectangular shaped houses appears to have been rather later than that of thin-rectangular shaped houses in the study area. On the basis of Table 3.5, which presents the results of simple and outlier analyses, by way of comparison, the best estimates for the start and end dates, based on 19 radiocarbon determinations (14 houses in the seven settlement sites, refer to Appendix 12-b) from rectangular shaped houses, ranges between *1488 BC and 1000 BC (95% probability)* for the start and from *378 BC to 101 BC* for the end dates *(95% probability)* respectively. In addition, the modelled distribution of 19 dates is demonstrated in Figure 3.14 and the modelled summed probability distribution is shown in Figure 3.15.

In order to show the results visually, modelled start and end date graphs were arranged using the same scales, as seen in Figure 3.18.

Square house shape

Finally, square-shaped houses were considered. A length-breadth ratio from 1:1 to 1.5:1 denotes a square house (Lee et al. 1998b: 427) According to the results of previous research (Kim 2006c; Lee 2009), these seem to have emerged from the Middle Bronze Age

TABLE 3. 5. MODELLED START AND END DATE RANGES (CAL BC, 68% INCLUDED), AND USE-SPAN FOR RECTANGULAR SHAPED HOUSES IN THE STUDY AREA, TREATING 19 RADIOCARBON DETERMINATIONS FROM SETTLEMENTS AS A SINGLE PHASE OF ACTIVITY (RESULTS OF 'ORIGINAL' DATA INDICATES MODELLED CALIBRATED OUTCOMES BEFORE APPLYING TO THE OUTLIER ANALYSIS (CHARCOAL, 1).

Rectangular	n	start	68%	start	95%	end	68%	end	95%	Amodel	span	68%	span	95%
Original	19	1371	1169	1517	1104	370	256	388	142	82.6	850	1110	768	1303
Outlier	19	1346	1102	1488	1000	353	223	378	101	89.1	810	1094	696	1283

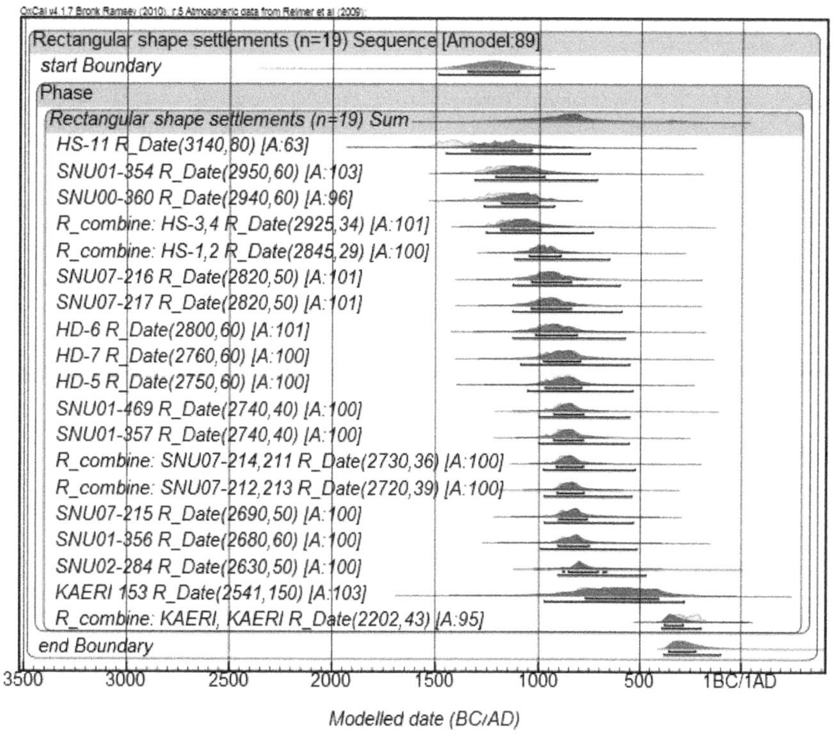

FIGURE 3. 14. MODELLED DISTRIBUTIONS BASED ON AN OUTLIER ANALYSIS OF 19 RADIOCARBON DETERMINATIONS ON CHARCOAL FROM SETTLEMENTS WITH RECTANGULAR SHAPED HOUSE IN THE STUDY AREA, TREATED AS A SINGLE PHASE OF ACTIVITY.

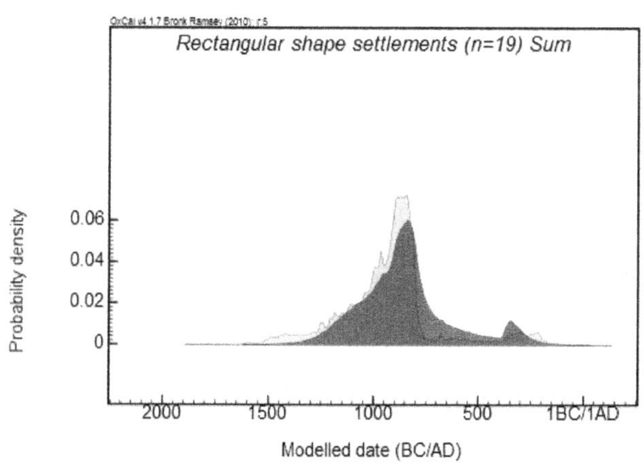

FIGURE 3. 15. MODELLED SUMMED PROBABILITY DISTRIBUTION BASED ON AN OUTLIER ANALYSIS OF 19 RADIOCARBON DETERMINATIONS ON CHARCOAL FROM SETTLEMENTS WITH RECTANGULAR SHAPED HOUSES IN THE STUDY AREA.

in the Korean peninsula[23]. To ascertain whether this corresponds to evidence gathered from the study area, 16 radiocarbon determinatons (12 houses in five settlement sites, Appendix 12-c) were identified from square-shaped houses and Bayesian modelling was conducted. The best approximations for the dates of the start and end dates of square shaped houses are from *1217 BC* to *702 BC* (*95% probability*) and ending between *695 BC and 336 BC* (*95% probability*) (Table 3.6). The span is between *0 and 807 years (95% probability)*. The modelled distribution of 16 radiocarbon determinations is presented in Figure 3.16 and the modelled summed probability distribution (Figure 3.17) is also displayed.

In order to show effectively the start and end ranges, the results were arranged in graph form and are presented in Figure 3.18. As can be shown, this house shape started later than the two other house shapes.

The analysed house-shape data are presented in Table 3.7 and Figure 3. 18. As can be seen in Figure 3.18, the house shape results seem to support the traditional chronology, that is, thin-rectangular-shaped houses were likely to have developed from the Early Bronze Age and square-shaped houses probably appeared from the Middle Bronze Age. Rectangular houses seem to have developed between the Early and the Middle Bronze Age. It is difficult to look at the relationship between the rectangular houses in the Late Neolithic period and those in the Early Bronze Age, due to the fact that unlike the other areas of the Korean peninsula, rectangular-shaped houses have not yet been confirmed in the Late Neolithic period for the research area.

[23] Among square shape houses, there is the 'Songgung-ni' type, which has round corner shapes and a shallow pit with postholes in the centre (Lee 2009: 29). This type developed in the south-western part of the Korean peninsula and opinion suggests that it appeared from the Middle Bronze Age (Kim 2006c: 4) or the Late Bronze Age (Lee 2009: 29).

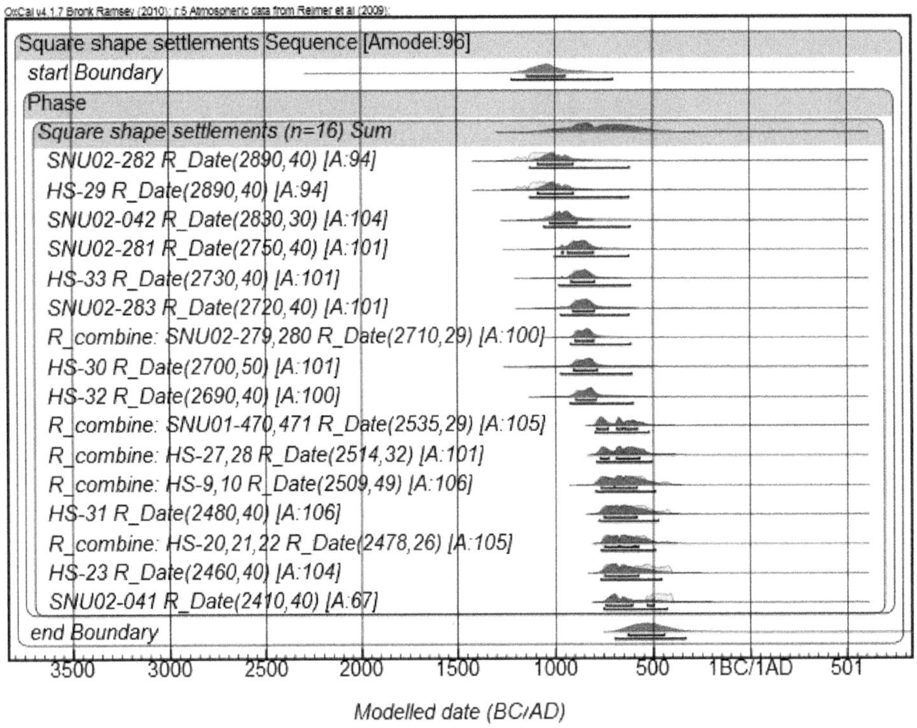

Figure 3. 16. Modelled distributions based on an outlier analysis of 16 radiocarbon determinations on charcoal from settlements with square shaped house in the study area treated as a single phase of activity.

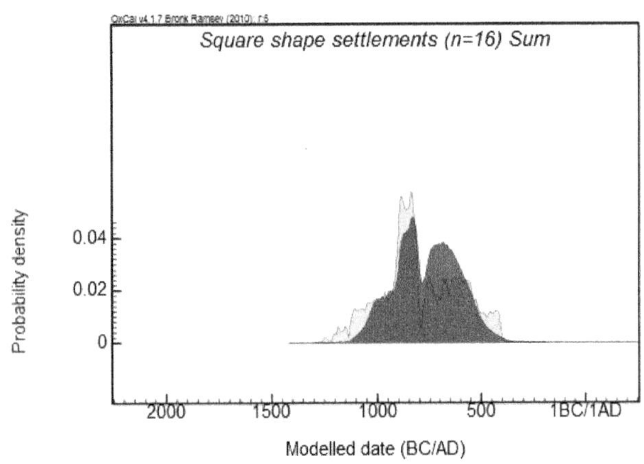

Figure 3. 17. Modelled summed probability distribution based on an outlier analysis of 16 radiocarbon determinations on charcoal from settlements with square shaped houses in the study area.

3.4 Summary of key findings

In order to find appropriate chronological models for long-term change in the research area, a total of 72 radiocarbon determinations from 16 settlements were calibrated and modelled using OxCal 4.1. Firstly, in order to identify the overall span of Bronze Age activity in the study area, the Bayesian model treats all of the radiocarbon data from settlements as fitting into a single phase of activity. To avoid an old wood effect, a charcoal outlier model was applied. According to the results of the outlier analysis, the use of Bronze Age settlements in the Gyeonggi area commenced within the period *1390-1127 BC (95.4% probability)* and ended *370-242 BC (95.4% probability*), spanning between *805 and 1093 years (95.4% probability*). These modelled start date ranges in the study area were somewhat later than the traditional chronology of the Korean Bronze Age, but, the start date duration practically corresponds with the Early Bronze Age period.

Table 3. 6. Modelled start and end date ranges (cal BC, 68% included), and use-span for square shaped houses in the study area, treating 16 radiocarbon determinations from settlements as a single phase of activity (Results of 'original' data indicates modelled calibrated outcomes before applying to the outlier analysis (charcoal, 1).

Square	n	start	68%	start	95%	end	68%	end	95%	Amodel	span	68%	span	95%
Original	16	1119	1003	1186	946	666	501	721	405	91.5	366	602	262	732
Outlier	16	1140	946	1217	702	629	446	695	336	96.1	359	644	0	807

TABLE 3. 7. MODELLED START AND END DATE RANGES (CAL BC, 68% INCLUDED), AND USE-SPAN ON AN OUTLIER ANALYSIS FOR HOUSE SHAPES IN THE STUDY AREA, TREATING EACH HOUSE SHAPE RADIOCARBON DETERMINATIONS FROM SETTLEMENTS AS A SINGLE PHASE OF ACTIVITY.

House shape	n	start	68%	start	95%	end	68%	end	95%	Amodel	span	68%	span	95%
Thin-rectangular	19	1504	1318	1616	1193	307	40	338	95	88.8	1096	1413	976	1619
Rectangular	19	1346	1102	1488	1000	353	223	378	101	89.1	810	1094	696	1283
Square	16	1140	946	1217	702	629	446	695	336	96.1	359	644	0	807

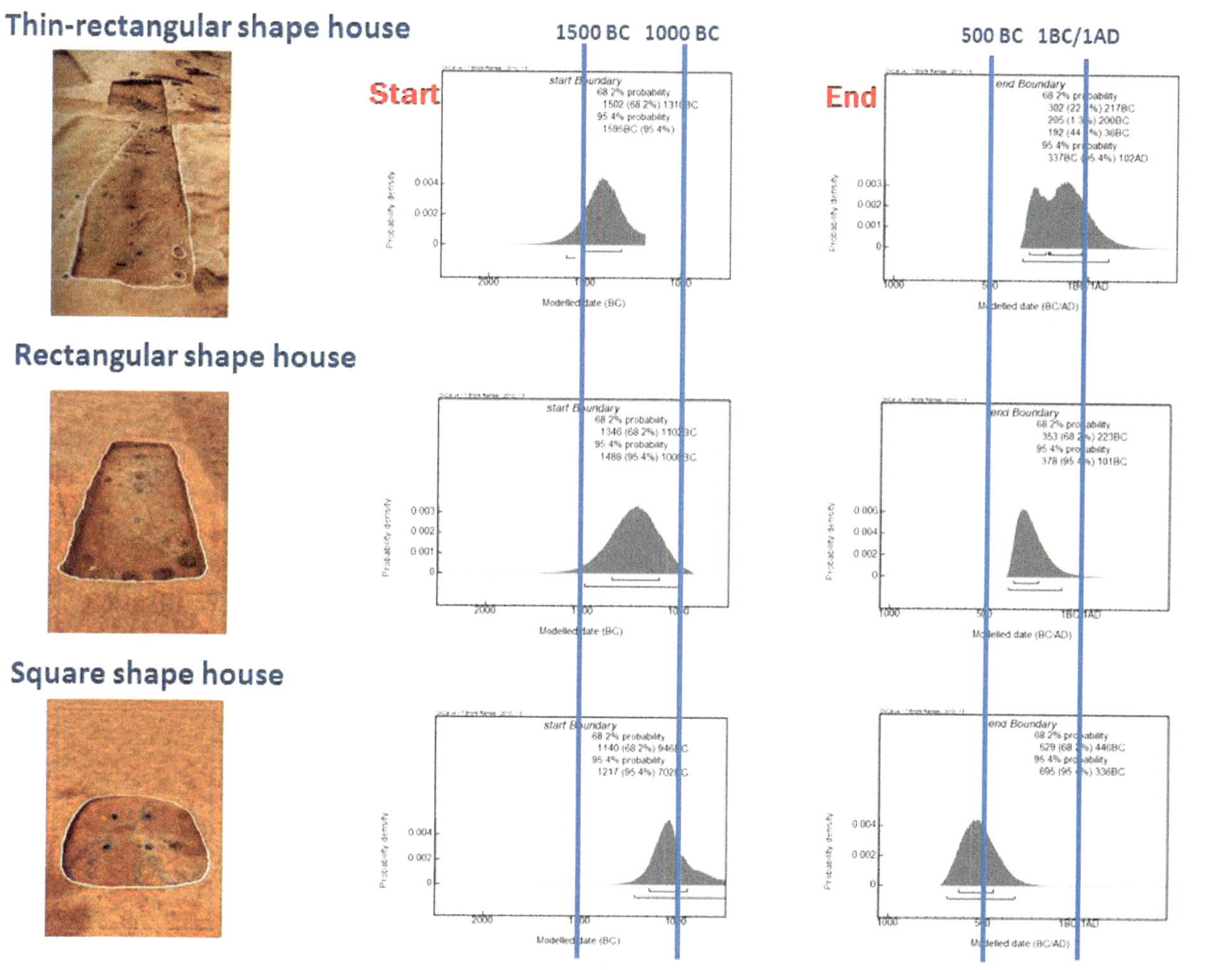

FIGURE 3. 18. MODELLED START AND END DATES BASED ON AN OUTLIER ANALYSIS OF RADIOCARBON DETERMINATIONS OF CHARCOALS FROM SETTLEMENTS WITH THREE DIFFERENT TYPES OF HOUSE SHAPE IN THE STUDY AREA (ALL INFORMATION ON EACH GRAPH IS PRESENTED IN TABLE 3.7). (NO. 1 PHOTO WAS PERMITTED BY GYEONGGI INSTITUTE OF CULTURAL PROPERTIES, SOURCE: (GYEONGGI INSTITUTE OF CULTURAL PROPERTIES AND GYEONGGI PROVINCIAL MUSEUM 2009: 57). NO. 2 AND 3 PHOTOS WERE PROVIDED BY THE KOREA INSTITUTE OF HERITAGE (HENCEFORTH KIH), SOURCE: (KOREA INSTITUTE OF HERITAGE AND YM CONSTRUCTION CO. LTD. 2008: 7 AND 9).

Secondly, in order to identify temporally sensitive characteristics, dating models for the five main pottery types (pottery with doubled rims with slant lines, pottery with perforated rims, pottery with notched rim, Heunamri type pottery, and red-burnished ware) from the research area were examined. As can be seen in Figure 3.5, it is noteworthy that the results of the five pottery types seem not to be indicative of the chronological divisions of the Bronze Age in the study area, as the five types of pottery seem to have coexisted, with the exception that the emergence of red-burnished pottery was around the Middle Bronze Age. Therefore, in order to find another reference point, thin-rectangular, rectangular and square house shapes were investigated. As can be seen in Figure 3.18, the house shape results show clearer starting ranges for each house shape than those of pottery types, although there are still difficulties in dividing the Bronze Age into three divisions, solely on the basis of house shape results.

Consequently, it is difficult to divide the Bronze Age into three periods according to only pottery types or house shapes. However, if both elements are considered together, it seems to be possible to identify the Middle Bronze Age according to the appearance of red-burnished ware and the square shaped house type. Together with these features, if the Late period potteries of Bronze Age based on artefact assemblages, such as pottery with clay stripes[24], hard pottery, which were fired at temperatures of between 700-850°C (Choi 2008a: 175), and vessels with imprinted design[25] were considered, it seems to be possible to divide the Bronze Age roughly into six divisions (refer to Table 3.8 and Appendix 17) rather than three divisions.

TABLE 3. 8. THE DIVISIONS OF THE BRONZE AGE ON THE BASIS OF HOUSE SHAPES AND POTTERY TYPES

Periods	House shapes	Pottery types	Number of settlement
Early	Thin-rectangular, Rectangular	Without red-burnished pottery	7
Early to Middle	Thin-rectangular, Rectangular Square	With red-burnished pottery	12
Early to Late	Thin-rectangular, Rectangular Square	With red-burnished pottery Later period pottery	9
Middle	Square	Red burnished pottery	8
Middle to late	Square	Red burnished pottery Later period pottery	5
Late		Later period pottery	4

These categories were applied to 45 settlements in the study area in order to look at long-term changes in the settlements in the mid-western part of the Korean peninsula (refer to Appendix 6). In order to examine long-term changes for monuments in the research area, settlement periodisation was utilized due to the lack of chronological evidence from the monuments themselves. Making the broad assumption that monuments within certain boundaries based around a settlement probably shared similar chronology with their associated settlements, this will allow at least a preliminary analysis of long-term developments in the related monuments. This assumption may involve possible dangers, especially in cases where a settlement and surrounding monuments within certain boundaries did not have close relationships. However, this method will be a suggestive practice through which to infer past behaviours. This will be dealt with in Chapter 5.3.

Finally, it is worthwhile mentioning the limitations of dating. Firstly, when radiocarbon determinations, which are related with pottery types, were confirmed, the frequency of pottery was not considered. If Bayesian modelling can consider the frequency of each pottery type present at a site, we might obtain the peak period for each pottery type and could utilise this information for periodisation. In addition, if enough radiocarbon determinations concerning representative pottery styles of the Late Bronze Age could be obtained, more reliable divisions of the Late period could be formulated. Another limitation is that the data from the 'Early to Middle', 'Early to Late' and 'Middle to Late' categories cannot be properly utilised in this analysis. These groups need other standards by which to analyse them, such as material culture elements. This analysis will be the next task, as this research is focused mainly on the landscape perspective. The long-term changes of settlements and monuments according to the above divisions will be discussed in Chapter 6.

[24] One radiocarbon determination (1770 ± 40 BP) related to this type of pottery in the study area has been identified (Im et al. 2002a: 71); therefore, it is impossible to run a Bayesian model and check its start and end dates at this stage.

[25] This is an earthenware vessel beaten with a paddle to compress the clay sides and with the imprint of a cord or a lattice design (Kim et al. 2004: 72)

Chapter 4. Environmental element analyses and GIS methodology

4.1 Environmental elements: Pedology, Hydrology, and Topography

In this chapter, the focus is on elements of the physical environment in order to examine how changes in the subsistence economy, especially in the development of agriculture, affected Bronze Age people's planning for their shelters and burials, and to investigate what long-term changes can be traced in the study area. This chapter presents the analysis and results concerning the relationships between settlements/monuments and natural features, such as, soil types and distance from water sources as well as aspect, slope, and elevation. Chapter 5 considers cultural characteristics, for example: what were the perceptions of these places from a human standpoint, such as viewsheds and movements to and from sites and how these features might have influenced the positioning of sites? Following on from these analyses the research will explore what a Bronze Age world view might have encompassed.

4.1.1 Background information regarding agriculture

As briefly mentioned in Chapter 2, it is thought that unlike the case of what is termed the 'Neolithic Revolution' (Childe 1934) in the Near East and Europe, agriculture in Korea, as in the Far East, is likely to have appeared around the middle of the Neolithic period, through the cultivation of dry-field crops and then, step by step culminating in the adoption of wet-rice agriculture (Ahn 1998c; Ahn 1998d; Choi 2001; Im 2005a). The 3 *hop* (approx. 0.54 *l*) of carbonised crops found within comb-pattern pottery represents the earliest archaeological evidence in the Korean peninsula. They were discovered in No. 2 house at Jitopri Bongsan-gun Hwanghae province (황해도 봉산군 지탑리, 黄海道 鳳山郡 智塔里) and were assumed to be foxtail millets (*Setaria italic var.germanica*) or barnyard grasses (*Panicum cus galli/ Echinochloa utilis*). It was estimated that they dated from the first half of the third millennium BC by North Korean archaeologists (Ahn 1998c: 383; Im 2005a: 342-343).

Rice cultivation appears towards the end of Neolithic period. Carbonised grains of rice (*Oryza sativa L.*) and foxtail millet were found in a peat layer at Gahyeonri Tongjinmyeon Gimposi, Gyeonggi province (경기도 김포시 통진면 가현리). The peat layer was dated to 4020 ± 26 BP (no lab no. 2618-2472 BC at 2 sigma) (Im 2005a: 347). Dry-field crops and rice were likely to have been cultivated together during the Early Bronze Age (ca. 1500 BC ~1000 BC) and the Middle Bronze Age (ca. 1000 BC ~ 600 BC, refer back to Table 2.3). Carbonised rice, barley (*Hordeum sativum J.*), foxtail millet, and sorghum (*Andropogon sorghum*) were unearthed at No. 12 house in Heunamri Yeojugun Gyeonggi province (경기도 여주군 흔암리). Radiocarbon dates from this house are presented in Table 5.1 (Im 1978: 17-18, 30-31). After this period, it is likely that intensive rice agriculture took hold during the late Bronze Age (ca. 600 BC ~ 400 BC) particularly in the southern part of the Korean peninsula (Kang et al. 1979: 58, 148; Lee 2005a: 66, refer to Table 4.2) on the basis of archaeological evidence (Ahn 1998c: 383-386; Im 2005a: 341-351; Choi 2003: 3; Choi 2010: 7-14).

TABLE 4. 1. RADIOCARBON DATES FROM HEUNAMRI SITE. (CALIBRATED USING OXCAL 4.1 BY THE AUTHOR, NOS. 1 AND 2 ARE THE SAME SAMPLE, DIVIDED IN TWO FOR QUALITY CONTROL PURPOSES. ONE SAMPLE WAS SENT TO KAERI (KOREA ATOMIC ENERGY RESEARCH INSTITUTE) AND THE OTHER WAS SENT TO RIKEN (RIKAGAKU KENKYUSHO, JAPAN)).

No.	Site name	Provenance	Material	Lab code	^{14}C BP	±	cal BC (95%)	
1	Yeoju Heunamri	House no.12	Charcoal	KAERI-70	3210	70	1668	1317
2	Yeoju Heunamri	House no.12	Charcoal	RIKEN	2920	70	1370	924
3	Yeoju Heunamri	House no.12	Charcoal	KAERI	2620	100	996	416
4	Yeoju Heunamri	House no.12	Charcoal	RIKEN	2980	70	1400	1014

TABLE 4. 2. RADIOCARBON DATES FROM SONGGUNG-NI SITE (KANG ET AL., 1979: 148; LEE, 2005A: 66) (CALIBRATED USING OXCAL 4.1. BY THE AUTHOR)

No.	Site name	Provenance	Material	Lab code	^{14}C BP	±	cal BC (95%)	
1	Buyeo Songgung-ri	House no.54-1	Charcoal	KAERI-186	2665	60	976	670
2	Buyeo Songgung-ri	House no.54-1	Charcoal	KAERI-187	2565	90	894	410
3	Buyeo Songgung-ri	House no.54-5	Charcoal	No lab. no.	2580	90	900	415

In order to understand rice cultivation, one needs to look at the transmission of rice to the Korean peninsula. Rice seems to have been introduced from China, due to the fact that wild rice has not yet been discovered in Korea (Heo 1991: 86). This involves three hypotheses about the possible transmission routes: the northern, southern, and combined paths (Ahn 1998a: 62-63). In the northern route theory, there are two different paths, one is from the northeast of China to the northern part of the Korean peninsula alongside the Yellow Sea coastal line, occurring during the Early Bronze Age (ca. 1500~1000 BC), coinciding with the appearance of semi-lunar shaped stone knives (Choe 1982: 524-525; Shim 1991: 44-54). The second path followed the course of the Huai river (회하, 淮河) to the Shandong peninsula (산동반도, 山東半島), then on to the Liaodong peninsula (요동반도, 遼東半島) and terminated at the west coast of the Korean peninsula via a sea route, dating to around 1000 BC (refer to Figure 5.1) (Heo 1991: 88-91; Shim 1991: 44-54). Secondly, the southern route theory also involves two ways: one is from Southeast Asia to the southern part of the Korean peninsula probably by using the Black Current (흑조, 黑潮) during the Bronze and Early Iron Age (Kim 1981: 76-77) and the other is from the Yangtze River valley to the west coast region of Korea, across the Yellow Sea on the basis of the discovery of carbonised rice, measured at 4020 ± 26 BP (no lab no. 2618-2472 BC at 2 sigma) (Im 2005a: 346-347). Finally, the third theory is a recognition of both routes' importance in the diffusion of rice, combining the northern land route from northern China, dating from around the second millennium BC and the southern sea route from the Yangtze River to the south-western part of the Korean peninsula, starting from the Yangtze River, on to the Shandong peninsula and then across the Yellow Sea to central Korea (Kim 1982: 516-517). According to the archaeological evidence in China, it is thought that rice cultivation first began in the lower and middle Yangtze River area from around 8050 *cal* BC (Jiang and Liu 2006) and according to current research by Bar-Yosef (2011) (although still debated), archaeological evidence for cultivated millet has been found at Xinglonggou (8050 *cal* BC – 6050 *cal* BC) in the north of China and evidence of rice has been discovered at Jiahu (7050 cal BC - 5850 cal BC) which is located below the Yellow River. Also, it has been suggested that communities based in the lower Yangtze River area shifted their subsistence economy, focusing on rice between 6000 BC and 3000 BC when rice can be demonstrated to be fully domesticated morphologically (Fuller and Qin 2010: 154).

It is thought that the agriculture diversified during the Bronze Age in Korea and that sorghum (*Andoropogon sorghum* or *Sorghum bicolour*), soybean (*Glycine max* (Merrill)), red bean (*Vigna angularis* or *Phaseolus angularis*), barley (*Hordeum vulgar*, *Hordeum sativum J.*) and wheat (*Triticum aestivum*) were introduced in the Bronze Age, whereas foxtail millet (*Setaria italic*) and broomcorn (*Panicum miliaceum*) seem to be grown continuously from the Neolithic period onwards (Ahn 1998e: 45; 1998b: 401-403) based on Jitap-ri site. It has been suggested that dry-field agriculture predominated rather than rice cultivation in the early stage of agriculture on the basis of the geographical occasions of early agricultural sites, excavated grains, and ancient sources (Ahn 1998d: 28).

Among the Bronze Age sites at Hunam-ri in Gyeonggi province, rice was discovered with foxtail millet, sorghum, broomcorn and barley. This site was dated from the Early Bronze Age to the Middle Bronze Age (Kim et al. 1972·1973; Im 1978). Based on this evidence it has been inferred that rice agriculture had been established in the early first millennium BC in this region, gradually becoming more important as a staple than dry-field crops. Other features worth mentioning are that regional variation in the rice cultivation should be considered and it would be useful to consider current archaeological issues about intensive rice agriculture in Korea (Ahn 2000; Song 2001; Choi 2010). It has been discussed that the so called, 'Songgung-ni' (송국리, 松菊里) type material culture assemblage[26] seems to be strongly related to the rice dominated, agricultural society existing in the late Middle and Late Bronze Age and that this type of site was located and discovered in, by and large, southern parts of the Korean peninsula. It seems quite probable that current archaeological results support the third theory of rice transmission; that is, rice diffused along both a northern route and a southern route.

4.1.2 Research questions pertaining to environmental element analyses

Such a change in the subsistence economy might prompt the alteration of a landscape by people in order to adapt and create new settings for agriculture. The traces of this remoulding can be read through the distribution of monuments and settlements and the patterns they form. In order to look at what elements affect how settlements and monuments were positioned in the environment in Bronze Age, several questions will be raised as follows:

1. How near were the most fertile soils for rice and dry-field agriculture to the settlements and monuments?

2. How did their positions change through time?

3. What were the relationships between monuments and settlements and water?

4. What were their topographical features, such as, aspect, slope and elevation, of settlements and monuments?

[26] The 'Songgung-ni' type culture assemblage has included, for example, circle or square house plans with oval-shaped hearths and two post holes in the centre of houses, egg-shaped pottery with outcurved rims, polished stone daggers with one-stepped handles, triangular stone knives, stone adzes, and Bipa-shaped bronze daggers (refer to Figure 2.16 and Table 2.14 in Chapter 2).

4.2 GIS Methodology

Several different analyses were applied in this research, for example, soil analysis, distance from water, the topographical features of sites, landform-preference, viewshed and movement. The specific methodology for each is introduced in its relevant section. However, there is a common way to extract the value from the DEM, in order to test the statistical significance of site distributions for each analysis.

In order to test the significance of a certain pattern, firstly certain values of the study area were obtained, for example those for slope. It is important to clarify what exactly is meant by the 'slope of the study area'. This is the value of each cell within the study area and it is useful to expand further on how the values were obtained. Spatial data are represented in a digital model and the GIS software operates by utilizing this digital model of the world. In GIS, there are two types of data structure, namely, vector data and raster data. Vector data are related to one or more coordinates and are represented by points, lines and polygons; while raster data are composed of cells or pixels, in which are contained continuous values (Wheatley and Gillings 2002: Chapter 2; Conolly and Lake 2006b: Chapter 2). When the results of certain analyses are obtained on the raster data set within the research area, they have to be converted into vector data values (centre point of each cell), which is represented by each cell value. These point values stand for the study area value, for example: 'the slope of study area'. This is the most advantageous point of using the GIS for the analysis to find statistical significance between the overall tendency of the study area and the location of sites.

4.3 Pedology: The relationship between soils and sites

4.3.1 Soil division

The traditional theory is that dry-field cultivation began first in the Middle Neolithic period and that rice agriculture was likely to have started at the end of the Neolithic or the start of the Early Bronze Age. Subsequently, dry-field crops and rice were cultivated together and rice seems to have become more important in the Middle Bronze Age, leading to intensive rice cultivation in the Late Bronze Age particularly centring on the southern part of the Korean peninsula (Ahn 1998d: 14-22; Im 2005a: 341-351). In order to test this theory, the hypothesis has been developed that the settlements and monuments of the Early Bronze Age were located on or near to fertile soil for dry-field crops, but that as rice agriculture developed, those of the Middle Bronze Age were located on or near to fertile soil for rice. To test the hypothesis, the relationship of soil types to settlement and monument locations was examined. There is the problem of the degradation of soils (Gaffney and Stančič 1991: 36-38), but due to the lack of firm palaeo-environmental data, modern soil data are often used as a variable in GIS analysis.

The agricultural sector of the Korean government operates an online programme '*Heuktoram,* 흙토람' (http://asis.rda.go.kr), providing useful soil information for the farming community. According to information provided by the NAAS (The National Academy of Agricultural Science), there are over 20,000 categories of raw soil data. Therefore, they have been re-categorised specifically for rice and dry-field cultivation on the basis of soil survey information post-dating 1964 by the NAAS.

The soil maps include information about the physical and chemical characteristics of soil, the soil aptitude rating, crop cultivation suitability, current usage, and soil groupings. Firstly, each item has sub-categories: for example, the category of physical characteristics includes gravel content, degree of erosion and the character of the topsoil. Further still, the sub-category of gravel contents includes the colour and character of deep soil, soil depths, and drainage grade. Secondly, the chemical characteristic of soil consists of the categories of acidity, organic content, phosphoric acid, kalium, calcium, magnesium, and silicic acid. Thirdly, the soil aptitude rating includes paddy fields, dry fields, orchards, grasslands, and woodlands. Fourthly, current soil usage includes the main soil usage and the recommended soil usage. Finally, soil grouping contains the topography of distribution, soil main material, soil accumulation, order and suborder (KREI: Korea Rural Economic Institute 한국농촌경제연구원).

The soil types are divided as follows:

1. Rice
    1) Rice_Good: normal and immature rice paddy
    2) Rice_Poor: sandy, humid, salty, and peculiar acid rice paddy
    3) Unranked_Rice: All areas are used for flooded rice paddy during wet summers and most areas are also used for non-irrigated barley during the dry winter and spring seasons.
2. Dry-field
    1) Dry-field_Good: normal dry field
    2) Dry-field_Poor: sandy, middle point, plateau, immature and volcanic ash dry field.
    3) Unranked_Dry-field: Most gently sloping areas are cultivated for barley, soybean, red pepper, potato, cabbage, radish, sweet potato and similar crops. Most hilly and some rolling areas grow pine forest, shrubs, wild grasses, and some mixed forest.
    4) Limited_Dry-field: These soils are used for woodlands and a few are cultivated for dry-field crops.
3. Both: mixed soils for Rice_Good and Dry-field_Poor
4. Forest: Most areas of these soil types are used for pine, hard wood, shrub, and mixed forest.

5. Related Water: inundated areas by river and by sea, tidelands, and reservoirs.
   The presence of settlements and monuments in this category presents three possibilities, such as, sea level change[27], the formation of reservoirs[28], and data errors[29].
6. No Data: although there is one monument in this category, the soil map of this particular area (an area close to the border line with North Korea) did not allow reference to this sector due to security reasons.

4.3.2 The relationships between soil types and sites

To begin with, suitable soils for rice and dry-field crops within the Gyeonggi province were classified (refer to Figure 4.1 and 4.2). Figure 4.1 presents a more detailed classification and Figure 4.2 shows simplified categories. In order to test the statistical significance of the relationship between the soil types of the total study area (which was mentioned in the Chapter three) and settlements or monuments, chi-square tests were run. There are statistically significant differences at the 95% confidence level between soil types and settlements (Figure 5.2: $\chi^2 = 18.13$, $df = 10$, and $p = 7.64E\text{-}05$), Figure 5.3: $\chi^2 = 13.84$, $df = 5$, and $p = 0.017$) and between soil types and monuments (Figure 5.2: $\chi^2 = 77.99$, $df = 10$, and $p = 1.24E\text{-}12$, Figure 5.3: $\chi^2 = 18.13$, $df = 5$, and $p = 6.1E\text{-}13$). The test results show that settlements and monuments were not distributed equally cross the soil types. The positive association of settlements is on the Dry-field_Good category while negative significance is found in the Forest and the Related_water categories. Similarly, the negative association of monuments is in the Related_water and the Forest areas and the positive association is in the Dry-field_Good and the Rice_Good classifications. The results of monuments are similar to those of the regional analysis of the island of Hvar, Croatia; that is, the location of cairns and tumuli were seen to be significantly related to good soil types (Gaffney and Stančič 1991: 65). In addition, the agrarian structures of the Tafí culture, which are recognised as the first agricultural communities in Northwest Argentina, were also located in fertile areas found on alluvial fans and glacis (Sampietro Vattuone et al. 2008: 191): 'the paleosol shows optimal morphological and chemical characteristics for the good development of plants in the agricultural terraces' (*ibid*: 198).

In Figure 4.2, the percentage of monuments is almost double that of settlements on poor soil for the rice category and from Figure 4.3 it can be seen that monuments were located more frequently on soils associated with rice production than were settlements, and that settlements were situated more often on the soils normally used for the cultivation of dry-field crops. This pattern might be related to the matter of site preservation. As soils for rice have been cultivated for a long time, settlement sites are more likely to have been destroyed, while monuments would be more likely to have maintained their positions. Alternatively, there might be other cultural reasons for their longevity of situation. This will be discussed in Chapter 6.

If we accept Gabriel Cooney's hypothesis (1983) that monuments of the Neolithic period in Ireland tend to be situated near settlement sites, perhaps a greater number of settlements might be located in fertile soil areas based on the presence of monuments there. In addition, if we consider scattered sites near monuments that have been surveyed, for example, the four scattered sites (Gyeonggi Provincial Museum 2001) near the dolmens in Jinsangri Yeoncheon-gun (site code No. 4), the five scattered sites around the dolmens in Byeonsan-ri Yangpyeong-gun (site code No. 167), the five scattered sites close to the dolmens in Sangjapo-ri Yangpyeong-gun (site code No. 171), and lastly the three scattered sites near dolmens in Gajwa-dong Goyang-si (site code No. 26) (Gyeonggi Provincial Museum 2002), we might hope to obtain information about the relationship between soil types and sites for the living and the dead. However, it has been very difficult to identify the X and Y coordinates of scattered sites in this research, because the scales of paper maps did not matched with the base DEM. Therefore, this analysis considered only confirmed sites and a consideration of scattered sites will need further investigation.

Referring to Figure 4.2, settlements are found in a similar proportion to that of the soil type distributions in the study area in the Unranked_Dry-field category. By contrast, in the Limited_Dry-field and Dry-field_good sections the proportion of settlements exceeds that of the study area. This being the case, why were a higher proportion of settlements than expected located in areas with soil more suitable for dry-field cultivation, rather than the wet rice cultivation that is thought to have dominated the agricultural regime of the Bronze Age? There are five possibilities. The first is that highly suitable land for rice cultivation tended to be ploughed over the long term and as a result, it can be conjectured that a disproportionate number of settlement sites may have been destroyed. On the other hand, a colossal megalithic structure is less vulnerable to destruction and is unlikely to be moved to other locations, although some destruction and movement from original locations has been documented (Beak and Oh 2007; Gyeonggi provincial museum 2007). The second possibility is that, in terms of traditional thought, dry-field and dry rice cultivation started earlier than wet-rice planting. If this traditional thinking is correct, the numbers of settlements on suitable soil for dry-field farming are likely to exceed those on suitable soil for rice, because the history of the practice of dry-field farming is longer than that of rice agriculture. The methods of dry-field agriculture including slash and burn have been compared to those of the Early Bronze Age on the basis of the location of

[27] Although there were regional variations, it has been estimated that the rise of the sea level in the Western seas and in the South seas around the Korean peninsula, was between ca. 6000 BP and 5000 BP five metres at its highest (Shin 1992: 38-45).

[28] Large-scale rescue excavations were executed in the now submerged districts by the construction of a *Paldang* dam in 1972 in the study area (Han et al. 1974).

[29] Due to the fact that a scanned map of archaeological sites has been used and geo-referenced rather than using the X and Y coordinates of sites, there are some errors and they will be reconsidered.

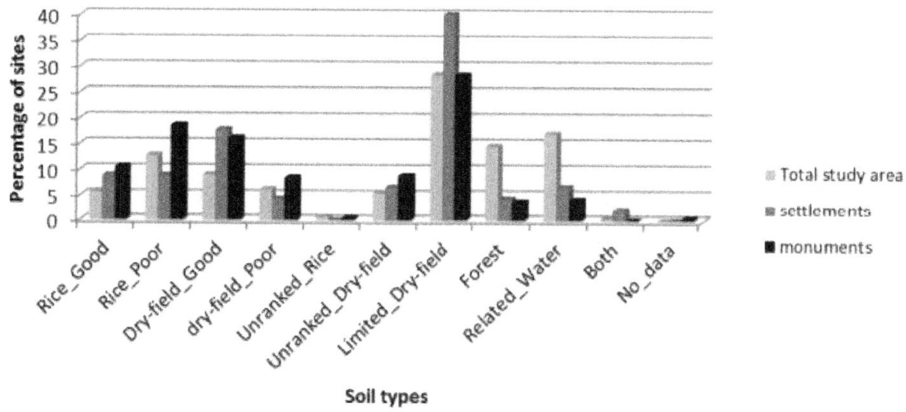

FIGURE 4. 1. THE RELATIONSHIPS BETWEEN SOIL TYPES AND SETTLEMENTS/MONUMENT SITES

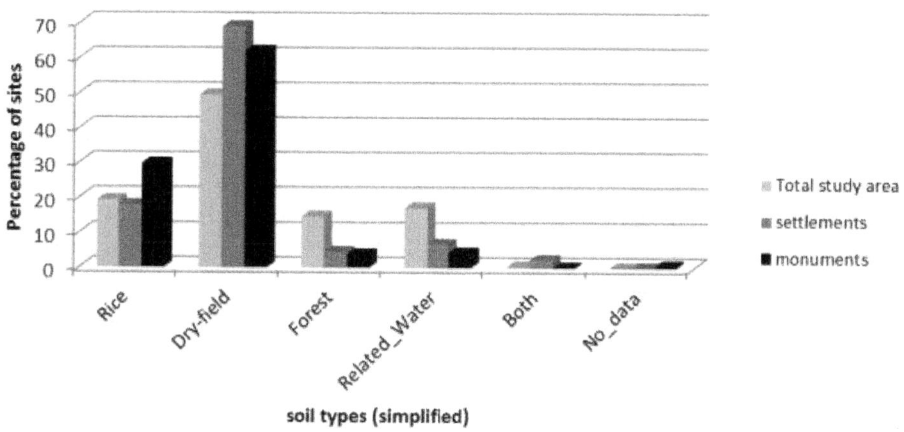

FIGURE 4. 2. THE RELATIONSHIPS BETWEEN SOIL TYPES AND SETTLEMENTS/MONUMENT SITES (SIMPLIFIED VERSION)

settlements and the material culture tool sets identified at the sites (Ahn 2000: 49-51). However, it is difficult to directly connect a settlement location and an agricultural strategy, because it is possible to use slash and burn procedures whilst living in settlements near river valleys, like the Iban tribe in Sarawak, Malaysia, according to ethnographical data (Ko 2010: 29-30, 42), equally not necessary to practice slash and burn on upland soils. The third possibility is that Bronze Age people did not have the appropriate technology to utilise good quality soil for rice agriculture at that time. For example, before the development of agricultural tools like the plough and the use of draft animals, it may have been difficult to prepare the heavier soils for planting. Despite the stone ploughshares discovered from the Jitap-ri site, dating from the Middle Neolithic period (Im 2005a: 343), it seems the widespread usage of ploughs came about only with the production of iron farming appliances in the Iron Age (after ca. 400 BC). Fourthly, the climatic conditions such as average temperature and precipitation in the study area might not have been appropriate for intensive wet-rice agriculture. According to research into environmental changes in the Korean central region (Yi et al. 2008: 112), after a mid-Holocene Climatic Optimum (between ca. 5000? and 3000 *cal* BC), the climate became cooler until circa 1500 *cal* BC. 'During this period, evergreen and deciduous broadleaved trees were replaced by conifers and cool-loving deciduous broadleaved trees of *Picea*, *Pinus* (*Diploxylon*), *Larix*/*Pseudotsuga* and *Betula*' (ibid). In addition, according to research by the Rural Development Administration, the optimum average temperature for rice maturing is approximately 22°C (Kim 5th, Feb. 2007.). To this day, this region has still not become the main granary of the Korean peninsula, although there have been enormous developments in agricultural technology and some places, for example, Icheon and Gimpo, have become well known for producing good quality rice. Finally, there might well be other cultural reasons and this will be discussed in Chapter 6.

On the other hand, the numbers of monuments in the Rice_Good, Rice_Poor, and Dry-field_Good sectors are found in higher than expected proportions given the representation of these soil types in the overall study area. According to archaeological evidence, the settlements of the Neolithic period tended to be established near to the sea and main rivers (refer back to Figure 2.9) and their subsistence economy appears to have been related to fishing, hunting, gathering and slash-and-burn farming (Ahn 1993: 75-80). Although there is evidence for rice cultivation from the Middle Neolithic period as mentioned before, it has been thought that the main shift from a subsistence economy to rice agriculture began in the Bronze Age. Therefore, as indicated by Bradley (1998) (albeit for a very different part of the world), the construction of monuments seems to reflect a change in the lifestyle of those that built them and perhaps indicates the value placed on such fertile soils by Bronze Age people. The relationship between monuments and soil types for agriculture could provide supporting evidence for such a thesis.

4.3.3 Long-term change

If, as can be assumed, long-term change in human activities can be read through the shifting landscape settings of sites as it can be through material culture (Gosden 2006), it should be possible to infer social change through the Bronze Age in Korea from the Neolithic period to the Early Iron Age. In Chapter 7, this will be discussed in comparison to the Neolithic period and the Iron Age. Therefore, to begin with, in order to investigate long-term changes from earlier periods to later periods in Bronze Age, the settlements were divided into three phases on the basis of chrono-typology and radiocarbon dating (see Chapter 3 for details).

As seen in Figures 4.3, 4.4 and 4.5 (especially, Figure 4.5), there are some patterns emerging in relation to soil types and its relationship to settlement location over time, although the potential problems of taphonomy and the destruction of sites should be considered. That is, settlements tended to be situated on soil suitable for dry-field crops (Figure 4.4) throughout the Bronze Age. The long-term changes of settlements and monuments will be discussed in Chapter 6.

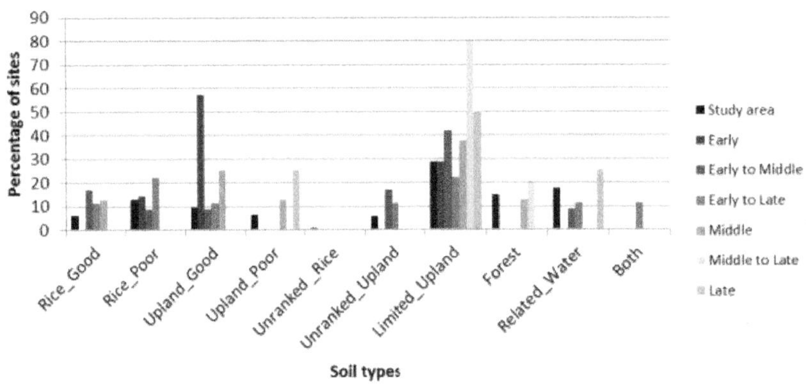

FIGURE 4. 3. RELATIONSHIPS BETWEEN SOIL TYPES AND TIME IN SETTLEMENT LOCATION

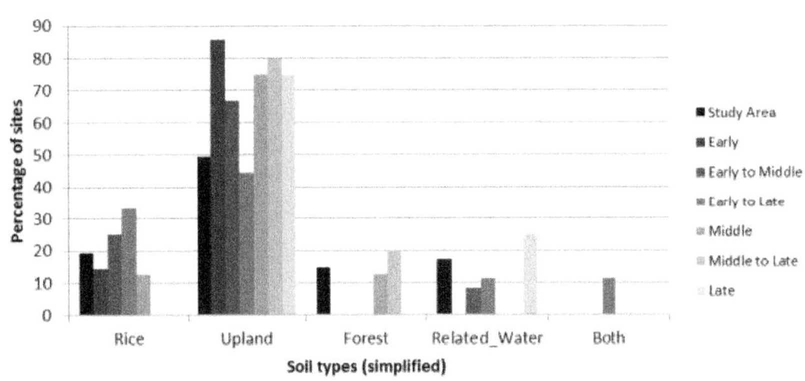

FIGURE 4. 4. RELATIONSHIPS BETWEEN SOIL TYPES AND TIME IN SETTLEMENT LOCATION (SIMPLIFIED SOIL TYPES)

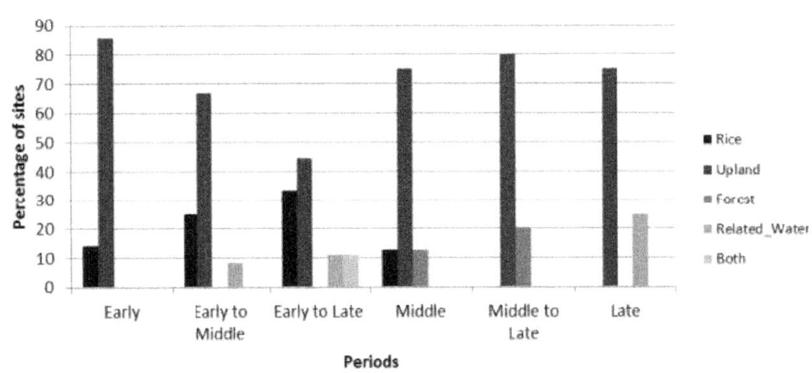

FIGURE 4. 5. RELATIONSHIPS BETWEEN SOIL TYPES AND TIME IN SETTLEMENT LOCATION (BY PERIODS)

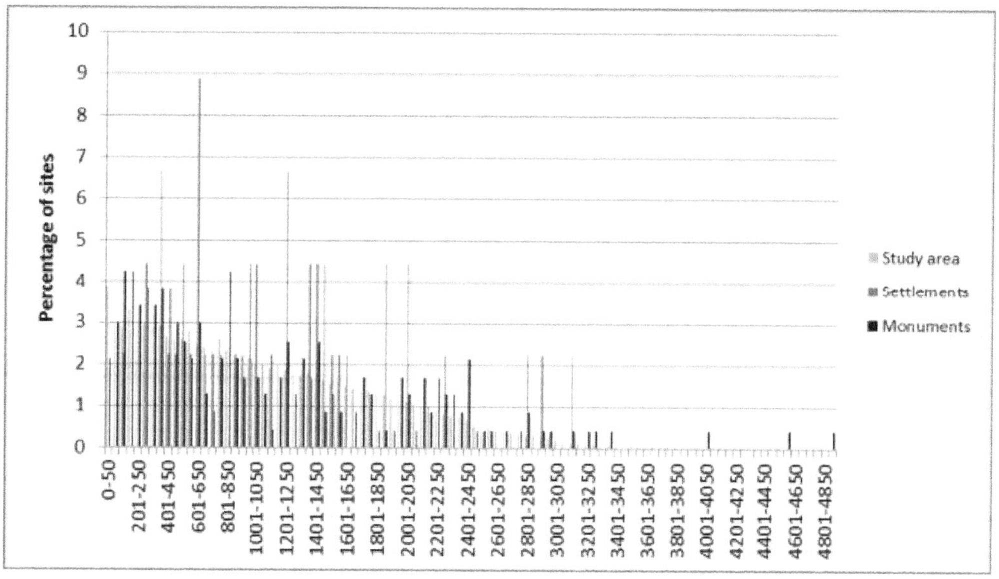

FIGURE 4. 6. DISTANCE IN METERS FROM TRIBUTARIES (SHREVE STREAM 1000)

4.4 Hydrology: Distance from water

Water is an essential resource for the existence of humans and animals. If the cultivation of dry-field crops and rice were the primary subsistence practices during the Bronze Age, it is relevant to investigate the distance from water sources to identified sites and it will be crucial to explore any connections between agricultural fields and water availability.

In order to analyse the distance of the sites to water in GIS, several steps need to be taken, as outlined below.

4.4.1 The modelling of hydrology

Firstly, water will always flow from steep slopes to flat areas. Therefore, once the flow direction of each cell on a digital elevation model (DEM) is recognized, it is feasible to decide stream size depending on the number of cell. However, if there are sinks, which are depressions where water collects and does not flow out of, they should be filled in order that streams flow (Please refer to Hydrological modelling flowchart from http://help.arcgis.com/en/arcgisdesktop/10.0/help/Deriving runoff characteristics).

After these steps, the Shreve method was selected here because in this system main rivers are expressed by the addition of all of its tributaries; therefore, it is likely to meet the research questions of the analysis relating to differences seen primarily in stream size between tributaries and main rivers.

Following the above steps, according to the equivalence between the base digital elevation model (SRTM 90m grid) by CGIAR-CSI and 1:25,000 DEM by the National Geographic Information Institute (NGII), Ministry of Land, Transport and Maritime Affairs, the Republic of Korea, two river systems were generated for analyses. One is the Shreve 1000 model and the other is the Shreve 100 model. In the Shreve 1000 model, streams were created by filling 1000 cells on the base DEM.

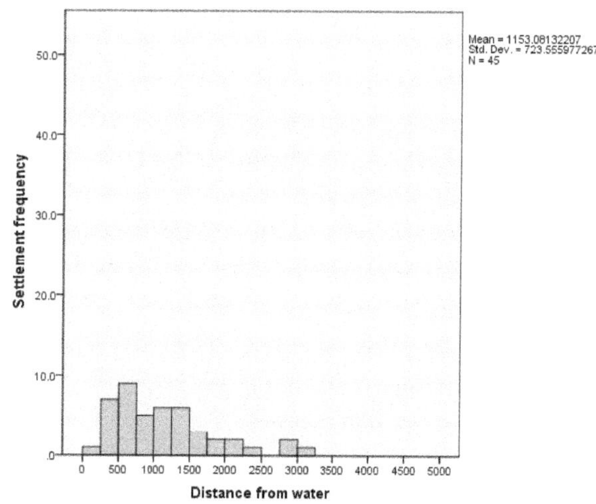

FIGURE 4. 7. DISTANCE FROM TRIBUTARIES TO SETTLEMENTS (SHREVE STREAM 1000)

4.4.2 Distance from tributaries and main rivers on the Shreve 1000 model

Following the steps recounted above, the map for the distance from tributaries of the study area to settlements and monuments and the map for the distance from main rivers of the study area to these sites were obtained (Figures 4.6 and 4.7). Tributaries and main rivers were generated by the correspondence between the base DEM (SRTM 90m grid) by CGIAR-CSI and the DEM by NGII, The Ministry of Land, Transport and Maritime Affairs, for the Republic of Korea. In addition, as mentioned in Chapter 3, it is important to clarify the 'distance from tributaries of the study area'. This is the value of each cell from the nearest tributary within the study area. This method encapsulates the advantage of using GIS for the analysis to assess statistical significance between the overall tendency of the study area and those of the locations of sites.

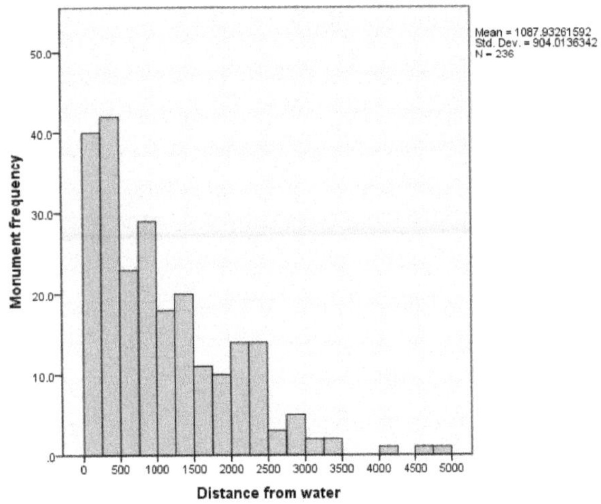

FIGURE 4. 8. DISTANCE FROM TRIBUTARIES TO MONUMENTS (SHREVE STREAM 1000)

Regarding the relationship between tributaries and settlements, the distance between a settlement and the nearest stream ranged between 0 and approx. 3.1km, with an average distance of 1153 metres (Figure 4.7). There is no statistical significance ($\chi^2 = 79.97$, $df = 97$, and $p = 0.895$). Also, according to the column for the number of houses and the distance from tributaries in Appendix 14, larger settlements, with large numbers of houses (more than 25), seem to be located nearer tributaries than were smaller settlements, although this is not statistically significant (Mann-Whitney U test, p value = 0.248). Settlements with large number of houses tended to be established from the Early Bronze Age and to have a long occupational history on the basis of settlement periodization (refer to Appendix 14).

According to the chi-square results for the distance from tributaries to monuments ($\chi^2 = 72.89$, $df = 97$, and $p = 0.968$), monuments were also distributed at random distances from streams. The distance between a monument and the nearest stream ranged between 0 and 5km, with an average distance of 1088 metres (Figure 4.8). The bar chart of the distance of monuments to tributaries does not show a clear pattern, although there are some concentrations closer to 0-550 m and 750-800 m from streams (Figure 4.7).

One feature worth mentioning is the exceptional sites, which are situated at a far distance from water sources. On the basis of Appendix 14, settlements with enclosures (72. Anseong Banjeri, 76. Osan Gajangdong, and 8. Bucheon Gogangdong) tend to be situated at a considerable distance from tributaries, with the exception of the enclosure site in Hwaseong Donghaksan. One commonality of these three settlements (No. 72, 76, and 8) is that they belong to the 'Middle to Late' category according to the chronological divisions used here (refer to Table 3.8). In addition, there may be other reasons to construct settlements or monuments in these types of locations, far from tributaries. It may be that these regions were related to metal resources or sacred places from an early period; for examples, Richard Bradley argues that people placed great importance on the natural places which were related to material resources, for example, quarries, as sacred places in their lives (Bradley 2000: 81-84). Anseong (72) region is not a quarry, but this area in Gyeonggi Province is known for its copper and zinc deposits and is famous for brassware (The Academy of Korean Studies 1991).

In addition, depending on the test results for the distance from main rivers to sites, statistical significance is shown in monuments ($\chi^2 = 56.10$, $df = 37$, and $p = 0.023$) and is not shown in settlements ($\chi^2 = 26.27$, $df = 37$, and $p = 0.906$). These results may be related to the long-term changes of site location and movement analysis. It will be addressed in Chapter 6.

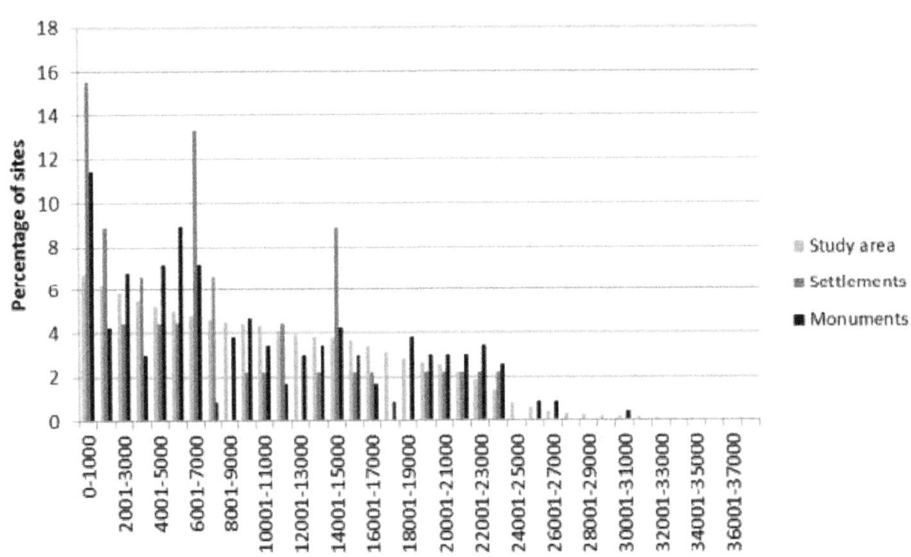

FIGURE 4. 9. DISTANCE IN METERS FROM MAIN RIVERS (SHREVE STREAM 1000 >= 17)

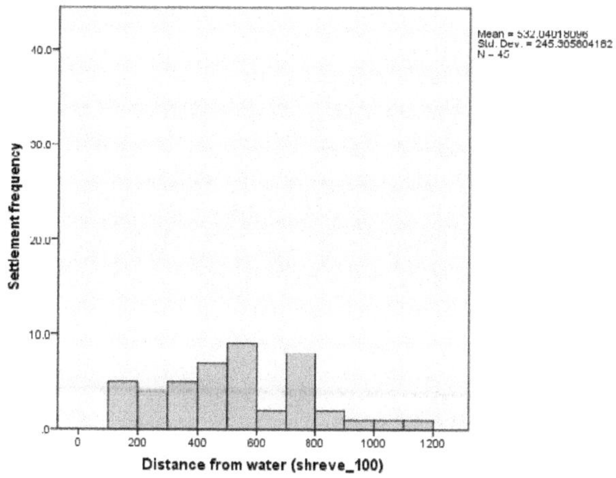

FIGURE 4. 10. DISTANCE FROM TRIBUTARIES TO SETTLEMENTS (SHREVE STREAM 100)

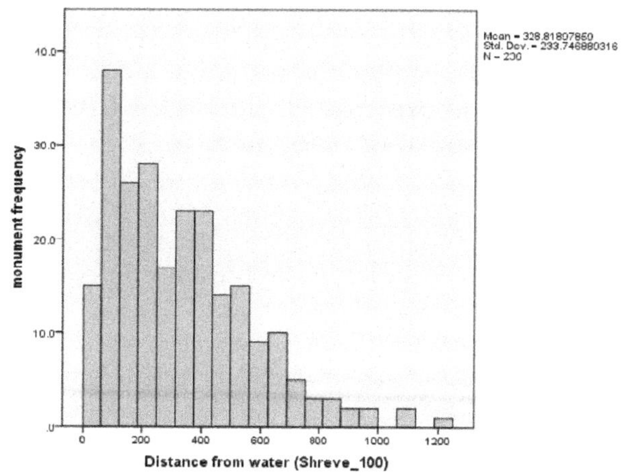

FIGURE 4. 11. DISTANCE FROM TRIBUTARIES TO MONUMENTS (SHREVE STREAM 100)

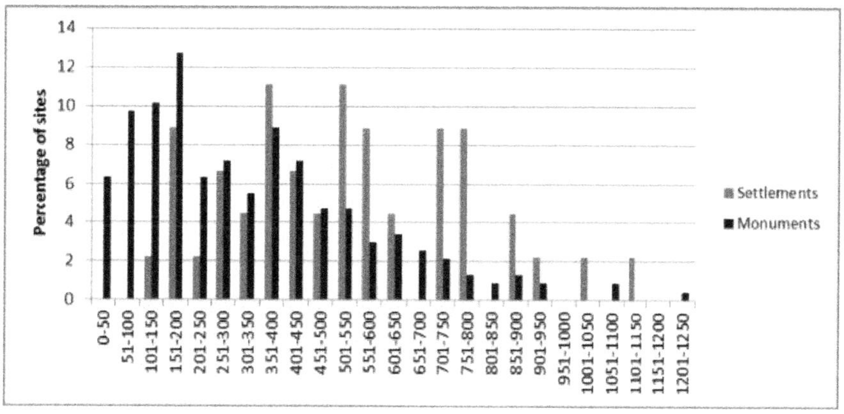

FIGURE 4. 12. DISTANCE IN METRES FROM TRIBUTARIES (SHREVE STREAM 100)

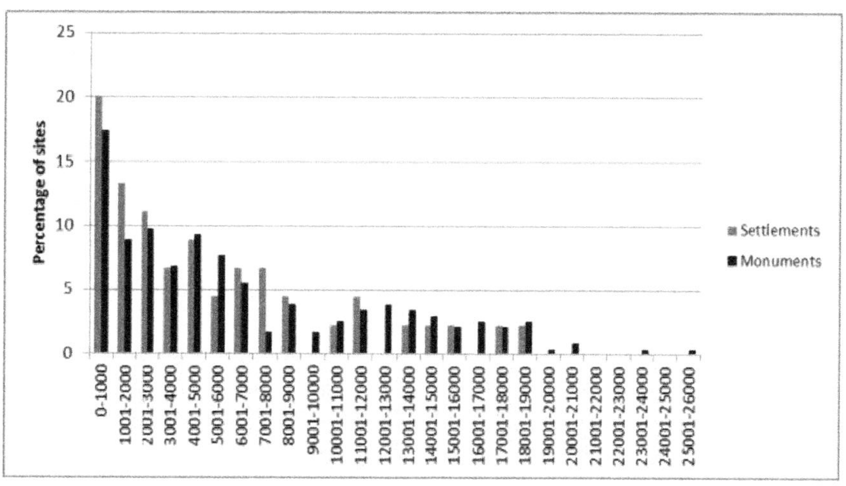

FIGURE 4. 13. DISTANCE IN METRES FROM MAIN RIVERS (SHREVE STREAM 100 >= 75)

4.4.3 Distance from tributaries and main rivers on the Shreve 100 model

Although some patterns in monuments emerge from the hydrological analysis based on Shreve's 1000 cells, when the numerical value for the average distances from water to settlements (1153 ± 904 metres: Figure 4.7) and to monuments (1088 ± 724 meters: Figure 4.8) were obtained, sites seemed surprisingly distant from water sources. Therefore, in order to obtain more reliable values, a second stream system was created on the basis of 100 cells using the Shreve method. Having applied this analysis, average values from water were 532 ± 245 metres (Figure 4.10) in the case of settlements and 329 ± 234 meters (Figure 4.11)) for monuments.

These average distances are more compatible with the results of Ha *et al*'s (2004) research in the Yeoncheon area. He indicated that the average distance from dolmens to water sources in this area was 200 meters. Further afield, these results recall those found elsewhere in the world, such as regarding prehistoric, where settlement did not occur at a distance greater than 300-500 meters from a water source (Kuna and Adelsbergerrová 1995: 122), although there are exceptional cases in these settlement results.

The results for settlements and monuments are presented in Figures 4.12 and 4.13. For this analysis, the value of distance from water of the study area was not considered, because of the number of data points involved are 23,082,866 points and also due to the identified relationship between the study area and settlements and monuments already presented in 1000 cells analysis. Instead, the relationship between settlements and monuments and their distance from water can be compared, with a view to discerning a pattern. According to the results, monuments tend to be located in closer proximity to water sources than settlements. Therefore, there seemed to be regional configuration of settlements and monuments in this study area (this point will be discussed later), the results of hydrologic analysis seem to be different with Gabriel Cooney's hypothesis (1983: 179). Cooney argued that there are strong relation between dwelling sites and megalithic tombs in Ireland during the Neolithic period, where human occupation evidences either house structures tend to be discovered under megalithic tombs. He concluded that 'the landscape of the living and the landscape of the dead may well have been indivisible for the builders of the Irish megalithic tombs' (*ibid*: 189).

TABLE 4. 3. ASPECT AND CALCULATED DEGREES

Aspect	Degree
N	0 – 22.5
NE	22.5 – 67.5
E	67.5 – 112.5
SE	112.5 – 147.5
S	147.5 – 192.5
SW	192.5 – 237.5
W	237.5 – 282.5
NW	282.5 – 337.5
N	337.5 – 360
Flat	-1

4.5 Topography: aspect, slope, and elevation of sites

This section considers aspect, slope, and elevation as one of a collection of environmental elements involved in landscape analysis. These analyses were carried out in order to identify the topographical characteristics of the locations of settlement and monument sites. This section will investigate where the Bronze Age people decided to settle and where they chose to be buried in the landscape and these results will be compared with the results of cultural element analyses in Chapter 5.

4.5.1 Aspect analysis

Aspect analysis is a means by which to identify the slope direction of the study area and where sites are located. Aspect is estimated in degrees from zero to 360 clockwise. Zero and 360 degrees indicate due north and -1 represents flat areas (ArcGIS 10 Help 2011b, refer to Table 4.3).

Firstly, in order to identify Bronze Age people's preference for the aspects that they chose for their living and the dead, data were produced by overlaying surface analysis across spatial analysis using GIS. At present, Koreans prefer a southerly orientation for their houses. In addition, since the influence of Buddhism in the Three Kingdom period (삼국시대, 三國時代) in Korea (after around the fourth century AD) (Choi et al. 2002b: 243), it has been thought that spirits go to the Western Paradise (the Buddhist Elysium, 서방 정토, 西方 淨土) after people die. Whether these or similar ideas extend further back in time is not known, but it is not inconceivable that they had earlier antecedents and so an investigation of the subject is worthwhile.

As Table 4.4 and Figure 4.14 indicate, northwest, southeast and south in order are the most common aspects for settlements, but these tendencies are clearly not statistically significant ($\chi^2 = 6.35$, $df = 8$, and $p = 0.61$). Most commons for monuments are east, southwest, and south aspects, while they tend to avoid a western aspect, and this also does not show statistical significance topographically ($\chi^2 = 11.09$, $df = 8$, and $p = 0.2$).

TABLE 4. 4. THE ASPECT PERCENTAGE AND FREQUENCY OF STUDY AREA, SETTLEMENTS AND MONUMENTS

Aspect	Study_Area (percentage)	Settlements (percentage)	Settlements (frequency)	Monuments (percentage)	Monuments (frequency)
N	11.15	13.33	6	7.20	17
NE	11.37	8.89	4	12.71	30
E	12.82	11.11	5	17.37	41
SE	12.29	17.78	8	11.86	28
S	11.81	13.33	6	13.56	32
SW	12.63	6.67	3	13.56	32
W	14.10	8.89	4	11.02	26
NW	12.62	20.00	9	12.29	29
Flat	1.20	0.00	0	0.42	1
Total	100.00	100.00	45	100.00	236

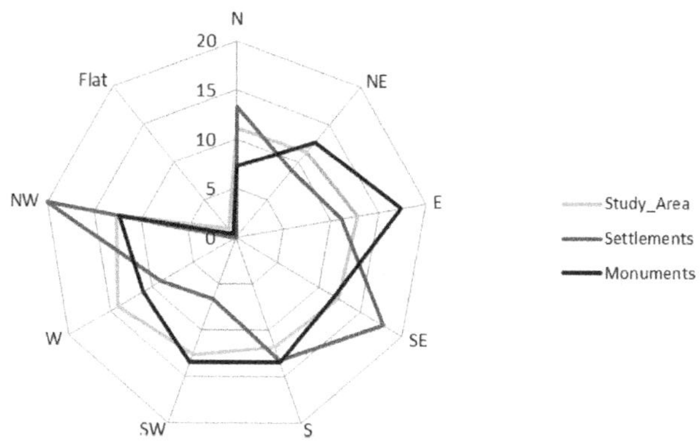

FIGURE 4. 14. THE ASPECT OF THE OVERALL STUDY AREA, SETTLEMENTS AND MONUMENTS (UNITS IN PERCENTAGE)

It is important not to confuse aspect analysis with analysis of orientation of each monument or house in Chapter 5.4. Therefore, it is difficult to compare it directly with other results concerning analysis of monument orientation in Europe (Barrett et al. 1991a; Darvill 2004). A surprising result is that one of the most common aspects for settlements was towards the Northwest as it is supposed that a northwest aspect is to be avoided, due to the fact that there are extremely cold winter winds in the Korean peninsula because of the Siberian anticyclone, as mentioned in Chapter 2.1. Therefore, the locations of these settlements were examined and it as taken as given, that the arable areas of the settlements were also situated in a Northwest direction.

4.5.2 Slope analysis

Turning now to slope analysis, a slope on the one hand is related to the formation of soil type and on the other, to a viewshed perspective and also to movement. In this section the basic results of slope analysis will be presented. Slope analysis under surface analysis in GIS was used for this analysis.

According to the results of slope analysis (Table 4.5 and Figure 4.15), 95.6% of settlements were situated on a 0-5° slope and 4.4% of settlements were on a slope of between 5.1° and 10°. As regards monuments, 80.9% were on a 0-5° slope and 17.4% were on a 5.1°-10° slope. In addition, 1.7% were on a 10.1°-15° slope. In brief, 100% of settlements were discovered on gentle (0-10°) slopes, 98.3% of monuments were situated on 0-10° slopes and 1.7% were located on slightly steeper 10.1°-15° slopes.

In order to test the significance of this pattern, the chi-square test values of settlements ($\chi^2 = 43.51$, $df = 9$, and $p = 1.7373E\text{-}06$) and that of monuments were obtained ($\chi^2 = 129.97$, $df = 9$, and $p = 1.2029E\text{-}23$), with both, as might be expected, displaying a significant departure from the study area values; specifically, both settlements and monuments are preferentially located on flatter land.

What, then, is the meaning of slope analysis for the present research? As recommended by the NAAS, slope can be directly related to land use. For example, slopes under 15° degrees are deemed suitable for rice cultivation and

TABLE 4. 5. THE DISTRIBUTION OF SLOPE (IN DEGREES) FOR THE STUDY AREA AND SITES

Slope	Study area	Settlement percentage	Monument percentage	Study area Frequency	Settlement Frequency	Monument Frequency
0-5	46.65	95.56	80.93	728968	43	191
5.1-10	20.87	4.44	17.37	326151	2	41
10.1-15	14.64	0	1.69	228707	0	4
15.1-20	9.87	0	0	154178	0	0
20.1-25	5.19	0	0	81154	0	0
25.1-30	2.06	0	0	32173	0	0
30.1-35	0.60	0	0	9341	0	0
35.1-40	0.12	0	0	1848	0	0
40.1-45	0.01	0	0	167	0	0
45.1-50	0.00	0	0	5	0	0
	100	100	100	1562692	45	236

Table 4. 6. The slope mean, median and mode of settlements and monuments

Slope	Settlements	Monuments
Average	2.0	2.8
Median	1.5	2.1
Mode		0.8

for dry-field fields. Slopes between 15° and 30° are fit for fruit trees, mulberry plantations, and (medicinal) herbs, those between 30° and 60° are appropriate for grassland, or, if severely eroded, for forestry. Lastly, slopes above 60° are deemed suitable only for woodland. It is possible to infer that settlements and monuments in the Bronze Age were located in areas suitable for rice and dry-field agriculture, based on the fact that the majority of both sites were located in the 0-10° slope region.

In addition, slope is related to questions of visibility and this will be considered further in the viewshed analysis (Chapter 5.2). Together with these points, the consideration of slope would surely be an important factor when people moved from one place to another. The energy consumption of moving to/in a steep region would be higher than that of a flat region. This concept of 'relative cost' will be considered in Chapter 5.3 in which movement analysis will also be conducted.

4.5.3 Elevation analysis

The final analysis in this section concerns elevation. In order to identify the elevation of settlements and monuments, the spatial and surface analysis in the GIS contour tool was used.

The range of elevation in the study area is from zero to 1236 metres above sea level (Figure 4.16). A total of 93.3% of settlements and 96.6% of monuments are located between 0 and 140 metres height above sea level and 6.7% of settlements and 3.6% of monuments were located between 141-300 metres height. Exceptionally, one settlement (No. 25 Seoul Ilwondong) was situated at 255 metres and one monument (No. 211 Ganghwa Gocheonri) was located at a height of 281 meters. According to Table 4.8, the average elevation of settlements is 77 meters and the median is 66 meters, while the average elevation of monuments is 65.2 metres and the median is 57.5 metres.

In order to examine whether there existed preferences for selecting an elevation in order to build settlements and monuments, the elevation relationships between the study area and settlements and between the study area and monuments were investigated separately. According to the test results (settlements: $\chi^2 = 47.23$, $df = 29$, and $p = 0.01764$); monuments: $\chi^2 = 159.66$, $df = 29$, and $p = 5.321E-20$), they both display statistical significance. Bronze Age people might have considered the location of their settlements in terms of security. This assumption might explain the reason why settlements have not been discovered at between zero to 20 metres in elevation. Unlike the Neolithic sites that have been discovered near the coast, where the lowest land lies (refer back to Figure 2.9), Bronze Age sites seemed to be rarely identified near the coast (refer to Figure 2.45). This might be due to taphonomic factors, but since Neolithic sites have survived in the archaeological record, it seems that this pattern may reflect a shift in the character of subsistence economy, and by extension the landscape setting of settlement, occurring between the Neolithic period and the Bronze Age.

Table 4. 7. The elevation of study area and sites

Elevation	Study area	Settlements percentage	Monuments percentage	Study area frequency	Settlement frequency	Monuments frequency
0-20	15.8	0.0	9.3	247149	0	22
21-40	12.8	22.2	21.2	200159	10	50
41-60	9.9	20.0	23.3	154004	9	55
61-80	8.9	24.4	18.6	138837	11	44
81-100	7.7	4.4	12.7	120811	2	30
101-120	6.7	17.8	5.5	103989	8	13
121-140	5.4	4.4	5.9	83611	2	14
141-160	4.4	2.2	0.9	68032	1	2
161-180	3.7	2.2	0.9	57557	1	2
181-200	3.2	0.0	0.0	49446	0	0
201-220	2.8	0.0	0.4	43067	0	1
221-240	2.4	0.0	0.9	37424	0	2
241-260	2.1	2.2	0.0	33118	1	0
261-280	1.9	0.0	0.0	29125	0	0
281-300	1.6	0.0	0.4	25781	0	1
>300	10.9	0.0	0.0	170166	0	0
	100.0	100.0	100.0	1562276	45	236

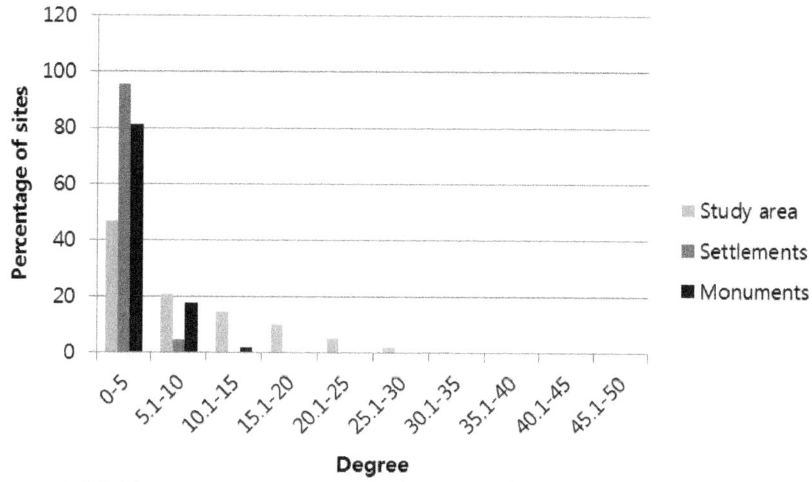

FIGURE 4. 15. THE DISTRIBUTION OF SLOPE (IN DEGREES) FOR THE STUDY AREA AND SITES

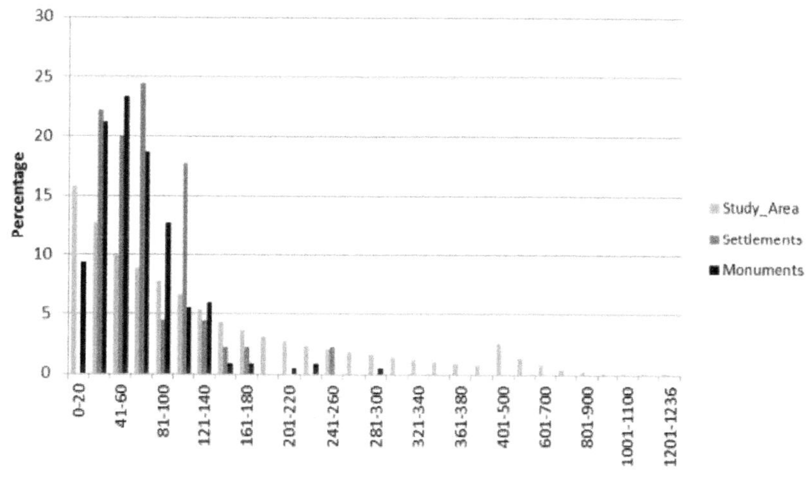

FIGURE 4. 16. THE ELEVATION OF STUDY AREA AND SITES

TABLE 4. 8. THE ELEVATION MEAN, MEDIAN AND MODE OF SETTLEMENTS AND MONUMENTS

Elevation	Settlements	Monuments
Average	77	65.2
Median	66	57.5
Mode	35	33.0

As mentioned above, the average elevation of settlements is higher than that of monuments in the study area. How is this difference in elevation reflected in terms of visibility of settlements and monuments? If the sites prove to have high visibility, could this fact give an insight into the Bronze Age perception and consequently their use of the landscape? The results of a cumulative viewshed and binary viewshed for settlements and monuments show some differences (as will be discussed in Chapter 5.2).

4.6 Summary of key findings

In this chapter, the environmental variables were examined in order to investigate how the change to the subsistence economy, especially in the development of agriculture, affected Bronze Age people's planning for their shelters and burials through a process of negotiation between the landscape and the society that inhabited that land and how environmental elements affect Bronze Age people to choose their placement of the living and the dead.

To sum up the relationships between settlements/ monuments and natural features, firstly, according to the soil type analyses, settlements were shown to have positive association in the Dry-field_Good category and a negative significance in the Forest and the Related_ water categories. Similarly, the negative significance of monuments was seen in the Related_water and Forest areas and a positive association was presented for the Dry-field_Good and the Rice_Good classifications. However, the proportions of monument sites in the Rice_Good and Rice_Poor sectors were found to be higher than those of settlements. The relationship between monuments and soil types for agriculture could provide supporting evidence for a hypothesis posited by Bradley (1998) in a European context: he argued that the advent of agriculture brought about a new sense of time and space and that stone monuments appear to be linked with the land itself. In addition, according to the results of long-term changes during the Bronze Age, settlements tended to be situated on soil suitable for dry-field crops throughout this period.

Secondly, the relationship between settlements and monuments and their distance from water were compared. According to the hydrological results, monuments tend to be located in closer proximity to water sources than settlements and this result reflects that monuments seem to be more related to arable lands.

Thirdly, on the basis of topographical results, settlements were situated commonly in the northwest, southeast and south aspects in order and that monument sites were located frequently in the east, southwest and south aspects, although these did not show statistical significance. In addition, most of settlements and monuments in the study area were located on slopes of 0-10° and these both show statistical significance, in that such areas, not surprisingly, were clearly being sought. According to soil information from the National Academy of Agricultural Science, soils with slopes under 15° degrees are deemed suitable for rice cultivation and for dry-field fields. Therefore, the slope information for settlements and monuments seems to reflect that these sites were also related to agriculture in the Bronze Age. Finally, approximately 95% of settlements and monuments are located at between 0 and 140 metres height above sea level and they both present statistical significance. Settlements were not identified in the category of between 0-20 metres elevation and the average and median elevation of settlements is higher than those of monuments. These patterns might be reflected in the transition of lifestyle from the Neolithic period to the Bronze Age.

Through the results of pedological, hydrological and topographical analyses, it has been possible to identify locational information concerning settlements and monument sites in the Bronze Age and to infer from that their subsistence economy. However, the environmental element analyses have not been sufficient to wholly extrapolate the characteristics of Bronze Age settlements and monuments, although natural features indicate the fundamental circumstances that surely determined the places to be people lived and chose to be buried. Therefore, further investigation of the cultural elements will be required; this will follow in Chapter 5.

Chapter 5. Cultural feature analyses

Although environmental elements must have played an important role in the decision of where to place settlements and monuments, it is difficult to say that the locations of sites were decided upon only by objective environmental factors, such as soil quality, distance from water, and topography. For example, it has been assumed that settlements would be placed near to good soil for rice. However, settlements tend to be located on soils associated with dry-field crops through the Bronze Age and, in their distance from water, settlements were situated further than monuments from water sources. Therefore, there might be other factors involved in the decisions on where to live and to be buried. Although it is a challenge to define what culture is (Ingold 1994: 329), due to the fact that it has been not easy to separate environmental factors and cultural factors, in this chapter, from the standpoint of human perceptions (Lock 2009), cultural elements, such as landform preferences, viewshed, movement and site orientation, will be considered, with a special concentration upon localised knowledge (Gosden 1994: 79) of the Bronze Age people in the Korean peninsula and phenomenological approaches (Tilley 1994).

5.1 Landform analysis

5.1.1 Aim

Before the viewshed analyses were conducted, feature analyses were carried out in order to identify which landforms, such as pit, channel, pass, ridge, peak, and plane, were preferred by prehistoric people, as a means to choose the locations of their shelters and burials. These elements themselves look like purely environmental factors. However, these features can alternatively be viewed as closely related to human decision-making, that is, a visible experience that absorbs environmental and cultural features into a conceptualised interaction with the landscape (Wheatley and Gillings 2000: 3). Therefore, landform preference analyses can be included within the category of cultural elements. In addition, in order to compare this research with other researchers' results, monument types, mainly table and capstone types, will be examined.

5.1.2 Methodology – Modelling features

In order to analyse what features have been chosen for the location of monuments and settlements, first of all, the features have to be identified from the digital elevation model (DEM) through the 'LandSerf, 2.3' software (Jo Wood, Department of Information Science, City University, London).

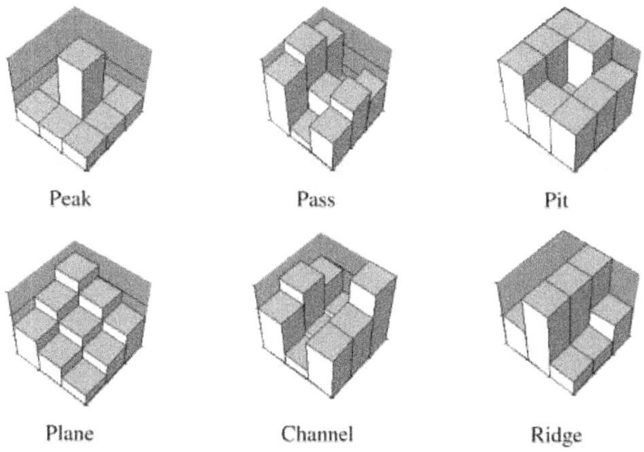

FIGURE 5. 1. THE SIX MORPHOMETRIC CLASSES AS REPRESENTED BY A GRIDDED ELEVATION MODEL (FROM FISHER ET AL., 2004: 108, WITH THE AUTHOR'S PERMISSION)

LandSerf software divides the physical landscape into six categorised features: pit, channel, pass, ridge, peak, and plane (Figure 5.1).

After the exportation of DEM from ArcGIS to LandSerf 2.3, the window cell size is chosen and then the 'Feature extraction' analysis is run under the 'Surface parameter' analysis. The morphological characteristic of the centre cell is decided by surrounding cells as can be seen in Figure 5.1. The classification of features followed the definition by Wood (Wood 1996: Chapter five; Fisher et al. 2004: 107-109). If all adjacent cells are lower than the core cell, the latter will be identified as a 'Peak' and, on the contrary, if all surrounding cells are higher than a centre cell, it can be termed a 'Pit'. In addition, if the centre displays three contiguous cells that are higher than the rest of the cells, it will be termed a 'Ridge'. If, however, these contiguous cells are lower relative to all other cells, then they will be identified as a 'Channel'. Compared to a 'Channel', a 'Pass' is identified as a passage between neighbouring cells. Finally, if a centred cell and surrounding cells have a similar height and a similar slope degree, the cell of interest is termed a 'Plane'. It should be emphasised that this does not mean that all the cells have a zero or lower degree of slope and a low elevation in the sense of a plain. That is, 'plane' should not be confused with 'plain', particularly as a 'Plane' can represent both a flat 'plain' and a steeply sloping 'plain'.

In order to find a compatible feature map with the DEM, with its 10 metre contour lines, the feature extraction in LandSerf was carried out using various sizes of window cells. For example, 3 × 3, 5 × 5, 7 × 7, 9 × 9, 11 × 11 (11 × 11 is approximately 1 km×1 km, because one cell size is 90 m×90 m), up to 25 × 25 (approximately 10 km × 10 km). After features were extracted, each different cell size produced a feature map and this was transformed into raster data in GIS; then each map was matched with contours in DEM, one by one, in order to select the map which was the most representative of the actual landscape. After trial and error, the 11 x 11 feature map was selected for the analyses, due to the fact that its characterisations are the most representative of the 10 metre contour in the DEM programme.

5.1.3 Results

Following the above steps, the feature category of each site was extracted from the 11 × 11 feature map. According to the results of landform analyses on the settlements (confirmed by excavation reports) and monument sites (Table 5.1 and Figure 5.2), 60% of identified settlements and 20.3% of monuments are situated on 'Ridges', 26.7% of settlements and 59.3% of monument sites are located in 'Planes', 8.9% of settlements and 0.9% of monument sites are on 'Peaks', 4.4% of settlements and 2.1% of monument sites were situated in 'Passes', and finally, 15.7% and 1.7% of monument sites were located in 'Channels' and 'Pits' respectively.

TABLE 5. 1. THE FEATURE PERCENTAGE OF STUDY AREA AND SITES

Value	Landform	Study area	Settlements	Monuments
1	Pit	0.27	0.00	1.69
2	Channel	22.20	0.00	15.68
3	Pass	1.36	4.44	2.12
4	Ridge	28.73	60.00	20.34
5	Peak	0.45	8.89	0.85
6	Plane	47.00	26.67	59.32
		100.00	100.00	100.00

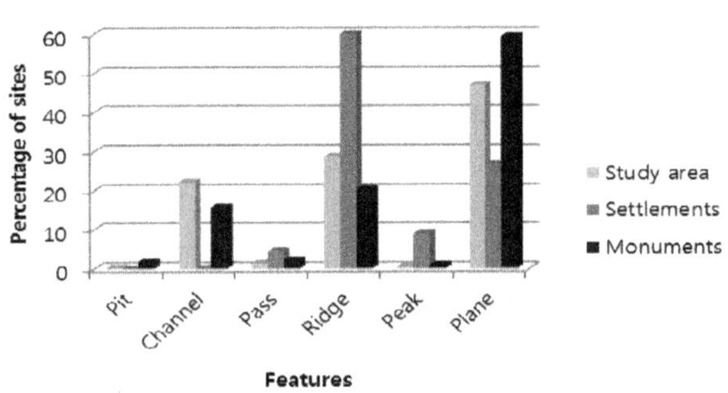

FIGURE 5. 2. THE LANDFORMS OF STUDY AREA AND SITES

That is, 60% of settlements were located on 'Ridges' and 59.3% of monuments were situated on 'Planes'. Importantly these results are statistically significant when compared to the expected proportions based on landforms in the total study area, if sites were randomly distributed (settlements: χ^2 =103.75, *df* = 5, and $p < 0.0000$, monuments: $\chi^2 = 37.5$, *df* = 5, and $p = 4.8 \times 10^{-7}$, refer to Table 5.2 and 5.3). In the case of settlements, people positively selected 'Ridge' and 'Peak' as their living place and they seemed to avoid 'Channel' for settlements. On the other hand, people preferred 'Plane' and 'Pit' for their monuments and 'Ridge' was not their first choice when identifying potential locations.

After the results are obtained, they must be re-checked, to verify their reliability, due to the fact that feature analysis is strongly dependent on the chosen window scale, for example, although certain cells were designated as 'Plane' in the approximate 1 km × 1 km unit cell analysis, if the analysis is conducted in the larger window scale, the 'Plane' cell may be altered to a different feature, such as, 'Ridge' (John Pouncett pers comm 2011). In order to check this point, 25 × 25 (approximately 10 km × 10 km) window cell analyses were carried out on the monuments and the results can be viewed in Table 5.4.

As can be seen in Table, 5.4, there are no significant differences in expected monument frequency between feature 11 and feature 25 analyses. As well as the analysis of 10 km × 10 km, a smaller scale five × five (450 m × 450 m) window cells analysis was also run. The monument frequency (Table 5.5) shows some differences compared to the two above analyses, but there was not such a

TABLE 5. 2. FEATURE_11 PERCENTAGE IN STUDY AREA AND THE FREQUENCY OF SETTLEMENTS AND ITS CHI-SQUARE TEST RESULT

Value	feature_11	Study area	Settlement Frequency	Expected	(Oi-Ei)^2	(Oi-Ei)^2/Ei
1	Pit	0.27	0	0.12	0.01	0.12
2	Channel	22.20	0	9.99	99.80	9.99
3	Pass	1.36	2	0.61	1.93	3.15
4	Ridge	28.73	27	12.93	198.01	15.32
5	Peak	0.45	4	0.20	14.42	71.21
6	Plane	47.00	12	21.15	83.72	3.96
		100.00	45	45.00		103.75
	df=(6-1)*(2-1)					
	df=5					
	0.05 significance					
	c2 =	103.75				
	p =	0.0000				

TABLE 5. 3. FEATURE_11 PERCENTAGE IN STUDY AREA AND THE FREQUENCY OF MONUMENTS AND ITS CHI-SQUARE TEST RESULT

Value	feature_11	Study area	Monument frequency	Expected	(Oi-Ei)^2	(Oi-Ei)^2/Ei
1	Pit	0.27	4	0.64	11.31	17.75
2	Channel	22.20	37	52.39	236.91	4.52
3	Pass	1.36	5	3.21	3.21	1.00
4	Ridge	28.73	48	67.80	392.15	5.78
5	Peak	0.45	2	1.06	0.88	0.83
6	Plane	47.00	140	110.92	845.65	7.62
		100.01	236	236.02		37.50
	df=(6-1)*(2-1)					
	df=5					
	0.05 significance					
	c2 =	37.50				
	p =	0.00000048				

TABLE 5. 4. FEATURE_25 PERCENTAGE IN STUDY AREA AND THE FREQUENCY OF MONUMENTS AND ITS CHI-SQUARE TEST RESULT

Value	feature_25	Study area	Monument frequency	Expected	(Oi-Ei)^2	(Oi-Ei)^2/Ei
1	Pit	0.41	4	0.97	9.20	9.50
2	Channel	19.52	37	46.07	82.21	1.78
3	Pass	2.05	5	4.84	0.03	0.01
4	Ridge	25.13	48	59.31	127.84	2.16
5	Peak	0.76	2	1.79	0.04	0.02
6	Plane	52.13	140	123.03	288.09	2.34
		100.00	236	236.00		15.81
	df=(6-1)*(2-1)					
	df=5					
	0.05 significance					
	c2 =	15.81				
	p =	0.00740800				

TABLE 5. 5. FEATURE_5 PERCENTAGE IN STUDY AREA AND THE FREQUENCY OF MONUMENTS AND ITS CHI-SQUARE TEST RESULT

Value	feature_5	Study area	Monument frequency	Expected	(Oi-Ei)^2	(Oi-Ei)^2/Ei
1	Pit	0.38	0	0.90	0.80	0.90
2	Channel	41.31	53	97.49	1979.50	20.30
3	Pass	1.49	5	3.52	2.20	0.63
4	Ridge	50.08	66	118.19	2723.67	23.05
5	Peak	0.45	1	1.06	0.00	0.00
6	Plane	6.29	111	14.84	9245.90	622.85
		100.00	236	236.00		667.73
	df=(6-1)*(2-1)					
	df=5					
	0.05 significance					
	c2 =	667.73				
	p =	0.00000000				

considerable gap between the numbers, therefore; it can be assumed that the results of feature 11 analyses are reliable and as a result, that they can be examined and interpreted.

The differences in the locations of the six morphological characteristics between settlements and monuments seem to be clear, though two potential problems should be considered: the morphological definition of certain categories of features and the accuracy of excavation report maps and site location descriptions.

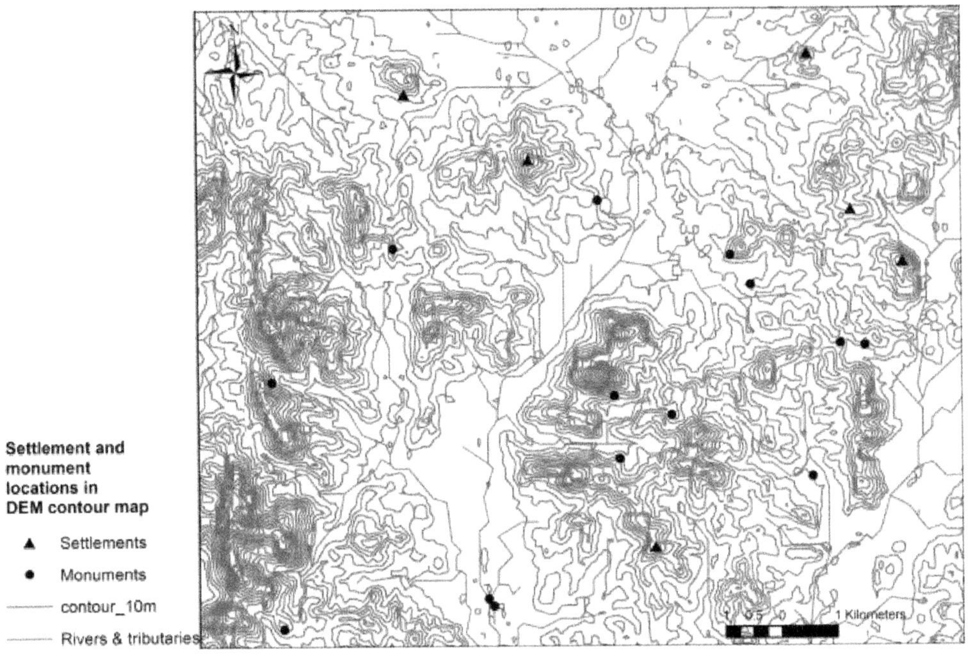

FIGURE 5. 3. SETTLEMENTS AND MONUMENTS LOCATION ON A DEM CONTOUR MAP

TABLE 5. 6. FEATURE_11 PERCENTAGE IN STUDY AREA AND THE FREQUENCY OF TABLE TYPE DOLMENS AND ITS CHI-SQUARE TEST RESULT

Value	feature_11	Study area	Table type Dolmen_ frequency	Expected	(Oi-Ei)^2	(Oi-Ei)^2/Ei
1	Pit	0.27	4	0.30	13.7	46.2
2	Channel	22.20	11	24.42	180.1	7.4
3	Pass	1.36	0	1.50	2.2	1.5
4	Ridge	28.73	33	31.60	2.0	0.1
5	Peak	0.45	4	0.50	12.3	24.8
6	Plane	47.00	58	51.70	39.7	0.8
		100.00	110			80.7
	df=(6-1)*(2-1)					
	df=5					
	0.05 significance					
	c2 =	80.7				
	p =	6.025E-16				

TABLE 5. 7. FEATURE_11 PERCENTAGE IN STUDY AREA AND THE FREQUENCY OF CAPSTONE TYPE DOLMENS AND ITS CHI-SQUARE TEST RESULT

Value	feature_11	Study area	Capstone type dolmen_ frequency	Expected	(Oi-Ei)^2	(Oi-Ei)^2/Ei
1	Pit	0.27	19	0.9	329.1	383.3
2	Channel	22.20	39	70.6	998.3	14.1
3	Pass	1.36	8	4.3	13.5	3.1
4	Ridge	28.73	99	91.4	58.3	0.6
5	Peak	0.45	7	1.4	31.0	21.7
6	Plane	47.00	146	149.5	12.0	0.1
		100.00	318			423.0
	df=(6-1)*(2-1)					
	df=5					
	0.05 significance					
	c2 =	423				
	p =	3.32185E-89				

It can be seen in the above results for landform preference between settlements and monuments, that they display a substantial contrast, although it is difficult to make a clear distinction between the characteristics of the spaces allocated for the living and the dead, due to fact that scattered sites have been discovered near dolmens, as mentioned in Chapter 4.2.2.

According to site maps and the explanations of site locations in the excavation reports, (Figure 5.3) settlements tend to be situated on ridges in the same way indicated by landform analyses and, consequently, they tend to be at a higher elevation and with a substantially better view than that for monuments. This point will be analysed in the viewshed and final discussion sections. By contrast, monuments that are identified in the 'Plane' category tend to be located at the end of ridgelines, which appear to represent the transitional zones between the end of a mountain and the start of plain, encompassing views over the nearest arable land. The viewshed analyses presented in the next section show a much clearer perspective supporting the results of landform analyses.

In addition, this result seems to be supportive of Yu's results seen in Table 2.6, concerning the location of dolmen in Ganghwa island: 61 % of dolmens were situated in the 'Slope' group, as a 'Plane' category in this research can represent both a flat 'plain' and a steeply sloping 'plain'. However, it is difficult to compare these data with Woo's result in Table 2.10 that suggests dolmens in the Gyeonggi region were located in the flatlands (26%) and on hill and mountain ridges (74%), due to the fact that he did no clearly define the categories.

Together with these features, it is worthwhile examining the preferred landform for table type and capstone type dolmens, in order to compare the results with those of other researchers (Yu, 2001, 2002). Yu mentioned that table type dolmens in Ganghwa Island were located more often on ridges and mountain tops than in the plains (see Table 2.7). There might be difficulties in comparing results in this research directly with Yu's results due to the fact that the study areas are not the same. But it is relevant to clarify the differences and why these might have occurred. For this analysis, in order to aid the comparison of the results, instead of monument site codes, the information for individual monuments was utilised. According to Tables 5.6 and 5.7, the landform results of both types of dolmens in the research area are statistically significant. However, monument types that were found in the 'Planes' and 'Ridge' categories do not seem to be too different from the baseline study area. This result is similar to the result of the chi-square test found in footnote 7. That is, they contribute very little to the chi-square (refer to Tables 5.6 and 5.7). Therefore, it is difficult to state that a certain type of dolmen is connected to a particular landform.

5.2 Viewshed analysis

5.2.1 Aims

This section focuses on visibility analyses. The aims of viewshed analysis are to investigate how visibility affects the location of settlements and monuments in their landscape and what, if any, differences exist between the viewsheds of settlements and monuments on the basis of the hypothesis that visual factors affect people's perceptions of their environment (Wheatley and Gillings 2000: 3). The matter of where people take a view seems to be closely related to their value of thinking and decision-making. Therefore, viewshed can be termed a cultural element.

5.2.2 Methods

The definition of viewshed

If the cells on the raster data are recognised from one or multiple observation points or lines, then, it can be called a viewshed (ArcGIS 10 Help 2011a). If only a single observation point is chosen, a value of one (1) is given to each cell which can be seen from the observation points and a value of zero (0) is designated to all cells which cannot be seen from the observation point (*ibid*). This analysis results in what is called binary viewshed. If multiple observation points are chosen, each cell is presented with a value, which represents how many observed points can see the point (*ibid*). This analysis is called cumulative viewshed.

Cumulative viewshed and binary viewshed are applied to the analyses of settlements and monuments in this study. Cumulative viewshed can obtain visible values and identify the most observable area from all settlements or all monuments and binary viewshed can procure the visible and invisible areas from each site and can compare the range of visible cell numbers. The scenario posited by this method is that where people[30] stand near a dolmen or at a settlement and are looking at the horizon, they command a potential 360 degree panoramic view. This assumes that people consider all directions from their standpoints when they decide on where to settle and where to be buried.

Limitation

Several criticisms have been applied to viewshed analyses, for example, the lack of consideration of past vegetation patterns by researchers using viewshed analysis, who utilise current environmental data due to the lack of reliable information about past landscapes (Lock and Stančič 1995: 34; Chapman and Gearey 2000: 316-319). Additional limitations highlighted are the issue of mobility, DEM and scale-dependant results and edge effects (Wheatley

[30] The default value (150cm) was chosen as a viewpoint after taking into account the average heights of male (167.4 cm) and female (150.8 cm) adults on the basis of ancient human skeletons in Yeanri Gyeongnam site (Busan University Museum 1993)

and Gillings 2000: 5-12). Bearing in mind the restrictions, certain decisions were taken with regards to the viewshed analyses applied to the study sites:

1. Viewshed analysis in this section is defined by static standpoints due to the fact that each settlement and monument site was analysed on the basis of XY coordinates.

2. Although the sites were not all constructed at the same time, the analyses were conducted on the basis of the consideration of all sites synchronically instead of diachronically. Settlements might be affected more than monuments due to the fact that monuments would be more visible in the landscape once they were built and that they will be cumulative.

3. The distance effect from the viewer is not considered in this section, even though there are different effects experienced by the viewer between near and far surroundings (which can be examined through the Higuchi viewshed or a distance banded viewshed) (Wheatley and Gillings 2000: 16-20), due to the fact that this research intends to concentrate on the broader viewshed patterns of settlements and monuments.

4. In order to minimise edge effects (Wheatley and Gillings 2000: 11-12; Conolly and Lake 2006a: 91), the analyses were executed including a buffer area surrounding the study region. Approximately 185 km × 153 km raster data was chosen, although the study region is approx. a 131 km × 143 km irregular shape.

Viewshed analysis remains an important tool to examine the relationship between the location of monuments and settlements and the possible decision-making processes by which they were placed, although there are certain limitations as mentioned above. In order to identify the patterns from the results of settlements and monuments, the results were examined from both cumulative and binary viewsheds (refer to Figure 5.5).

5.2.3 Results

5.2.3.1 Cumulative viewshed

Although there are criticisms (Fleming 1999b: 204; 2005; Wheatley and Gillings 2002) regarding the lack of formal methodology to Tilley's phenomenological approaches (Tilley 1994), his research has prompted much debate and has impacted significantly upon later studies (Cummings and Whittle 2003; Cummings and Fowler 2004). In order to examine whether this approach can be applied to Seoul·Incheon·Gyeonggi province and to find out whether monuments in the study area were oriented towards distinguished natural outcrops or certain prominent locations, a cumulative viewshed analysis was run.

Firstly, the results for the most visible area faced by all monuments were obtained from the cumulative viewshed (refer to Figure 5.5). The highest value obtained is 52, meaning that 52 sites out of 236 monument sites looked out towards one place. This location is Bukhan mountain (북한산, 北漢山) (refer to the dark circle on Figure 5.4). Incidentally, the palace of the Joseon dynasty (조선시대, 朝

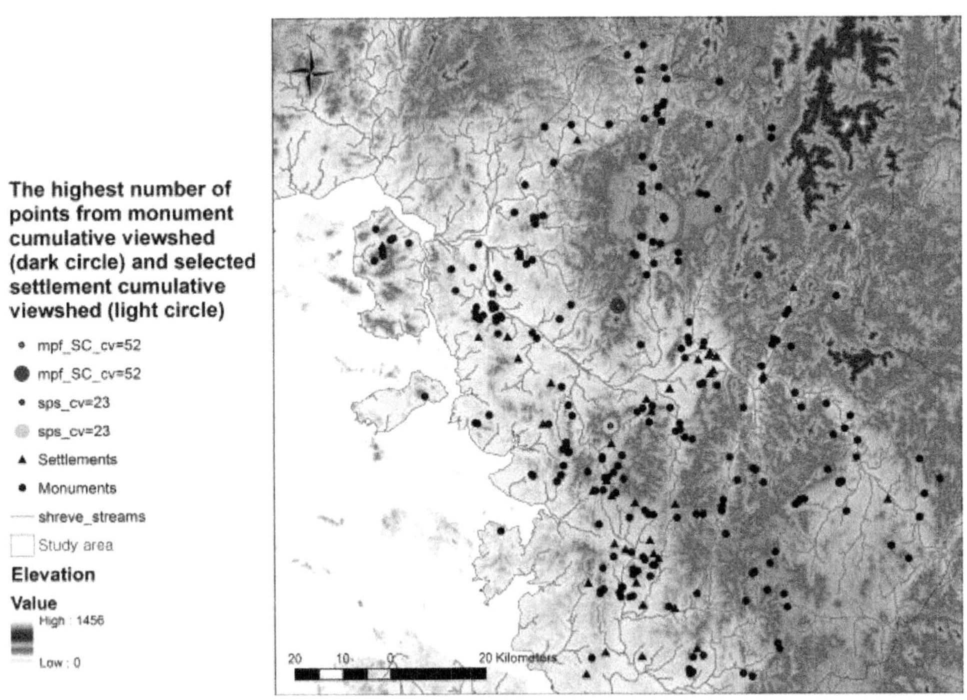

FIGURE 5. 4. THE HIGHEST NUMBER OF POINTS FROM MONUMENT CUMULATIVE VIEWSHED (DARK GREY CIRCLE) AND SETTLEMENT VIEWSHED (LIGHT GREY CIRCLE)

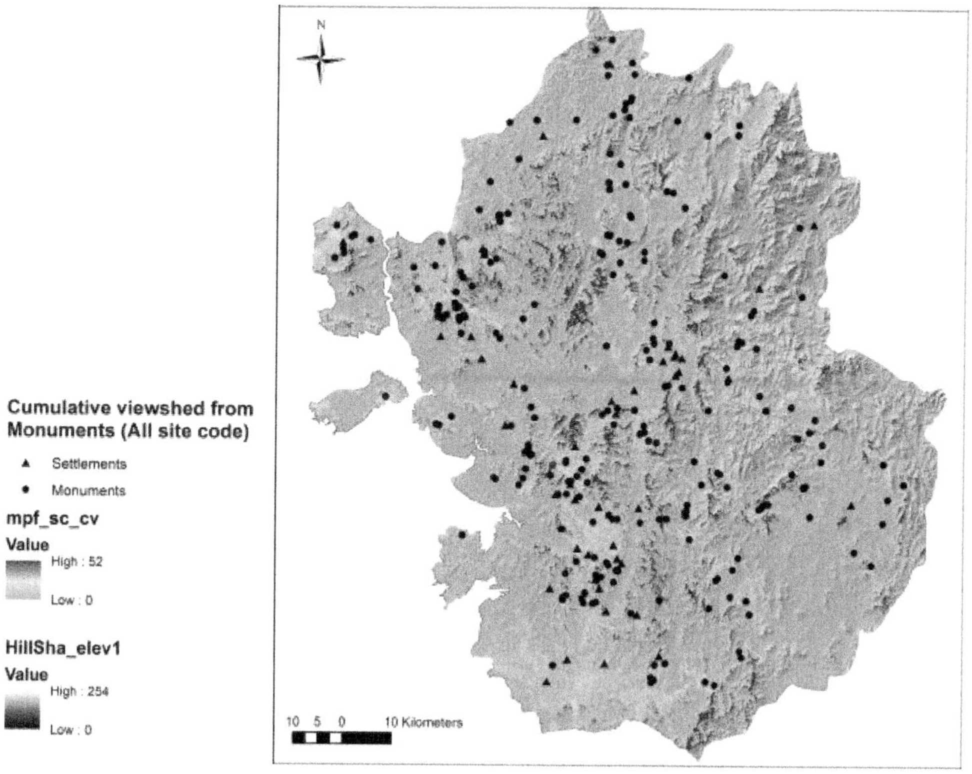

FIGURE 5. 5. CUMULATIVE VIEWSHED MAP FROM MONUMENTS (ALL SITE CODES)

鮮時代; 1392 – 1910 AD) and also the current presidential residence (청와대, 青瓦臺) are located near this mountain. According to C.J. Choe (1992: 59-61; 1993), when the Goryeo (고려, 高麗; 918 - 1392) and Joseon dynasties decided on the location of their capital or a palace of their kingdom, they considered the significance of topographical features, due to the fact that they believed certain topographical features were auspicious and thus conferred eternal prosperity on their kingdom. The interesting point is that from the Bronze Age, many monuments were oriented towards this area; this will be discussed together with other results in the final section.

In addition, according to the results of the cumulative viewshed, settlements which obtained high numbers from all monuments, are, in order: site code no. 25, Seoul Ilwondong (16: cumulative viewshed number from monuments, which means that Ilwondong site can be seen from 16 monuments); no. 44, Osan Gajangdong (11, enclosure site); no. 12. Hwaseong Gogeumsan (7); no. 8, Bucheon Gogangdong (7, enclosure site); no. 24, Seoul Myeongildong (7); no. 26, Namyangju Suseokri (6), and no. 36, Hanam deokpungdong ritual site (6). The remaining settlements obtained figures between zero and five. The commonality of these sites is that they are located at rather high elevations, 122.3 ± 63.7 m, compared to the settlement average of 77 m (see Chapter 5, Table 5.14).

Monument sites with the highest cumulative viewshed values are site codes no. 211, Ganghwa Gocheonri (9: cumulative viewshed numbers from monuments); no. 26. Goyang Gajwadong (9); no. 128. Pyeongtaek Yanggyori (7); no. 125, Pyeongtaek Naecheonri (7); no. 214, Ilsan-seogu Gusandong (7); no. 71. Gimpo Unyangdong 1 (7); no. 113, Hwaseong Bansongri (6); no. 230, Incheon Daegokdong A (6), and no. 232, Incheon Daegokdong C (6). The elevation average (78.3 ± 81.5 m) of these sites is somewhat higher than the monument site average of 65.2 ± 41.8 m, but, compared to the settlement cases, they appear to lack a common factor making them harder to interpret.

The location that has the highest value of cumulative viewshed from all settlements (refer to Figure 5.6) is Gwanak mountain (관악산, 冠岳山, refer to the light circle on the Figure 5.4), where new government buildings have been located on the southern side of the mountain and Seoul National University has been situated on its northern slope. The shape of the mountain peak is believed to look like a flame. In accordance with *Pungsu,* a traditional Korean geographically-focused conceptual theory, this particular mountain corresponds to the idea of a 'Fire mountain' and therefore, nearby settlements (in this case Seoul) risk conflagrations due to their proximity to the dangerous peak (Gwacheon Cultural Centre 1991). It is difficult to know what the Bronze Age people did think about Gwanak mountain, but it can be conjectured that it might have embodied symbolic meanings for them due to the fact that this mountain dominated the landscape and was visible to many Bronze Age settlements.

As well as having this feature, the settlements which are the most visible from all other settlements, are sites no. 25, Seoul Ilwondong (12: cumulative viewshed number from settlements); no. 12, Hwaseon Gogeumsan (9); no. 26, Namyangju Suseokri (8); no. 36, Hanam Deukpungdong Ritual site (8); no. 19, Peyongtaek Hyeongokri (7), and no. 8, Bucheon Gogangdong (6, Enclosure). The remaining

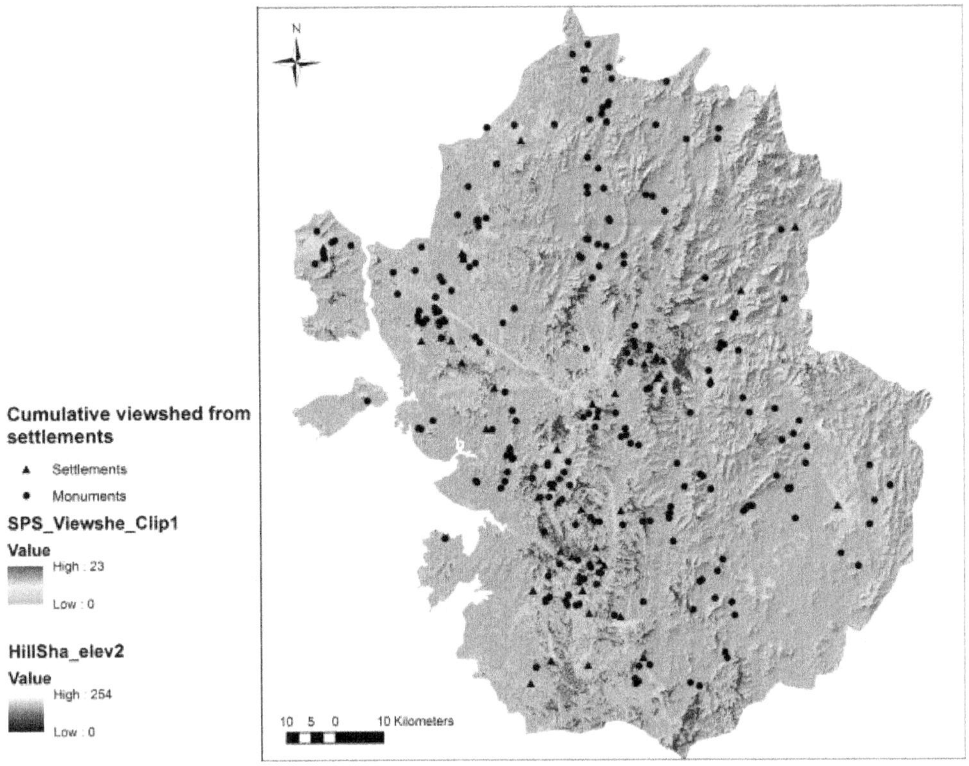

FIGURE 5. 6. CUMULATIVE VIEWSHED FROM 45 SELECTED SETTLEMENTS

settlements presented figures between zero and five. Five sites (nos. 25, 12, 26, 36, and 8) are the same as the results for the monuments' cumulative viewshed.

In addition, the monuments, which are the most visible from all settlements, are sites no. 128, Pyeontaek Yanggyori (5); no. 111, Hwaseong Sugiri (5); no. 131, Hanam Gyosandong (4); no. 221, Seoul Umeondong (4); no. 95, Anyang Pyeongchondong (3); no. 51, Guri Sanodong (3); no. 108, Suwon Homesildong (3); no. 97, Gunpo Sanbondong (3) and no. 109, Suwon Gyodong (3). Although these monuments have no similarity in elevation, they have a rather higher visibility than the average visibility of monuments. The range of visibility will be dealt with in the next section.

According to the results of cumulative viewshed, it has been possible to suggest that there may have been an element of continuity from the Bronze Age to the pre-modern/ modern period on the phenomenological aspect. That is, the most visible area from all the monuments, the Bukhan mountain, and the most visible area from all the settlements, the Gwanak mountain, have been significant locations throughout history. Although the mountains are at one level 'just' environmental and topographical elements, natural elements can at the same time indicate cultural significance in accordance with how people view, conceptualise and interpret their landscape, though the meanings may alter period by period. Likewise, there are some meaningful results from the cumulative viewshed of monuments and settlements in the research area. But, at the same time, the topography of a landscape has a significant impact upon the value of the results of a cumulative viewshed analysis. When used in a European setting, where the land is (relative to this study area) very flat, elevation is a significant marker in the analysis. However, where the landscape is mountainous, as is the case for the study area, elevation becomes less significant. Therefore, binary viewshed analysis was carried out in order to find a clearer pattern between the monuments and the settlements in the study area.

5.2.3.2 Binary viewshed analysis

The visible and invisible cell numbers (from the attribute table) of the binary viewshed from each of 45 selected settlements (see Appendix 15) and 236 monuments (see Appendix 7) were obtained and then the different viewshed ranges between settlements and monuments were compared. The average visible cell numbers from settlements is 12098.7 ± 10054.5 (Table 5.8 and Figure 5.7) and the average cell number from monument is 4176.2 ± 5060.6 (Table 5.8 and Figure 5.8). As can be seen, the mean viewshed of settlements is approximately three times larger than that of monuments. It is difficult to argue at this stage that there was a clear division between settlements and monuments, due to the fact that four settlement sites (no. 2, Paju Dayulri; no. 3, Paju Okseokri; no. 4, Paju Gyohari; and no. 45, Gwangmyeong Gahakdong) were discovered under dolmens when they were excavated. However, it does appear to be the case, that often when Bronze Age people in the Korean peninsula decided the location of their habitation, they seemed to prefer a site with an uninterrupted view of the surrounding landscape, making this a priority for the positioning of a settlement rather than for that of their monuments.

TABLE 5. 8. THE VIEWSHED RANGES OF SETTLEMENTS AND MONUMENTS

Viewshed	Settlements	Monuments
Mean	12098.7	4176.2
Standard deviation	10054.5	5060.6
Median	9337.0	2552.0
Interquartile range	10822.0	4805.0

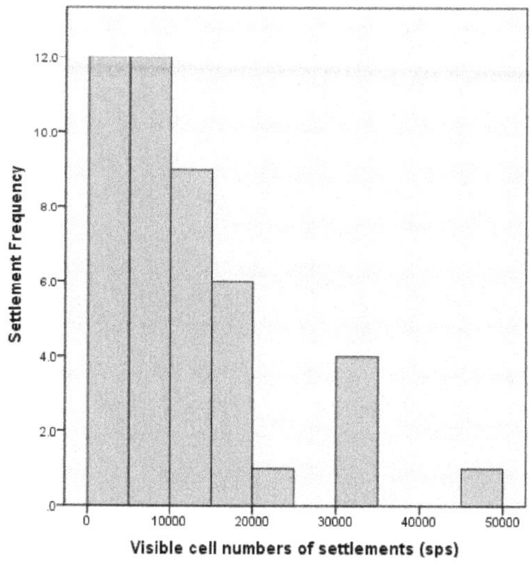

FIGURE 5. 7. THE VISIBLE CELL NUMBERS AND FREQUENCY OF 45 SELECTED SETTLEMENTS

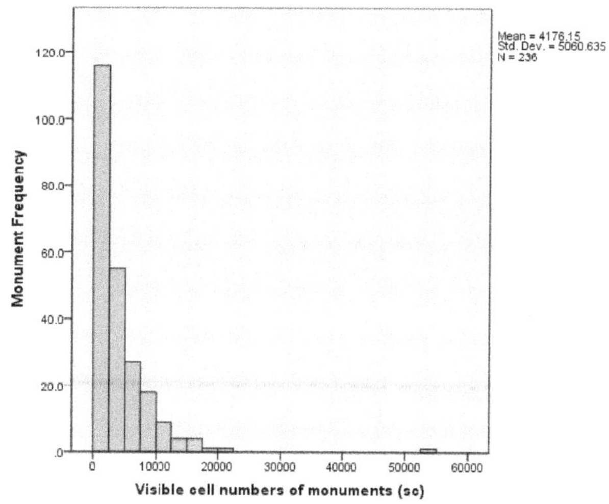

FIGURE 5. 8. THE VISIBLE CELL NUMBERS AND FREQUENCY OF MONUMENTS

According to the results of the binary viewshed cell numbers for settlements (figure 5.7), two exceptional cases can be identified. No. 25 Seoul Ilwondong site has the highest number (47594) of visible cells among settlement sites, as can be seen in figure 5.9. This site has a fine prospect along the main Han river (한강, 漢江) and this location seems to have been deliberately chosen. It is estimated that this settlement dates to the late Bronze Age on the basis of the house shapes (rounded corner shape)

TABLE 5. 9. INFORMATION CONCERNING NO. 25. SEOUL ILWONDONG

Site code	Town	Village	Period	Visible cell numbers	Elevation	Feature_11
25	Seoul	Ilwondong	Late	47594	255	Ridge

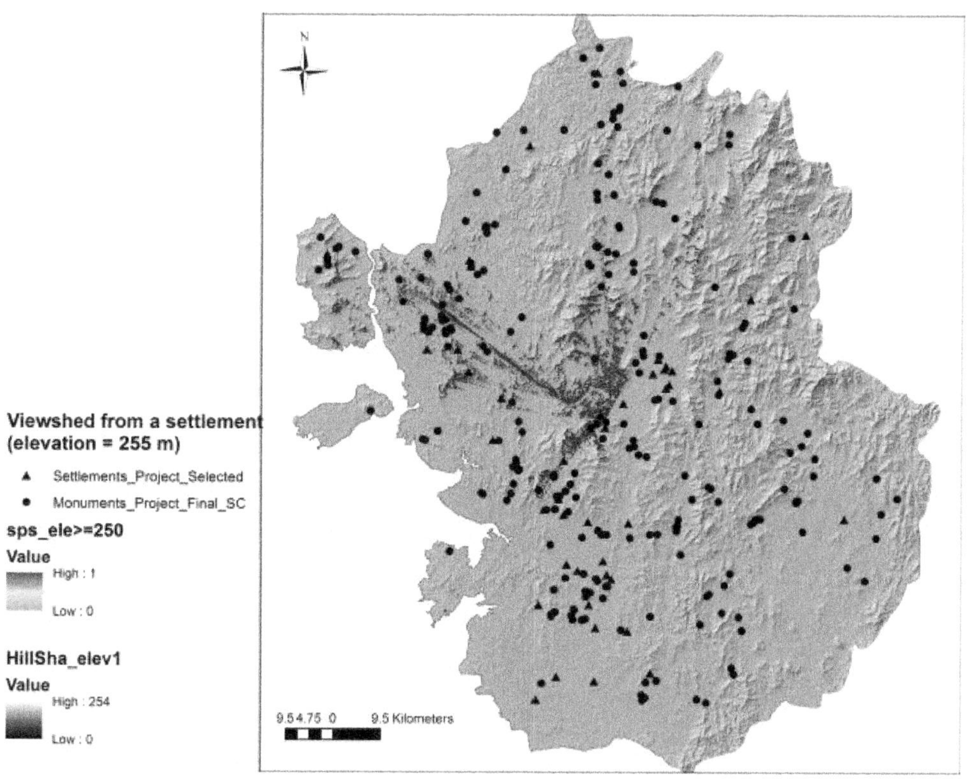

FIGURE 5. 9. VIEWSHED FROM NO. 25 SEOUL ILWONDING SITE

TABLE 5. 10. THE INFORMATION OF FOUR EXCEPTIONAL SITES

Site code	Town	Village	Period	Visible cell numbers	Elevation	Feature_11	Enclosure	River vs. Inland
8	Bucheon	Gogangdong	Middle to Late	33469	119	Ridge	Y	
19	Pyeongtaek	Hyeongokri	Early to Middle	31852	66	Ridge		Anseong river
41	Pyeongtaek	Bangchukri	Middle	31553	55	Peak		Anseong river
44	Osan	Gajangdong	Middle to Late	30060	111	Ridge	Y	

and pottery sherds excavated, which are characterised by a bowl type with a round shaped stripe, which has been identified as late Bronze Age pottery (Choi 2008a: 22, 62-65). This site will be discussed further in Chapter 6.

Secondly, other exceptional sites in Figure 5.7 are no. 8 Bucheon Gogangdong (33469), no. 19 Pyeongtaek Hyeongokri (31852), no. 41 Pyeongtaek Bangchukri (31553), and no. 44 Osan Gajangdong (30060). According to Table 5.10 (also refer to the Appendix 15), with the exception of no. 19 Pyeongtaek Hyeongokri, the dating period for these three sites is applicable to the Middle or Middle to Late Bronze Age. Among them, both nos. 8 and 44 are located at over 110 m (115 ± 5.7 m, compared to the settlement average of 77 m) and both had enclosures. The commonality between nos. 19 and 41 is that both settlements are situated near the Anseong River.

The lowest visible cell number is 667 in no. 1, Yeoncheon Samgeori site (the next lowest number is 1126 in no. 45. Gwangmyeong Gahakdong). In the excavation report, six Neolithic houses were discovered under three Bronze Age houses and charcoal in house 9 was dated to 2930 ± 50 BP (NCIRF (National Centre for Inter-University Research Facilities) at Seoul National University (No lab no. 1307-996 BC (2 sigma), Figure 5.10) (Song et al. 2002: 160). On the basis of radiocarbon dating, this site seems to belong to the Early Bronze Age and according to

FIGURE 5. 10. PLOT OF THE CALIBRATED DATE OF HOUSE NO. 9 IN SAMGEORI, YEONCHEON (CALIBRATED USING OXCAL 4.1. BY THE AUTHOR).

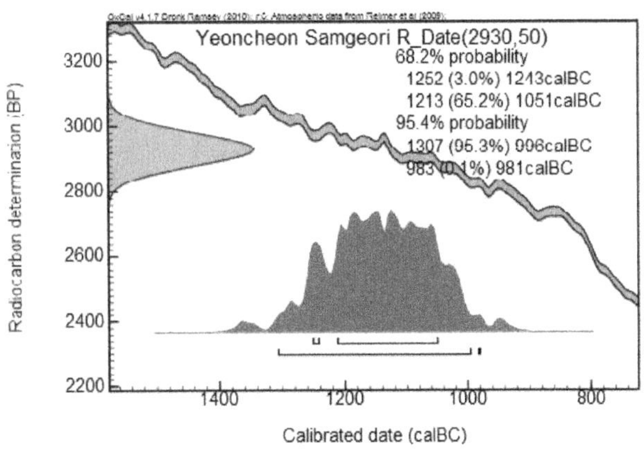

the analysis results in Chapter 4, this site comes under the Early to Middle Bronze Age period. Possibly Bronze Age people tended to consider visibility as a more important factor in determining settlement location as time went by.

Turning now to one exceptional visible cell numbers of monuments: monument no. 128 Pyeongtaek Yanggyori has the highest visible cell number (54322, Figure 5.11). This monument is located at 107 metres above sea level (compared to the monument average of 65.2 ± 41.8 m) in a rather flat area compared to others in the study area. Its surrounding settlements (no. 18 Pyeongtaek Hyeonhwari (14412), no. 19 Pyeongtaek Hyeongokri (31852), and no. 41 Pyeongtaek Bangchukri (31553, Figure 5.12) also have fairly broad viewsheds.

The correlation between the view range and the elevation of settlements and monuments was examined in order to look at the reasons why the average viewshed of settlements is approximately three times larger than that of monuments. The relationships between the viewsheds and elevations of settlements and monuments can be seen in Figures 5.13, 5.14 and 5.15. There is a positive correlation of $r^2 = 0.36$ (p value = 0.000014) between the range of viewsheds and the elevation of settlements (Figure 5.13) while that for dolmens is insignificant ($r^2 = 0.0067$, Figure 5.15). If the exceptional settlement (No 25 Ilondong site) is excluded as an outlier, a positive correlation of r^2 becomes 0.16 (p value = 0.00679, Figure 5. 14).

As mentioned briefly in the viewshed histogram and taken together with the results of landform analysis, elevation seems to be more important in relation to settlement location than that of monuments. That is, people preferred locations for their settlements with uninterrupted views and higher elevations, perhaps partly because they were more suitable for defence. Conflicts in the Korean Bronze Age have not been extensively researched, but it is possible to assume that there might have been conflicts in/between groups based on archaeological evidence: broken points of stone arrowheads and polished stone daggers, which were found in dolmens (Lee, 2002: 280); daggers and arrowheads made of stone or bronze, discovered in dolmens (National Museum of Korea 1992: 10-23); as well as houses with evidence of destruction by fire (Kim and Yun, 1967: 39; Bae and Gang, 2000: 74, 109; Lee et al, 2006: 65-66; Gijeon Cultural Properties Institute, 2004: 32; Department of Archaeology and Anthropology and

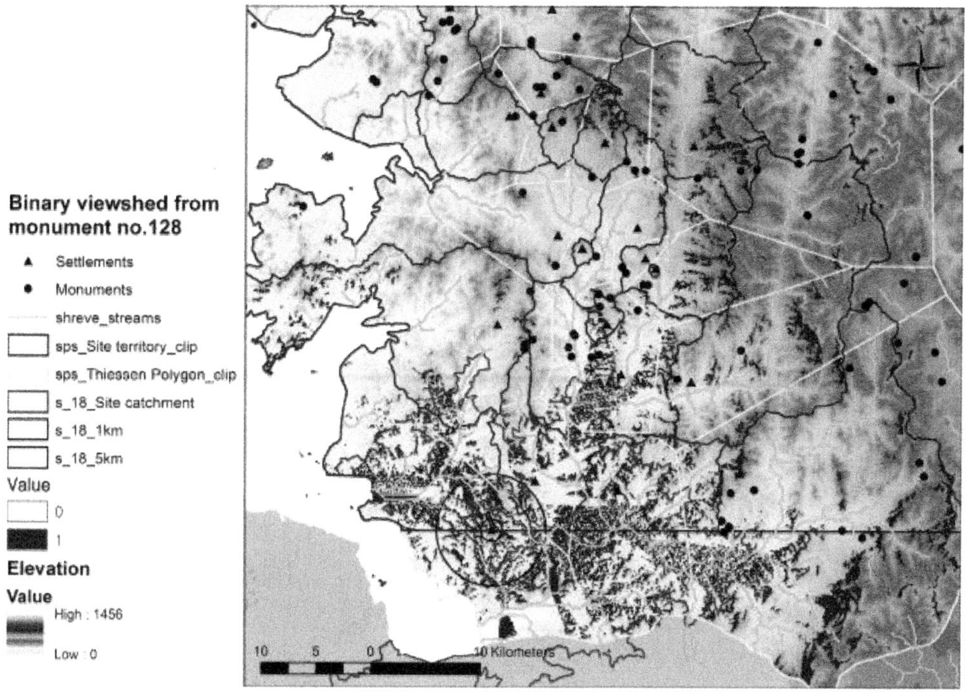

FIGURE 5. 11. BINARY VIEWSHED FROM MONUMENT SITE NO.128 PYEONGTAEK YANGGYORI.

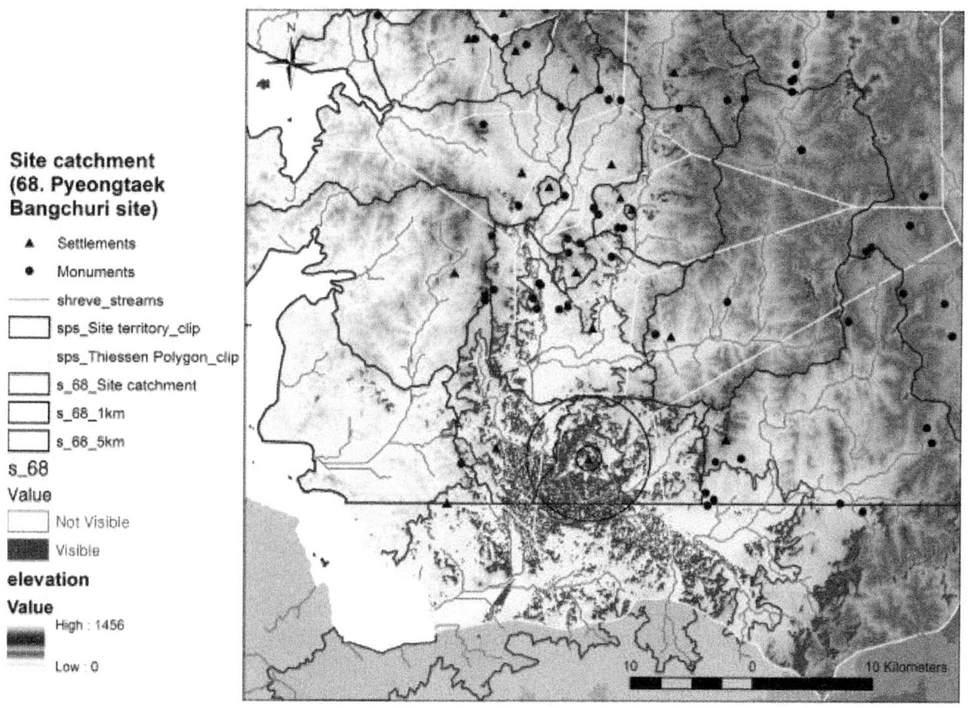

FIGURE 5. 12. BINARY VIEWSHED FROM SETTLEMENT NO. 41. PYEONGTAEK BANGCHUKRI.

the University Museum, 1976: 10; Park et al, 2007: 58, 98). They also appear to have chosen ridge settings for their settlements and favoured a location for monuments within a border zone marking the end of mountains and the start of plains. These results will be discussed in the final interpretation with the results of movement analyses.

Among the settlements, five sites (8. Bucheon Gogangdong, 14; Hwaseong Dohaksan, 15; Suwon Yuljeondong, 42; Anseong Banjeri, and 44. Osan Gajangdong) have enclosures. Further investigation is needed, because the interpretations of some enclosure sites in the study area are somewhat different. For example, at both no.8. Bucheon Gogangdong and no. 42 Anseong Banjeri site, no houses were found inside the enclosures. Instead of houses, both sites have common features, that is, their enclosures surround the peak of the mountain and at the centre of the enclosures there is a rock bed in no.8 Bucheon Gogangdong

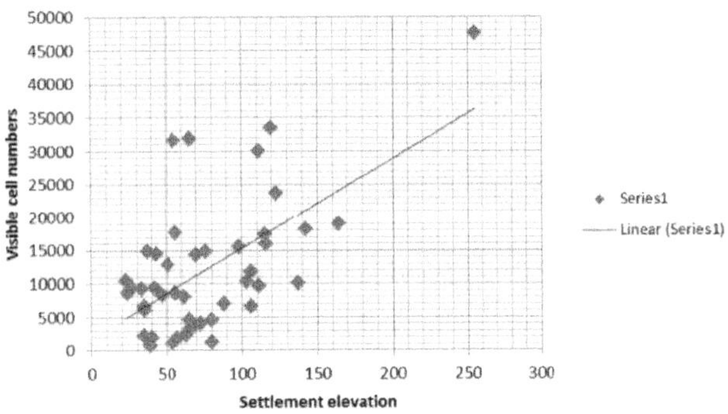

FIGURE 5. 13. THE CORRELATION BETWEEN ELEVATION AND VISIBLE CELL NUMBERS FOR SETTLEMENTS ($R2 = 0.36$, P VALUE = 0.000014)

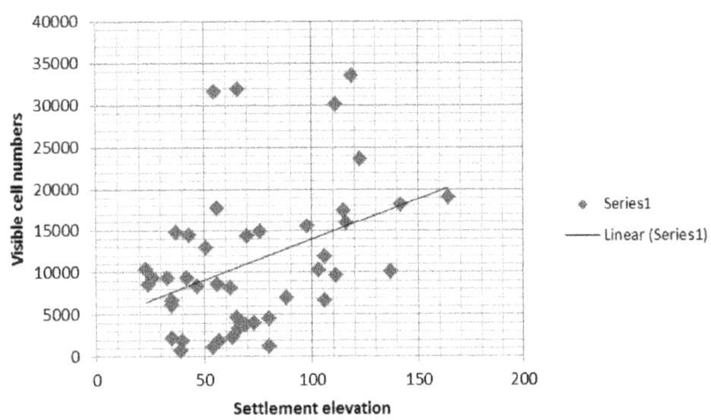

FIGURE 5. 14. THE CORRELATION BETWEEN ELEVATION AND VISIBLE CELL NUMBERS FOR SETTLEMENTS (EXCLUDING ONE OUTLIER FROM FIGURE 6.13 ($R2 = 0.16$, P VALUE = 0.00679)

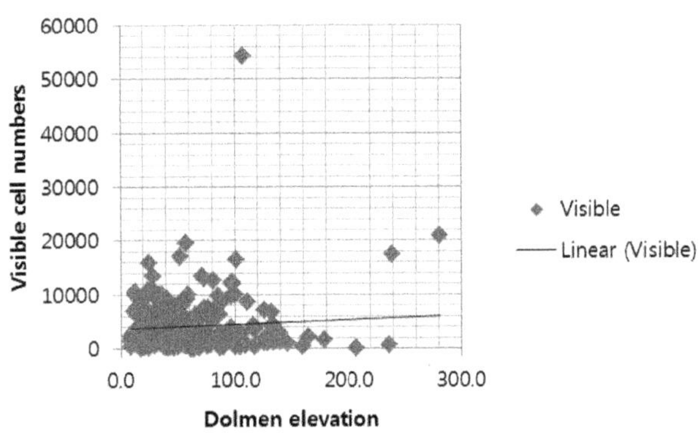

FIGURE 5. 15. THE CORRELATION BETWEEN ELEVATION AND VISIBLE CELL NUMBERS FOR DOLMENS ($R2 = 0.0067$)

site and a mound of piled stone in no.42 Anseong Banjeri site (Lee 2007: 100-107). Therefore, these enclosure sites could be interpreted as ritual sites instead of functioning as defensive structures (Lee 2007: 100-114). The differences in elevation between enclosure sites and non-enclosure sites can be assessed. It might be assumed, for example, that enclosure sites would be more likely to be situated on high ground, whether for ceremonial and/or defence purposes. As the two types of site display more or less

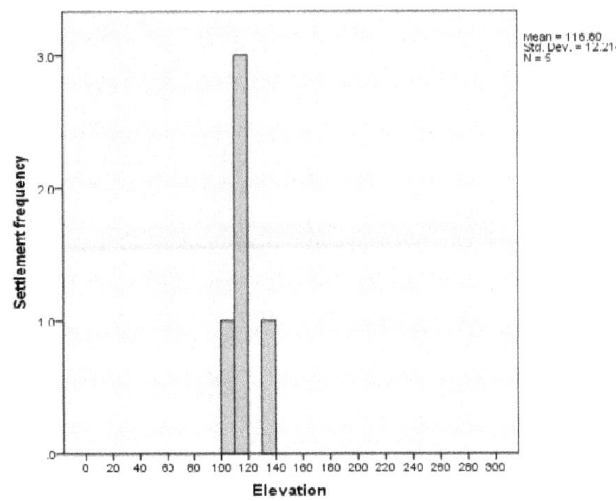

FIGURE 5. 16. THE ELEVATION AND SETTLEMENT FREQUENCY FOR ENCLOSURE SITES

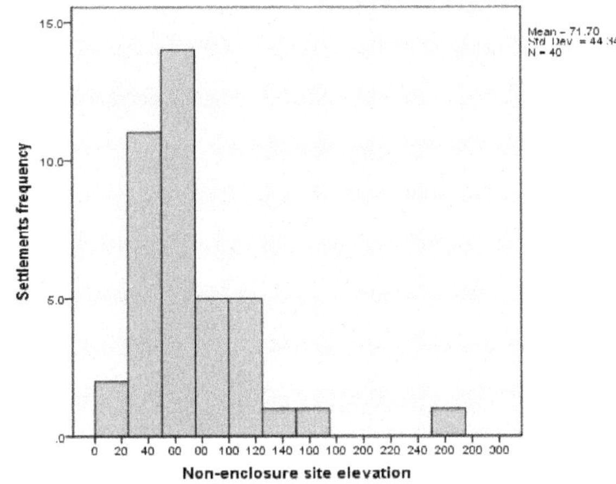

FIGURE 5. 17. THE ELEVATION AND SETTLEMENT FREQUENCY FOR NON-ENCLOSURE SITES

normal distributions (refer to Figure 5.16 and 5.17), a t-test (enclosure sites: Mean = 116.8 ± 12.2 m (median: 111 ± 8 (IQR) m), n = 5; non-enclosure sites: Mean = 71.70 ± 43.34 (median: 63 ± 40.5 (IQR) m), n = 40) was conducted and a p-value of 3.45E-05 obtained. That is, there is a clear elevation difference between enclosure sites and non-enclosure sites. Among the non-enclosure sites, however, there is an obvious outlier. It is no. 25 Seoul Ilwondong, and this site will be discussed in Chapter 6.

This result raises the question of whether there is a difference in viewshed between enclosure and non-enclosure sites above 100 metres elevation. In order to identify whether enclosure sites were deliberately chosen for their uninterrupted views, the following analysis was carried out and the results were as follows: (enclosure sites: mean = 19007 ± 11735 (median: 11812 ± 20016 (IQR) m), n = 5; non-enclosure sites: mean = 19814 ± 12391 (median: 17748.5 ± 5617.5 (IQR) m), n = 8, non-enclosure sites are no.12. Hwaseong Gogeumsan; no. 16. Suwon Imokdong; no.21. Yongin Jukjeon; no.25. Seoul Ilwondong; no.28. Yeoju Heunamr; no.48. Hanam Deokpungdong ritual site; no.54. Uiwang Idong and no. 75. Paju Sikhyeonri).

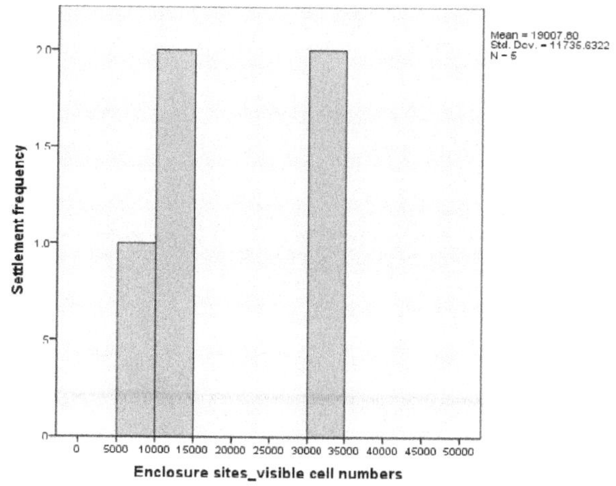

FIGURE 5. 18. THE VISIBLE CELL NUMBERS AND SETTLEMENT FREQUENCY FOR ENCLOSURE SITES

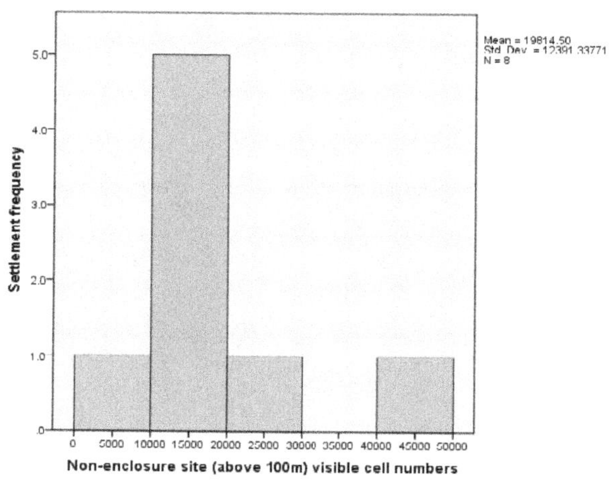

FIGURE 5. 19. THE VISIBLE CELL NUMBERS AND SETTLEMENT FREQUENCY FOR NON-ENCLOSURE SITES

Due to the fact that the distribution of the two site types does not show a normal distribution pattern (refer to Figure 5.18 and 5.19), a non-parametric Mann-Whitney test was carried out and there was found to be no difference in viewshed between the enclosure sites and the non-enclosure sites above 100 metres sea level (p = 0.77). However, as documented in Appendix 16, a difference was identified in the house numbers category between enclosure sites and non-enclosure sites above 100 metres elevation (enclosure sites: mean = 10 ± 8 (median: 9 ± 13 (IQR)), n = 5; non-enclosure sites: mean = 5 ± 5.5 (median: 2 ± 6 (IQR)), n = 8). By and large, enclosure sites tended to have more houses than non-enclosure sites. As indicated above, two sites with enclosures seemed to have different functions due to the fact that within the separate enclosure areas there are found natural bed rock (approx. 4.1 m × 3.2 m) in the case of no.8 Bucheon Gogangdong and a mound of piled stones (6 m × 6 m) at no. 42. Anseong Banjeri, instead of houses (Lee 2007: 100-107, 112). Interestingly, one ritual site was included in the non-enclosure sites above 100 metres elevation category. Similar to nos. 8 and 72, the natural bed rock was exposed and several rocks faced each other above the bed rock, although no enclosure was discovered surrounding the ritual sites. Stone structures are common among the three sites and these structures seem to be created for ritual ceremonies or else to fuction as objects of worship themselves (Choi 2007: 225-227). Using tentative settlement periodization applied to five identified enclosure settlements, one site (no. 14. Hwaseong Donghaksan) was classified as Early to Middle Bronze Age and four sites (no. 8. Bucheon Gogangdong, no.15. Suwon Yuljeondong, no. 42. Anseong Banjeri, no. 44. Osan Gajangdong) appear to date from the Middle to the Late Bronze Age. In addition, among eight non-enclosure settlements, three sites (no. 16. Suwon Imokdong, no. 36. Hanam Deokpungdong ritual site and no. 43. Paju Sikhyeonri) were categorised as Middle Bronze Age and one site (no. 25 Seoul Ilwondong) was included in the Late Bronze Age period. Another four sites displayed long-term use (from Early to Middle and from Early to Late Bronze Age). Therefore, it is difficult to make conclusive remarks, but generally, it would appear that people tended to prefer higher locations (over 100 m above sea level) for their settlements after the Middle Bronze Age period and this tendency is discussed further in Chapter 6.

As mentioned in the landform analysis section in Chapter 5, in order to compare this study's results with those of other reseachers, it may be useful to examine what differences, if any, exist in viewsheds between table type and captone type dolmens. Table type dolmens (termed 'northern type') dolmens are distributed mainly in the area north of the Han river (Choi 2000: 11); capstone dolmens, however, are prevalent in all regions of the Korean peninsula[31] and Baduk board-type (termed 'southern type') dolmens are allocated to mostly the area south of the Han river (*ibid*: 12). It is difficult to unpick the origins of dolmen types here, because the main focus of this study is their landscape setting. In addition there are only two examples of Baduk board-type dolmens in the research area. Therefore, only a comparison of viewsheds between table type and capstone type dolmens was carried out.

Firstly, it was examined whether or not table and capstone type dolmens have different viewsheds (among 236 monument sites, 25 sites have both types). In order to compare the patterns of viewshed range between the two types of dolmens (refer to Table 5.11), monument clusters rather than individual monuments were utilised. As can be seen in figures 5.20 and 5.21, they do not confirm with the pattern expected for a normal distribution: the median visible cell number of 51 table type dolmen sites is 2947 ± 5285 (IQR) and the median visible cell numbers of 125 capstone type dolmen sites is 2552 ± 4805 (IQR).

TABLE 5. 11. THE VIEWSHED RANGES OF TABLE TYPE DOLMEN SITES AND CAPSTONE TYPE DOLMEN SITES

Viewshed	Table type	Capstone type
Mean	4430.0	4845.4
Standard deviation	4540.7	6038.5
Median	2947.0	2552.0
Interquartile range	5285.0	4805.0

[31] North Korean archaeologist suggests that the table type dolmen was developed from this capstone type dolmen (Seok 2002: 11, 248).

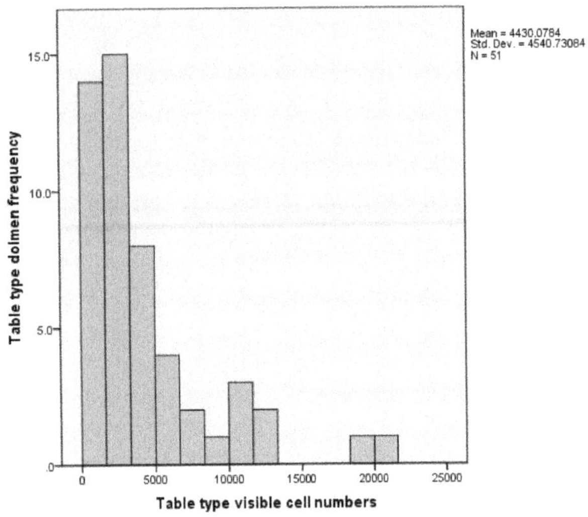

FIGURE 5. 20. VISIBLE CELL NUMBERS AND FREQUENCY OF TABLE TYPE DOLMEN SITES

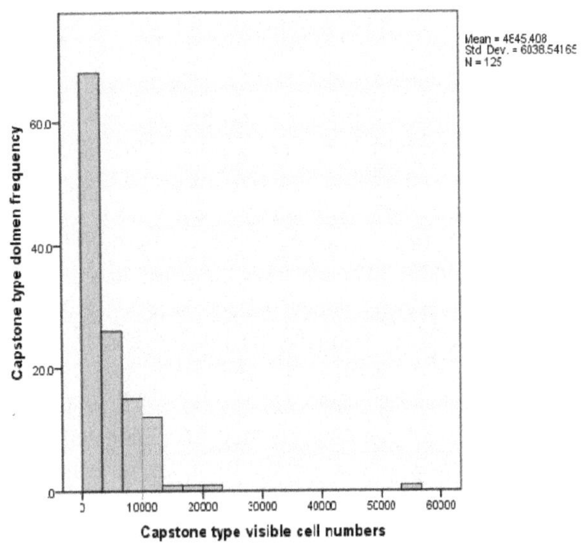

FIGURE 5. 21. VISIBLE CELL NUMBERS AND FREQUENCY OF THE CAPSTONE TYPE DOLMEN SITES

As expected from a visual examination of Figures 5.20 and 5.21, a Mann-Whitney test finds no difference in the visible cell numbers between table and capstone type dolmen sites (p value = 0.89). Secondly, the elevation of table type and capstone type dolmen sites was considered in order to investigate the correlation between the viewshed and elevation of table type and capstone type dolmen sites. The median elevation of 51 table type dolmen sites is 60 ± 56.8 (IQR) metres and the median elevation of 125 capstone type dolmen sites is 56 ± 40 (IQR) metres (refer to Table 5.12, Figures 5.22 and 5.23). There is no distinction in the difference in relative elevation between the two types of dolmen sites (Mann-Whitney U-test, p value = 0.71).

Then, what was the distribution pattern of the two types of dolmen sites? According to Figures 5.24 and 5.25, table type dolmen sites are concentrated in the northernmost three-quarters of the study area and capstone type dolmen sites are situated almost all over the research area.

TABLE 5. 12. THE ELEVATION OF TABLE TYPE DOLMEN SITES AND CAPSTONE TYPE DOLMEN SITES

Elevation	Table type	Capstone type
Mean	67.5	62.4
Standard deviation	50.0	41.1
Median	60.0	56.0
Interquartile range	56.8	40.0

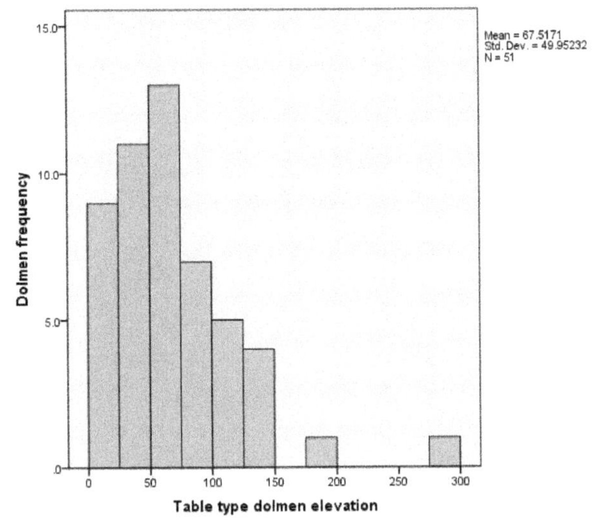

FIGURE 5. 22. THE ELEVATION AND FREQUENCY OF TABLE TYPE DOLMEN SITES

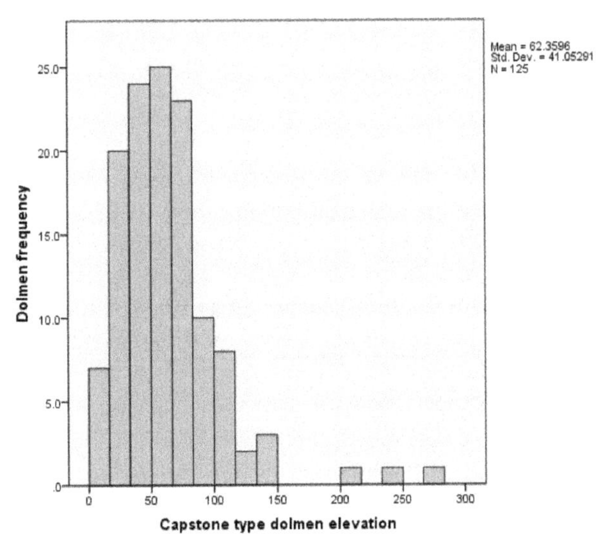

FIGURE 5. 23. THE ELEVATION AND FREQUENCY OF CAPSTONE TYPE DOLMEN SITES

As can be shown above, it is difficult to identify any clear distinctions between table type dolmen sites and capstone type dolmen sites on the basis of viewshed range and elevation. Only the distribution of the two dolmen types across the study area suggests a difference in terms of the concentration of table type dolmens in the northern sector as previous researchers have indicated.

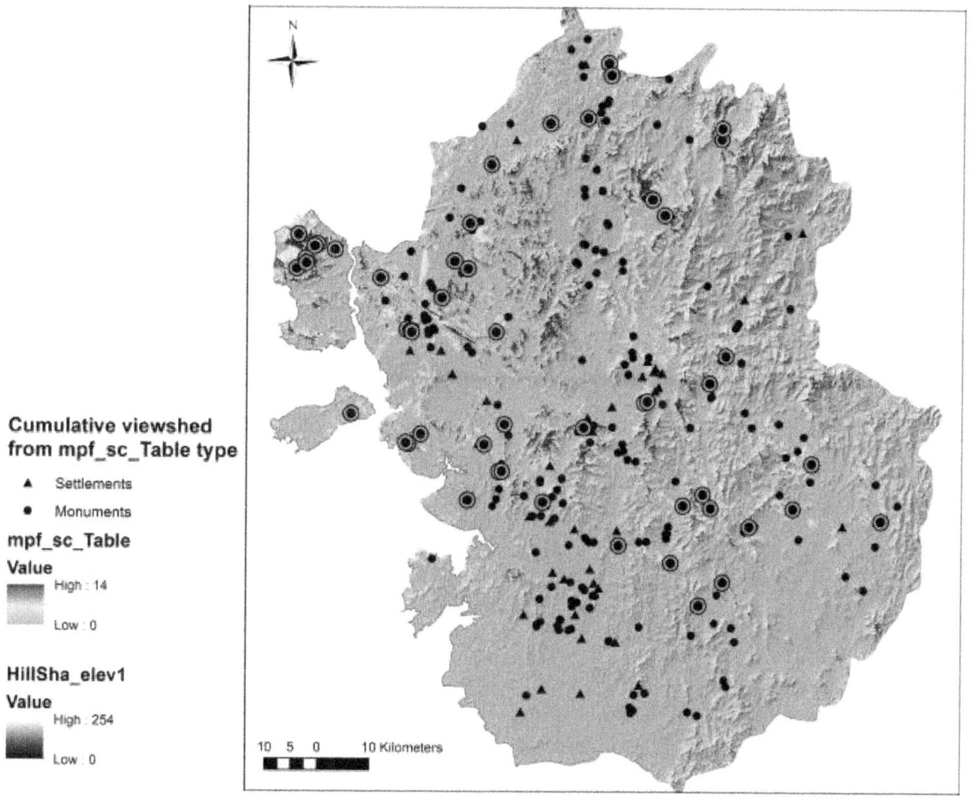

FIGURE 5. 24. DISTRIBUTION AND CUMULATIVE VIEWSHED OF TABLE TYPE DOLMEN SITES (BIG CIRCLE)

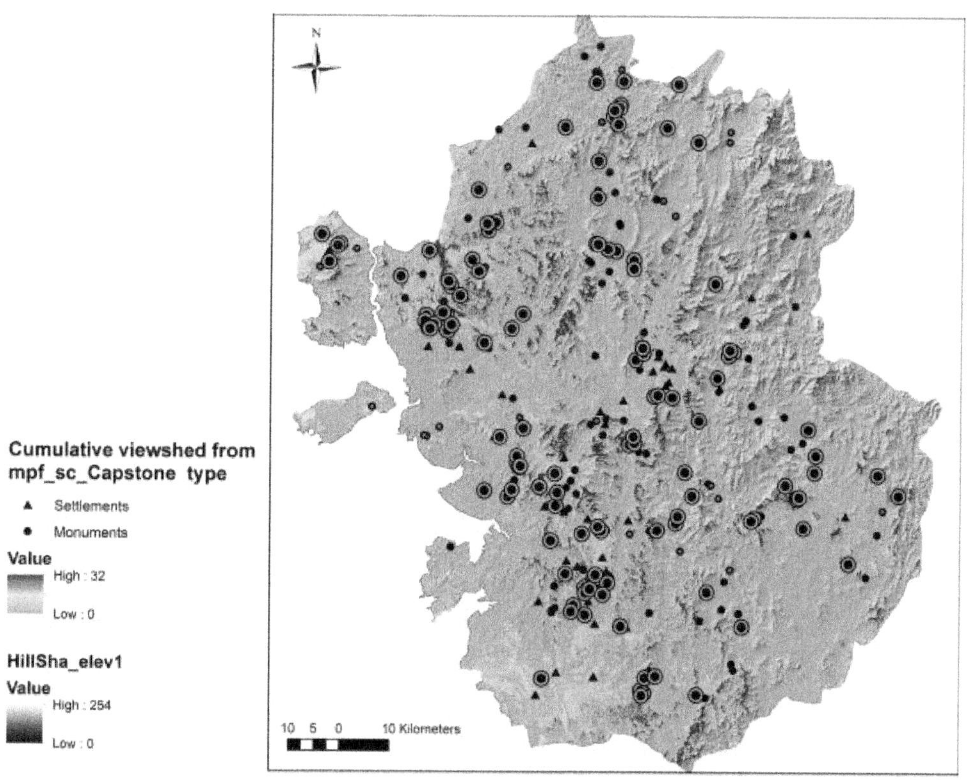

FIGURE 5. 25. DISTRIBUTION AND CUMULATIVE VIEWSHED OF CAPSTONE TYPE DOLMEN SITES (BIG CIRCLE)

According to the results of the binary viewshed analyses, there are differences between the placement of settlements and monuments. The mean viewshed of settlements is approximately three times larger than that of monuments. The relationships between the viewsheds and elevations of settlements and monuments are a positive relation between the range of viewsheds and the elevation of settlements while that for dolmens is not significant. In addition, what is surprising is the finding that the cumulative viewshed results of settlements and monuments had view of locations important in later periods of Korean history. The decision by which locations were selected were invested with symbolic meaning, for example, in order for historic Korean dynasties to enjoy prosperity and to avoid mishaps certain types of site were specifically chosen (Choe 1992: 60-61; Choe 1993). Therefore, if a royal palace was located in a certain area, it suggests that the location was considered a very auspicious place by the rulers of the kingdom of that period. This finding and the results of the next movement analyses are suggestive of the concept of '*Pungsu*' (풍수, 風水) and this will be discussed further in Chapter 6.

5.3 Movement analysis

5.3.1 Aims

This section will concentrate on movement analyses. The aims of movement analysis are to investigate how movement affects the location of settlements and monuments in their landscape and how movement can be interpreted as a cultural element. In order to address this question, GIS and cost surface analysis have been utilised to generate site catchment boundaries. The consideration of slope is an important factor when people move from one place to another, although slope is not the only factor in determining movement (Lock and Bell 2000: 91-92; Lock and Pouncett 2010). The energy consumption of moving to/in a steep region would be higher than that of a flat region. In order to find more realistic patterns of human mobility on the basis of energy expenditure, site catchment was obtained for each settlement. After these procedures, the number of monuments within 1 km and 5 km Euclidean distance and 1 km and 5 km site catchments adjusted for energy consumption (henceforth adjusted 5 km site catchment) were extracted (Table 5.13).

5.3.2 Methods

Modelled 1 km and 5 km adjusted site catchment boundaries were created taking into consideration topography and relative cost in order to compare the boundaries of the 1 km and 5 km radius Euclidean distance buffers.

The 1 km radius was chosen according to the idea of 'reward limitation' in agricultural subsistence economy suggested by Chisholm (1966: 45-49) and Vita-Finzi and Higgs (1970: 16) described a circle with a 5 km radius, as the economic threshold for intensive agricultural subsistence in their research, after an examination of Levant coastal sites, which are thought to be where early forms of agriculture were practised. In addition, according to Young-moon Lee, there is a trend for small clusters of dolmens located

Table 5. 13. Two procured boundaries

	Euclidean distance	Cost distance
Single site	1km and 5km buffers	1 km and 5 km site catchment adjusted for energy expenditure

in valleys, or hills and basins within approximately 5 km diametres from a neighboring mountain in the south-western part of the Korean peninsula (Lee 2002b: 308). Also, the distance among Iron Age hillforts in the study area maintained more or less 5 km intervals from each site (Choi 1993: 259). Based on above researches, 1 km and 5 km radii were decided for movement analyses.

Firstly, a cost surface must be generated. Cost raster includes criteria such as slope and land-use. Often it is difficult to compare different criteria. Therefore, each criterion should be reclassified to an ordinal scale. Cost is the energy consumed, as one moves from a destination to a targeted point (Lock and Bell 2000: 86). The cost is determined by an algorithm, which is based on the distance between two points and the relative cost. The concept of relative cost that was utilised is the definition and calculation posited by Lock and Bell (*ibid*: 88-89).

$$\text{relative cost} = \frac{\tan(\text{slope})}{\tan(1°)}$$

In order to create the 1 km and 5 km site catchment adjusted for energy expenditure areas, both cost distance and path distance were generated. Cost distance or path distance tools compute the least weighted distance, instead of evaluating the actual distance between the destination and the source or targeted point (ArcGIS 10 Help 2011c). The distinction between the cost distance and the path distance is that the latter considers not only the least cost distance, but also several other factors, such as: road conditions, whether movement is uphill or downhill, wind speed and wind direction (Pouncett 2009: 13; ArcGIS 10 Help 2011d). As can be seen in Figure 5.26, site catchment boundaries were obtained from the cost distance analysis (black line) and site catchment boundaries from path distance analysis (grey line). They are not dissimilar, although there are some gaps between the two lines. Therefore, the cost distance site catchment boundaries were used for the site catchment figures. The adjusted 5 km site catchment boundaries look like they were simply determined by environmental elements, such as geographical features. Yet one wonders how closely related these results are to culturally determined ideas of the ideal location for habitation in the study area during the Bronze Age? According to the results (see next section), they seem to be attributable to an experienced and localised knowledge of the land that the people inhabited (Bourdieu 1990b: 53-55; Gosden 1994: 117; 1999a: 489) rather than to a more general conceptual framework of "landscape". How environmentally determined landscape is intertwined with culturally interpreted landscape will be examined in Chapter 6.

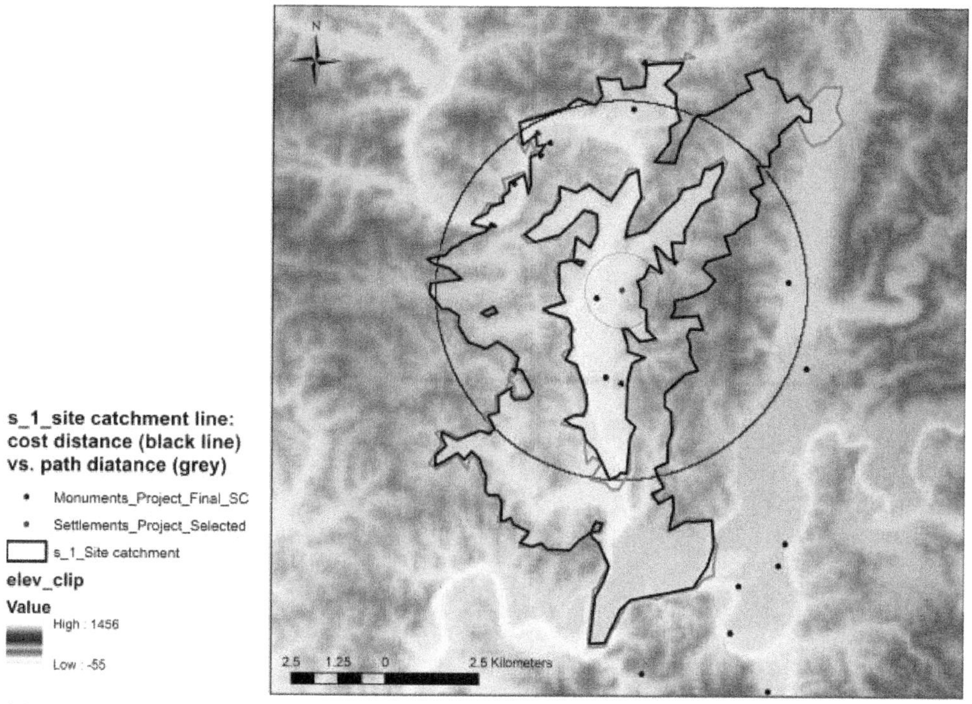

FIGURE 5. 26. NO.1 YEONCHEON SAMGEORI SITE CATCHMENT BOUNDARIES ON THE BASIS OF THE COST DISTANCE (BLACK LINE) AND THE PATH DISTANCE (GREY LINE)

5.3.3 Results

5.3.3.1 Site catchment boundaries

In order to examine the relationship between settlements and monuments, 1 km and 5 km Euclidean buffers (see black radii from each settlement, see Figures 5.27 - 5.32) and 1 km and 5 km adjusted site catchment boundaries (see grey irregular lines from each settlement, refer to Figures 5.27 – 5.31) from 45 settlements were obtained (Refer to Appendix 19).

As can be seen in Figure 5.27 and 5.28. settlements that are situated near to main rivers, namely the Han (Figure 5.27) and the Anseong (Figure 5.28) rivers, have very broad 5 km site catchments when this area is adjusted for energy consumption, compared to the settlements located inland (refer to Figure 5.29, 5.30, and 5.31). Therefore, in order to avoid overlapping data, a 5 km Euclidean buffer was utilised in the case of settlements that are located near to main rivers. The reason why different standards were applied to these analyses is that the site catchments of settlements near to main rivers overlapped considerably and as a consequence, it was difficult to designate which monument sites belonged to a certain settlement. Therefore, according to the settlements' periodization (refer to Table 3.8), information on monument sites was extracted within an adjusted 5 km site catchment area from settlements which were situated inland and within a 5 km Euclidean buffer from settlements which were located near to main rivers. In order to look at the long-term changes of monument sites, monument data, which were only related to the settlements of 'Early', 'Middle', and 'Late' Bronze Age categories in Table 4.8, were obtained (see Appendix 18). The long-term changes of monument sites will be discussed in Chapter 6. This means was somewhat experimental, but, at the same time, was the best way available to obtain chronological information from monuments where evidence was limited.

On the basis of the site catchment maps generated for inland settlements (Figure from 5.29 to 5.31), it is quite clear that a pattern has emerged. That is, by and large catchments tend to be surrounded by mountains and within their defined areas they often include tributaries. Among 45 analysed settlements, with the exception of the third (14 sites) that are located near to main rivers, two-thirds (31 sites) display similar configurations. This positioning in terms of topographic locations, seems to be related directly to Myeongdang, and embodies the notion of a propitious location as defined by the concept of *Pungsu*, although where the boundaries from two or three settlements overlap this occasion can place limits on the interpretation. This concept will be addressed in the Chapter 6.

In addition, monuments occur within the 5 km site catchment adjusted for energy expenditure boundaries of most (29 out of 31, 94%) of these settlements (refer to Figure 5.32), with an average monument number of 6 (± 5.3) and a median number of 5 (± 6.5). Moreover, of the 236 included in this project, 80% (185) occur within the 5 km site catchment adjusted for energy expenditure boundaries of a settlement. Clearly, the settlements and monuments relate to one another within the landscape in which they were created.

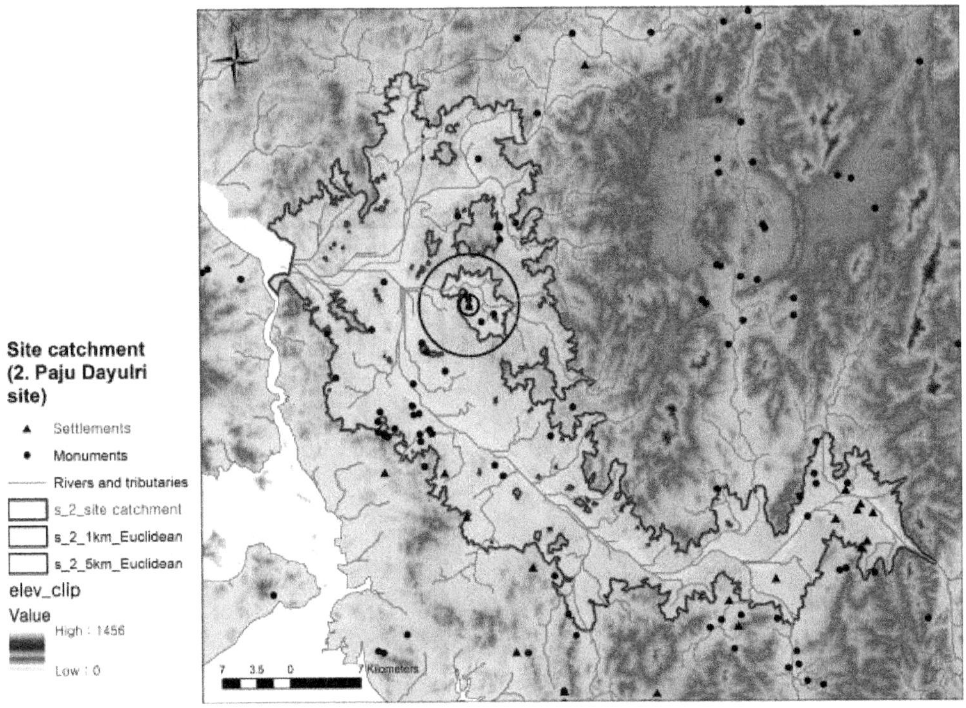

FIGURE 5. 27. NO.2 PAJU DAYULRI SITE CATCHMENT BOUNDARIES

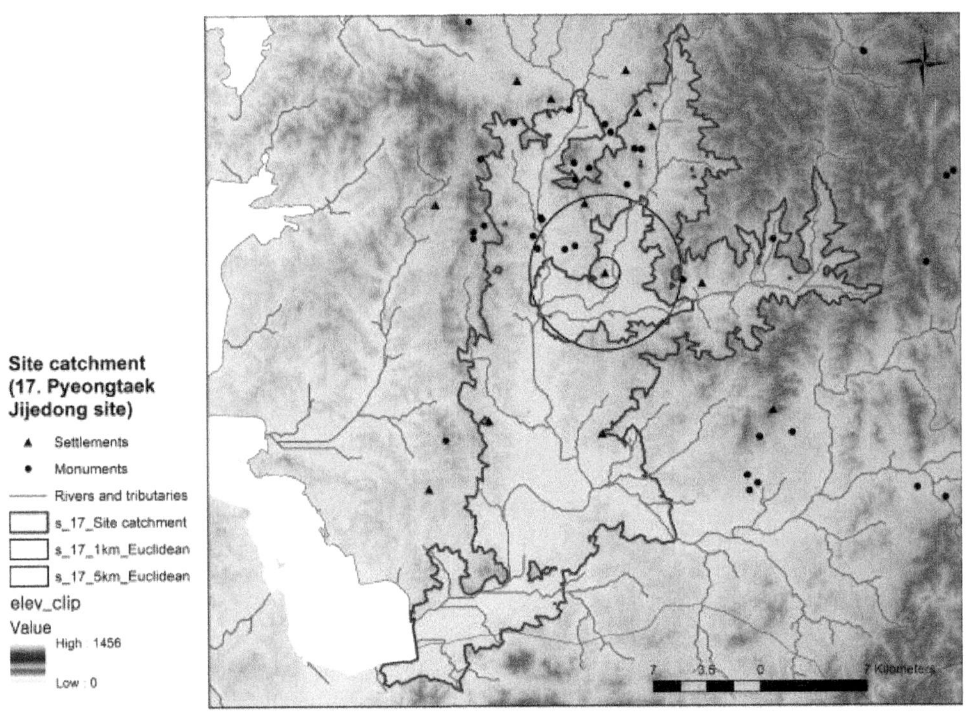

FIGURE 5. 28. NO.17 PYEONGTAEK JIJEDONG SITE CATCHMENT BOUNDARIES

5.4 Orientation

5.4.1 Aims

In order to observe the regional variation of settlements and monuments, their orientations were examined as further examples of the cultural context of these sites. It can be considered that house and dolmen orientations are culturally determined, because the decisions involved are related to human perception, although it could also be due to natural elements, such as ridgelines and the direction in which rivers flowed. Another reason why the orientations of sites were investigated, is that previous publications have indicated that houses or monuments were constructed parallel to ridgelines or flowing rivers (Kim 1981; Ji 1987b). Orientation was also significant before the Three Kingdom period (삼국시대, 三國時代), as the eastwards orientation of the deceased's head had symbolic meaning in terms of their potential resurrection (Lee et al. 1984: 7; Choe 1992: 170). It might also be interesting to compare the orientation of

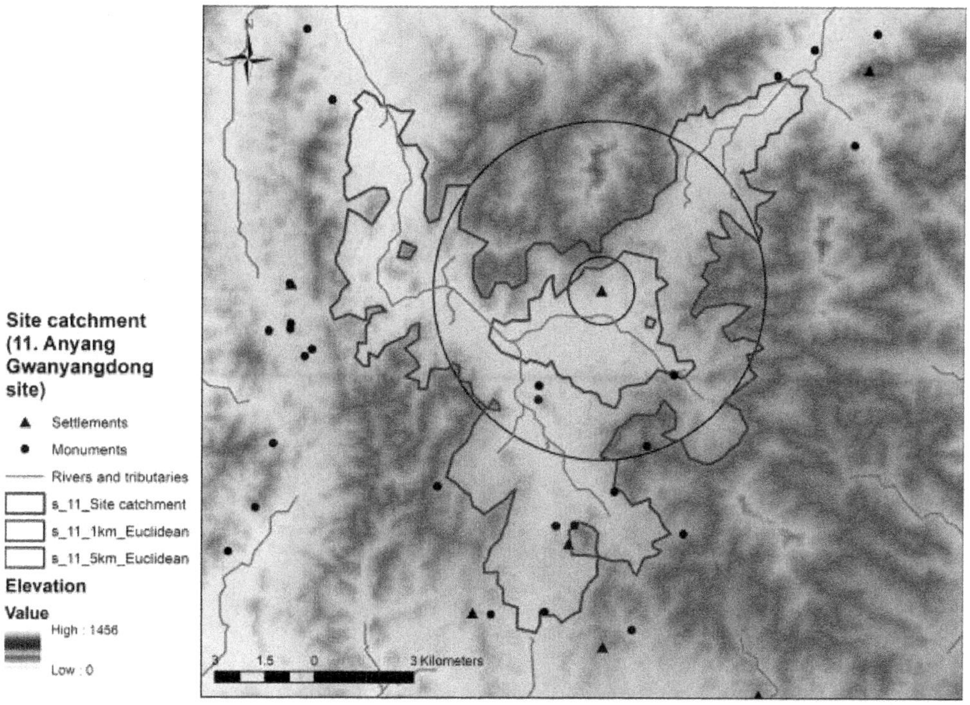

FIGURE 5. 29. NO.11 ANYANG GWANYANGDONG SITE CATCHMENT BOUNDARIES

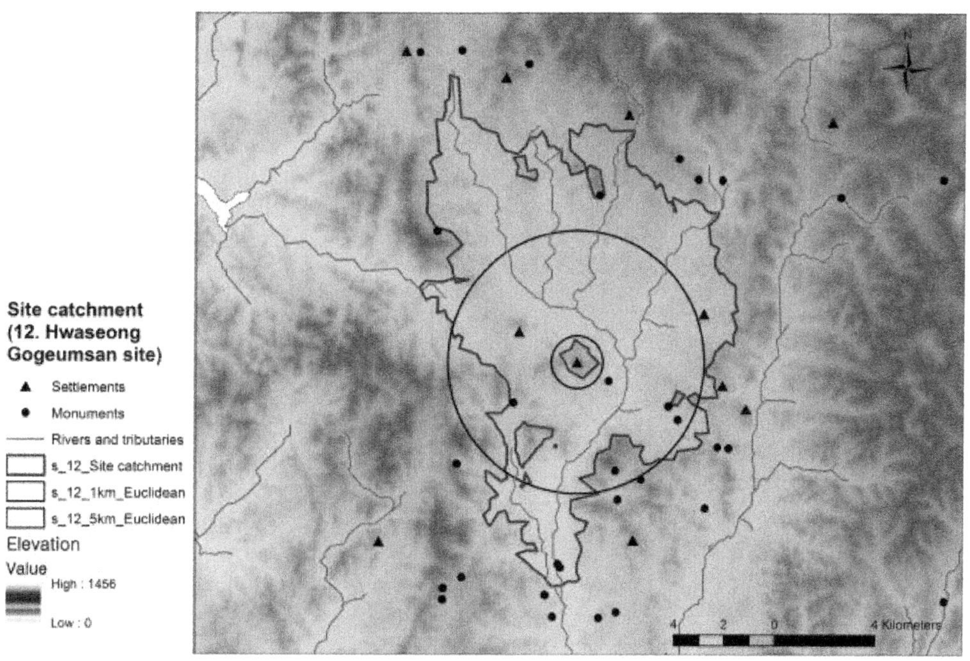

FIGURE 5. 30. NO.12 HWASEONG GOGEUMSAN SITE CATCHMENT BOUNDARIES

monuments in the study area with those of monuments in Europe, which tend to relate to the directions of astronomical observations, demonstrating an interest in the sky and the changing seasons that might be expected to be widespread cross-culturally. For example, the axis of the inner structure of Stonehenge faces the midsummer sunrise (McClintock 2006), the passage tomb of Newgrange faces the winter solstice sunrise (Stout and Stout 2008), and approx. 36% (if all those facing the eastern half of the compass are added up, the figure increases to 85.5%) of the long barrows in Cotswold-Seven, are oriented to the east (Darvill 2004: 98 Figure 37).

5.4.2 Methods

In order to ascertain whether houses and dolmens were established parallel to contour lines or adjacent to streams or not, the orientations identified from excavation reports (refer to Chapter 4) for 147 of 314 individual houses from 45 settlement sites and for 375 of 706 individual dolmens

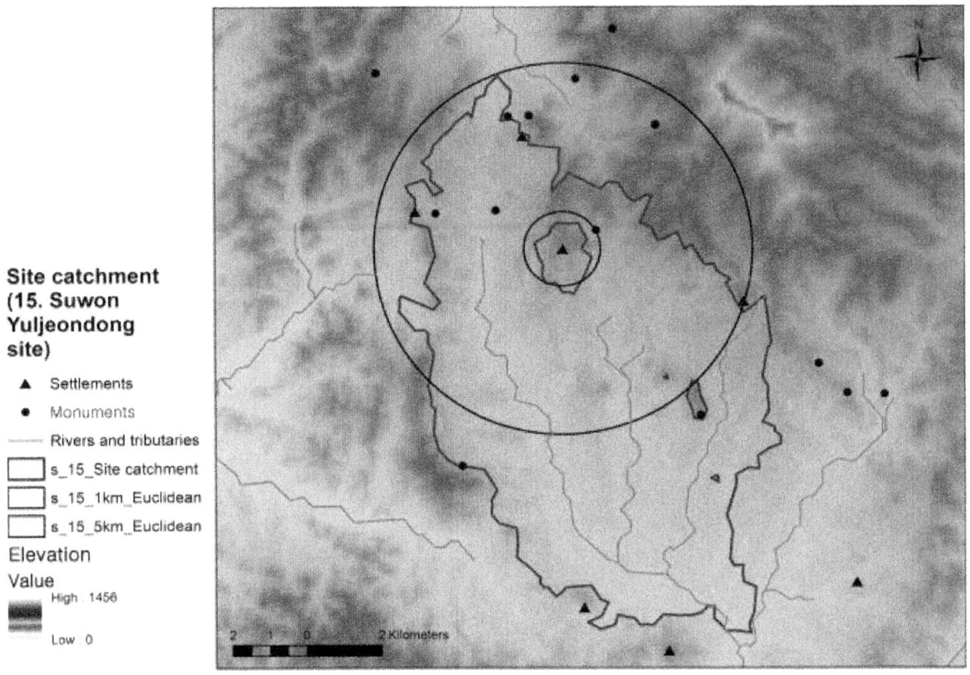

FIGURE 5. 31. NO.15 SUWON YULJEONDONG SITE CATCHMENT BOUNDARIES

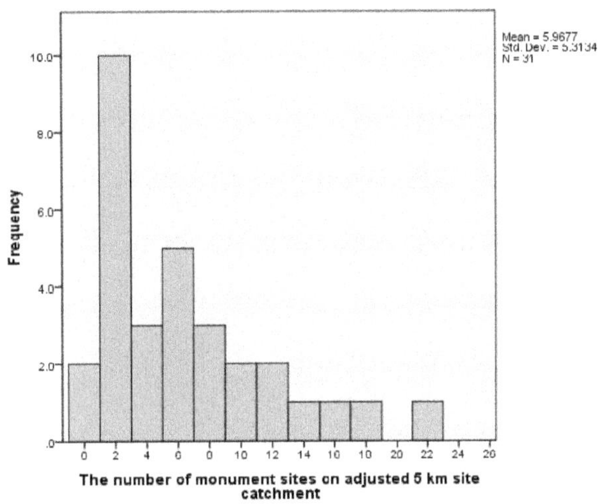

FIGURE 5. 32. THE NUMBER OF MONUMENT SITES ON ADJUSTED 5 KM SITE CATCHMENT

from 219 monument sites (Gyeonggi provincial museum 2007; Woo 2006; Choi et al. 2005), formed the basis of the analysis. In addition the aspect results of 45 settlement sites and 219 monument sites were also utilised for the orientation analysis. The long axes of the houses and dolmens were utilised, due to the fact that it was difficult to identify house entrances and the head direction of burials. These axes were cross-tabulated and chi-square tests were applied to the data using SPSS v.18.

5.4.3 Results

The orientation of the Bronze Age houses and dolmens in the research area tended to follow their natural surroundings, for example, the aspects of sites, contour lines and stream directions (Houses: Table 5.14, chi-square test result: Table 5.15; Monuments: Table 5.16, chi-square test result: Table 5.17).

As can be seen in Tables 5.15 and 5.17, the chi-square *p* values are 0.000 and 0.003 respectively and the relationship between the orientation of houses and dolmens to the natural topography of the landscape, such as, direction of contour lines and aspects of site locations seems to be significant. That is, these results support the discoveries of other researchers that dolmen and house construction in the study area was influenced by topographical features. However, it seems to be difficult to compare the majority of monument orientations, which in Europe often take into account astronomical measurements (Darvill 2004: 98-99), because the analyses were carried out on the basis of the direction of the long axes of the houses and dolmens, instead of the entrances of houses and head direction of burials.

Due to the fact that the Korean peninsula consists of approx. 70 per cent mountainous areas (refer to Chapter 2's topography section), it would seem to be inappropriate to construct houses and dolmens following the direction of distinct astronomical phenomena, such as the midsummer sunrise and/or the winter solstice. Instead, they tend to follow the natural topography of the landscape. Korean Bronze Age people's perceptual response towards the landscape they inhabited seems to have determined and formed the cultural framework in and by which they lived; they seem not to have divided themselves from nature and appear to have thought that they were a part of the ecosystem in which they lived and died. Therefore, their structures for the living and the dead tended to follow natural topographic features. Harmony with nature seems to have been an important issue in their culture and that is the reason why it has been difficult to divide environmental and cultural elements clearly in this research.

TABLE 5. 14. CROSS-TABULATION BETWEEN 314 HOUSE ORIENTATIONS AND ASPECT

		Aspect								Total
		E	N	NE	NW	S	SE	SW	W	
Orientation	Unidentified	8	25	69	13	12	10	26	4	167
	E-W	7	12	2	3	2	9	4	3	42
	NE-SW	0	1	1	4	2	4	3	0	15
	NW-SE	0	1	2	6	12	4	6	0	31
	S-N	1	25	8	4	4	11	4	2	59
Total		16	64	82	30	32	38	43	9	314

TABLE 5. 15. CHI-SQUARE TEST RESULTS OF THE RELATIONSHIP BETWEEN 314 HOUSE ORIENTATIONS AND ASPECT

	Value	df	Asymp. Sig. (2-sided)
Pearson Chi-Square	129.350a	28	0.000
Likelihood Ratio	121.557	28	0.000
N of Valid Cases	314		

TABLE 5. 16. CROSS-TABULATION BETWEEN 706 DOLMEN ORIENTATIONS AND ASPECT

		Aspect									Total
		E	F	N	NE	NW	S	SE	SW	W	
Orientation	Unidentified	47	2	21	30	42	88	34	23	44	331
	E-W	22	0	9	13	24	19	13	7	15	122
	NE-SW	9	0	7	8	7	12	7	14	5	69
	NW-SE	16	0	2	5	12	7	12	6	5	65
	S-N	12	0	16	15	16	19	19	13	9	119
Total		106	2	55	71	101	145	85	63	78	706

TABLE 5. 17. CHI-SQUARE TEST RESULTS OF THE RELATIONSHIP BETWEEN 706 DOLMEN ORIENTATIONS AND ASPECT

	Value	df	Asymp. Sig. (2-sided)
Pearson Chi-Square	58.648a	32	0.003
Likelihood Ratio	56.327	32	0.005
N of Valid Cases	706		

5.5 Summary of key findings

In this chapter, cultural elements analyses related to landform preference, viewshed, movement, and orientation were examined in order to identify how Bronze Age people perceived their surroundings and how they decided the locations for the living and the dead in the landscape.

- According to landform analyses, 60% of settlements were located on 'Ridges' and 59.3% of monuments were situated in inclined 'Planes'.

- On the basis of the cumulative viewshed analyses, the highest value from all monument sites is 52 and their location is on Bukhan mountain (북한산, 北漢山). The location that has the highest value of all the settlements is found on Gwanak mountain (관악산, 冠岳山).

- Based on the binary viewshed, the mean viewshed of settlements (12098.7 ± 10054.5) is approximately three times larger than that for monuments (4176.2 ± 5060.6). There is a positive correlation of $r^2 = 0.36$ (p value = 0.000014) (if one outlier is excluded, a positive correlation of r^2 is 0.16 (p value = 0.00679) is attained) between the range of viewsheds and the elevation of settlements, while that for dolmens is not significant ($r^2 = 0.0067$).

- There were differences (t-test, p-value of 3.45E-05, 95% confidence level) in elevation between five enclosure sites (Mean = 116.8 ± 12.2 m (median: 111 ± 8 (IQR) m) and 40 non-enclosure sites (Mean = 71.70 ± 43.34 (median: 63 ± 40.5 (IQR) m).

- There was found to be no difference (Mann-Whitney U-test, $p = 0.77$, 95% confidence level) in viewshed between the five enclosure sites (mean = 19007 ± 11735 (median: 11812 ± 20016 (IQR) m) and the eight non-enclosure sites located 100 metres above sea level.

- A Mann-Whitney test found no difference in the visible cell numbers between 51 table (2947 ± 5285 (IQR) and 125 capstone type (2552 ± 4805 (IQR) dolmen sites (*p* value = 0.89).

- There is no distinction in the difference in the relative elevation between 51 table type (60 ± 56.8 (IQR) metres) and 125 capstone type (56 ± 40 (IQR) metres) dolmen sites (Mann-Whitney U-test, *p* value = 0.71).

- As can be seen, it is difficult to identify any clear distinctions between table type dolmen sites and capstone type dolmen sites on the basis of viewshed range and elevation analysis. Only the distribution of the two dolmen types across the study area suggests a difference in terms of the concentration of table type dolmens in the northern sector as previous researchers have indicated (see Figures 6.24 and 6.25). People seem to have had similar ideas on where to place their monuments, but chose different monument forms based on their cultural affinities and historical practices.

- According to movement analyses, among 45 analysed settlements, with the exception of the third (14 sites) that are located near to main rivers, two-thirds (31 sites) display similar configurations. That is, by and large catchments tend to be surrounded by mountains and within their defined areas they often include tributaries. This positioning in terms of topographic locations, seems to be related directly to Myeongdang (명당, 明堂), and embodies the notion of a propitious location as defined by the concept of *Pungsu* (풍수, 風水).

- Monuments occur within the 5 km site catchment adjusted for energy expenditure boundaries of 94% of inland settlements. 80% of monument sites in this project occur within the adjusted 5 km site catchment boundaries of settlements.

- On the basis of orientation analyses, the relationship between the orientation of houses and dolmens to the natural topography of the landscape, such as, direction of contour lines and aspects of site locations appears to be significant (chi-square test, houses: *p* values = 0.000 and dolmens: *p* values = 0.003 respectively, 95% confidence level).

Chapter 6. Discussion

This study has investigated the relationship between the locations of the living and the dead and their landscapes in the Korean Bronze Age. In this chapter, the results of chapter 3, 4, and 5 will be discussed within the broader scope of Korean archaeology. In order to avoid the repetition of previous results (see sections 3.4, 4.6 and 5.5), this chapter mainly focuses on the third research questions (*long-term changes*) set out in chapter 1, and the comparisons between new findings in this research and the traditional approaches applied to Korean Bronze Age. In addition, the main research contributions made to Korean archaeology concerning the Bronze Age period will be summarised. The summary of key findings concerning the first (*What environmental elements affected how settlements and monuments were positioned in the landscape*?) and second (*Which cultural elements affected how settlements and monuments were positioned in the landscape?*) research questions introduced in chapter 1 will be presented in chapter 7.

This study has investigated the relationship between the locations of the living and the dead and their landscapes in the Korean Bronze Age. In this chapter, the results of chapters 3, 4, and 5 will be discussed within the broader scope of Korean archaeology and in order to avoid the repetition of previous results (see sections 3.4, 4.6 and 5.5), this chapter will mainly focus on the third set of research questions (*long-term changes*) set out in chapter 1. Also comparisons between new findings in this research and traditional approaches applied to the Korean Bronze Age will be examined. In addition, the main research contributions made to Korean archaeology concerning the Bronze Age period will be summarised. The first and the second research questions (1. Which environmental elements affected how settlements and monuments were positioned in the landscape? 2. Which cultural elements affected how settlements and monuments were located in the landscape?) raised in chapter 1 will be presented in chapter 7.

1. *What were the environmental and cultural motives behind their decisions to select specific locations for the living and the dead? How did site locations change through the Bronze Age, in terms of the Early, Middle, and Late Bronze Age periods?*

The first observation regarding long-term changes in settlements and monuments is that settlements tended to be situated on soil suitable for dry-field crops (Figure 6.1 and 6.2) throughout the Bronze Age. On the other hand, monuments were also located on this same soil type, but they appear more consistently on the soil type associated with rice, although there are very few 'dated' sites for this time (Figure 6.3, refer to Appendix 18).

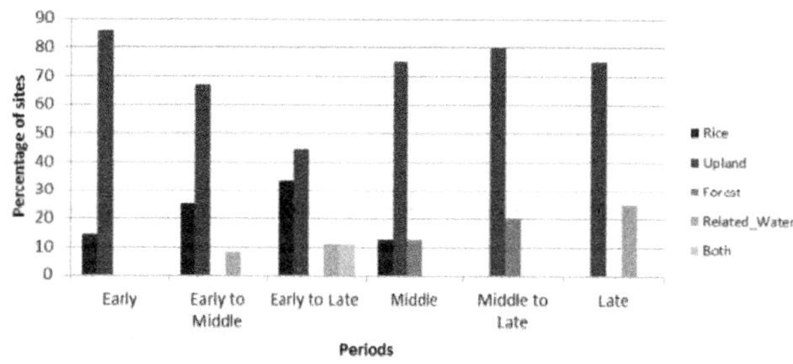

FIGURE 6. 1. SETTLEMENTS. LONG-TERM CHANGES IN SOIL TYPES THROUGH THE BRONZE AGE

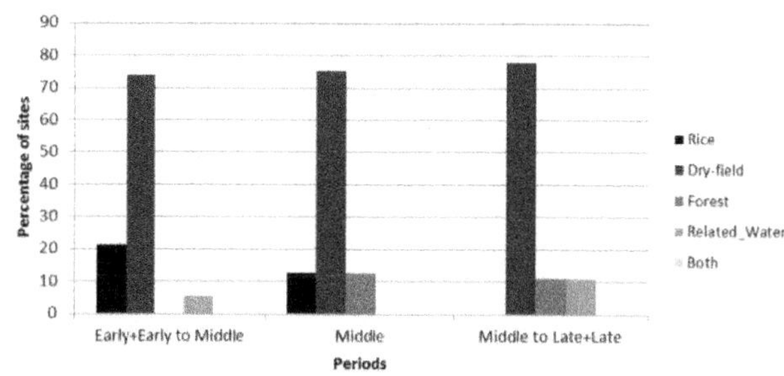

FIGURE 6. 2. SETTLEMENTS. LONG-TERM CHANGES IN SOIL TYPES (SIMPLIFIED) THROUGH THE BRONZE AGE

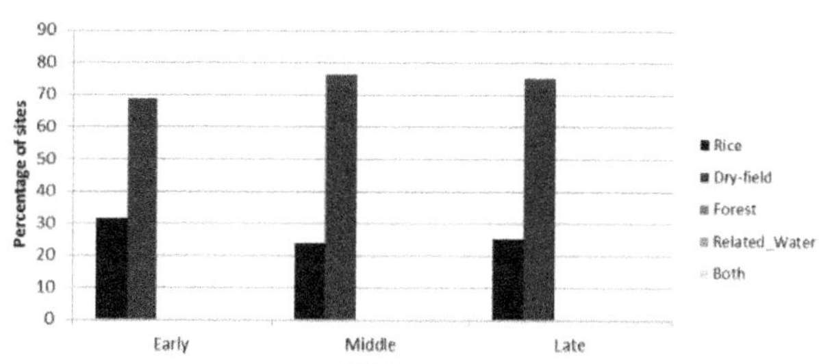

FIGURE 6. 3. MONUMENTS. LONG-TERM CHANGES IN SOIL TYPES THROUGH THE BRONZE AGE

In addition to this, aspect, elevation and viewshed (Table 6.1 and 6.2) were analysed, as a means of making a simple comparison between settlements and monuments through time, though only the Early, Middle, and Late categories were compared. As can be seen in Table 6.1, by and large, settlements were located at a higher elevation than monuments throughout the Bronze Age. Based on the median values, both settlements and monuments were located at the highest elevation during the Middle Bronze Age, although the exceptional high elevation (255 metres) site seems to be Late Bronze Age. Also, the viewshed range of both types of site steadily increased over time, with the median viewshed value of settlements overall being three times broader than that of monuments. These results may be interpreted in terms of people's decisions to find locations for settlements which commanded a clear view over their landscape and provided security from invaders. There seems to have been conflicts in the Korean Bronze Age based on available archaeological evidence: broken pieces of stone arrowheads and daggers have been found in dolmens (Lee, 2002: 280), different types of bronze weapons were developed throughout the Bronze Age (National Museum of Korea, 1992) and a considerable number of houses in the study area seemed to have been destroyed by fire (Kim and Yun, 1967: 39; Bae and Gang, 2000: 74, 109; Lee et al, 2006: 65-66; Gijeon Cultural Properties Institute, 2004: 32; Department of Archaeology and Anthropology and the University Museum, 1976: 10; Park et al, 2007: 58, 98). Together with these features, it has been difficult to identify wounded skeletons by weapons in the Korean peninsula due to the acid soils, but it is possible to infer that there would be conflicts at this time based on the evidence of a thoracic vertebrae injured by a polished stone dagger in the Sudare site (スダレ 遺跡) and the femur damaged by a polished stone arrowhead in the Sinmachi site (新町 遺跡), Fukuoka ken (福岡県), Japan in the Yayoi period (弥生時代: approx. 300 BC-AD 300), which corresponds to the Bronze Age (Turumoto and Naitou 1989: 110).

TABLE 6. 1. ELEVATION OF SETTLEMENTS AND MONUMENT SITES IN THE EARLY, MIDDLE, AND LATE BRONZE AGE (UNIT: METRES)

Elevation (m)		Early (n=7)	Middle (n=8)	Late (n=4)
Settlements	Average	66.1	83.5	108.5
	Standard deviation	21.6	34.7	98.4
	Median	65.0	76.5	66.0
	Interquartile range	25.5	46.0	67.0
		Early (n=16)	Middle (n=21)	Late (n=4)
Monuments	Average	51.1	63.6	34.5
	Standard deviation	30.8	24.0	4.7
	Median	44.5	64.0	33.5
	Interquartile range	19.8	36.0	3.5

TABLE 6. 2. VIEWSHED RANGE OF SETTLEMENTS AND MONUMENT SITES IN THE EARLY, MIDDLE, AND LATE BRONZE AGE (UNIT: VISIBLE CELL NUMBER IN THE DEM)

Viewshed		Early	Middle	Late
Settlements	Average	9277.1	13410.9	22121.0
	Standard deviation	5059.6	8981.9	17424.5
	Median	8605.0	12538.5	16266.5
	Interquartile range	7812.5	9266.5	11922.0
Monuments	Average	4434.3	5830.5	5991.3
	Standard deviation	3635.4	5071.2	4101.4
	Median	3364.0	5369.0	5877.0
	Interquartile range	5001.8	8489.0	6721.8

By contrast, monuments seem to have been constructed more frequently on lower land than settlements and nearer the arable area of presumably associated settlements, at least in a general sense, even if we cannot point to connections between specific settlements and monuments. It might be suggested that these monuments functioned as territorial markers. Due to the topographic characteristics of the Korean peninsula which consists largely of mountainous regions, results produced from the 5 km site catchment boundaries adjusted for energy expenditure, show that sites tend to be situated within a location type that was surrounded by mountains and that they often include tributaries (refer back to Figure 5.29, 5.30, and 5.31). Among 45 analysed settlements, approximately two-thirds (31 sites) were located within the above configurations, while approximately one-third of sites (14 sites) not showing this pattern were located near to main rivers or the coast. In terms of their topographic location, inland settlements sites can be interpreted as consistent with the concept of *Myeongdang* (명당, 明堂) (Figure 6.11), which embodies the notion of a propitious location, as defined by the concept of *Pungsu.* Monument sites occur within adjusted 5 km site catchment boundaries of 94% of inland settlements and 80% of monument sites were found within these settlement boundaries. Therefore, there seems to be close relationships between settlements and monuments in the Bronze Age.

2. *Can we identify social change in landscape preference from the end of the Neolithic period to the beginning of the Iron Age in the study area, through analysis of the Bronze Age landscape?*

This study examined pottery types, house shape, the placement of settlements, the number of houses located within settlement sites, the development of monuments and enclosures (Appendix 20) on the basis of landscape perspectives. According to the available archaeological evidence, settlements of the Neolithic period tended to be established near to main rivers and to the sea (refer back to Figure 2.9) and their subsistence economy appears to have comprised fishing, hunting and gathering and slash-and-burn farming. Although there is evidence of rice cultivation (refer to Chap. 5) from the Middle Neolithic period, it has been thought that intensive rice agriculture did not begin until the Middle Bronze Age. By contrast, the settlements of the Bronze Age period, located in the study area, were distributed both near to and at a distance from the tributaries of the region (Figure 6.4). Settlements in the Early Bronze Age (appendix 17) were, on the whole, situated near to the main rivers of the study area; this is especially the case where features of the Early Bronze Age sites suggest continuity with the Neolithic period and this result corroborates the findings of previous research in this field (Choi et al. 1993; Lee 2005c).

In addition to the above aspects, the results of this study indicate that the distinctive features of the Late Bronze Age (refer to Appendix 22) seem to have been the emergence of settlements which were functionally differentiated

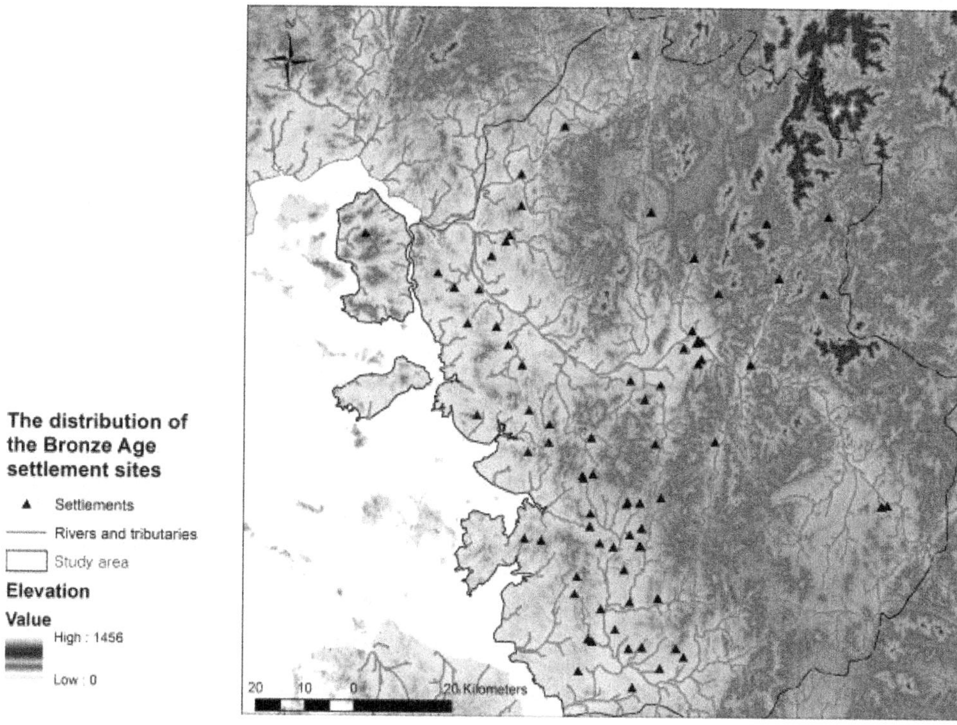

FIGURE 6. 4. THE DISTRIBUTION OF THE BRONZE AGE SETTLEMENT SITES

compared to previous settlements, that is, settlements in later periods seemed to be precursors of the Iron Age hillforts. Settlements at this time have overall wide viewsheds, although they were not situated at high elevations, with the exception of one site (255 m) with only one house. In addition, three of four settlements in the Late period were located near the main Han River (refer to Figure 6.5, 6.6 and 6.7) and one site was situated on the west coast (Figure 6.8). Their locations seem to have been carefully selected in order to observe the traffic on the river and around the coastline, suggesting that these sites might have functioned as observation points on the basis of records, such as, *Shiji* (사기, 史記) *Joseonyeoljeon* (조선열전, 朝鮮列傳) by *Sima Qian* (사마천, 司馬遷, 145 BC – 87 BC) and *Sanguo Zhi Weizhi Dongyijeon* (삼국지 위지 동이전, 三國志 魏志 東夷傳) by *Chen Shou* (진수, 陳壽, AD 233–297) (Choi 2008b: 105-114) indicating that the basin of the Han River was disputed by various groups at that time. That is, settlements in the Late Bronze Age are likely to be related to the emergence of the hillfort in the Iron Age. For example, the Acha mountain hillfort (아차산성, 峨嵯山城), was constructed in AD 286 by Chaekgae king (책계왕, 責稽王, ? – AD 298) during the Baekjae Kingdom (백제, 百濟, 18 BC-AD 660) according to the *Samguksagi* (삼국사기, 三國史記) (Im et al. 2000; National Research Institute of Cultural Properties Korea 2001: 304). This hillfort was located at a diagonal orientation across the Han River from the Ilwondong site (Figure 6.6) and was at an elevation of 285 meters, with a broad viewshed over the Han River. According to the M.L. Choi (2008a: 202-203), the Ilwondong site can be classified as a ritual site. It is probable that this site was used for ritual practices, due to the fact that only one house (at that time 2.4 m × 1.4 m, at an elevation of 279.4 metres) was discovered in 1999. However, according to the viewshed results and due to the its elevation, Ilwondong might be seen as an antecedent of the Iron Age hillfort. According to current research (Choi 2007), a large rock with cup-marks was situated near to where a Bronze Age house was discovered. A large rock is a common structure seen at other ritual sites and it is likely that this particular site also had an important role as a hillfort during the Baekje kingdom (백제, 百濟, 18 BC-AD 660) due to the fact that it had an advantageous viewshed for defensive purposes during the Three Kingdoms period. Another example is the Iseong hill fort in Hanam (이성산성, 二聖山城). This site, located at an elevation of 209.8 metres, also had a fine view of the surrounding area of the Han River. It has been estimated that Iseong hill fort was constructed during the fifth century by the Silla Kingdom (신라, 新羅) (Cultural Heritage Administration 2000).

Besides these features, the number of surrounding monuments near these settlements is very low. Only fourteen individual monuments within four monument sites, which are related to the four settlements sites, were confirmed (Appendix 22). According to the Chinese historical records, *Shiji* (사기, 史記, Records of the Grand Historian), Sānguó Zhì (삼국지, 三國志) *Wei Zhi* (위지, 魏志) *Dongyizhuan* (동이전, 東夷傳), *Hòuhàn Shū* (후한서, 後漢書, Book of the Later Han) *Dongyi liezhuan* (동이열전, 東夷列傳), during the Early Iron Age (400 BC and 1 BC) there seemed to be several complex societies, such as, Wiman Joseon (위만조선, 衛滿朝鮮), Buyeo (부여, 夫餘), Goguryeo (고구려, 高句麗), Okjeo (옥저, 沃沮), Dongye (동예, 東濊), and Samhan (삼한, 三韓) existing in the Korean peninsula and Manchuria. The Late Bronze Age is the period just before the Early Iron Age. Therefore, more élite or 'state'- controlled worship seems to have begun during the Late Bronze Age.

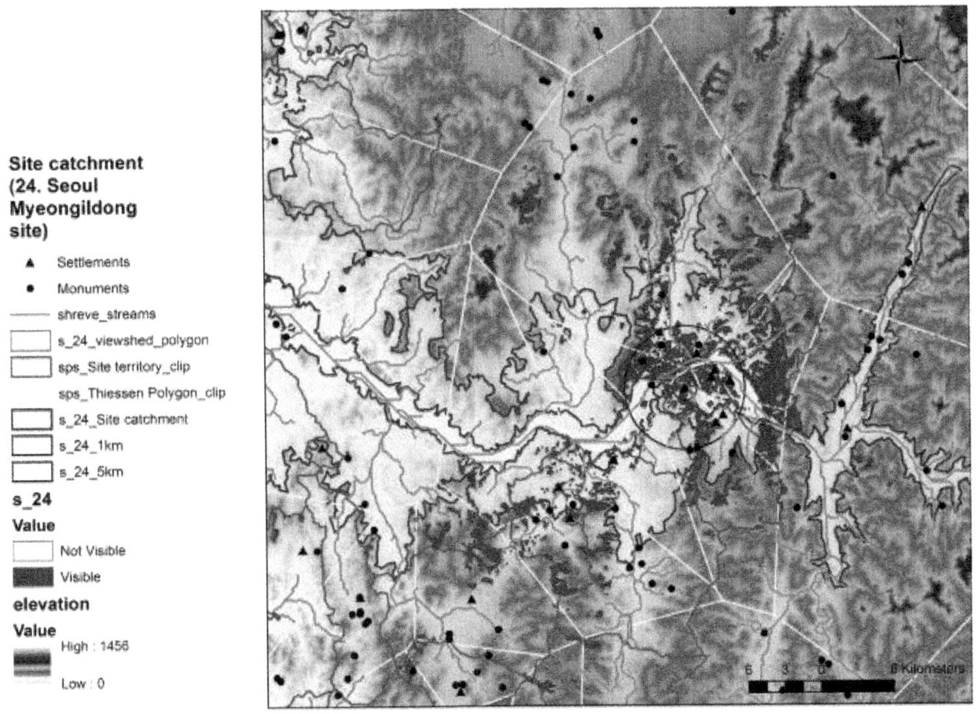

FIGURE 6. 5. THE VIEWSHED RANGE FROM SETTLEMENT (24. SEOUL MYEONGILDONG SITE) IN THE 'LATE' PERIOD

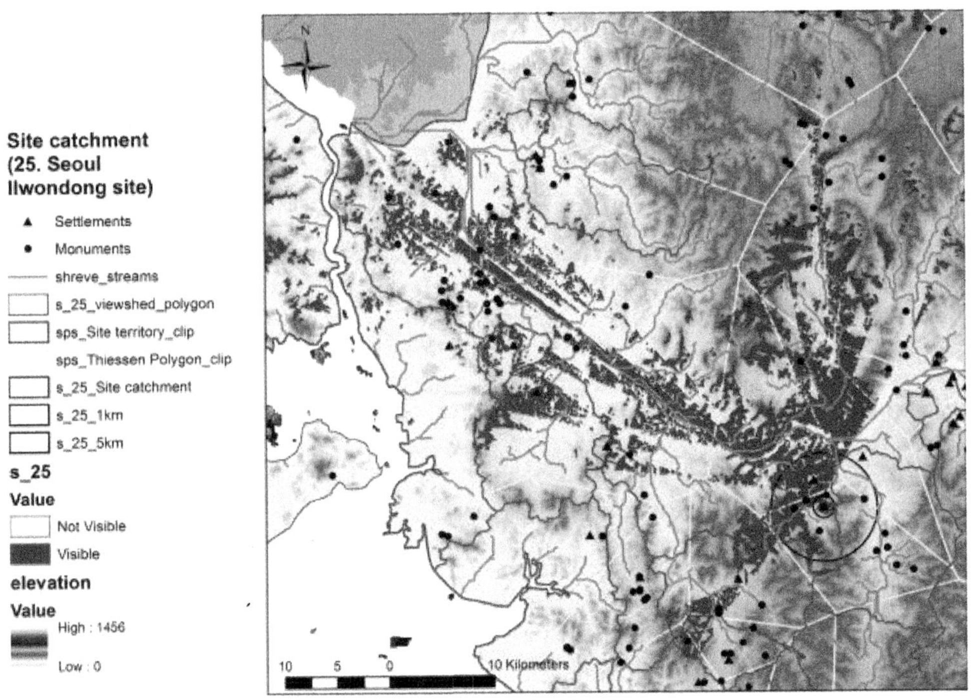

FIGURE 6. 6. THE VIEWSHED RANGE FROM SETTLEMENT (25. SEOUL ILWONDONG SITE) IN THE 'LATE' PERIOD

3. *What are the new findings and new perspectives expounded in this research? How do the results presentd in this research support and/or contradict traditional interpretations of Korean Bronze Age archaeology?*

Firstly, the traditional divisions of the Korean Bronze Age have been suggested on the basis of the development of different pottery types (Choi 2008b: 20-23). While the present research applied Bayesian modelling in order to divide the Bronze Age into three phases and, therefore, to look at long-term change, this was not possible, due to the fact that, according to the results, representative pottery types in Gyeonggi province seemed to be used almost simultaneously throughout the entire Bronze Age, except for the red burnished pottery (refer to Chapter 3.3.2, Figure 3.5). Therefore, in this research, Bayesian models based on house shape have been also utilised and a consideration of both pottery types and house shapes provides six tentative divisions. From the results, several significant patterns can be identified. For example, as mentioned before, society had become more complex on the basis of the appearance of ritual and enclosure sites (refer to Appendix 16), as well as an increase in the number of houses (refer to Appendix 20).

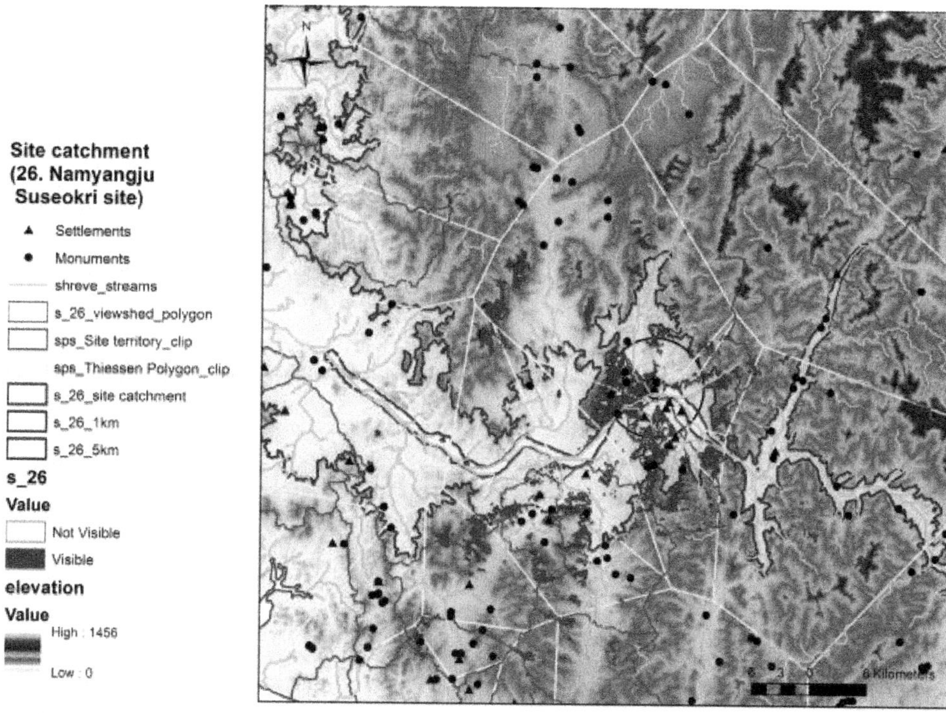

FIGURE 6. 7. THE VIEWSHED RANGE FROM SETTLEMENT (26. NAMYANGJU SUSEOKRI SITE) IN THE 'LATE' PERIOD

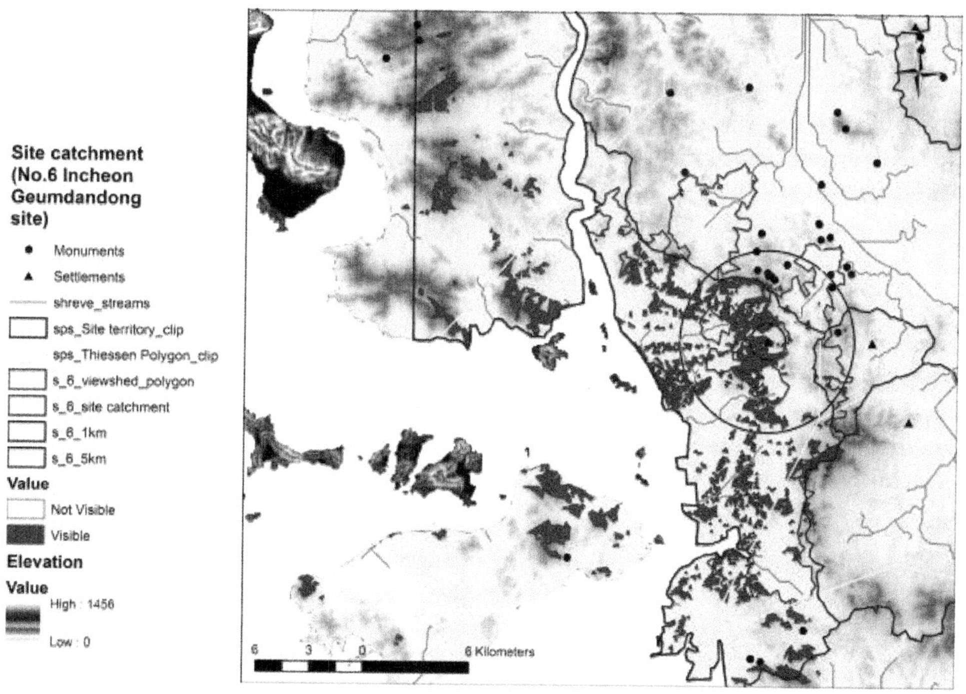

FIGURE 6. 8. THE VIEWSHED RANGE FROM SETTLEMENT (6. INCHEON GEUMDANDONG SITE) IN THE 'LATE' PERIOD

Secondly, another feature worth mentioning is the shift in the typology of dolmens and their volumes. As time went by, the number of table type dolmens seems to have decreased and effectively to have disappeared after the Middle Bronze Age in the study area (see Appendix 21). In contrast, capstone type dolmens likely continued into the late Bronze Age, although their numbers also decreased. In addition, it can be suggested that the volumes of the two types of dolmens reached their largest values during the Middle Bronze Age (refer to Table 6.3), although only one table type dolmen site was identified in this period, if the provisional dating proposed here can be accepted. These results seem to be in contrast to earlier findings (Yu 2002; Kang 2002b), which argued that the heaviest dolmens seemed to have been constructed in the Late Bronze Age, on the basis of the relationship between capstone weight and population numbers, these opinions being based on assumptions about the evolutionary 'progress' of society (Fried 1967; Service 1962). The main point of these studies is that there is an assumption that the Late Bronze Age was a complex society and had large populations, with a hierarchy of chiefs. According to the interpretation by

M.L. Choi (1984), dolmen society was a chiefdom society and dolmens appear to have represented the chief's burial. T.Y. Yu (2003) also argues that dolmens were constructed by the descendant of a dominant lineage, like a chief, in order to maintain their kin's power. These assumptions are plausible, but have not yet been fully proved. Consequently, better independent chronologies for the monuments are required in order to reveal the structures of Bronze Age societies. It is difficult to reconstruct how the power system was developed and what order of social hierarchy existed in the Bronze Age based on these analyses. However, on the tentative basis of the capstone volumes, it could be interpreted that the construction of monuments functioned as the consolidation of communities in the Korean Bronze Age, just as the construction of ditches has been suggested to have performed a similar function during the British Bronze Age (Hodder 1990; Whittle et al. 1999; Gosden 2011).

Thirdly, the difference in viewsheds between table type and capstone type dolmens was explored. In order to avoid biased results when sites have large numbers of monuments, monument clusters rather than individual monuments were utilised. The median visible cell number of 51 table type dolmen sites is 2947 ± 5285 (IQR) and the median visible cell numbers of 125 capstone type dolmen sites is 2552 ± 4805 (IQR). As neither shows a normal distribution, a Mann-Whitney test was employed, and no difference was found in the visible cell numbers between table and capstone type dolmen sites (p value = 0.89, 95% confidence level). Next, the elevation of table type and capstone type dolmen sites was considered in order to investigate the correlation between the viewsheds and elevations of table type and capstone type dolmen sites. The median elevation of 51 table type dolmen sites is 60 ± 56.8 (IQR) metres and the median elevation of 125 capstone type dolmen sites is 56 ± 40 (IQR) metres. There is no distinction in the difference in relative elevation between the two types of dolmen sites (Mann-Whitney U-test, p value = 0.71). As can be seen, it is difficult to identify any clear distinctions between table type dolmen sites and capstone type dolmen sites on the basis of viewshed range and elevation. Only the distribution of the two dolmen types across the study area suggests a difference in terms of the concentration of table type dolmens in the northern sector as previous researchers have indicated (see Figures 5.24 and 5.25). People seem to have had similar ideas on where to place their monuments, but chose different monument forms based on their cultural affinities and historical practices.

TABLE 6. 3. THE CAPSTONE VOLUMES OF TABLE AND CAPSTONE TYPES

Volume	m3	Early	Middle	Late
Table type capstone	Average	17242.0	80440.5	
	Standard deviation	8103.2		
	Median	14080.0		
	Interquartile range	13380.0		
Capstone type capstone	Average	26879.0	66817.7	9563.1
	Standard deviation	77256.4	72075.6	7778.2
	Median	13345.0	37065.0	6557.2
	Interquartile range	13931.1	104348.3	5785.3

Fourthly, several studies (Yu 2002; Kang 2002b; Ha 2007) have attempted to explain where monuments were located in the landscape. These studies examined site locations, but it was impossible to test whether their results were statistically significant or not, due to the fact that they did not take the geography (especially topography) of the region into consideration. However, the most advantageous point of using GIS in this research is to obtain data regarding the overall tendency of the study area, so that it is possible to test the relationships between the study area and the sites to see if and where they depart from what would be expected given a more or less 'random' distribution of sites across the landscape.

4. *Future research*

Two topics related to the research presented here have not been fully explored, and await future research. Firstly, rituals related to agriculture and the roles of leaders in Korean Bronze Age societies and secondly, the concept of *Pungsu* need further investigation. Enclosure sites (Appendix 16) and at least one ritual site (no. 48. Hanam Deokbung-dong) seem to have developed, by and large, from the Middle Bronze Age. These site-types can be interpreted in relation to the establishment of rice agriculture as the main subsistence economy. Consequently, the optimum conditions, especially precipitation, for rice agriculture would have been an important concern for Bronze Age peoples, although the optimal agricultural condition in the Bronze Age may not be the same as at present. Rituals for the supplication of the appropriate conditions under which rice could be grown might be conducted when they were most needed, for example, after sowing when rainfall would be required to germinate the grains. An implication of this behaviour is the possibility that the community leader of this period might have had a role to play as a ritual leader or shaman[32]. This is supported by the discovery of

[32] It is believed that the concept of a 'shaman' originated with the Evenks, a people who live in North Asia and speak a tungusic language. Their culture was studied by Russian anthropologists and through later publications became known to the wider, international academic community (Price 2011: 984-986). The 'shaman' performs rituals, through which he is believed to act as a mediator between the domain of the living and either those of the spirits of nature or those of the dead (*ibid*: 985). However, according to Price, the notion of 'shamanism' is still a contested concept and he cautions that variable and flexible approaches for the definition of shamanic practices are required, due to the fact that archaeological evidence from across a wide number of regions, does not allow for a narrow definition of 'shamanism' (*ibid*: 996-998).

Figure 6. 9. Bronze mirror from Nonsan (Diameter: 21.2cm, National Museum of Korea, 1992: 34)

bronze artefacts, such as bronze mirrors and bronze bells, which to have been utilised when shamans performed their ritual ceremonies (Jeong 1981; Lee 1987a) (Figure 6.9 and Figure 6.10). The existence of ritual and sacred places continued into the Iron Age as *Sodo* (소도, 蘇塗)[33] according to the *Wei Zhi* (위지, 魏志) records.

The second topic is *the concept of Pungsu* (풍수, 風水). The topographic location of inland settlement sites can be interpreted as consistent with the concept of *Myeongdang* (명당, 明堂) (Figure 6.11), which exemplifies the notion of an auspicious location by *Pungsu* concept.

It could be argued that, though the theory of *Feng-shui* had been known from approximately AD 300 in China and had profoundly influenced Korean *Pungsu,* subsequently, the concept of *Pungsu* in Korea seems to be related to the change to a subsistence economy, especially the advent of rice cultivation (Choe 1992: 58-63; Han 1993: 119-124). This conceptual framework of propitious location allowed the people of the Bronze Age to negotiate and to adapt to their environments, to find the most appropriate site, to interpret locations culturally and to symbolise them for the living and their dead.

According to Choe, Chang-Jo (1992), the foremost *Pungsu* specialist in Korea, a propitious location, in theory, is a rounded valley, surrounded by mountains termed the four spirits: East - the green dragon (좌청룡, 左青龍), West - the white tiger (우백호, 右白虎), South - the red phoenix (남주작, 南朱雀), and North - the black turtle (북현무, 北玄武). Such valley locations are also advantageous for defensive and practical reasons of course, especially in places where there are strong, cold winds, as in Korea, which experiences gales from the north-west during the winter[34].

Pungsu has been a conceptual framework for the interaction of human beings with the natural world throughout considerable periods of Korean history. The symbolic order of the four spirits has been found to be depicted in mural paintings in the Goguryeo tomb dating from the fourth century AD. The four spirits seem to have been painted primarily when tomb locations were not in the ideal, auspicious place, as prescribed by *pungsu,* in order to make up for their weak aspects (Jeon 2004: 24). Of course, there is a considerable gap between the end of

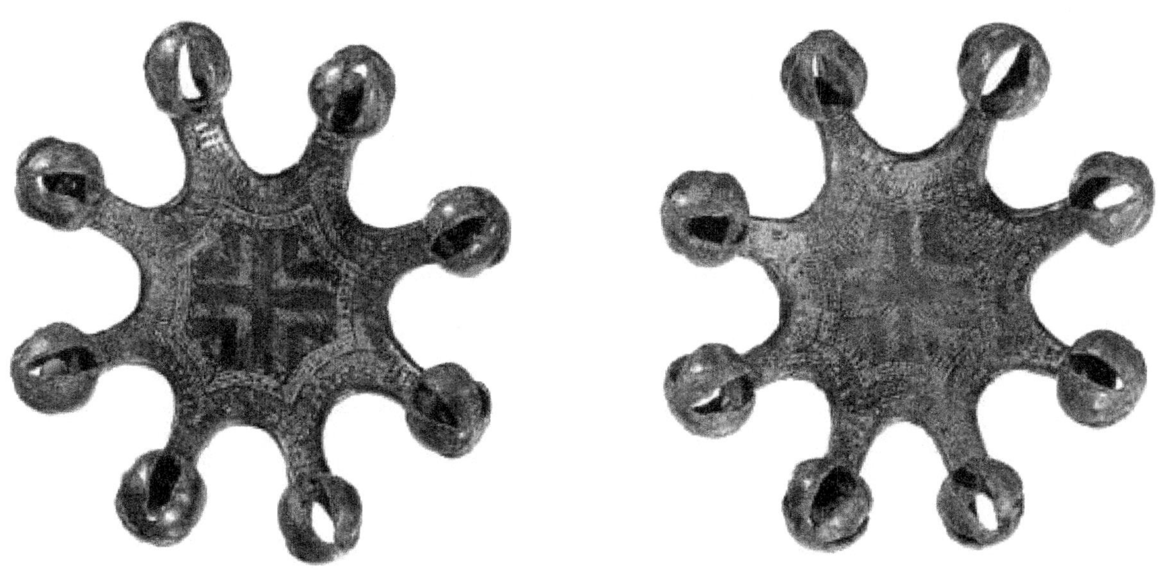

Figure 6. 10. Bronze bells from Yesan (Reported) (Diametre: approx. 12cm, National Museum of Korea, 1992: 36)

[33] Shaman ritual place: a site of a religious ceremony of the Later Iron Age (AD 1-300), where a tall wooden pole was erected and decorated with bells and a drum (Kim et al. 2004: 183; Hudson 1992: 147).

[34] Nine settlements among 45 settlements were situated on a North-West aspect and they share common geographical features: arable areas were located on the north-west side of those settlements.

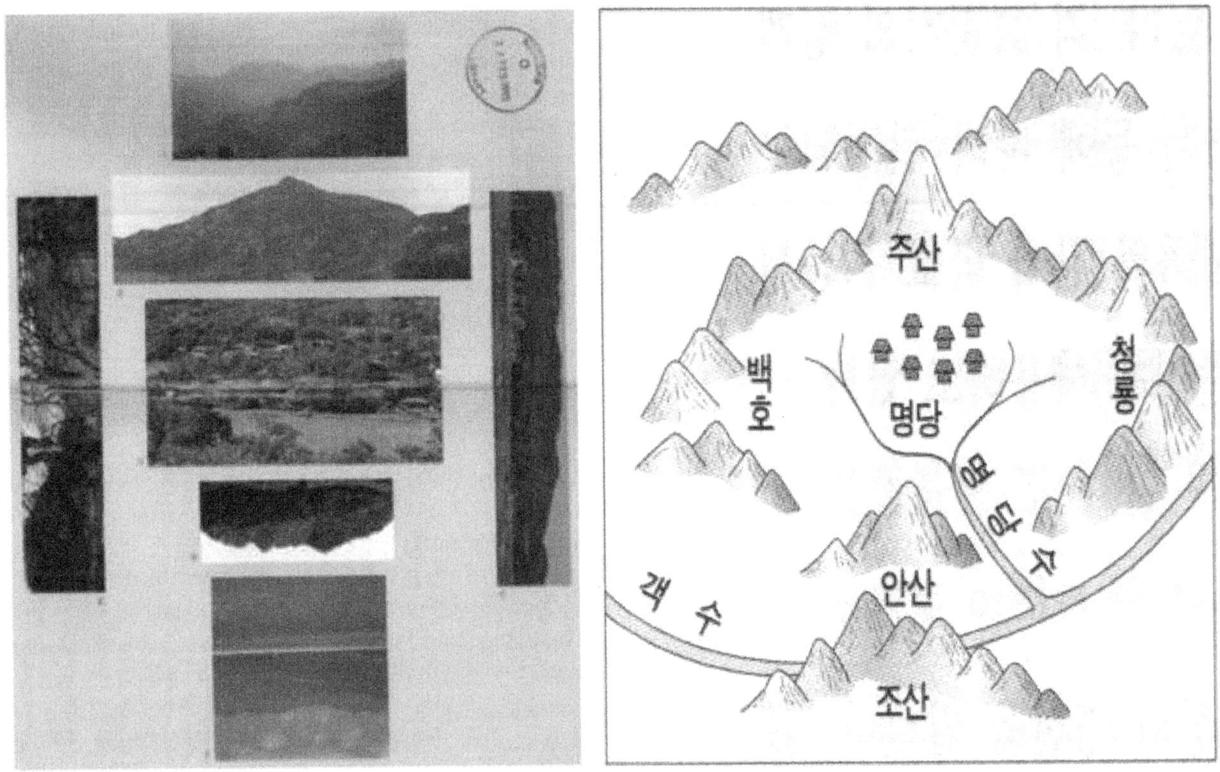

FIGURE 6. 11. SCHEME OF MYEONGDANG (명당, 明堂)
(LEFT: (CHOE 1992: 2-3, WITH THE AUTHOR'S PERMISSION), RIGHT: (LEE 2002A: 296, WITH THE PUBLISHER'S PERMISSION))

the Bronze Age (approx. 400 BC) and surviving evidence for the depiction of the four spirits in mural paintings. However, if the worship of Jumong (주몽, 朱蒙, 58-19 BC), who established Goguryeo (고구려, 高句麗, 37 BC-AD 668), can be related to indigenous cultural practices in the Goguryeo Kingdom, such as that of the depiction of the four spirits, it is possible to begin to narrow the apparent break between the two periods (Jeon, 2004: 353-356), although there still remains a hiatus of approximately 400 years. From the ninth to the tenth centuries, at the end of the Silla Kingdom (신라, 新羅, 57 BC-AD 935), the writings of Doseon (도선, 道詵, 827-898), a monk in the Late Silla Kingdom as well as a master of *Pungsu*, seem to have influenced Wanggun (왕건, 王建, AD 877-AD 943), who laid the foundation of the Goryeo (고려, 高麗, AD 918-AD 1392) dynasty, when he established the capital in Songak (송악, 松嶽, the old name of Gaeseong, 개성, 開城) (Choe, 1992: 85-87). Similarly, Lee Seong-gae (이성계, 李成桂, AD1335-1408), who was the founder of the Joseon dynasty (조선, 朝鮮, AD1392-1897) moved the capital to Hanyang (한양, 漢陽), which is in same location as that of the current capital, Seoul, in the Republic of Korea (Choe 1993; Han 1993: 182-184). Arguably, the influence of the concept of *Pungsu* can be identified throughout Korean history, and, it is suggested here, seems to be traced back into prehistory. One of the more significant findings to emerge from this study is that the locations of settlements and monuments are closely related to the 5 km site catchment for adjusted energy expenditure boundaries and that the topographical features associated with the sites are reminiscent of the propitious area as defined by *Pungsu*.

Chapter 7. Conclusion

Many of the significant changes that took place in the Korean Bronze Age (c.1500-400 BC) can be attributed to the development of rice agriculture as the staple of the subsistence economy (Ahn 1998d; Choi 2001; Im 2005a). This research has investigated Bronze Age people's decision-making when choosing locations in which to live and to be buried and what elements affected their decision in the central Korean peninsula. In addition, features indicative of long-term changes, which can be traced in their landscape, were explored. To address these questions, GIS was utilized for the spatial analysis of 45 settlements and 236 monument sites in Seoul·Incheon·Gyeonggi province. Bayesian modelling using 72 radiocarbon determinations from 16 settlements in the research area was conducted in order to provide some chronological framework for the spatial analyses. Environmental elements, such as, pedology, hydrology, and topography, were analysed and cultural elements embodying landform preference, viewshed, movement and orientation, were investigated.

This chapter will present a summary of the main findings of the above analyses and prompted by this research, suggested areas for future research will be addressed.

Firstly, the results of environmental element analyses are summarised. According to the pedological findings, settlements were shown to have positive association in the Dry-field_Good category and similarly, a positive association for monument sites was presented for the Dry-field_Good and the Rice_Good classifications. The proportions of monument sites in the Rice_Good and Rice_Poor sectors were found to be higher than those of settlements. The relationship between monuments and soil types for agriculture could support a hypothesis postulated by Bradley (1998): he argued that the advent of agriculture provoked a new sense of time and space and that stone monuments appear to be related to the land itself. In addition, on the basis of hydrological results, monument sites tend to be situated in closer vicinity to water sources than settlements and this result, together with the pedological results seems to reflect that monuments were related to arable land. Also, based on the topographical outcomes, settlements and monuments seem to have commonly preferred aspects, but neither set of results are statistically significant. Slope results support those of soil analysis, that is, most settlement and monument sites were found in the 0-10° slope region, which is an area of soil suitable for rice and dry-field crop cultivation. This seems to reflect the nature of the main subsistence economy in the Bronze Age.

Through the environmental element analysis, the locational information of settlements and monument sites in the Bronze Age has been identified and from that information a linked subsistence economy can be inferred. However, the results relating to natural features have not fully explained the locations of settlements and monuments. In consequence, further investigations of the cultural elements, such as, landform preference, viewshed, movement and orientation were carried out.

In this second part the results of cultural feature analyses are summarised. According to landform-preference analyses, 60% of settlements were located on 'Ridges' and approximately 60% of monuments were situated in inclined 'Planes'. According to site maps (Figure 5.3), settlements tended to be located on ridges in the same way indicated by landform analyses and, consequently, they tend to be at a higher elevation and with a substantially better view than that seen for monuments. By contrast, monument sites that are identified in the inclined 'Plane' category tend to be located at the transitional zones between the end of a mountain range and the start of a plain, encompassing view over the nearest arable land. Together with these results and on the basis of binary viewshed analyses, the mean viewshed of settlements (12098.7 ± 10054.5) is approximately three times larger than that of monuments (4176.2 ± 5060.6). There is a moderate positive correlation of $r^2 = 0.36$ (p value = 0.000014) (if an outlier is excluded from Figure 6.13, the positive correlation is considerably reduced, though remains significant, $r^2 = 0.16$ (p value = 0.00679) would be attained) between the range of viewsheds and the elevation of settlement while that for dolmens is not significant ($r^2 = 0.0067$). That is, people seem to prefer locations for their settlements with uninterrupted views and higher elevations; it is thought that this is partly due as the locations were more suitable for defence on the basis of the evidence of conflicts during this period in the archaeological record.

Based on the results of movement analyses, due to the topographic characteristics of the Korean peninsula which consists largely of mountainous regions, results produced from the 5 km site catchment boundaries adjusted for energy expenditure area, show that sites tend to be situated within a location type that was surrounded by mountains and that they often include tributaries (Figures 5.29, 5.30, and 5.31). Among 45 analysed settlements, approximately two-thirds (31sites) were located within the similar configurations, while approximately one-third of sites (14 sites) not showing this pattern, are located near to main rivers or the coast. These sites in terms of topographic location can be interpreted as consistent with the concept of *Myeongdang* (명당, 明堂) (Figure 6.11), which embodies the notion of a propitious location. In addition, monuments occur within the 5 km site catchment adjusted for energy expenditure boundaries of most (29 out of 31 94%) these settlements (refer to Figure5.32). Moreover, of the 236 monument sites included in this project, 80% (185) occur within the adjusted 5 km site catchment boundaries of a settlement. Clearly, settlements and monuments were related to one another within the landscape in which they were created. Also worth mentioning are the results of the orientation analysis. The relationship between the orientation of the long axes of houses and dolmens to the natural topography of the landscape, such as, the direction of contour lines and aspects of site locations, are statistically significant and these results are supportive of the opinions of previous researchers (Kim 1981; Ji 1987a).

These results of cultural feature analyses have provided locational information for settlements and monument sites in the Korean Bronze Age alongside those of the environmental element analyses. However, some results seem to be closely related to the fact that the Korean peninsula consists of approximately 70 per cent mountainous areas. Arguably, Korean Bronze Age peoples' perceptual response towards the landscape they inhabited seems to have been influenced by their surrounding environment, interpreting the land and its forms within a cultural framework in and by which they lived. It appears that they did not set themselves apart from the natural world but instead considered that they themselves were an element of the landscape in which they lived and died. The distinction between 'environmental' and 'cultural' seems to be irrelevant for the Bronze Age in the study area, and presumably throughout the rest of Korea at this time, though confirmation of this also awaits future investigation.

To conclude, life and death rituals cannot exist without interplay between each state (Whittle, 2003:48-49; Schulting, 2004:22) as well as symbolic perspectives; human behaviour is determined not just by subsistence necessities but also through cultural orientations (Hodder, 1990; Tilley 1994). Therefore, the motives and decisions of human behaviour seem to be determined simultaneously, by both environmental and cultural perspectives. Furthermore, in order to understand human behaviour in a more contextual manner, it is necessary to consider the unique landscape within which people existed (Gosden, 1994: 79). Although research questions in this work began with a division between environmental elements and cultural elements, according to the results of analyses, Bronze Age people seemed to decide their placement of the living and the dead on the basis of a more holistic point of view. This conclusion was suggested by the consideration of viewshed and movement, rather than location being exclusively environmentally determined, such as, depending on the 'best' soil types (though this itself will vary due to various factors, including the crops grown and the level of technology available). Harmony with nature seems to have been an important issue in their culture and it seems to be that environmental and cultural elements were fundamentally intertwined to Bronze Age people in Korea. In consequence, the incidence of a proto-*Pungsu* way of thinking that encompassed a sociocultural-led approach to the environment in which Bronze Age communities existed, could be a mechanism by which to provide insights into the identity of the peoples of the Korean Bronze Age.

Finally, due to the fact that this research was conducted with a broader scope, in order to identify long-term changes in the study area on the basis of landscape archaeology, it was possible to show rough trends emerging from period to period. It was difficult to analyse at a more micro-level, allowing for an examination of communal or individual identities, as the data are patchy and as yet what there is has not been fully collated. Therefore, material culture investigations are needed to evaluate cultural exchanges and interactions as well as to trace detailed identities. In addition, another limitation is that the data from the 'Early to Middle', 'Early to Late' and 'Middle to Late' categories cannot be properly utilised in this analysis. These groups need other standards by which to analyse them. This analysis will be the next task to pursue and better independent chronologies for the monuments are required in order to reveal the structures of Bronze Age society. Also, the procurement of more isolated settlement information within the study area and across the border in North Korea will allow a comparative study to be undertaken with the results from this research. Finally, more palaeo-environmental evidence is needed to better place the onset of wet rice agriculture. This would reveal whether it coincides with the other changes identified in this research.

Bibliography

AHN, J. H. 2000. The formation of agricultural society in Korea. *The Journal of Korean Archaeological Society* 43 (In Korean).

AHN, S. M. 1993. Neolithic culture in Han River valley. *In:* CHOI, M. L., LEE, S. B., AHN, S. M. & PARK, S. B. (eds.) *The history of Han River valley.* Seoul: Minumsa.

AHN, S. M. 1998a. Cereals and Farming tools in Korean Prehistory. *In:* AHN, S. M. (ed.) *Prehistoric Farming and Subsistence in East Asia* Seoul: Hakyeon Publications (In Korean).

AHN, S. M. 1998b. Dietary life in Korean prehistory. *In:* AHN, S. M. (ed.) *Prehistoric Farming and Subsistence in East Asia* Seoul: Hakyeon Publication (In Korean).

AHN, S. M. 1998c. Neolithic agriculture in East Asia through cultivated crops. *Prehistoric Farming and Subsistence in East Asia* Seoul: Hakyeon Publications (In Korean).

AHN, S. M. 1998d. The outcomes and tasks of prehistoric farming in Korea. *Prehistoric Farming and Subsistence in East Asia* Seoul: Hakyeon Bublications (In Korean).

AHN, S. M. 1998e. The present conditions and future works of the Bronze Age in Korea. *Prehistoric Farming and Subsistence in East Asia.* Seoul: Hakyeon Publications (In Korean).

AHN, S. M. 1998f. Social aspects and subsistence economy of Gangwon province in the Neolithic period. *In:* AHN, S. M. (ed.) *Prehistoric Farming and Subsistence in East Asia* Seoul: Hakyeon Publication (In Korean).

ARCGIS 10 HELP. 2011a. *Analyze Visibility* [Online]. [Accessed 2nd, Aug. 2011].

ARCGIS 10 HELP. 2011b. *How Aspect works* [Online]. [Accessed 5th April 2012].

ARCGIS 10 HELP. 2011c. *Understanding cost distance analysis* [Online]. [Accessed 26th, Aug. 2011].

ARCGIS 10 HELP. 2011d. *Understanding path distance analysis* [Online]. [Accessed 26th, Aug. 2011].

ARCGIS.COM & ESRI.COM. *Deriving runoff characteristics* [Online]. Available: http://help.arcgis.com/en/arcgisdesktop/10.0/help/index.html#//009z0000005p000000.htm [Accessed 7 March 2008].

ARIMITSU, K. 1959. A study of Korean polished stone dagger. *In:* PUBLICATION COMMITTEE (ed.) *1990 The Collection of Arimitsu Kyoichi's Works.* Tokyo: Dongmyeong-sa (In Japanese).

BAE, G. D. & LEE, H. J. 2002. Bucheon Gogangdong Prehistoric site -The 5th excavation report. Seoul: Bucheon-si and The Institute of Cultural Properties, Hanyang University (In Korean).

BAR-YOSEF, O. 2011. The transition to cultivation in North and South China: a view from the Levant Part 1. Paper given at UCL, ICCAHA (International Centre for Chinese Heritage and Archaeology).

BARRETT, J., BRADLEY, R. & GREEN, M. 1991a. *Landscape, Monuments and Society.* Cambridge: Cambridge University Press.

BARRETT, J., BRADLEY, R. & GREEN, M. 1991b. *Papers on the Prehistory of Cranborne Chase.* Oxford: Oxbow books monograph 11.

BARTZ, P. M. 1972. *South Korea.* Oxford: Clarendon Press.

BAYLISS, A., BRONK RAMSEY, C., VAN DER PLICHT, J. & WHITTLE, A. 2007. Bradshaw and Bayes: Towards a timetable for the Neolithic. *Cambridge Archaeological Journal,* 17: 1-28.

BEAK, J. O. & OH, D. Y. 2007. The present condition and character of dolmens in Gyeonggi province. *A retrospective and prospective study of dolmens in Gyeonggi province.* Gyeonggi Provincial Museum (In Korean).

BOURDIEU, P. 1990b. The Logic of Practice. Trans. R. Nice Cambridge: Polity Press.

BRADLEY, R. 1998. *The Significance of Monuments: On the Shaping of Human Experience in Neolithic and Bronze Age Europe.* London, New York: Routledge.

BRADLEY, R. 2000. *An Archaeology of Natural Places.* London, New York: Routledge.

BRONK RAMSEY, C. 2009. Bayesian analysis of radiocrbon dates. *Radiocarbon,* 51: 337-360.

BRONK RAMSEY, C. 2009b. Dealing with outliers and offsets in radiocarbon dating. *Radiocarbon,* 51: 1023-1045.

BUCK, C. E., CHRISTEN, J. A., KENWORTHY, J. B. & LITTON, C. D. 1994. Estimating the duration of archaeological activity using 14C determinations. *Oxford Journal of Archaeology,* 13: 229-240.

BUCK, C. E., KENWORTHY, J. B., LITTON, C. D. & SMITH, A. F. M. 1991. Combining archaeological and radiocarbon information: a Bayesian approach to calibration. *Antiquity,* 65: 808-821.

BUCK, C. E., LITTON, C. D. & SMITH, A. F. M. 1992. Calibration of radiocarbon results pertaining to related archaeological events. *Journal of Archaeological Science,* 19: 497-512.

BUSAN UNIVERSITY MUSEUM 1993. Gimhae Yeanri Ancient tombs II. Busan: Busan University (In Korean).

CGIAR-CSI (CONSULTATIVE GROUP ON INTERNATIONAL AGRICULTURE RESEARCH - CONSORTIUM FOR SPATIAL INFORMATION). *DEM (SRTM 90m grid)* [Online]. Available: http://srtm.csi.cgiar.org/ [Accessed October 2008].

CHAPMAN, H. P. & GEAREY, B. R. 2000. Palaeoecology and the perception of prehistoric landscapes: some

comments on visual approaches to phenomenology. *Antiquity,* 74: 316-319.
CHAPMAN, R. 1981. The emergence of formal disposal areas and 'the' problem' of megalithic tombs in prehistoric Europe. *In:* CHAPMAN, R., KINNES, I. & RANDSBORG, K. (eds.) *The Archaeology of Death.* Cambridge: Cambridge University Press.
CHILDE, G. 1957. *The Dawn of European Civilization (6th ed).* London: Routledge & Kegan Paul LTD.
CHILDE, V. G. 1934. *New light on the most ancient East: The oriental Prelude to European Prehistory.* London: Kegan Paul.
CHISHOLM, M. 1966. *Rural Settlement and Land Use.* London: Hutchinson.
CHOE, C. J. 1992. *Where is the good place? The theory and practice of Korean Pungsu.* Seoul: Seohae munjip (In Korean).
CHOE, C. J. 1993. The discussion about the designation of 'Seoul' as the capital of the Joseon Dynasty on the basis of the 'True Record of the Joseon Dynasty'. *In:* CHOE, C. J., CHOI, W. S., SUNG, D. H., HAN, D. H. & GWON, S. J. (eds.) *Pungsu, Kŭsam ŭi chiri saengmyŏng ŭi chiri.* Seoul: Purŭn namu (In Korean).
CHOE, J. P. 1982. The diffusion route and chronology of Korean plant domestication. *The Journal of Asian Studies,* 41: 519-530.
CHOI, B. S. 2007. The study of historical and geographical characteristics of Daemo hillfort in Seoul. *In:* CHOI, M. L. (ed.) *The Archaeology of Gyeonggi Province.* Seoul: Juluesung (In Korean).
CHOI, G. L. 2001. The commencement of rice agriculture and natural environment. *In:* THE KOREAN ARCHAEOLOGICAL SOCIETY (ed.) *Korean Archaeological Conference.* Busan University: The Korean Archaeological Society (In Korean).
CHOI, G. P., HA, M. S., HWANG, B. G., LEE, G. J., CHOI, M. J. & RYU, Y. S. 2002a. Hanam Misadong. Seoul: Sejong University Museum and Hanam-si (In Korean).
CHOI, J. P., HA, M. S., HWANG, B. G., KIM, J. H., OH, D. Y. & MOON, C. H. 2007. Excavation Report of the Deukpung Vally in Hanam City. Seoul: Sejong University Museum and Hanam City (In Korean).
CHOI, J. P., HA, M. S., HWANGBO, K., CHOI, M. J. & RYU, Y. S. 2003a. The Dolmen in Yeoncheon. Seoul: Sejong University Museum (In Korean).
CHOI, J. P., HA, M. S., HWANGBO, K., CHOI, M. J. & RYU, Y. S. 2003b. Pyeongtaek Bangchuri. Seoul: Sejong University Museum.
CHOI, J. P., HA, M. S., HWANGBO, K., CHOI, M. J. & RYU, Y. S. 2005. Report on the Field Survey of Dolmen, Ganghwa. Seoul: Sejong University Museum, Ganghwa-Gun (In Korean).
CHOI, M. L. 1978. Types and Classification of Dolmens in South Heolla Region. *The Korean Historical Review (Yeoksa Hakbo),* 78: 1-50 (in Korean).
CHOI, M. L. 1981. Dolmen Societies and their Political Evolution in Chŏlla Namdo Province. *Han'guksa Yŏn'gu,* 35: 1-14 (In Korean).
CHOI, M. L. 1982. A Relative Chronology of the Archaeological materials discovered from Cholla-Namdo province, South-west Korea. *Jindan Hakpo,* 53: 1-10 (In Korean).
CHOI, M. L. 1984. *A Study of the Yongsan River Valley Culture: The rise of Chiefdom Society and State in Ancient Korea.* Seoul: Dong Song Sa.
CHOI, M. L. 1993. Baekje in Hanseong period. *In:* CHOI, M. L., LEE, S. B., AHN, S. M. & PARK, S. B. (eds.) *The history of Han River valley.* Seoul: Minumsa (In Korean).
CHOI, M. L. 1999. Originand Diffusion of Korean Dolmens. *In:* CHOI, M. L., LEE, C. G., LEE, Y. M. & LEE, S. J. (eds.) *The Synthetic Research and Study of Korean Dolmens site.* Seoul: Korean Cultural Properties Administration and Seoul National University Museum (In Korean).
CHOI, M. L. 2000. Origin and Diffusion of Korean Dolmens. *In:* CHOI, M. L. & KIM, S. W. (eds.) *The Theory and Method for the Study of Korean Dolmens.* Seoul: Juluesung (In Korean).
CHOI, M. L. 2003. A General Introduction. *In:* GUKSA PYEONCHAN WIWONHOE (ed.) *The History of Korea 1.* Guksa Pyeonchan Wiwonhoe.
CHOI, M. L. 2008a. *The Korean Bronze • Iron Age and the Restoration of Korean Ancient History.* Seoul: Juleusung (In Korean).
CHOI, M. L. 2008b. New perspectives in the research of the Korean Bronze, and Former & Later Iron Ages: The Origin of the Korean Culture and Northeast Asia in terms of the Polyhedral Theory and Establishing New Chronology *In:* CHOI, M. L. (ed.) *The Korean Bronze • Iron Age and the restoration of Korean ancient history (In Korean).* Seoul: Juleusung (In Korean).
CHOI, M. L. The new chronology of Songgukri site in Buyeo. Korean Bronge Age Society on the basis of Songguksi site in Buyeo, 1, Oct. 2010 The Korean National University of Cultural Heritage. The Korean National University of Cultural Heritage, Korean Ancient Historical Society (In Korean).
CHOI, M. L., CHOI, W. G. & SHIN, Y. W. 2002b. *Korean History: High School Textbook.* Seoul: Ministry of Education, Science and Technology (In Korean).
CHOI, M. L., LEE, C. G., LEE, Y. M. & LEE, S. J. 1999. *The Synthetic Research and Study of Korean Dolmens site.* Seoul: Korean Cultural Properties Administration and Seoul National University Museum (In Korean).
CHOI, M. L., LEE, S. B., AHN, S. M. & S.B., P. 1993. *The history of Han River valley.* Seoul: Minumsa (In Korean).
CHOI, M. L. & RHEE, S. N. 2001. Korean archaeology for the 21st Century: from Prehistory to State formation. *Seoul journal of Korean Studies,* 14: 117-147.
CHOI, N. S. 1927. From the worship of rock to the megalithic culture. *Donggwang*: 12-25 (As quoted in Woo. 2006: 19) (In Korean).
CHOI, S. K. 1987a. A view on the sites and artefacts before the establishment of archaeology. *In:* PUBLICATION COMMITTEE (ed.) *The collection of treatises in the*

celebration of retirement of Prof. Won-yong Kim I. Archaeology. Seoul: Iljisa (In Korean).
CHOI, S. R. 1987b. A characteristic of Plain pottery culture in Jeonnam region. *In:* PUBLICATION COMMITTEE (ed.) *The Collection of Treatises in the Celebration of Retirement of Prof. Won-yong Kim.* Seoul: Iljisa (In Korean).
CHOI, S. R. 1997. Iron age (1) Settlement. *In:* THE NATIONAL HISTORY COMPILATION COMMITTEE (ed.) *Korean History 3. Bronze Age and Iron Age.* Seoul: Tamgudang Munhwasa.
CONOLLY, J. & LAKE, M. 2006a. *Geographical Information Systems in Archaeology.* Cambridge: Cambridge University Press.
CONOLLY, J. & LAKE, M. 2006b. *Geographical nformation Systems in Archaeology.* Cambridge: CAmbridge University Press.
COONEY, G. 1983. Megalithic tombs in their environmental setting: A settlement perspective. *In:* REEVES-SMYTH, T. & HAMOND, F. (eds.) *Landscape Archaeology in Ireland.* Oxford: BAR British Series 116.
CRAWFORD, G. W. & LEE, G. A. 2003. Agricultural origins in the Korean Peninsula. *Antiquity,* 295: 87-95.
CULTURAL HERITAGE ADMINISTRATION. 2000. *Iseong-sanseong* [Online]. Available: http://www.cha.go.kr/korea/heritage/search/Culresult_Db_View.jsp?mc=NS_04_03_02&VdkVgwKey=13,04220000,31 [Accessed 27th Dec. 2011].
CUMMINGS, V. & FOWLER, C. (eds.) 2004. *The Neolithic of the Irish Sea: Materiality and traditions of practice,* Oxford: Oxbow Books.
CUMMINGS, V. & WHITTLE, A. 2003. Tombs with a view: landscape, monuments and trees. *Antiquity,* 77: 255-266.
DARVILL, T. 2004. *Long Barrows of the Cotswolds and Surrounding Areas.* Stroud: Tempus.
DEPARTMENT OF ARCHAEOLOGY AND ANTHROPOLOGY & THE UNIVERSITY MUSEUM SEOUL NATIONAL UNIVERSITY 1974. The Heunamri Site: A Prehistoric Village Site on the Han River. Seoul: Department of Archaeology and Anthropology and The University Museum, Seoul National University (In Korean).
DEPARTMENT OF ARCHAEOLOGY AND ANTHROPOLOGY & THE UNIVERSITY MUSEUM, S. N. U. 1976. The Heunamri Site 3: A Prehistoric Village Site on the Han River. . Seoul: Department of Archaeology and Anthropology and The University Museum, Seoul National University (In Korean).
DEPARTMENT OF ARCHAEOLOGY AND ANTHROPOLOGY & THE UNIVERSITY MUSEUM, S. N. U. 1978. The Heunamri Site 4: A Prehistoric Village Site on the Han River. Seoul: Department of Archaeology and Anthropology and The University Museum, Seoul National University (In Korean).
ESRI.COM. 2011. *World countries* [Online]. [Accessed 25th, Sept 2012].
FISHER, P., WOOD, J. & CHENG, T. 2004. *Where is Helvellyn? Fuzziness of Multiscale Landscape Morphometry* [Online]. Transactions of the Institute of British Geographers, 29(1): 106-128. Available: http://www.soi.city.ac.uk/~jwo/tibg/ [Accessed 6th, May 2011].
FLEMING, A. 1999a. Phenomenology and the megaliths of Wales: a dreaming too far? *Oxford Journal of Archaeology,* 18: 119-125.
FLEMING, A. 1999b. Phenomenology and the megaliths of Wales: a dreaming too far? . *Oxford Journal of Archaeology,* 18: 119-125.
FLEMING, A. 2005. Megaliths and post-modernism: the case of Wales. *Antiquity,* 79: 921-932.
FLEMING, A. 2006. Post-processual Landscape Archaeology: a Critique. *Cambridge Archaeological Journal,* 16: 267-280.
FRIED, M. H. 1967. *The Evolution of Political Society : An Essay in Political Anthropology.* New York: Random House.
FULLER, D. Q. & QIN, L. 2010. Declining oaks, increasing artistry, and cultivating rice: the environmental and social context of the emergence of farming in the Lower Yangtze Region. *Environmental Archaeology,* 15: 139-159.
GAFFNEY, V. & STANČIČ, Z. 1991. The Hvar case study. *GIS Approached to Regional Analysis: A Case Study of the Island of Hvar: Preface by Kenneth Kvanne.* Ljubljana: Znanstveni inštitut Filozofske fakultete.
GOSDEN, C. 1994. *Social Being and Time.* Oxford and Cambridge: Blackwell.
GOSDEN, C. 1999a. The organisation of society. *In:* BARKER, G. (ed.) *Companion Encyclopedia of Archaeology.* London: Routledge.
GOSDEN, C. 2006. Material Culture and Long-term Change. *In:* ROWLANDS, M., TILLEY, C. & SPYER, P. (eds.) *Handbook of Material Culture.* SAGE.
GOSDEN, C. 2011. English landscape and identities. Paper at the English Faculty, University of Oxford.
GOSDEN, C. & LOCK, G. 1998. Prehistoric histories. *World Archaeology,* 30: 2-12.
GOWLAND, W. 1895. Notes on the Dolmens and other Antiquities of Korea. *The journal of the Anthropological Institute of Great Britain and Ireland,* 24: 316-331.
GRÄSLUND, B. 1987. *The Birth of Prehistoric Chronology : Dating Methods and Dating Systems in Nineteenth-Century Scandinavian Archaeology.* Cambridge: Cambridge University Press.
GWACHEON CULTURAL CENTRE. 1991. *Mountains in Gwacheon* [Online]. Gwacheon. Available: http://www.gccc.or.kr/source/data/gc/data_list_view2.html?Dsdv=3&Dsid=139 [Accessed 2012 17th, April].
GWAK, J. C. Prehistory and ancient rice and dry field in Korea. The Formation of Agriculture in Korea, 2001 Busan University. The Korean Archaeological Society, 21-73 (In Korean).

GWON, D. H. 2011. *Korean Landform.* Paju: Hanwul Academy (In Korean).
GWON, O. Y., LEE, H. W., SHIN, S. H. & PARK, J. G. 2007. *Excavation Report on the Settlement of the Bronze Age of Bansongri, Hwaseong.* Osan: Hanshin University Museum (In Korean).
GYEONGGI INSTITUTE OF CULTURAL PROPERTIES & GYEONGGI PROVINCIAL MUSEUM 2009. *The Gyeonggi Excavations: 10 Years of Discovery.* Seoul: Gyeonggi Institute of Cultural Properties and Gyeonggi Provincial Museum (In Korean).
GYEONGGI PROVINCIAL MUSEUM. 2001. *The Distribution Map of Cultural Sites in the Imjin River Valley (1:100,000).* Yongin: Gyeonggi Provincial Museum (In Korean).
GYEONGGI PROVINCIAL MUSEUM. 2002. *The Distribution Map of Cultural Sites in the Han River Valley (1:100,000).* Yongin: Gyeonggi Provincial Museum (In Korean).
GYEONGGI PROVINCIAL MUSEUM 2007. *Dolmens in Gyeonggido.* Seoul: Gyeonggi provincial museum (In Korean)
GYEONGSANGNAM-DO & DONG-A UNIVERSITY MUSEUM. 1999. Cultural Remains of the Nam River (In Korean).
HA, M. S. 1985. *A Study of Korean Dolmen Culture.* MA dissertation (In Korean), Yonsei University.
HA, M. S. 1988. A comparative research on dolmen culture between Guem river and Namhan river. *In:* PUBLICATION COMMITTEE (ed.) *The Collection of Archaeology and Anthropology Treatises in the Celebration of Retirement of Prof. Bo-Gi Son.* Seoul: Jisiksanupsa (In Korean).
HA, M. S. 1997. *Studies on the Aortheast Asian Dolmen Culture.* PhD thesis (In Korean), Soongsil University.
HA, M. S. 1999. *The Dolmen of Old Choson: centering around the dolmens of Liaoning and Jilin Provinces in China and the northern region of the Korean Peninsula.* Seoul: Baeksan Jaryowon (In Korean).
HA, M. S. 2004. Mangwol-dong settlement site. *In:* NATIONAL RESEARCH INSTITUTE OF CULTURAL HERITAGE KOREA (ed.) *Dictionary of Korean Archaeology-Bronze Age-.* Seoul: Hakyeon Munhwasa.
HA, M. S. 2007. Dolmen culture in the basin of the Namhan river. *In:* GYEONGGI PROVINCIAL MUSEUM (ed.) *Dolmens in Gyeonggido.* (In Korean).
HA, M. S., KIM, J. Y. & LEE, J. Y. 2004. New perspectives on natural environment of dolmen sites based on the model of GIS: centering on Yeoncheon area. *Gijeongogo,* 4**:** 277-299 (In Korean).
HAN, B. S., KIM, J. C., JIN, H. S., CHOI, S. K., JEONG, Y. H., SON, B. G., LEE, Y. J., LEE, H. G., JO, Y. J., HWANG, Y. H., KIM, J. B., IM, B. T., JI, G. G. & CHOI, M. L. 1974. The Synthetic Research Report of the submerged districts by *Paldang·Soyang* Dam. Korean Cultural Properties Administration (In Korean).
HAN, D. H. 1993. You can see the site for living, if you know Pungsu. *In:* CHOI, C. J. (ed.) *Pungsu, Kŭsam ŭi chiri saengmyŏng ŭi chiri.* Seoul: Purŭn namu (In Korean).
HEO, M. H. 1991. The origin and transmission of cultivated rice in Korea. *Journal of Korean Archaeological Society,* 27**:** 59-95 (In Korean).
HODDER, I. 1984. Burials, houses, women and men in the European Neolithic. *In:* MILLER, D. & TILLEY, C. (eds.) *Ideology, Power and Prehistory.* Cambridge: Cambridge University Press.
HODDER, I. 1990. *The Domestication of Europe: Structure and Contingency in Neolithic Societies.* Cambridge: Blackwell.
HODDER, I. & HUTSON, S. 2003. *Reading the Past: Current Approaches to Interpretation in Archaeology (3rd edition).* Cambridge: Cambridge University Press.
HUDSON, M. J. 1992. Rice, Bronze, and Chieftains: An archaeology of Yayoi Ritual. *Japanese Journal of Religious Studies,* 19**:** 139-189.
IM, H. J. 1978. The Hunamri Site 4: A prehistoric village-site on the Han River progress report 1976, 1977. Seoul: The University Museum and Department of Archaeology, Seoul National University.
IM, H. J. 2005a. Agriculture in Korean prehistory *In:* IM, H. J. (ed.) *Development of Korean Neolithic Culture.* Seoul: Hakyeon Publications, (In Korean).
IM, H. J. 2005b. *Development of Korean Neolithic Culture.* Seoul: Hakyeon Publications (In Korean).
IM, H. J., CHOI, J. T., YOON, S. D. & JANG, E. J. 2000. Acha-Sanseong. Seoul: Institute of Humanities, Seoul National University (In Korean).
IM, H. J., KIM, S. N. & LEE, J. M. 2002a. Excavation Report of Hwasung Gogumsan Site. Seoul: Seoul Nstional University Museum (In Korean).
IM, H. J., KIM, S. N. & LEE, J. M. 2002b. Hwaseong Gogeumsan site. Seoul: Seoul National University Museum.
IM, H. J. & YANG, S. H. 1999. Dolmens in Kanghwa Island. Seoul: The Institute of Humaanities in Seoul National University and Kanghwa County (In Korean).
INCHEON METROPOLITAN CITY & CULTURAL HERITAGE INVESTIGATION COMMITTEE 2002. *Cultural Heritage in Ganghwa.* Incheon: Incheon Metropolitan City and Jogye Order of Korean Buddhism Cultural Heritage Investigation Committee (In Korean).
INCHEON METROPOLITAN CITY COUNCIL & INHA UNIVERSITY MUSEUM 2005. Daegokdong Dolmens. Incheon: Incheon Metropolitan City Council and Inha University Museum (In Korean).
INGOLD, T. 1994. Introduction to culture. *In:* INGOLD, T. (ed.) *Companion Encyclopedia of Anthropology.* London, New York: Routledge.
JANG, G. H., KIM, S. T., KIM, A. G., SEO, B. S. & SEO, G. D. 2002a. *Siheung Gyesu-dong Angol site.* Suwon: Siheung-si and Gijeon Cultural Properties Institute (In Korean).
JANG, G. H., KIM, S. T., KIM, S. S., KIM, Y. H. & SEO, G. D. 2004. *Suwon Yuljeon-dong Site.* Suwon:

Gijeon Cultural Properties Institute and Korea Housing Company (In Korean).
JANG, G. H., KIM, S. T., SO, S. Y., KIM, G. T., SEO, G. D. & KIM, H. S. 2002b. *Anyang Gwanyang-dong Prehistoric Site Excavation Report.* Suwon: Gijeon Cultural Properties Institute and Korea Water Resources Company (In Korean).
JEON, H. T. 2004. *The World of Koguryo mural paintings.* Seoul: Seoul national university press (In Korean).
JEONG, G. H. 1981. Dangun society and Bronze culture. *Hanguk Hakbo,* 23.
JI, G. G. 1982. A Study of the Dolmen Distributed on the Northeastern Asia. *Journal of Korean Archaeological Studies (Hanguk Gogo hakbo),* 12: 245-261 (In Korean).
JI, G. G. 1987a. The megalithic culture of the East and the West. *In:* PUBLICATION COMMITTEE (ed.) *The collection of treatises in the celebration of retirement of Prof. Won-yong Kim. Part 1.* Seoul: Iljisa (In Korean).
JI, G. G. 1987b. The megalithic culture of the East and the West. *The collection of treatises in the celebration of retirement of Prof. Won-yong Kim. Part 1. (In Korean)* Seoul: Iljisa.
JIANG, L. & LIU, L. 2006. New evidence for the origins of sedentism and rice domestication in the Lower Yangzi River, China. *Antiquity,* 80: 355-361.
JO, H. L. 2000. Nature and Human geography. *In:* ARRANGEMENT COMMITTEE FOR 29TH INTERNATIONAL GEOGRAPHICAL CONFERENCE (ed.) *Geography of Korea.* Seoul: Gyohaksa (In Korean).
JO, Y. J. 1992. Bronze Age. *In:* CHOI, M. L., JO, Y. J., BAE, G. D., SHIN, S. J. & LEE, S. J. (eds.) *The History of Research on the Korean Prehistory and Archaeology (Hanguk Seonsa Gogohak sa).* Seoul: Kkachi Publisher (In Korean).
KANG, D. S. 2002a. *The Study of a Settlement Pattern of Dolmen Society in the Northern Part of Ganghwa.* MA dissertation Seogang University (In Korean).
KANG, D. S. 2002b. The analysis of structure and distribution of dolmens in Ganghwa. *The Journal of Inha University Museum,* 4: 43-64 (In Korean).
KANG, D. S. 2007. Dolmens in Ganghwa Island. *In:* GYEONGGI PROVINCIAL MUSEUM (ed.) *Dolmens in Gyeonggido.* Yongin: Gyeonggi provincial museum.
KANG, I. K., LEE, G. M., HAN, Y. H. & LEE, G. S. 1979. *Songguk-ri.* Seoul: National Museum of Korea (In Korean).
KIM, B. C. 2005. Middle Bronze Age Regional Settlement Patterns in the Middle and Lower of Geum River. *The Journal of Korean Archaeological Society* 57: 99-124 (In Korean).
KIM, B. C. 2006a. Household Archaeology of Songgukri-Type Settlements in the Lower and Middle Reaches of Geum River: Analysis of Household Wealth/Status Variabllity Using MDS. *Journal of the Korean Archaeological Society,* 51: 79-108 (In Korean).
KIM, B. C. 2006b. The Political Economy of Wet-rice production in the Bronze Age, Central-western Korea. *The Journal of Korean Archaeological Society,* 58: 40-65 (In Korean).
KIM, B. C. 2011. Dwelling patterns and Household developmental cycle during the Early Bronze Age: With special reference to Yeoksam-dong and Heunamri-type settlements of Hoseo rigion. *Journal of Korean Ancient Historical Society (Hanguk Sanggosa Hakbo),* 72: 31-60 (In Korean).
KIM, B. M. 1981. The study of the Megalithic culture origin in Korea *The Journal of Korean Archaeological Society,* 10·11: 55-78 (In Korean).
KIM, G. T. 2002a. *A study of the Boseong river valley culture: The growth of complex society in southwest Korea.* PhD., The Graduate School of the University of Oregon.
KIM, J. B. 1975. Bronze Artifacts in Korea and their Cultural Historical Significance. *In:* PETER H. LEE (ed.) *The Traditional Culture and Society of Korea: Prehistory.* Honolulu: The Center of Korean Studies, University of Hawaii.
KIM, J. B. 1987a. The Bronze Age Culture. *A Guide to the Study of Korean History (Hanguksa yeongoo immune).* Seoul: Jisik Sanupsa (In Korean).
KIM, J. H. 1978a. *Prehistory of Korea.* Honolulu: The University of Hawaii.
KIM, J. H. 1978b. A study of Bronze Age Culture in Korea. *Hanguk Kogo Hakbo (Journal of Korean Archaeological Studies),* 5: 1-16 (In Korean).
KIM, J. H. 1984. The sovereign area on the basis of archaeology. *Jeongshin Munwha Yeongu,* 21 45-56 (In Korean).
KIM, J. H. 1987b. The Gojoseon on the basis of archaeology. *In:* THE ACADEMY OF KOREAN STUDIES (ed.) *Hanguk sanggosaui jemunje.* Seoul: The Academy of Korean Studies (Hanguk Jeonsin Munhwa Yeonguwon).
KIM, J. I. 2002b. An Archaeology of Death. *Seoul Journal of Korean Studies,* 15: 101-128.
KIM, J. S. 2001. Reconsidering the Heunamri Assemblages: Origin and Date. *Youngnam Archaeology,* 28: 35-64 (In Korean).
KIM, J. W. 2008. Mountainous morphology. *In:* KIM, J. W., LEE, M. B., KONG, W. S. & KIM, T. H. (eds.) *Physical Geography of Korea.* Seoul: Seoul National University Press (In Korean).
KIM, J. W. & YUN, M. B. 1967. The Okseok-ri site *In:* NATIONAL MUSEUM OF KOREA (ed.) *A Study of Korean Dolmens.* Seoul: National Museum of Korea Publications (In Korean).
KIM, K. O., LEE, C. G., G.G., L., YOON, Y. I., JO, E. J., YU, H. J. & EDITED BY WHITFIELD, R. 2004. *Dictionary of Korean Art and Archaeology.* Seoul: Hollym International Corp. (In Korean).
KIM, S. H. 5th, Feb. 2007. *The optimum condition of high quality rice production in Korea* [Online]. Seoul: The Agriculture, Fisheries, and Livestock News. Available: http://www.aflnews.co.kr/aflnews/news/news_contents.asp?news_code=2007020501119&c_code=0103 [Accessed 4th, May 2011].

KIM, S. O. 2006c. Chronology and social changes in dwellings in the Korean Bronze Age. *Journal of Korean Archaeological Society,* 60: 4-37 (In Korean).

KIM, W. Y. 1961a. A bronze dagger tomb of Shiertaiyingzi. *Yeoksa Hakbo,* 16: 109-121 (In Korean).

KIM, W. Y. 1981a. Korean Archaeology Today. *Korean Journal,* 21: 21-43.

KIM, W. Y. 1982. Discoveries of Rice in Prehistoric Sites in Korea. *The Journal of Asian Studies,* 41: 513-518.

KIM, W. Y. 1986a. *Introduction to Korean Archaeology.* Seoul: Iljisa (In Korean).

KIM, W. Y. 1986b. *The Korean Archaeology Outline.* Seoul: Iljisa.

KIM, W. Y. 2002c. *Introduction to Korean Archaeology.* Seoul: Iljisa (In Korean).

KIM, W. Y., IM, H. J. & CHOI, M. L. 1972·1973. The Hunamri Site. Seoul: Seoul National University Dept. of Archaeology and Art history (In Korean).

KIM, Y. S. & IM, B. T. 1968. Yeoksamdong settlement excavation report. *Sahak yeongu,* 20: 23-51 (In Korean).

KO, I. H. 2010. Reconsideraing Early Bronze Age Farming Strategies: A critical examination of Slash and Burn Farming. *The Journal of Korean Ancient Historical Society,* 67: 25-44 (In Korean).

KOO, J. J. 2005. A study of the Daecheon-ri Neolithic Dwelling Site at Okcheon-gun. *The Journal of Korean Ancient Historical Society,* 47: 5-36 (In Korean).

KOREA INSTITUTE OF HERITAGE & YM CONSTRUCTION CO. LTD. (eds.) 2008. *Sosa-site in Korea,* Seoul: Korea Institute of Heritage.

KREI: KOREA RURAL ECONOMIC INSTITUTE 한국농촌경제연구원. Available: http://www.krei.re.kr/kor/info/infor_qnaview.php?bn_idx=5121&cpage=1& [Accessed 25 January 2011.

KUNA, M. & ADELSBERGERROVÁ, D. 1995. Prehistoric location preferences: an application of GIS to the Vinorsky potok project, Bohemia, the Czech Republic. *In:* LOCK, G. & STANCIC, Z. (eds.) *Archaeology and Geographical Information Systems: A European Perspective.* London Taylor & Francis.

LEE, B. G. 1974a. The excavated plain potteries and polished stone tools in Gyeonggi province. *Archaeology,* 3.

LEE, B. G. 1974b. *A study on plain coarse pottery from Kyunggido area.* M.A., Seoul National University (In Korean).

LEE, B. G. 1984. On the excavated artefects in Heunam-ri. *The 60th Anniversary Collection of Dr. Yoon, M.B.* Seoul: Toncheon Munhwasa (In Korean).

LEE, B. G. 1986. On the chronology of early plain pottery in the Han river basin. *Youngnam Archaeology,* 2: 31-57 (In Korean).

LEE, C. G. 1988. The cultural development of plain pottery in South Korea and the Gong-yeol pottery culture. *The Journal of Korean Ancient Historical Society,* 1: 37-92 (In Korean).

LEE, G. M. 1987a. *The Study of Korean Ritual Artefacts.* Hanyang University (In Korean).

LEE, G. M. 1992a. Korean type bronze dagger culture. *The Bronze Culture in Korea.* Seoul: Bumwoo Publishing Co. (In Korean).

LEE, G. M. 1992b. Liaoning type bronze dagger culture in Korea. *The Bronze Culture in Korea.* Seoul: Bumwoo Publishing Co. (In Korean).

LEE, H. G. 1987b. The study of dolmens in the Balhae coast region. *Jeongshinmunwha Yeongoo,* 32: 203-221 (In Korean).

LEE, H. W. 2009. *Settlement Patterns and Social Structures in Korean Bronze Age.* Seoul: Seogyeong Publishing Company (In Korean).

LEE, J. M. 2004. A study on the relationship betweeen Yeoksamdong and Songgungni assemblages in Cetral Korea. *Journal of the Korean Archaeological Society,* 54: 35-62 (In Korean).

LEE, J. M. 2005a. The study of Early and Middle plain pottery period in middle part of Korea. *In:* ARCHAEOLOGICAL ENVIRONMENT INSTITUTE AT THE KOREA UNIVERSITY (ed.) *The cultural system of agricultural society through the Songguk-ri culture.* (In Korean).

LEE, K. B., TRANSLATED BY, WAGNER, E. W. & SHULTZ, E. J. 1984. *A New History of Korea.* Seoul: Iljogak (In Korean).

LEE, N. G., GWON, O. Y., LEE, H. W., LEE, G. S., SHIN, S. H., JO, S. S. & KIM, Y. J. 2006. *Excavation Report on the Settlement of the Bronze Age of Cheoncheon-Ri, Hwaseong.* Osan: Hanshin University Museum (In Korean).

LEE, N. S., LEE, H. & LEE, H. S. 1998a. *Baekseok-dong site.* Gongju: Gongju University Museum•Chungcheong namdo Cheonan-si (In Korean).

LEE, N. S., LEE, H. & LEE, H. S. 1998b. Baekseok-dong site. Cheonan: Gongju University Museum.

LEE, S. G. 2003. The Dwelling Transitions and Structural Features in the Neolithic Age of the Korean Peninsula. *Gomunhwa,* 61: 3-29 (In Korean).

LEE, S. G. 2005b. *New trend of Korean Neiolithic culture.* Seoul: Hakyeon Publishing company.

LEE, S. G. 2005c. *The New Trend of Neolithic Culture in the Korean Peninsula.* Seoul: Hakyeon Munhwasa (In Korean).

LEE, S. J. 1992c. Neolithic Period. *In:* CHOI, M. L., JO, Y. J., BAE, G. D., SHIN, S. J. & LEE, S. J. (eds.) *The history of research on the Korean prehistory and archaeology (Hanguk Seonsa Gogohak sa).* Seoul: Kkachi publisher (In Korean).

LEE, S. Y. 2007. The study of enclosure character in Gyeonggi region. *In:* CHOI, M. L. (ed.) *The Archaeology of Gyeonggi Province.* Seoul: Juluesung (In Korean).

LEE, W. P. (ed.) 2002a. *Dictionary of Geography terms,* Seoul: Shinwonbook (In Korean).

LEE, Y. M. 1993. *A Study of Dolmen Society in Jeonnam Region.* PhD. Thesis, Korea National University of Education (In Korean).

LEE, Y. M. 1999. Dolmens in Hwasun. *In:* CHOI, M. L., LEE, C. G., LEE, Y. M. & LEE, S. J. (eds.) *The*

Synthetic Research and Study of Korean Dolmens site. Seoul: Korean Cultural Properties Administration, Seoul National University Museum (In Korean).

LEE, Y. M. 2002b. *A study of Dolmen Society in Korea.* Seoul: Hakyeon Munhwasa (In Korean).

LOCK, G. 2009. Human activity in a spatial context. *In:* CUNLIFFE, B., GOSDEN, C. & JOYCE, R. A. (eds.) *The Oxford Handbook of Archaeology.* Oxford University Press.

LOCK, G. & BELL, T. 2000. Topographic and cultural influences on walking the Ridgeway in later prehistoric times. *In:* LOCK, G. (ed.) *Beyond the Map.* Amsterdam, Oxford: IOS Press.

LOCK, G. & DALY, P. 1999. Looking at Change, Continuity and Time in GIS: an example from the Sangro Valley, Italy. *In:* BARCELÓ, J. A., BRIZ, I. & VILA, A. (eds.) *New Techniques for Old Times CAA 98: Computer Applications and Quantitative Methods in Archaeology, Proceeding of the 26th Conference, Barcelona, March 1998.* Oxford: BAR International Series 757.

LOCK, G. & POUNCETT, J. 2010. Walking the Ridgeway Revisited: The methodological implications of scale dependency for the derivation of slope and the calculation of least-cost pathways. *In:* FRISCHER, B., CRAWFORD, J. W. & KOLLER, D. (eds.) *Making History Interactive: Computer Applications and Quantitative Methods in Archaeology (CAA).* Oxford: BAR International Series 2079.

LOCK, G. & STANČIČ, Z. 1995. *Archaeology and Geographical Information Systems-A European Perspective.* London: Taylor & Francis.

MCCLINTOCK, J. 2006. *The Stonehenge Companion.* London: English Heritage.

MIN, D. S. 1997. Defence facilities. *In:* THE NATIONAL HISTORY COMPILATION COMMITTEE (ed.) *Korean History 3. Bronze Age and Iron Age.* Seoul: Tamgudang Munhwasa (In Korean).

MIYAZATO, O. 2005. Settlement patterns of Yeoksam-dong assemblage in Cetral-western Korea. *Journal of the Korean Archaeological Society,* 56: 49-92 (In Korean).

NAHM, A. C. 1996. *Korea: Tradition & Transformation (the 2nd edition).* New Jersey, Seoul: Hollym International Corp.

NATIONAL MUSEUM OF KOREA 1992. *The Bronze Culture in Korea.* Seoul: Bumwoo Publishing Co. (In Korean).

NATIONAL MUSEUM OF KOREA 1993. *Pre- & Proto-Historic Pottery of Korea.* Seoul: Sinyu Publisher (In Korean).

NATIONAL RESEARCH INSTITUTE OF CULTURAL HERITAGE KOREA 2004. *Dictionary of Korean Archaeology-Bronze Age-.* Seoul: Hakyeon munhwasa (In Korean).

NATIONAL RESEARCH INSTITUTE OF CULTURAL PROPERTIES KOREA 2001. *Dictionary of Korean Archaeology.* Seoul: Hakyeon munhwasa (In Korean).

NELSON, S. M. 1993. *The Archaeology of Korea.* Cambridge: Cambridge University Press.

OH, C. K. 1958. *Handbook of Korea.* New York: Pageant Press, INC.

PARK, H. H. 1984. The study of Korean dolmen culture. *The study of Korean history (Hanguksa yeongu),* 46.

PARK, S. H. 2006. A Study on the Locational Pattern of Settlement in the Bronze Age-in the Midwest of the Korean Peninsula- *Journal of Korean Ancient Historical Society (Hanguk Sanggosa Hakbo),* 54: 21-46 (In Korean).

PARK, S. J., GWON, H. S. & LEE, Y. J. 1996. *Pyeongtaek Hyeonhwari site.* Pyeongtaek: Pyeontaek-si and Prehistoric Culture Institute at Chungbuk University (In Korean).

PEARSON, G. W. & STUIVER, M. 1986. High-precision calibration of the radiocarbon time scale, 500-2500 BC. *Radiocarbon,* 28: 839-862.

POUNCETT, J. 2009. Workshop 2: Inter site spatial analysis. Oxford: Institute of Archaeology.

PRICE, N. 2011. Shamanism. *In:* INSOLL, T. (ed.) *The Archaeology of Ritual and Religion.* Oxford: Oxford University Press.

REIMER, P. J., BAILLIE, M. G. L., BARD, E., BAYLISS, A., BECK, J. W., BLACKWELL, P. G., BRONK RAMSEY, C., BUCK, C. E., BURR, G. S., EDWARDS, R. L. E., FRIEDRICH, M., GROOTES, P. M., GUILDERSON, T. P., HAJDAS, I., HEATON, T. J., HOGG, A. G., HUGHEN, K. A., KAISER, K. F., KROMER, B., MCCORMAC, F. G., MANNING, S. W., REIMER, W. R., RICHARDS, D. A., SOUTHON, J. R., TALAMO, S., TURNEY, C. S. M., VAN DER PLICHT, J. & WEYHENMEYER, C. E. 2009. IntCal09 and Marine09 Radiocarbon Age Calibration Curves, 0–50,000 Years cal BP. *Radiocarbon,* 51: 1111–1150.

RENFREW, C. 1976. Megaliths, territiriesand populations. *In:* DELAET, S. J. (ed.) *Accultration and continuity in Atlantic Europe.* Brugge: De Tempel. .

SAMPIETRO VATTUONE, M. M., NEDER, L., ROLDAN, J. & VATTUONE, M. A. 2008. Mother Earth: soil and people relationships during the prehistoric period (Northwest Argentina). *World Archaeology,* 40: 190-205.

SCHULTING, R. 2004. An Irish sea change: some implications for the Mesolithic-Neolithic transition. *In:* CUMMINGS, V. & FOWLER, C. (eds.) *The Neolithic of the Irish Sea: Materiality and traditions of practice.* Oxford: Oxbow books.

SCHULTING, R. J. 1998. *Slighting the Sea: The Mesolithic-Neolithic Transition in Northeast Europe.* PhD., University of Reading.

SCHULTING, R. J. 2009. Archaeological Practical. Institute of Archaeology, University of Oxford.

SEOK, G. J. 2002. *The study of dolmens in Joseon.* Seoul: Joongsim Publisher (In Korean).

SEONG, N. J. 1997. Burials. *In:* THE NATIONAL HISTORY COMPILATION COMMITTEE (ed.) *Korean History 3. Bronze Age and Iron Age.* Seoul: Tamgudang Munhwasa (In Korean).

SERVICE, E. R. 1962. *Primitive Social Organization : An Evolutionary Perspective.* . New York Random House

SEUNG, C. T., LEE, S. J., TSUCHIDA, J. K. & CHOI, G. H. 2007. *Hwaseong Banwoldong.* Daejeon: Paekjae Research Institute, Chungnam National University (In Korean).

SHIM, B. G. 1991. The rice cultivation of Korean prehistory. *The Journal of Korean Archaeological Society* 27: 5-57 (In Korean).

SHIN, S. J. 1992. The natural environment of Neolithic period in Korea. *The Journal of Korean Ancient Historical Society,* 10: 17-81 (In Korean).

SIM, B. G. 1981. Relationship between the dolmens of Korea and Japan. *Journal of Korean Archaeological Studies,,* 10•11: 79-108.

SIM, B. G. 1999. Japan. *In:* CHOI, M. L., LEE, C. G., LEE, Y. M. & LEE, S. J. (eds.) *The Synthetic Research and Study of Korean Dolmens site.* Seoul: Korean Cultural Properties Administration and Seoul National University Museum (In Korean).

SON, B. H. 1987. The burial of Korean prehistory. *In:* PUBLICATION COMMITTEE (ed.) *The Collection of Treatises in the Celebration of Retirement of Prof. Won-yong Kim. Part 1.* Seoul: Iljisa (In Korean).

SON, J. T. 1934. The study of Joseon dolmens. *Gaebyeok (The Creation),* 1: 16-26 (In Korean).

SON, J. T. 1948. The research of Chosen dolmens. *The study of Joseon national culture*: 1-41.

SONG, H. J. 1990. *The Study of the Location of Gojoseon and Its' Ethnic Group.* M.A. dissertation, Seoul National University (In Korean).

SONG, H. J., LEE, B. H., KIM, D. J., KIM, J. C. & KIM, H. J. 2004. *Historical Atlas of Korea.* Seoul: Sagyejeol.

SONG, M. Y. The structuture and transform of village at the formative period of agriculture in South Korea. The formation of agriculture in Korea, 2001 Busan University. The Korean Archaeological Society 75-108 (In Korean).

SONG, M. Y., LEE, S. H. & PARK, G. S. 2002. Yeoncheon Samgeori site. Kyonggi provincial museum.

STOUT, G. & STOUT, M. 2008. *Newgrange.* Cork: Cork Univsersity Press.

STUIVER, M. & PEARSON, G. W. 1986. High-precision calibration of the radiocarbon time scale, AD 1950-500 BC. *Radiocarbon,* 28: 805-838.

THE ACADEMY OF KOREAN STUDIES. 1991. *Anseong brassware* [Online]. Seoul: Woongjin publisher. Available: http://terms.naver.com/entry.nhn?docId=579809 [Accessed 2nd, April 2012].

THE KOREAN OVERSEAS INFORMATION SERVICE 2003. *Handbook of Korea (11th edition).* Seoul: The Korean Overseas Information Service.

THE NATIONAL ACADEMY OF AGRICULTURAL SCIENCE (NAAS), R. D. A. I. K. *'Heuktoram'* 흙토람 [Online]. Available: http://asis.rda.go.kr [Accessed 14 August 2010].

TILLEY, C. 1994. *A Phenomenology of Landscape: Places, Paths and Monuments.* Oxford: Berg.

TRIGGER, B. 1990. Monumental architecture: a thermodynamic explanation of symbolic behaviour. *World Archaeology,* 22: 119-132.

TURUMOTO, T. & NAITOU, Y. 1989. Disease and trauma. *In:* NAGAI, M., KOBAYASHI, K., KANASEKI, H. & SAHARA, M. (eds.) *The study of Yayoi culture 1. Yayoi people and their environment.* Tokyo: Youzan kaku.

VITA-FINZI, C. & HIGGS, E. S. 1970. Prehistoric economy in the Mount Carmel area of Palestine: Site Catchment Analysis. *Proceedings of the Prehistoric Society.* Cambridge: Department of Archaeology and Anthropology. University of Cambridge. .

WHEATLEY, D. & GILLINGS, M. 2000. Vision, perception and GIS: developing enriched approaches to the study of archaeological visibility. *In:* LOCK, G. (ed.) *Beyond the Map.* Amsterdam and Oxford: IOS press.

WHEATLEY, D. & GILLINGS, M. 2002. *Spatial Technology and Archaeology: The Archaeological Applications of GIS.* London, New York: Taylor & Francis.

WHITTLE, A. 2003. *The Archaeology of People.* London and New York: Routledge.

WHITTLE, A., BARCLAY, A., BAYLISS, A., MCFADYEN, L., SCHULTING, R. J. & WYSOCKI, M. 2007. Building for the Dead: Events, Processes and Changing Worldviews from the Thirty-eighth to the Thirty-fourth Centuries cal. BC in Southern Britain. *Cambridge Archaeological Journal,* 17: 123-147.

WHITTLE, A., POLLARD, J. & GRIGSON, C. 1999. *The Harmony of Symbols: The Windmill Hill Causewayed Enclosure, Wiltshire.* Oxford: Oxbow.

WOO, J. M. 2005. *A Study on Dolmen culture in Gyeonggi Region.* PhD, Gyeonggi University (In Korean).

WOO, J. M. 2006. *A Study of Dolmens in Geyonggi Region: Dolmens in Geyonggi, Seoul, and Incheon.* Seoul: Hakyeon Publications (In Korean).

WOOD, J. 1996. *Morphometric Characterisation in The Geomorphological Characterisation of Digital Elevation Models, PhD Thesis, University of Leicester* [Online]. City University, London. Available: http://www.soi.city.ac.uk/~jwo/phd/05feat.php [Accessed 6th, May 2011].

YI, S. B. 1988. *Introduction to Archaeology.* Seoul: Iseonggwa Shilcheon (in Korea).

YI, S. H., KIM, J. Y., YANG, D. Y., OH, K. C. & HONG, S. S. 2008. Mid- and Late-Holocene palynofloral and environmental change of Korean central region. *SienceDirect,* 176-177: 112-120.

YONHAP NEWS AGENCY 1997. *Korea Annual. 34th Annual Edition.* Seoul: Yonhap News Agency (In Korean).

YOON, S. Y. & LEE, H. J. 1994. *Misari.* Seoul: Misari site excavation committee and Gyeonggi province public management committee (In Korean).

YU, T. Y. 2001. *A Study of Dolmen Society in Prehistoric Korea: Focused on the Problems of Social Stratification of Dolmen Building Society.* Hanyang University (In Korean).

YU, T. Y. 2002. Construction of dolmens and the formation of the chiefdom society in Ganghwa Island. *The Journal of Inha University Museum,* 4: 13-42 (In Korean).

YU, T. Y. 2003. *A study of dolmen society in Korea.* Seoul: Juluesung Publishing Co. (In Korean).

Appendix 1

THE RADIOCARBON DATES (CALIBRATED BY OXCAL 4.0) OF NEOLITHIC SITES IN KOREA (IM, 2005: 101-103)

Site	Site of type	Material	Lab. No.	Date BP	±	+1σ cal BC	-1σ cal BC	+2σ cal BC	-2σ cal BC
Amsa-dong	structure (10th)	Charcoal	KAERI-188	5510	110	-4483	-4241	-4584	-4050
Amsa-dong	structure (2th)	Charcoal	KAERI-189	5000	70	-3937	-3703	-3950	-3659
Amsa-dong	structure (4th)	Charcoal	KAERI-?	4871	200	-3941	-3378	-4225	-3097
Amsa-dong	structure (5th)	Charcoal	KAERI-?	4610	200	-3632	-3095	-3907	-2876
Amsa-dong	structure (1975)	Charcoal	N	6230	110	-5315	-5050	-5469	-4934
Amsa-dong	structure (1975)	Charcoal	N	6050	105	-5201	-4801	-5283	-4714
Amsa-dong	structure (1975)	Charcoal	AERILK	4950	200	-3975	-3521	-4315	-3196
Misa-ri	IV layer	Charcoal	KSU-497	5100	140	-4041	-3712	-4243	-3640
Si-do	III district	Charcoal	AERILK-11	3049	59	-1405	-1221	-1433	-1128
Si-do	stone grave	Charcoal	AERILK-12	2870	60	-1129	-934	-1260	-901
Si-do	stone grave	Charcoal	AERILK-13	3100	60	-1436	-1299	-1500	-1211
Soya-do		Shell	KSU-442	3860	42	-2457	-2235	-2465	-2205
Oyi-do		Shell	KSU-617	4080	45	-2848	-2499	-2865	-2487
Seonyu-do		Charcoal	AERILK-?	4812	44	-3649	-3530	-3696	-3386
Osan-ri	V-V layer	Charcoal	KSU-616	6130	50	-5207	-4997	-5216	-4940
Osan-ri	V-V layer	Charcoal	KSU-615	6070	30	-5022	-4941	-5192	-4851
Osan-ri	B-Raised design Pottery layer	Charcoal	KSU-515	7050	120	-6028	-5798	-6209	-5714
Dongsam-dong	Mokdo period	Charcoal	GX-0378	5890	140	-4940	-4588	-5207	-4454
Dongsam-dong	Busan period	Charcoal	GX-0379	4915	135	-3938	-3533	-3979	-3374
Dongsam-dong	Dudo period	Charcoal	GX-0493	3400	120	-1877	-1536	-2016	-1436
Dongsam-dong	V layer	Charcoal	Gak-6666	5820	140	-4837	-4505	-5007	-4361
Dongsam-dong	V layer	Charcoal	Gak-6667	5500	100	-4456	-4253	-4545	-4053

Site	Site of type	Material	Lab. No.	Date BP	±	+1σ cal BC	-1σ cal BC	+2σ cal BC	-2σ cal BC
Dongsam-dong	V layer	Charcoal	Gak-6669	5190	130	-4229	-3806	-4325	-3712
Dongsam-dong	V layer	Charcoal	Gak-6668	5160	120	-4223	-3795	-4312	-3703
Dongsam-dong	III layer	Charcoal	Gak-6664	4690	120	-3635	-3361	-3707	-3093
Dongsam-dong	III layer	Charcoal	Gak-6662	4510	120	-3368	-3024	-3520	-2906
Dongsam-dong	III layer	Charcoal	Gak-6663	1140	120	773	1016	656	1154
Dongsam-dong	III layer	Charcoal	Gak-6661	3800	110	-2457	-2056	-2566	-1941
Dongsam-dong	III layer	Charcoal	Gak-6660	3470	100	-1922	-1667	-2035	-1525
Dongsam-dong	III layer	Charcoal	AERILK-27	4400	90	-3317	-2909	-3346	-2893
Dongsam-dong	III layer	Charcoal	AERILK-23	4020	100	-2856	-2409	-2876	-2293
Dongsam-dong	III layer	Charcoal	AERILK-24	3980	100	-2829	-2301	-2866	-2204
Dongsam-dong	III layer	Charcoal	AERILK-25	3930	100	-2571	-2235	-2855	-2137
Dongsam-dong	III layer	Charcoal	AERILK-26	3880	100	-2477	-2202	-2621	-2036
Dongsam-dong	II layer	Charcoal	AERILK-22	4170	100	-2886	-2630	-3010	-2473
Dongsam-dong		Charcoal	N-1132	5180	125	-4227	-3802	-4318	-3711
Dongsam-dong		Charcoal	N-1213	4480	160	-3362	-2931	-3635	-2761
Dongsam-dong		Charcoal	AERILK-?	4950	100	-3928	-3643	-3968	-3527
Suga-ri	V layer (I period)	Charcoal	N-3448(a)	4510	105	-3363	-3030	-3515	-2912
Suga-ri	V layer (I period)	Shell	N-3448(b)	4490	70	-3340	-3095	-3367	-2931
Suga-ri	V layer (I period)	Shell	N-3452	4430	90	-3324	-2928	-3352	-2906
Suga-ri	III layer (II period)	Shell	N-3457	4380	70	-3096	-2906	-3333	-2889
Suga-ri	III layer (II period)	Shell	N-3456	4290	90	-3087	-2702	-3326	-2621
Suga-ri	I layer (III period)	Shell	N-3453	3390	70	-1862	-1541	-1881	-1523
Suga-ri	I layer (III period)	Shell	N-3451	3130	80	-1496	-1311	-1608	-1134
Sandal-dong		Shell	KSU-618	4440	40	-3322	-3018	-3334	-2926

Appendix 2

THE LIST OF RADIOCARBON DATES (CALIBRATED BY OXCAL 4.0) OF BRONZE AGE SITES IN GYEONGGI AND GANGWON PROVINCE (YOUN ET AL., 2007A; 2007B)

Site	Site of type	Material	Lab. No.	Date BP	±	+1 σ cal BC	-1σ cal BC	+2σ cal BC	-2σ cal BC
Geoduri Series	Settlement	Charcoal	SNU01-347	2530	80	-795	-539	-805.5	-411.5
Geoduri Series	Settlement	Charcoal	SNU01-348	2710	60	-904.5	-808.5	-995	-793.5
Geoduri Series	Settlement	Charcoal	SNU01-349	2820	40	-1014.5	-914	-1113.5	-851
Geoduri Series	Settlement	Charcoal	SNU01-350	2400	40	-520.5	-399.5	-747.5	-391
Geoduri Series	Settlement	Charcoal	SNU01-351	2720	40	-900	-825	-969.5	-802
Geoduri Series	Settlement	Charcoal	SNU01-352	2720	70	-925	-805	-1040.5	-786.5
Geoduri Series	Settlement	Charcoal	SNU01-353	2760	70	-977	-829	-1110	-799
Gwangyang-dong Series	Settlement	Charcoal	SNU01-354	2950	60	-1260.5	-1054	-1377	-999
Gwangyang-dong Series	Settlement	Charcoal	SNU01-355	2370	90	-746.5	-372	-769.5	-207.5
Gwangyang-dong Series	Settlement	Charcoal	SNU01-356	2680	60	-894.5	-799.5	-974.5	-769
Gwangyang-dong Series	Settlement	Charcoal	SNU01-357	2740	40	-915	-832	-974.5	-808.5
Gwangyang-dong Series	Settlement	Charcoal	SNU01-358	2870	50	-1122	-946	-1211	-910
Jugjeon Series	Settlement	Charcoal	SNU02-26	2650	40	-839	-790.5	-898	-780
Jugjeon Series	Settlement	Charcoal	SNU02-27	2880	80	-1192.5	-933	-1304.5	-844.5
Jugjeon Series	Settlement	Charcoal	SNU02-28	2780	40	-995	-858	-1017.5	-827
Jugjeon Series	Settlement	Charcoal	SNU02-29	2550	60	-798	-550	-815.5	-416
Jugjeon Series	Settlement	Charcoal	SNU02-30	2640	60	-893.5	-772	-966.5	-553.5
Jugjeon Series	Settlement	Charcoal	SNU02-31	640	60	1286	1393.5	1270.5	1415
Jugjeon Series	Settlement	Charcoal	SNU02-32	660	50	1281	1389.5	1270.5	1402
Jugjeon Series	Settlement	Charcoal	SNU02-33	2440	60	-731.5	-411	-751.5	-404.5
Jugjeon Series	Settlement	Charcoal	SNU02-34	2920	80	-1257	-1008	-1375.5	-914
Angol Series	Settlement	Charcoal	SNU02-41	2410	40	-698	-402	-749	-394.5
Angol Series	Settlement	Charcoal	SNU02-42	2830	30	-1015	-925.5	-1109.5	-904
Angol Series	Settlement	Charcoal	SNU02-43	2580	40	-807.5	-667	-819.5	-547.5
Geoduri Series	Settlement	Charcoal	SNU02-374	2240	70	-387	-205	-408	-95.5
Geoduri Series	Settlement	Charcoal	SNU02-375	2320	40	-410	-258.5	-512.5	-210

Site	Site of type	Material	Lab. No.	Date BP	±	+1 σ cal BC	-1σ cal BC	+2σ cal BC	-2σ cal BC
Geoduri Series	Settlement	Charcoal	SNU02-376	2870	40	-1119	-978.5	-1191.5	-920.5
Geoduri Series	Settlement	Charcoal	SNU02-377	2940	40	-1254.5	-1055	-1289	-1013
Geoduri Series	Settlement	Charcoal	SNU02-378	710	40	1263	1380.5	1224	1389
Geoduri Series	Settlement	Charcoal	SNU02-379	2520	40	-779	-550.5	-795	-515.5
Geoduri Series	Settlement	Charcoal	SNU02-380	2480	40	-756	-536.5	-768.5	-414
Yongam Series	Settlement	Charcoal	SNU02-383	2430	200	-802	-257.5	-1005	-41.5
Yongam Series	Settlement	Charcoal	SNU02-384	2600	80	-839.5	-549.5	-917.5	-415.5
Yongam Series	Settlement	Charcoal	SNU02-385	2700	40	-894	-810.5	-918.5	-798
Yongam Series	Settlement	Charcoal	SNU02-386	2770	40	-972.5	-843	-1007.5	-826
Yongam Series	Settlement	Charcoal	SNU02-387	480	30	1420.5	1443.5	1407.5	1453
Cheonjeon Series	Settlement	Charcoal	SNU02-388	2320	60	-504.5	-230	-730	-201
Cheonjeon Series	Settlement	Charcoal	SNU02-389	2590	60	-825.5	-590.5	-894	-521.5
Cheonjeon Series	Settlement	Charcoal	SNU02-390	2410	40	-698	-402	-749	-394.5
Cheonjeon Series	Settlement	Charcoal	SNU02-391	2080	40	-162.5	-46	-199.5	5
Cheonjeon Series	Settlement	Charcoal	SNU02-392	2300	60	-407.5	-209	-700	-195
Nambugdong Series		Charcoal	SNU02-455	3500	40	-1881.5	-1769	-1929.5	-1694
Nambugdong Series		Charcoal	SNU02-456	3840	40	-2426.5	-2204	-2459.5	-2153
Nambugdong Series		Charcoal	SNU02-457	4440	50	-3325.5	-3012	-3334.5	-2923
Nambugdong Series		Charcoal	SNU02-458	4450	50	-3325.5	-3021	-3338.5	-2928
Nambugdong Series		Charcoal	SNU02-459	4650	40	-3506.5	-3365	-3620.5	-3355
Nambugdong Series		Charcoal	SNU02-460	4700	60	-3624.5	-3374	-3633	-3365
Nambugdong Series		Charcoal	SNU02-461	4620	60	-3516	-3340	-3627.5	-3104
Nambugdong Series		Brazier	SNU02-462	3810	40	-2333	-2147	-2456	-2136
Eulwang series	Ancient remains	Shell	SNU02-463	4010	60	-2619.5	-2465	-2854.5	-2344
Eulwang series	Ancient remains	Shell	SNU02-464	4080	60	-2850.5	-2496	-2869.5	-2475
Gwangyangdong Series	Settlement	Charcoal	SNU02-469	2740	40	-915	-832	-974.5	-808.5

Site	Site of type	Material	Lab. No.	Date BP	±	+1 σ cal BC	-1σ cal BC	+2σ cal BC	-2σ cal BC
Gwangyangdong Series	Settlement	Charcoal	SNU02-470	2580	40	-807.5	-667	-819.5	-547.5
Gwangyangdong Series	Settlement	Charcoal	SNU02-471	2490	40	-761.5	-539.5	-779	-415
Gwangyangdong Series	Settlement	Charcoal	SNU02-472	2440	60	-744.5	-408	-760	-401
Yongsuri Series		Charcoal	SNU02-161	1830	40	134	230.5	80	318.5
Yongsuri Series		Charcoal	SNU02-162	1880	60	70.5	215	-18.5	318.5
Yongsuri Series		Charcoal	SNU02-163	2550	40	-796.5	-591	-804.5	-538.5
Yangsuri dolmen	Dolmen	Charcoal	KAERI-95	3900	200	-2830.5	-2043	-2908	-1782
Sangjapori dolmen	Dolmen	Charcoal		2170	60	-357	-119.5	-380.5	-54.5

Appendix. 3

SUMMED PROBABILITY DISTRIBUTIONS IN CALIBRATED YEARS BC IN THE NEOLITHIC AND BRONZE AGE SITES

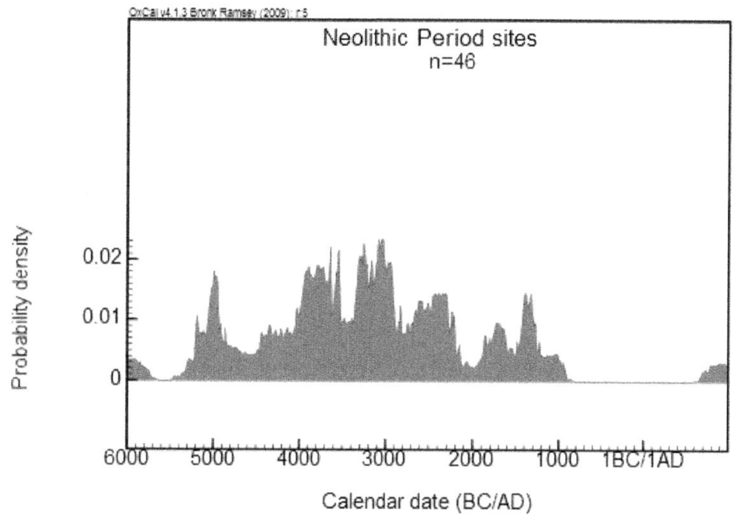

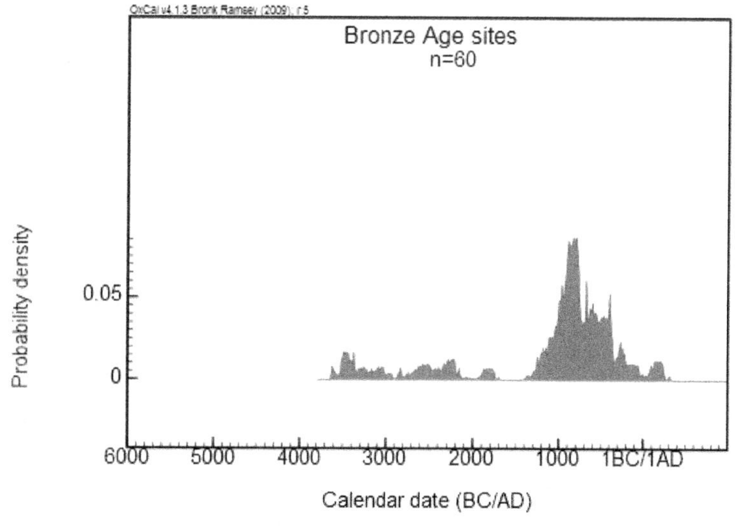

Appendix 4

SUMMED PROBABILITY DISTRIBUTIONS OF HEUNAM-RI, YEOKSAM, AND GARAK-DONG SITES BASED ON J.S. KIM'S DATA (KIM, 2001: 40-41)

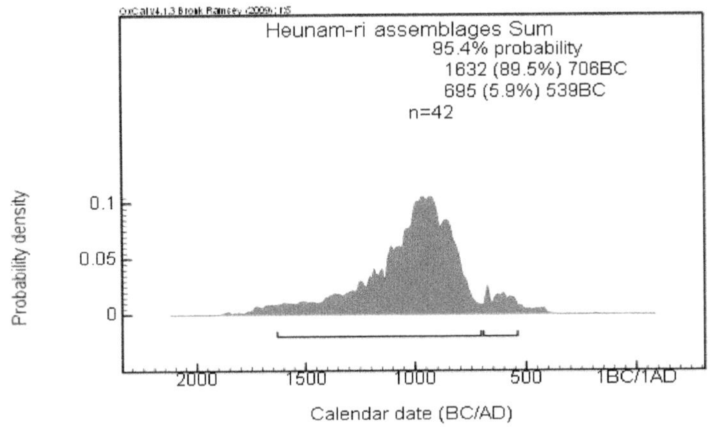

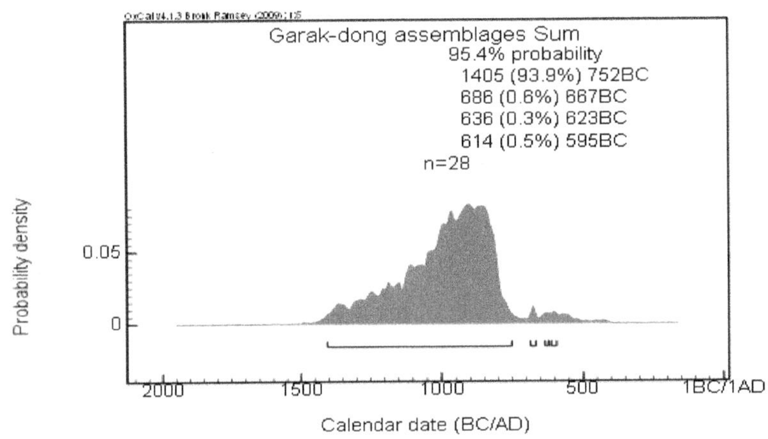

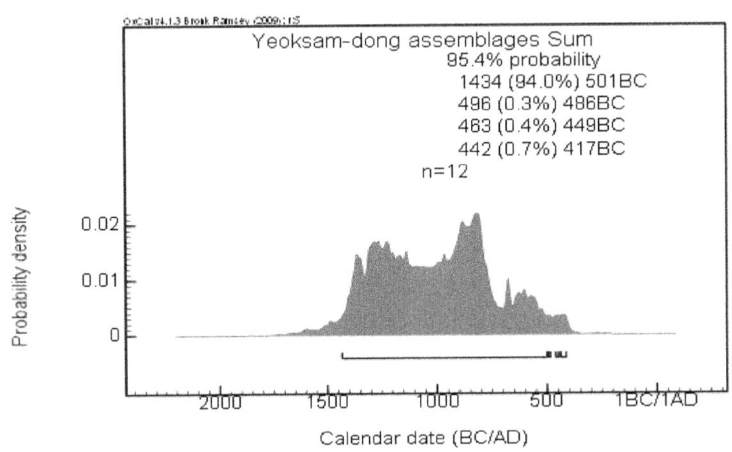

Appendix 5

MONUMENT SITE CODES AND THE NUMBER OF MONUMENT TYPES

Site_Code	Town	Village	Table	Capstone	Baduk board	Transformed	Unidentified	Menhir	Total
1	Yeoncheon	Hakgok-ri	2	3			1		6
2	Yeoncheon	Samgot-ri					1		1
3	Yeoncheon	Samgeo-ri					1		1
4	Yeoncheon	Jinsang-ri		2					2
5	Yeoncheon	Yangwon-ri	1						1
6	Yeoncheon	Chatan-ri	1						1
7	Yeoncheon	Tonghyeon-ri	2	7					9
8	Yeoncheon	Jeongok-ri		1					1
9	Yeoncheon	Jeongok-ri		2					2
10	Yeoncheon	Jeongok-ri		1					1
11	Yeoncheon	Eundae-ri		2					2
12	Yeoncheon	Choseong-ri		1			1		2
13	Paju	Hapo-ri	1						1
14	Paju	Samok-ri		1			2		3
15	Paju	Bongam-ri		3					3
16	Paju	Deokeun-ri	7	2			5		14
17	Paju	Deokeun-ri 3		8			2		10
18	Paju	Deokeun-ri 3		1					1
19	Paju	Seopae-ri		5					5
20	Paju	Sannam-ri		4					4
21	Paju	Dayul-ri	4	19			15		38
22	Paju	Dangha-ri 3					2		2
23	Paju	Sangjiseok-ri	1						1
24	Paju	Yadang-ri		4					4
25	Paju	Cho-ri					1		1
26	Goyang	Gajwa-dong	1	4					5
27	Goyang	Wondang-dong		1					1
28	Goyang	Hwajeong-dong	2	3					5
29	Yangju	Hapae-ri					2		2
30	Yangju	Seonam-ri		1					1
31	Yangju	Okjeong-dong					1		1
32	Yangju	Yuyang-dong 2		1			2		3

Site_Code	Town	Village	Table	Capstone	Baduk board	Transformed	Unidentified	Menhir	Total
33	Yangju	Yuyang-dong 2		1					1
34	Yangju	Majeong-dong		1			1		2
35	Yangju	Mansong-dong		1			2		3
36	Uijeongbu	Jail-dong		2			1		3
37	Uijeongbu	Singok-dong					1		1
38	Uijeongbu	Howon-dong					2		2
39	Uijeongbu	Gosan-dong		2	1		1		4
40	Dongducheon	Anheung-dong		1			1		2
41	Dongducheon	Songnae-dong					1		1
42	Dongducheon	Sangpae-dong					1		1
43	Pocheon	Chudong-ri		1			1		2
44	Pocheon	Mansegyo-ri		2					2
45	Pocheon	Suip-ri	1						1
46	Pocheon	Gisan-ri	1						1
47	Pocheon	Jajak-dong	1						1
48	Pocheon	Seondan-dong					1		1
49	Pocheon	Geumheon-ri	1						1
50	Pocheon	Neulgeo-ri		1					1
51	Guri	Sano-dong					1		1
52	Guri	Inchang-dong 2		6			1		7
53	Guri	Inchang-dong 3		1			1		2
54	Guri	Gyomun-dong		2			1		3
55	Namyangju	Jidun-ri		1			2		3
56	Namyangju	Gaun-dong 1					1		1
57	Namyangju	Geumnam-ri 2					6		6
58	Namyangju	Geumnam-ri 1					1		1
59	Namyangju	Sambongri 2		4					4
60	Namyangju	Sambong-ri 2		1					1
61	Namyangju	Jinjung-ri	2	1					3
62	Gapyeong	Hasaek-ri					1		1
63	Gapyeong	Seonchon-ri					1		1
64	Gimpo	Siam-ri		1			3		4
65	Gimpo	Seoktan-ri					1		1
66	Gimpo	Gojeong-ri	1	2					3
67	Gimpo	Gaheon-ri					1		1

Site_Code	Town	Village	Table	Capstone	Baduk board	Transformed	Unidentified	Menhir	Total
68	Gimpo	Seokmo-ri		1					1
69	Gimpo	Masan-ri 1		1					1
70	Gimpo	Masan-ri 3		3			2		5
71	Gimpo	Unyang-dong 2		2					2
72	Gimpo	Unyang-dong 3		2					2
73	Gimpo	Unyang-dong 3		1					1
74	Gimpo	Unyang-dong 5		4			3		7
75	Gimpo	Geulpo-dong 1		1					1
76	Gimpo	Geulpo-dong 2					1		1
77	Gimpo	Gamjeong-dong 1					1		1
78	Gimpo	Gamjeong-dong 2		1					1
79	Gimpo	Singok-ri 2		2					2
80	Gimpo	Singok-ri 3					3		3
81	Siheung	Gyesu-dong	1	8			2		11
82	Siheung	Geumi-dong	1						1
83	Siheung	Gunja-dong					1		1
84	Siheung	Jonam-dong					1		1
85	Siheung	Cheolsan-dong	1						1
86	Siheung	Haan-dong		1					1
87	Siheung	Gahak-dong 2	4	4			4		12
88	Siheung	Gahak-dong 3		3					3
89	Siheung	Gahak-dong 3		1					1
90	Siheung	Gahak-dong 4		1					1
91	Siheung	Gahak-dong 6		4					4
92	Ansan	Seonbu-dong	3	13					16
93	Ansan	Yangsang-dong		3			10		13
94	Ansan	Wolpi-dong		2					2
95	Anyang	Pyeongchon-dong 1		11		1			12
96	Anyang	Pyeongchon-dong 2					1		1
97	Gunpo	Sanbon-dong		11					11
98	Gunpo	Bugok-dong					2		2
99	Uiwang	Cheonggye-dong					1		1
100	Uiwang	Naeson-dong					15		15
101	Uiwang	Ojeon-dong					1		1
102	Uiwang	Gocheon-dong					1		1

Site_Code	Town	Village	Table	Capstone	Baduk board	Transformed	Unidentified	Menhir	Total
103	Uiwang	Wanggok-dong					1		1
104	Uiwang	I-dong	1	1					2
105	Uiwang	Sam-dong		1					1
106	Suwon	Iui-dong		2			3		5
107	Suwon	Woncheon-dong		1					1
108	Suwon	Homaesil-dong		1					1
109	Suwon	Gyo-dong		1			3		4
110	Hwaseong	Songsan-dong				1	1		2
111	Hwaseong	Sugi-ri		1		1			2
112	Hwaseong	Byeongjeom-ri		3		1	3		7
113	Hwaseong	Bansong-ri 1		1					1
114	Hwaseong	Bansong-ri 2		1					1
115	Hwaseong	Gwanhang-ri					4		4
116	Hwaseong	Dongo-ri					2		2
117	Hwaseong	Dongo-ri					4		4
118	Hwaseong	Guirae-ri		4					4
119	Hwaseong	Mangwol-ri		2					2
120	Hwaseong	Jegi-ri		1					1
121	Osan	Oesammi-dong		1		1			2
122	Osan	Jigot-dong		1					1
123	Osan	Geumam-dong		10			1		11
124	Osan	Gajang-dong		1					1
125	Pyeongtaek	Naecheon-ri					1		1
126	Pyeongtaek	Suwolam-ri		2			2		4
127	Pyeongtaek	Dongcheon-ri		1					1
128	Pyeongtaek	Yanggyo-ri		2					2
129	Hanam	Gwangam-dong	1	2		2			5
130	Hanam	Gami-dong	1	2					3
131	Hanam	Gyosan-dong		5			2		7
132	Seongnam	Taepyeong-dong		1					1
133	Seongnam	Sujin-dong		1					1
134	Seongnam	Sasong-dong		1			2		3
135	Seongnam	Sunae-dong					1		1
136	Gwangju	Samseong-ri		4					4
137	Gwangju	Jangji-dong		1					1

Site_Code	Town	Village	Table	Capstone	Baduk board	Transformed	Unidentified	Menhir	Total
138	Gwangju	Ssangdong-ri			1				1
139	Gwangju	Sani-ri	1						1
140	Gwangju	Gungpyeong-ri	1				2		3
141	Yongin	Wangsan-ri	2	7			3		12
142	Yongin	Sinwon-ri		1					1
143	Yongin	Yuun-ri		2					2
144	Yongin	Jeondae-ri					2		2
145	Yongin	Maseong-ri		1					1
146	Yongin	Jung-dong					1		1
147	Yongin	Sangha-dong	1						1
148	Yongin	Jubuk-ri	1						1
149	Yongin	Maeng-ri					1		1
150	Yongin	Saam-ri	1	6			1		8
151	Yongin	Geunsam-ri					2		2
152	Yongin	Jangpyeong-ri		1					1
153	Anseong	Ssangji-ri					2		2
154	Anseong	Myeongmok-ri		1					1
155	Anseong	Banje-ri		3					3
156	Anseong	Seungdu-ri		1					1
157	Anseong	Manjeong-ri 1		1					1
158	Anseong	Manjeong-ri 2		1					1
159	Anseong	Hyeonsu-dong		2					2
160	Anseong	Mijang-ri					1		1
161	Anseong	Janggye-ri					1		1
162	Yangpyeong	Munho-ri	1	1					2
163	Yangpyeong	Sureung-ri					1		1
164	Yangpyeong	Yangsu-ri					2		2
165	Yangpyeong	Daesim-ri					1		1
166	Yangpyeong	Jeonsu-ri					1		1
167	Yangpyeong	Byeongsan-ri					4		4
168	Yangpyeong	Daeseok-ri					6		6
169	Yangpyeong	Hoehyeon-ri		1					1
170	Yangpyeong	Angdeok-ri					5		5
171	Yangpyeong	Sangjapo-ri	1	1			16		18
172	Yeoju	Ipo-ri		1					1

Site_Code	Town	Village	Table	Capstone	Baduk board	Transformed	Unidentified	Menhir	Total
173	Yeoju	Jurok-ri		1					1
174	Yeoju	Oesa-ri		1			2		3
175	Yeoju	Seoku-ri		5			9		14
176	Yeoju	Sinjeop-ri	1						1
177	Yeoju	Sanggeo-ri		1					1
178	Yeoju	Dojeon-ri		1					1
179	Icheon	Hyeonbang-ri 2	1	4			3		8
180	Icheon	Hyeonbang-ri 3		5			1		6
181	Icheon	Hyeonbang-ri 4					12		12
182	Icheon	Namjeong-ri		1			4		5
183	Icheon	Suha-ri	1						1
184	Icheon	Doam-ri 1					4		4
185	Icheon	Doam-ri 3					2		2
186	Icheon	Sojeong-ri		1					1
187	Icheon	Sinwon-ri		1					1
188	Icheon	Haewol-ri	1						1
189	Yeoncheon	Hwoengsan-ri						1	1
190	Paju	Munji-ri						2	2
191	Yangju	Okjeong-dong						2	2
192	Uijeongbu	Nogyangdong						1	1
193	Uijeongbu	Ganeungdong						1	1
194	Hwaseong	Ssangjeong-ri						1	1
195	Hwaseong	Dongo-ri						1	1
196	Hwaseong	Sujik-ri						1	1
197	Yongin	Yuun-ri						2	2
198	Yongin	Jubuk-ri						2	2
199	Yongin	Chang-ri						1	1
200	Yongin	Saam-ri						4	4
201	Yongin	Duchang-ri						1	1
202	Anseong	Naeu-ri						1	1
203	Yeoju	Seoku-ri						1	1
204	Yeoju	Gaya-ri						1	1
205	Yeoju	Cheo-ri						1	1
206	Ganghwaup	Daesan-ri	1						1
207	Ganghwa, Songhae-myeon	Sangdo-ri	1	3					4

Site_Code	Town	Village	Table	Capstone	Baduk board	Transformed	Unidentified	Menhir	Total
208	Ganghwa, Hajeom-myeon	Bugeun-ri	6	4			2		12
209	Ganghwa, Hajeom-myeon	Samgeo-ri	7						7
210	Ganghwa, Naega-myeon	Osang-ri	6						6
211	Ganghwa, Naega-myeon	Gocheon-ri	15	3					18
212	Ganghwa, Yangsa-myeon	Gyosan-ri	7	2					9
213	Yeoncheon	Wondang 3 ri					1		1
214	Ilsanseo-gu	Gusan-dong					3		3
215	Suwon	Imok-dong					1		1
216	Suwon	Ha-dong					1		1
217	Osan	Sucheong-dong		2					2
218	Seongnam	Dochon-dong					1		1
219	Seoul	Godeok-dong					2		2
220	Seoul	Wonji-dong					1		1
221	Seoul	Umyeon-dong					1		1
222	Seoul	Yangjae-dong	1						1
223	Seoul	Jagok-dong					1		1
224	Seoul	Gaepo-dong					4		4
225	Seoul	Sinjeong-dong					1		1
226	Seoul	Anam-dong					1		1
227	Incheon	Juan-dong	1						1
228	Incheon	Unnam-dong (Yeongjong island)	1						1
229	Incheon	Wondang-dong					1		1
230	Incheon	Daegok-dong A	1						1
231	Incheon	Daegok-dong B		3					3
232	Incheon	Daegok-dong C		4			2		6
233	Incheon	Daegok-dong D	2	4			2		8
234	Incheon	Daegok-dong E	7	2					9
235	Incheon	Munhak-dong	1						1
236	Incheon	Hakik-dong	1						1
									730

Appendix 6

X AND Y COORDINATES AND OTHER INFORMATION OF 45 SETTLEMENT SITES

No.	Town	Village	Longitude	Latitude	Soil type	Elevation	Slope	Aspect	sh_1000	sh_1000_17	sh_100	sh_100_75	Landform	Period
1	Yeoncheon	Samgeori	127.021	38.091	Unranked_Upland	39.0	4.20	NW	577.08	6,486.34	577.08	787.24	Plane	Early to Middle
2	Paju	Dayulri	126.747	37.747	Upland_Good	35.0	1.45	N	1,242.95	6,680.86	785.36	4,317.87	Ridge	Early
3	Paju	Okseokri	126.777	37.817	Limited_Upland	98.0	2.54	SE	1,010.81	4,319.01	744.46	894.73	Ridge	Early
4	Paju	Gyohari	126.743	37.757	Upland_Good	51.0	2.19	NE	894.73	6,325.73	338.07	1,533.26	Ridge	Early
5	Ganghwa	Samgeori	126.421	37.761	Rice_Poor	66.0	4.19	NW	1,583.52	11,034.46	532.69	7,517.74	Ridge	Early to Late
6	Incheon	Geumdandong	126.654	37.598	Upland_Poor	47.0	1.14	W	1,851.30	7,517.74	443.91	4,154.60	Ridge	Late
7	Incheon	Wondangdong	126.722	37.599	Rice_Good	33.0	1.40	S	646.34	4,154.60	1,032.51	4,266.17	Ridge	Early to Late
8	Bucheon	Gogangdong	126.824	37.517	Limited_Upland	119.0	2.10	SE	3,111.49	6,549.53	188.34	8,832.96	Ridge	Middle to Late
9	Siheung	Gyesudong	126.807	37.442	Rice_Poor	40.0	0.89	SE	2,009.16	13,781.14	280.75	11,719.25	Ridge	Early to Middle
10	Gunpo	Daemiyadong	126.926	37.322	Upland_Good	88.0	0.31	SE	1,871.28	21,468.32	372.07	2,640.90	Ridge	Early
11	Anyang	Gwanyangdong	126.967	37.409	Limited_Upland	69.0	2.44	E	710.26	11,719.25	933.53	3,738.61	Plane	Early to Middle
12	Hwaseong	Gogeumsan	127.004	37.217	Unranked_Upland	123.0	0.86	NW	1,492.23	14,003.54	400.14	17,452.03	Peak	Early to Late
13	Hwaseong	Cheoncheonri	126.979	37.227	Limited_Upland	57.0	2.78	S	1,429.50	15,230.17	366.06	14,170.58	Ridge	Early to Middle
14	Hwaseong	Donghaksan	127.080	37.202	Rice_Good	106.0	2.96	NE	421.72	14,293.74	773.03	15,515.70	Ridge	Early to Middle
15	Suwon	Yuljeondong	126.970	37.314	Limited_Upland	111.0	2.84	S	2,027.58	22,217.73	475.01	13,230.66	Ridge	Middle to Late
16	Suwon	Imokdong	127.024	37.302	Forest	142.0	3.21	S	367.40	23,552.86	437.20	5,936.01	Ridge	Middle
17	Pyeongtaek	Jijedong	127.047	37.116	Limited_Upland	35.0	2.64	E	532.69	5,091.69	421.72	7,762.25	Plane	Early to Middle
18	Pyeongtaek	Hyeonhwari	126.918	36.989	Rice_Good	43.0	0.22	S	2,294.31	5,101.79	313.89	1,298.96	Ridge	Early to Middle
19	Pyeongtaek	Hyeongokri	126.962	37.029	Unranked_Upland	66.0	1.80	NE	989.88	3,685.06	532.69	2,472.59	Ridge	Early to Middle
20	Yongin	Bongmyeongri	127.119	37.112	Rice_Poor	65.0	1.53	W	628.18	10,878.01	599.69	3,685.06	Ridge	Early
21	Yongin	Jukjeon	127.116	37.301	Limited_Upland	164.0	2.29	W	784.42	20,116.61	779.38	5,106.37	Ridge	Early to Late
22	Seoul	Garakdong	127.098	37.512	Upland_Good	37.0	0.57	NW	1,422.25	1,925.77	188.34	1,726.69	Ridge	Middle
23	Seoul	Yeoksamdong	127.046	37.491	Upland_Good	70.0	1.47	SW	372.07	3,819.18	251.11	1,588.18	Ridge	Early
24	Seoul	Myeongildong	127.164	37.565	Related_Water	56.0	1.36	E	251.11	1,632.99	502.23	502.23	Plane	Late
25	Seoul	Ilwondong	127.057	37.469	Limited_Upland	255.0	6.43	NW	1,398.50	6,114.10	388.26	554.89	Ridge	Late
26	Namyangju	Suseokri	127.175	37.590	Limited_Upland	76.0	0.59	NW	376.67	554.89	221.96	480.16	Peak	Late
27	Hanam	Misari	127.209	37.572	Upland_Good	23.0	0.58	SW	480.16	480.16	297.78	297.78	Ridge	Early to Late

No.	Town	Village	Longitude	Latitude	Soil type	Elevation	Slope	Aspect	sh_1000	sh_1000_17	sh_100	sh_100_75	Landform	Period
28	Yeoju	Heunamri	127.611	37.316	Limited_Upland	115.0	2.64	NE	627.78	627.78	596.40	596.40	Ridge	Early to Late
29	Gapyeong	Daljeonri	127.508	37.813	Related_Water	80.0	3.46	N	148.89	1,850.77	160.05	1,591.44	Plane	Early to Late
30	Gapyeong	Daeseongri	127.383	37.699	Limited_Upland	63.0	8.93	SE	529.45	529.45	779.69	4,564.52	Plane	Middle to Late
31	Yangpyeong	Yangsuri	127.317	37.537	Upland_Good	35.0	0.25	N	297.78	297.78	178.95	11,034.46	Plane	Early to Middle
32	Incheon	Dongyangdong	126.748	37.560	Limited_Upland	26.0	1.89	SE	1,640.82	6,552.01	480.16	6,552.01	Plane	Early to Middle
33	Hanam	Mangwoldong	127.193	37.540	Related_Water	42.0	0.30	SE	621.48	621.48	621.48	621.48	Peak	Early to Middle
34	Hanam	Mangwoldong Gusan	127.189	37.573	Both	24.0	0.30	NW	1,201.84	1,201.84	400.14	1,203.69	Plane	Early to Late
35	Hanam	Deokpungdong Surigol	127.200	37.546	Limited_Upland	56.0	1.19	W	969.01	2,432.72	872.71	2,432.72	Plane	Early
36	Hanam	Deokpungdong Ritual site	127.193	37.540	Limited_Upland	116.0	1.61	E	1,136.97	3,358.65	737.81	3,358.65	Ridge	Middle
37	Uiwang	Idong	126.958	37.341	Limited_Upland	106.0	5.01	NW	1,459.01	19,181.11	639.06	18,679.44	Ridge	Early to Middle
38	Hwaseong	Banwoldong	127.060	37.235	Rice_Good	62.0	0.90	N	1,203.69	16,829.62	140.38	8,447.99	Ridge	Middle
39	Hwaseong	Bansongdong	127.069	37.210	Limited_Upland	73.0	1.14	SW	1,531.49	14,641.15	548.19	7,309.38	Ridge	Middle
40	Hwaseong	Gajaeri	126.919	37.154	Upland_Good	80.0	2.89	SE	662.16	9,983.55	572.80	6,769.64	Plane	Middle
41	Pyeongtaek	Bangchukri	127.046	37.023	Upland_Poor	55.0	0.40	N	1,381.13	2,280.10	887.82	2,280.10	Peak	Middle
42	Anseong	Banjeri	127.172	37.039	Forest	137.0	0.14	S	2,825.03	7,783.01	1,139.78	6,213.80	Pass	Middle to Late
43	Paju	Sikhyeonri	126.874	37.960	Limited_Upland	103.0	3.52	NW	903.50	903.50	741.81	903.50	Plane	Middle
44	Osan	Gajangdong	127.031	37.157	Limited_Upland	111.0	1.38	E	2,938.29	7,814.75	732.79	2,981.98	Ridge	Middle to Late
45	Gwangmeong	Gahakdong	126.862	37.408	Rice_Poor	54.0	0.79	N	1,032.75	14,361.90	534.54	10,634.28	Pass	Early to Late

Appendix 7

X AND Y COORDINATES AND OTHER INFORMATION OF 236 MONUMENT SITES

No.	Town	Village	Longgitude	Latitude	Soil type	Visible	Elevation	Slope	Aspect	sh_1000	sh_1000_17	sh_100	sh_100_75	Landform
1	Yeoncheon	Hakgok-ri	126.949	37.990	Upland_Good	2034	28.0	1.60	S	204.63	204.63	240.08	240.08	6
2	Yeoncheon	Samgot-ri	127.024	38.134	Upland_Good	1109	47.0	3.02	S	399.52	9,874.65	379.93	4,105.46	6
3	Yeoncheon	Samgeo-ri	127.013	38.089	Upland_Good	1578	33.0	0.57	N	408.06	6,920.06	22.20	376.67	6
4	Yeoncheon	Jinsang-ri	127.017	38.070	Rice_Good	1879	37.0	1.41	E	510.98	5,813.88	355.13	512.42	6
5	Yeoncheon	Yangwon-ri	127.031	38.000	Unranked_Upland	653	69.0	8.21	S	540.04	1,209.40	268.19	1,216.71	6
6	Yeoncheon	Chatan-ri	127.073	38.094	Upland_Good	1897	60.0	2.57	SE	338.07	3,983.59	110.98	3,983.59	2
7	Yeoncheon	Tonghyeon-ri	127.079	38.073	Upland_Poor	2288	76.0	1.44	N	865.63	1,643.37	204.63	1,643.37	6
8	Yeoncheon	Jeongok-ri	127.058	38.010	Upland_Poor	408	41.0	1.35	SW	156.95	156.95	161.59	161.59	6
9	Yeoncheon	Jeongok-ri	127.074	38.032	Rice_Good	1287	48.0	1.78	SE	268.19	268.19	259.79	259.79	6
10	Yeoncheon	Jeongok-ri	127.071	38.027	Upland_Poor	3175	68.0	1.95	SW	355.13	355.13	355.13	355.13	6
11	Yeoncheon	Eundae-ri	127.059	38.021	Upland_Poor	348	25.0	1.72	W	110.98	110.98	22.20	110.98	6
12	Yeoncheon	Choseong-ri	127.069	37.997	Rice_Good	1821	52.0	5.34	NE	556.66	1,018.58	556.66	556.66	4
13	Paju	Hapo-ri	126.820	37.917	Related_Water	73	18.0	3.24	W	548.19	548.19	62.78	548.19	2
14	Paju	Samok-ri	126.755	37.875	Limited_Upland	441	21.0	2.15	W	1,183.25	1,183.25	1,203.07	1,221.36	6
15	Paju	Bongam-ri	126.798	37.820	Limited_Upland	465	39.0	2.61	SW	795.64	5,147.93	795.64	5,165.46	6
16	Paju	Deokeun-ri 1	126.777	37.816	Limited_Upland	12346	98.0	2.54	SE	1,018.58	4,359.21	776.84	4,347.66	4
17	Paju	Deokeun-ri 2	126.781	37.816	Limited_Upland	1911	54.0	4.49	E	732.79	4,506.57	619.09	4,512.25	4
18	Paju	Deokeun-ri 3	126.781	37.805	Upland_Good	4920	44.0	4.99	E	1,101.98	5,646.62	392.68	5,004.20	4
19	Paju	Seopae-ri	126.694	37.713	Rice_Good	7155	37.0	6.30	NW	1,553.05	2,352.73	643.67	2,352.73	4
20	Paju	Sannam-ri	126.700	37.705	Limited_Upland	11919	98.0	4.04	NE	1,469.77	2,841.03	1,077.57	2,841.03	4
21	Paju	Dayul-ri•Dangha-ri	126.746	37.751	Upland_Good	3973	14.0	0.85	S	1,328.21	6,614.27	119.53	1,328.21	1
22	Paju	Dangha-ri 2	126.747	37.745	Limited_Upland	9289	41.0	1.21	S	1,265.15	6,658.66	500.75	1,628.16	6
23	Paju	Sangjiseok-ri	126.775	37.739	Rice_Good	2347	9.0	1.26	NE	470.84	9,166.76	393.31	1,401.13	6
24	Paju	Yadang-ri	126.762	37.732	Rice_Good	10057	36.0	0.61	S	582.61	7,923.81	439.45	1,850.23	4
25	Paju	Cho-ri	126.797	37.982	Related_Water	782	48.0	0.51	E	1,740.33	3,739.21	645.20	3,760.95	2

No.	Town	Village	Longgitude	Latitude	Soil type	Visible	Elevation	Slope	Aspect	sh_1000	sh_1000_17	sh_100	sh_100_75	Landform
26	Goyang	Gajwa-dong	126.721	37.688	Limited_Upland	10666	24.0	0.15	NW	790.36	3,422.72	476.56	3,422.72	4
27	Goyang	Wondang-dong	126.867	37.659	Rice_Good	1775	54.0	0.36	SW	2,029.53	8,210.82	315.46	8,239.69	4
28	Goyang	Hwajeong-dong	126.841	37.633	Upland_Good	6129	51.0	0.55	E	1,445.95	4,582.83	500.75	4,582.83	5
29	Yangju	Hapae-ri	127.027	37.880	Limited_Upland	3046	96.0	0.91	NW	1,261.25	13,666.47	757.58	2,714.22	3
30	Yangju	Seonam-ri	127.028	37.867	Limited_Upland	1309	92.0	1.71	SW	313.89	14,882.90	329.96	3,832.32	4
31	Yangju	Okjeong-dong	127.077	37.823	Unranked_Upland	2352	98.0	2.20	SW	424.05	20,337.52	424.05	8,916.42	6
32	Yangju	Yuyang-dong 1	127.032	37.785	Forest	989	70.0	4.55	SW	1,375.77	22,588.08	178.95	12,675.05	6
33	Yangju	Yuyang-dong 2	127.027	37.786	Forest	1674	70.0	4.08	S	1,793.59	22,187.24	99.26	12,597.16	6
34	Yangju	Majeong-dong	127.054	37.777	Unranked_Upland	2091	57.0	2.56	NW	110.98	23,574.72	110.98	13,613.11	6
35	Yangju	Mansong-dong	127.072	37.774	Limited_Upland	593	76.0	3.37	W	1,187.20	22,677.82	443.91	14,087.58	2
36	Uijeongbu	Jail-dong	127.114	37.758	Limited_Upland	2305	76.0	2.90	SW	1,327.66	19,887.25	110.98	11,737.92	2
37	Uijeongbu	Singok-dong	127.058	37.738	Rice_Poor	506	50.0	1.75	W	110.98	19,586.71	110.98	12,304.12	6
38	Uijeongbu	Howon-dong	127.042	37.716	Upland_Good	4282	59.0	4.33	E	288.54	18,122.02	288.54	11,693.20	6
39	Uijeongbu	Gosan-dong	127.114	37.743	Limited_Upland	997	87.0	0.35	SE	1,047.67	18,265.26	188.34	10,142.29	4
40	Dongducheon	Anheung-dong	127.027	37.932	Upland_Poor	1103	146.0	8.51	E	1,927.31	8,143.43	270.93	1,909.33	2
41	Dongducheon	Songnae-dong	127.065	37.877	Limited_Upland	1283	108.0	5.12	NW	816.12	14,271.73	628.57	2,973.37	4
42	Dongducheon	Sangpae-dong	127.052	37.913	Upland_Good	2212	64.0	5.13	SE	119.53	10,347.05	119.53	119.53	6
43	Pocheon	Chudong-ri	127.182	37.993	Rice_Good	1742	100.0	1.97	S	383.15	2,530.29	366.06	2,530.29	6
44	Pocheon	Mansegyo-ri	127.253	37.968	Upland_Good	1551	83.0	0.76	S	155.37	4,674.89	155.37	522.42	3
45	Pocheon	Suip-ri	127.327	37.988	Upland_Good	3949	117.0	2.61	SW	110.98	8,414.77	110.98	7,186.87	6
46	Pocheon	Gisan-ri	127.326	37.970	Related_Water	4297	132.0	0.51	NE	44.39	9,058.93	44.39	6,925.15	2
47	Pocheon	Jajak-dong	127.177	37.864	Upland_Good	8637	111.0	0.36	SE	219.72	16,419.25	140.38	12,068.68	6
48	Pocheon	Seondan-dong	127.162	37.866	Limited_Upland	2537	129.0	3.86	S	1,302.75	16,536.41	80.03	10,724.37	6
49	Pocheon	Geumheon-ri	127.205	37.838	Upland_Good	4350	134.0	1.06	NE	94.17	18,878.40	94.17	15,003.35	6
50	Pocheon	Neulgeo-ri	127.205	38.070	Related_Water	523	105.0	2.88	S	178.95	6,147.84	189.64	189.64	6
51	Guri	Sano-dong	127.141	37.632	Rice_Good	7400	34.0	1.52	E	643.67	5,791.50	198.52	621.48	6

No.	Town	Village	Longgitude	Latitude	Soil type	Visible	Elevation	Slope	Aspect	sh_1000	sh_1000_17	sh_100	sh_100_75	Landform
52	Guri	Inchang-dong 1	127.142	37.595	Upland_Poor	9984	34.0	0.38	NW	1,060.05	2,242.19	323.17	1,060.05	4
53	Guri	Inchang-dong 2	127.139	37.604	Rice_Poor	9065	33.0	0.66	SE	843.43	3,192.53	221.96	844.60	6
54	Guri	Gyomun-dong	127.124	37.583	Limited_Upland	2227	41.0	4.79	NE	1,851.96	1,851.96	66.59	1,867.73	2
55	Namyangju	Jidun-ri	127.301	37.720	Upland_Good	1323	100.0	3.37	E	603.78	8,075.91	31.39	8,075.91	2
56	Namyangju	Gaun-dong 1	127.167	37.720	Limited_Upland	2689	30.0	0.82	SE	332.93	1,176.36	332.93	1,132.84	3
57	Namyangju	Geumnam-ri 1	127.372	37.657	Limited_Upland	1050	38.0	2.34	E	424.05	424.05	135.01	393.31	6
58	Namyangju	Geumnam-ri 1	127.367	37.649	Upland_Good	1869	35.0	2.06	SW	110.98	548.19	110.98	548.19	6
59	Namyangju	Sambongri 1	127.339	37.604	Limited_Upland	1761	59.0	9.72	E	606.23	606.23	288.54	597.63	6
60	Namyangju	Sambong-ri 2	127.336	37.594	Forest	1357	41.0	5.63	E	751.05	751.05	94.17	770.48	6
61	Namyangju	Jinjung-ri	127.312	37.554	Rice_Poor	3406	33.0	1.49	E	177.56	788.18	177.56	764.38	6
62	Gapyeong	Hasaek-ri	127.474	37.808	Upland_Poor	544	159.0	11.08	NE	129.42	4,798.81	125.56	4,329.72	6
63	Gapyeong	Seonchon-ri	127.484	37.684	Forest	2242	65.0	6.41	SE	80.03	2,175.16	80.03	2,175.16	6
64	Gimpo	Siam-ri	126.649	37.766	Upland_Poor	10243	25.0	1.59	NE	926.12	926.12	744.13	926.12	6
65	Gimpo	Seoktan-ri	126.636	37.723	Rice_Good	13389	28.0	1.75	E	2,799.90	2,799.90	492.82	2,846.92	6
66	Gimpo	Gojeong-ri	126.585	37.719	Upland_Poor	6642	28.0	2.03	E	2,449.67	6,908.63	714.75	6,908.63	2
67	Gimpo	Gaheon-ri	126.596	37.680	Limited_Upland	3111	12.0	0.57	SE	1,178.04	6,456.00	251.11	6,448.06	6
68	Gimpo	Seokmo-ri	126.647	37.651	Rice_Good	9646	21.0	2.08	NE	2,219.55	4,080.24	484.76	4,080.24	6
69	Gimpo	Masan-ri 1	126.645	37.643	Unranked_Upland	1605	32.0	2.68	SW	2,955.26	4,715.34	278.11	4,715.34	6
70	Gimpo	Masan-ri 2	126.665	37.636	Limited_Upland	1656	25.0	1.17	NW	2,197.25	3,596.84	218.60	3,613.17	6
71	Gimpo	Unyang-dong 1	126.686	37.649	Rice_Good	7275	23.0	0.65	N	1,274.65	1,274.65	662.16	1,274.65	3
72	Gimpo	Unyang-dong 2	126.692	37.651	Rice_Good	9965	13.0	2.81	N	861.92	861.92	347.42	861.92	4
73	Gimpo	Unyang-dong 3	126.685	37.657	Rice_Poor	10433	13.0	0.79	SE	845.18	845.18	555.33	845.18	6
74	Gimpo	Unyang-dong 4	126.684	37.657	Rice_Poor	10529	13.0	0.79	SE	875.81	875.81	605.82	875.81	6
75	Gimpo	Geulpo-dong 1	126.704	37.636	Rice_Poor	5567	18.0	0.43	W	198.52	1,365.52	148.89	1,365.52	6
76	Gimpo	Geulpo-dong 2	126.707	37.633	Rice_Good	3387	15.0	0.77	W	284.24	1,487.27	267.27	1,483.78	4
77	Gimpo	Gamjeong-dong 1	126.693	37.632	Rice_Poor	2145	17.0	0.15	SW	94.17	2,354.19	94.17	2,354.19	6

No.	Town	Village	Longgitude	Latitude	Soil type	Visible	Elevation	Slope	Aspect	sh_1000	sh_1000_17	sh_100	sh_100_75	Landform
78	Gimpo	Gamjeong-dong 2	126.695	37.626	Rice_Good	6496	18.0	1.67	NE	587.66	2,762.43	88.78	2,762.25	6
79	Gimpo	Singok-ri 1	126.779	37.606	Limited_Upland	2439	23.0	1.08	W	806.71	806.71	430.96	806.71	4
80	Gimpo	Singok-ri 2	126.789	37.597	Rice_Poor	6920	12.0	0.10	NW	62.78	1,475.63	62.78	1,459.68	6
81	Siheung	Gyesu-dong	126.821	37.441	Limited_Upland	2502	68.0	1.93	N	1,509.30	13,254.51	945.07	8,230.51	6
82	Siheung	Geumi-dong	126.855	37.396	Upland_Good	1963	55.0	3.27	E	1,593.76	15,895.49	270.02	12,100.64	6
83	Siheung	Gunja-dong	126.784	37.349	Limited_Upland	419	20.0	2.76	NW	1,448.33	23,592.95	395.18	18,855.53	6
84	Siheung	Jonam-dong	126.857	37.366	Forest	201	42.0	2.94	N	1,450.88	18,680.22	188.34	15,369.22	2
85	Gwangmyeong	Cheolsan-dong	126.865	37.476	Limited_Upland	2698	28.0	3.34	SW	960.84	7,804.41	567.18	3,130.83	6
86	Gwangmyeong	Haan-dong	126.874	37.458	Rice_Good	7525	44.0	3.27	N	1,237.59	9,172.53	329.96	5,153.24	4
87	Gwangmyeong	Gahak-dong 1	126.862	37.396	Limited_Upland	171	47.0	0.90	S	1,791.39	15,496.45	329.96	11,962.65	5
88	Gwangmyeong	Gahak-dong 2	126.861	37.408	Rice_Poor	1106	54.0	0.79	N	988.89	14,386.72	502.23	10,638.54	3
89	Gwangmyeong	Gahak-dong 3	126.862	37.398	Rice_Poor	1025	54.0	1.22	E	1,678.08	15,352.21	355.13	11,805.96	4
90	Gwangmyeong	Gahak-dong 4	126.870	37.391	Rice_Poor	699	57.0	1.93	W	2,416.05	15,683.96	397.05	12,523.32	6
91	Gwangmyeong	Gahak-dong 5	126.867	37.389	Rice_Poor	1140	70.0	0.78	NE	2,118.02	15,966.02	400.14	12,731.13	4
92	Ansan	Seonbu-dong	126.788	37.346	Limited_Upland	607	37.0	3.04	SE	1,712.66	23,663.09	549.54	18,968.68	4
93	Ansan	Yangsang-dong	126.851	37.349	Limited_Upland	2953	87.0	6.02	S	548.19	20,592.34	400.14	17,302.91	4
94	Ansan	Wolpi-dong	126.843	37.337	Limited_Upland	1074	26.0	7.17	SE	529.45	22,134.22	534.54	18,712.68	6
95	Anyang	Pyeongchon-dong 1	126.947	37.379	Limited_Upland	6671	73.0	1.58	NW	357.89	14,992.97	357.89	14,992.97	4
96	Anyang	Pyeongchon-dong 2	126.947	37.383	Upland_Good	3781	45.0	1.97	NW	484.76	14,572.85	426.94	14,572.85	6
97	Gunpo	Sanbon-dong	126.931	37.356	Related_Water	7205	126.0	10.80	E	2,007.07	18,012.33	470.32	16,907.00	2
98	Gunpo	Bugok-dong	126.933	37.322	Limited_Upland	923	49.0	1.34	NE	1,351.74	21,435.05	44.39	17,224.45	6
99	Uiwang	Cheonggye-dong	127.993	37.387	Unranked_Rice	1685	55.0	5.22	N	99.26	14,210.76	91.51	14,211.40	6
100	Uiwang	Naeson-dong	126.984	37.368	Limited_Upland	17374	239.0	9.33	S	2,134.47	16,291.53	724.68	16,291.53	4
101	Uiwang	Ojeon-dong	126.973	37.355	Limited_Upland	1876	85.0	7.33	SW	486.79	17,645.45	448.88	17,645.45	6
102	Uiwang	Gocheon-dong	126.960	37.346	Limited_Upland	6807	132.0	6.49	NW	1,028.21	18,623.38	938.80	18,623.38	4
103	Uiwang	Wanggok-dong	126.997	37.345	Limited_Upland	1200	128.0	5.61	NW	2,299.14	18,900.93	110.98	17,960.16	6

No.	Town	Village	Longgitude	Latitude	Soil type	Visible	Elevation	Slope	Aspect	sh_1000	sh_1000_17	sh_100	sh_100_75	Landform
104	Uiwang	I-dong	126.954	37.346	Rice_Poor	2693	67.0	2.17	NW	1,233.40	18,660.43	387.63	18,660.43	6
105	Uiwang	Sam-dong	126.951	37.323	Limited_Upland	3218	58.0	1.16	W	834.33	21,225.77	198.52	16,844.84	6
106	Suwon	Iui-dong	127.047	37.287	Limited_Upland	3952	97.0	1.80	E	1,201.43	22,242.51	733.80	13,098.10	6
107	Suwon	Woncheon-dong	127.056	37.280	Limited_Upland	9913	100.0	1.80	E	443.91	21,636.47	421.72	12,641.91	6
108	Suwon	Homaesil-dong	127.942	37.261	Unranked_Upland	4301	66.0	7.64	N	2,024.18	19,541.21	677.60	10,680.76	6
109	Suwon	Gyo-dong	127.012	37.274	Limited_Upland	16434	101.0	3.24	S	496.31	20,393.82	487.29	10,968.19	4
110	Hwaseong	Songsan-dong	127.018	37.211	Rice_Poor	5922	35.0	1.27	E	732.45	13,419.13	178.95	4,219.78	6
111	Hwaseong	Sugi-ri	126.977	37.203	Limited_Upland	7552	73.0	2.78	W	1,689.20	12,565.44	600.92	3,529.09	6
112	Hwaseong	Byeongjeom-ri	127.045	37.203	Unranked_Upland	9279	58.0	2.77	SW	1,091.20	13,064.13	548.19	5,060.63	4
113	Hwaseong	Bansong-ri 1	127.067	37.189	Limited_Upland	5369	67.0	1.01	NE	1,376.12	12,474.62	887.82	6,264.37	6
114	Hwaseong	Bansong-ri 2	127.073	37.189	Unranked_Upland	790	51.0	0.89	S	932.21	12,667.12	603.78	6,690.58	6
115	Hwaseong	Gwanhang-ri	126.953	37.181	Limited_Upland	60	64.0	2.70	NE	2,110.44	10,840.90	662.16	3,989.40	6
116	Hwaseong	Dongo-ri	126.956	37.142	Upland_Good	9836	97.0	1.60	S	3,285.09	6,896.10	503.21	3,626.03	6
117	Hwaseong	Dongo-ri	126.968	37.139	Limited_Upland	9763	85.0	4.28	E	2,831.39	6,971.31	377.32	4,415.07	6
118	Hwaseong	Guirae-ri	126.993	37.137	Limited_Upland	3068	34.0	0.88	SW	455.41	5,148.31	366.06	643.67	4
119	Hwaseong	Mangwol-ri	126.998	37.148	Upland_Poor	1759	9.0	0.09	SE	0.00	6,325.73	0.00	0.00	6
120	Hwaseong	Jegi-ri	126.999	37.147	Related_Water	2270	10.0	0.11	NW	110.98	6,193.55	110.98	110.98	6
121	Osan	Oesammi-dong	127.049	37.198	Rice_Poor	3654	49.0	0.94	W	1,503.08	12,711.05	221.96	5,102.66	6
122	Osan	Jigot-dong	127.022	37.180	Limited_Upland	1285	72.0	7.51	S	1,366.24	10,111.52	407.46	2,102.49	4
123	Osan	Geumam-dong	127.033	37.177	Rice_Good	91	62.0	2.69	NW	2,364.53	10,065.38	523.83	3,085.90	6
124	Osan	Gajang-dong	127.024	37.170	Rice_Poor	1245	58.0	3.46	NE	2,228.86	9,077.43	266.35	2,269.27	2
125	Pyeongtaek	Naecheon-ri	127.016	37.129	Unranked_Upland	6903	33.0	1.19	NW	1,330.25	4,551.33	533.62	1,326.73	6
126	Pyeongtaek	Suwolam-ri	127.024	37.132	Unranked_Upland	3811	39.0	0.49	E	1,987.83	5,042.83	518.16	1,983.37	4
127	Pyeongtaek	Dongcheon-ri	127.105	37.113	Rice_Poor	2947	55.0	5.96	E	825.72	9,706.18	177.56	1,290.40	2
128	Pyeongtaek	Yanggyo-ri	126.931	37.017	Forest	54322	107.0	2.68	W	2,352.52	5,408.11	1,063.77	5,421.58	6
129	Hanam	Gwangam-dong	127.177	37.521	Upland_Poor	7536	77.0	5.43	NW	1,953.21	5,869.79	591.00	5,869.79	2

No.	Town	Village	Longgitude	Latitude	Soil type	Visible	Elevation	Slope	Aspect	sh_1000	sh_1000_17	sh_100	sh_100_75	Landform
130	Hanam	Gami-dong	127.170	37.519	Limited_Upland	2916	75.0	1.67	E	2,491.94	5,681.45	466.63	5,682.23	4
131	Hanam	Gyosan-dong	127.209	37.518	Limited_Upland	6319	86.0	10.14	W	891.42	4,080.60	883.65	4,065.66	2
132	Seongnam	Taepyeong-dong	127.123	37.447	Upland_Good	13326	71.0	2.25	E	296.13	9,314.22	296.13	2,943.99	6
133	Seongnam	Sujin-dong	127.125	37.436	Upland_Good	8727	53.0	0.99	SW	625.03	10,608.66	339.53	4,247.94	4
134	Seongnam	Sasong-dong	127.114	37.433	Upland_Good	6424	33.0	0.78	NW	332.93	10,682.03	344.57	4,578.63	6
135	Seongnam	Sunae-dong	127.136	37.421	Limited_Upland	3512	63.0	3.60	SW	484.76	12,409.35	484.76	5,992.38	6
136	Gwangju	Samseong-ri	127.271	37.478	Limited_Upland	381	100.0	7.57	S	2,308.34	2,308.34	0.00	2,330.53	2
137	Gwangju	Jangji-dong	127.242	37.387	Rice_Poor	1343	60.0	2.08	E	357.89	5,462.54	357.89	408.06	4
138	Gwangju	Ssangdong-ri	127.295	37.368	Upland_Good	1042	91.0	6.40	NE	826.02	6,067.83	31.39	4,550.09	2
139	Gwangju	Sani-ri	127.302	37.365	Rice_Poor	2780	106.0	11.73	NE	645.20	6,473.68	449.43	5,162.84	4
140	Gwangju	Gungpyeong-ri	127.320	37.343	Limited_Upland	1206	126.0	3.74	SW	856.47	9,328.07	424.05	7,590.55	4
141	Yongin	Wangsan-ri	127.259	37.346	Upland_Good	1175	89.0	8.33	NW	985.14	8,765.47	506.14	3,004.20	6
142	Yongin	Sinwon-ri	127.228	37.309	Unranked_Upland	2110	86.0	4.66	SW	507.11	13,493.76	364.03	6,583.06	4
143	Yongin	Yuun-ri	127.224	37.297	Upland_Poor	2481	72.0	1.52	NE	675.05	14,908.68	99.26	8,005.09	6
144	Yongin	Jeondae-ri	127.182	37.283	Upland_Poor	6424	79.0	1.38	E	625.03	15,667.76	568.92	8,823.11	6
145	Yongin	Maseong-ri	127.184	37.272	Forest	1667	135.0	6.13	E	2,849.69	17,892.55	221.96	10,676.22	2
146	Yongin	Jung-dong	127.165	37.282	Limited_Upland	743	120.0	3.59	SW	1,548.61	18,791.44	110.98	11,556.80	2
147	Yongin	Sangha-dong	127.120	37.276	Limited_Upland	481	68.0	2.29	S	0.00	21,843.67	31.39	14,714.97	6
148	Yongin	Jubuk-ri	127.235	37.248	Upland_Good	1785	100.0	3.18	NE	315.46	19,826.39	155.37	13,331.82	6
149	Yongin	Maeng-ri	127.329	37.186	Upland_Good	1545	126.0	1.96	W	1,711.36	25,589.93	129.42	15,900.14	6
150	Yongin	Saam-ri	127.298	37.176	Rice_Poor	1424	140.0	3.18	SE	1,983.74	26,098.64	190.93	18,566.14	6
151	Yongin	Geunsam-ri	127.372	37.140	Related_Water	4177	116.0	2.03	S	834.33	21,786.90	169.04	13,012.15	6
152	Yongin	Jangpyeong-ri	127.379	37.116	Unranked_Upland	2922	105.0	1.00	E	794.71	20,539.26	417.02	11,635.31	6
153	Anseong	Ssangji-ri	127.284	37.126	Upland_Poor	1686	133.0	3.15	SE	2,230.62	20,641.73	62.78	15,585.71	2
154	Anseong	Myeongmok-ri	127.187	37.026	Unranked_Upland	949	38.0	0.24	S	2,401.33	6,745.18	66.59	4,336.09	2
155	Anseong	Banje-ri	127.163	37.015	Rice_Poor	2196	71.0	1.69	S	3,110.07	5,894.87	218.60	5,203.47	6

No.	Town	Village	Longgitude	Latitude	Soil type	Visible	Elevation	Slope	Aspect	sh_1000	sh_1000_17	sh_100	sh_100_75	Landform
156	Anseong	Seungdu-ri	127.156	36.991	Upland_Poor	4939	34.0	0.17	W	823.93	2,374.92	198.52	2,374.92	4
157	Anseong	Manjeong-ri 1	127.154	37.000	Rice_Good	17122	52.0	0.55	NE	1,243.74	3,373.72	183.03	3,373.72	4
158	Anseong	Manjeong-ri 2	127.162	36.996	Rice_Poor	6079	23.0	0.81	SE	407.46	2,904.56	210.57	2,900.92	6
159	Anseong	Hyeonsu-dong	127.280	36.995	Rice_Poor	5058	36.0	0.48	NE	914.34	11,279.40	129.42	6,607.00	6
160	Anseong	Mijang-ri	127.363	37.040	Rice_Good	377	90.0	2.48	S	367.40	19,928.01	0.00	14,395.99	6
161	Anseong	Janggye-ri	127.358	37.051	Upland_Good	689	109.0	5.15	E	596.40	20,044.26	253.07	14,298.34	2
162	Yangpyeong	Munho-ri	127.347	37.601	Upland_Good	2567	36.0	1.02	NW	142.12	142.12	155.37	155.37	6
163	Yangpyeong	Sureung-ri	127.380	37.591	Rice_Poor	191	87.0	6.17	W	22.20	3,103.09	31.39	3,103.09	2
164	Yangpyeong	Yangsu-ri	127.315	37.530	Upland_Good	4523	27.0	0.17	F	408.06	408.06	408.06	408.06	6
165	Yangpyeong	Daesim-ri	127.391	37.506	Rice_Poor	2606	34.0	1.27	W	204.63	204.63	204.63	204.63	6
166	Yangpyeong	Jeonsu-ri	127.406	37.481	Rice_Poor	1329	81.0	5.20	W	639.06	2,175.16	639.06	2,175.16	6
167	Yangpyeong	Byeongsan-ri	127.464	37.488	Upland_Good	6139	65.0	2.23	N	983.14	983.14	188.34	993.85	4
168	Yangpyeong	Daeseok-ri	127.482	37.431	Upland_Poor	785	56.0	0.55	W	198.52	2,527.56	142.12	2,527.56	1
169	Yangpyeong	Hoehyeon-ri	127.508	37.466	Rice_Poor	1627	43.0	3.42	SE	173.35	2,005.97	173.35	173.35	2
170	Yangpyeong	Angdeok-ri	127.508	37.443	Upland_Good	4901	40.0	1.66	SW	94.17	94.17	94.17	94.17	6
171	Yangpyeong	Sangjapo-ri	127.539	37.421	Rice_Good	2956	41.0	2.36	W	267.27	267.27	248.15	248.15	6
172	Yeoju	Ipo-ri	127.537	37.391	Related_Water	3701	40.0	1.79	SE	297.78	297.78	296.13	296.13	6
173	Yeoju	Jurok-ri	127.470	37.368	Limited_Upland	90	207.0	3.16	W	1,830.96	6,734.73	44.39	6,370.27	2
174	Yeoju	Oesa-ri	127.502	37.343	Unranked_Upland	4184	61.0	1.36	SW	667.71	4,949.95	169.04	2,984.45	6
175	Yeoju	Seoku-ri	127.684	37.389	Unranked_Upland	767	78.0	2.30	W	244.15	9,605.11	169.04	9,605.11	6
176	Yeoju	Sinjeop-ri	127.696	37.326	Rice_Poor	1806	72.0	4.35	N	457.03	4,112.17	457.57	4,112.17	6
177	Yeoju	Sanggeo-ri	127.620	37.231	Limited_Upland	1878	132.0	5.42	E	2,347.38	5,993.99	518.16	5,993.99	6
178	Yeoju	Dojeon-ri	127.731	37.353	Limited_Upland	658	236.0	2.43	NE	1,426.23	8,414.71	455.41	8,421.24	6
179	Icheon	Hyeonbang-ri 1	127.499	37.344	Upland_Good	4159	61.0	1.10	E	332.93	5,336.72	209.39	2,877.21	6
180	Icheon	Hyeonbang-ri 2	127.496	37.345	Upland_Poor	4703	65.0	1.36	SE	377.32	5,491.46	358.58	3,165.88	6
181	Icheon	Hyeonbang-ri 3	127.497	37.343	Upland_Poor	3307	58.0	1.02	S	240.08	5,550.31	218.60	2,986.10	6

No.	Town	Village	Longgitude	Latitude	Soil type	Visible	Elevation	Slope	Aspect	sh_1000	sh_1000_17	sh_100	sh_100_75	Landform
182	Icheon	Namjeong-ri	127.402	37.308	Unranked_Upland	4964	80.0	0.67	SE	923.72	14,869.37	183.03	6,745.73	6
183	Icheon	Suha-ri	127.405	37.312	Upland_Good	1500	78.0	0.99	SW	1,089.62	14,345.43	80.03	6,587.33	6
184	Icheon	Doam-ri 1	127.411	37.313	Rice_Poor	1344	69.0	0.86	S	1,040.35	13,807.87	88.78	6,164.53	2
185	Icheon	Doam-ri 2	127.417	37.313	Rice_Poor	7116	83.0	0.92	NE	850.70	13,400.39	282.50	5,762.51	4
186	Icheon	Sojeong-ri	127.395	37.304	Rice_Poor	6379	86.0	0.87	SW	448.88	15,554.53	361.32	7,176.06	4
187	Icheon	Sinwon-ri	127.514	37.292	Unranked_Upland	3461	56.0	1.26	NW	308.35	8,388.65	338.07	1,257.14	6
188	Icheon	Haewol-ri	127.350	37.216	Forest	357	117.0	4.91	SW	2,098.39	23,495.43	110.98	13,602.99	4
189	Yeoncheon	Hwoengsan-ri	126.987	38.116		441	43.0	0.55	SE	156.95	10,162.38	110.98	3,199.93	1
190	Paju	Munji-ri	126.732	37.825	Limited_Upland	739	20.0	2.23	S	289.39	2,796.64	289.39	2,796.64	6
191	Yangju	Okjeong-dong	127.080	37.819	Rice_Poor	2902	95.0	0.99	SE	282.50	20,742.80	188.34	9,357.28	2
192	Uijeongbu	Nogyangdong	127.011	37.755	Forest	2897	139.0	7.36	E	1,775.64	23,173.43	200.99	16,241.57	2
193	Uijeongbu	Ganeungdong	127.016	37.752	Upland_Poor	3501	117.0	6.90	NE	1,233.40	22,649.90	228.52	16,041.17	2
194	Hwaseong	Ssangjeong-ri	126.717	37.245	Unranked_Upland	7791	14.0	3.39	SE	4,879.99	30,345.98	377.32	25,984.84	6
195	Hwaseong	Dongo-ri	126.948	37.135	Limited_Upland	8489	88.0	3.69	SE	2,409.52	6,665.17	268.19	4,535.93	6
196	Hwaseong	Sujik-ri	126.996	37.130	Unranked_Upland	2987	11.0	1.13	E	379.93	4,309.59	198.52	372.07	6
197	Yongin	Yuun-ri	127.227	37.298	Rice_Poor	2410	68.0	1.04	E	400.14	14,660.57	22.20	7,790.51	6
198	Yongin	Jubuk-ri	127.235	37.248	Upland_Good	1763	92.0	2.98	N	253.07	19,794.07	119.53	13,289.62	6
199	Yongin	Chang-ri	127.170	37.318	Rice_Poor	1080	42.0	0.26	SE	110.98	16,039.02	119.53	6,587.89	1
200	Yongin	Saam-ri	127.303	37.179	Rice_Poor	1267	134.0	0.66	NW	1,430.36	26,609.20	178.95	19,110.15	4
201	Yongin	Duchang-ri	127.334	37.147	Unranked_Upland	2077	164.0	7.73	E	2,130.77	25,139.00	421.72	16,454.50	2
202	Anseong	Naeu-ri	127.301	36.989	Upland_Good	2978	66.0	1.59	SW	221.96	12,992.20	221.96	8,458.86	6
203	Yeoju	Seoku-ri	127.687	37.393	Unranked_Upland	767	78.0	2.30	W	244.15	9,605.11	169.04	9,605.11	6
204	Yeoju	Gaya-ri	127.685	37.283	Upland_Good	3177	35.0	2.60	W	88.78	88.78	80.03	80.03	6
205	Yeoju	Cheo-ri	127.661	37.208	Limited_Upland	1483	86.0	2.15	S	567.18	2,512.90	567.18	2,512.90	2
206	Ganghwaup	Daesan-ri	126.485	37.765	Rice_Good	1465	9.0	1.34	W	1,460.53	5,466.50	88.78	5,466.50	6

No.	Town	Village	Longgitude	Latitude	Soil type	Visible	Elevation	Slope	Aspect	sh_1000	sh_1000_17	sh_100	sh_100_75	Landform
207	Ganghwa, Songhae-myeon	Sangdo-ri	126.447	37.773	Upland_Good	7007	11.5	1.23	N	1,712.66	8,581.38	22.20	8,581.38	6
208	Ganghwa, Hajeom-myeon	Bugeun-ri	126.441	37.770	Upland_Poor	10948	27.4	1.97	N	2,265.79	9,161.27	148.89	9,161.27	6
209	Ganghwa, Hajeom-myeon	Samgeo-ri	126.423	37.750	Limited_Upland	1611	178.4	9.29	NW	2,214.33	11,299.45	430.96	11,299.45	6
210	Ganghwa, Naega-myeon	Osang-ri	126.403	37.731	Limited_Upland	1198	53.0	5.63	SW	1,208.59	13,564.24	812.79	13,564.24	6
211	Ganghwa, Naega-myeon	Gocheon-ri	126.425	37.741	Limited_Upland	20838	281.3	5.83	NW	2,904.82	11,435.51	673.96	11,435.51	4
212	Ganghwa, Yangsa-myeon	Gyosan-ri	126.405	37.790	Limited_Upland	12605	80.7	5.71	SW	2,596.12	12,304.46	843.72	12,304.46	4
213	Yeoncheon	Wondang 3 ri	126.859	37.987	Upland_Good	2037	19.0	2.13	S	424.05	424.05	66.59	440.57	6
214	Ilsanseo-gu	Gusan-dong	126.685	37.676	Rice_Poor	15924	25.0	0.55	SW	177.56	177.56	177.56	177.56	4
215	Suwon	Imok-dong	126.977	37.320	Limited_Upland	306	69.0	1.42	S	2,342.65	21,729.43	80.03	15,901.63	2
216	Suwon	Ha-dong	127.067	37.280	Upland_Good	373	43.0	0.69	E	248.15	21,889.66	199.76	13,073.00	6
217	Osan	Sucheong-dong	127.062	37.168	Rice_Poor	695	30.0	0.74	E	1,320.21	10,244.73	204.63	5,703.61	2
218	Seongnam	Dochon-dong	127.153	37.418	Rice_Poor	1677	77.0	1.83	NW	679.42	11,676.20	91.51	6,890.81	2
219	Seoul	Godeok-dong	127.136	37.567	Related_Water	4628	25.0	1.87	E	0.00	0.00	0.00	0.00	6
220	Seoul	Wonji-dong	127.054	37.447	Rice_Poor	2333	57.0	6.15	NE	784.73	8,359.50	345.28	5,919.39	6
221	Seoul	Umyeon-dong	127.026	37.467	Rice_Poor	7940	48.0	2.60	SE	313.89	6,278.63	282.50	5,776.39	6
222	Seoul	Yangjae-dong	127.038	37.474	Rice_Poor	5229	26.0	0.43	E	199.76	5,891.86	199.76	4,439.11	2
223	Seoul	Jagok-dong	127.100	37.476	Limited_Upland	3409	55.0	4.78	S	985.64	5,783.55	332.93	1,336.35	4
224	Seoul	Gaepo-dong	127.061	37.479	Rice_Poor	6897	37.0	2.20	NE	1,167.75	5,039.61	129.42	2,712.31	6
225	Seoul	Sinjeong-dong	126.849	37.509	Limited_Upland	2641	48.0	1.60	NW	1,445.95	5,665.78	379.28	1,998.09	6
226	Seoul	Anam-dong	127.031	37.589	Limited_Upland	8117	54.0	3.46	SW	409.27	6,014.99	409.27	3,446.10	6
227	Incheon	Juan-dong	126.683	37.456	Rice_Good	2916	24.0	1.11	SW	1,997.60	19,257.30	315.46	17,400.88	6
228	Incheon	Unnam-dong (Yeongjong island)	126.529	37.487	Related_Water	19509	57.0	4.13	NE	3,357.91	23,872.85	443.91	23,872.85	4
229	Incheon	Wondang-dong	126.700	37.604	Limited_Upland	604	48.0	1.34	S	2,287.86	4,559.60	857.62	4,559.60	2
230	Incheon	Daegok-dong A	126.646	37.633	Rice_Good	6440	71.0	5.35	NW	3,231.72	5,136.00	527.58	5,136.00	6

No.	Town	Village	Longitude	Latitude	Soil type	Visible	Elevation	Slope	Aspect	sh_1000	sh_1000_17	sh_100	sh_100_75	Landform
231	Incheon	Daegok-dong B	126.652	37.632	Unranked_Upland	6217	55.0	5.60	NE	2,687.49	4,750.05	665.13	4,750.05	6
232	Incheon	Daegok-dong C-2	126.653	37.630	Rice_Good	13060	73.0	8.00	N	2,520.73	4,808.45	707.83	4,808.45	4
233	Incheon	Daegok-dong D	126.655	37.630	Rice_Good	10055	58.8	5.77	NE	2,420.23	4,706.55	613.90	4,706.55	6
234	Incheon	Daegok-dong E	126.658	37.629	Limited_Upland	4939	43.3	4.33	NE	2,152.97	4,677.94	673.96	4,677.94	6
235	Incheon	Munhak-dong	126.656	37.439	Rice_Poor	3678	23.0	6.61	N	4,039.65	22,223.58	426.36	20,266.57	6
236	Incheon	Hakik-dong	126.650	37.441	Rice_Poor	527	9.0	1.62	NW	4,592.92	22,346.01	91.51	20,740.72	6

Appendix 8

Radiocarbon determinations of Dolmens in the study area (no. 1-3) and the other regions (no. 4-10)

No.	Site_Code	Town	Village	Lab No.	Material	Date BP	±	+1 σ cal BC'	-1σ cal BC'	+2σ cal BC'	-2σ cal BC'	Note	Reference
1	164	Yangpyeong	Yangsuri	KAERI		3900	200	-2832	-2045	-2910	-1784		1
2	16	Paju	Okseokri	GX0554	charcoal	2590	105	-891	-540	-967	-408	Settlement data under BI dolmen	2
3	171	Yangpyeong	Sangjapori	KAERI		2170	60	-359	-121	-382	-56	Slender dagger, jade, Red-burnished pottery	3
4		Jecheon	Hwangseokri	GX0555	H u m a n bone	2360	370	-895	3	-1391	382		4
5		Daejeon	Biraedong	No Lab no.		2860	50	-1115	-941	-1210	-904	Bipa shaped Bronze dagger, Red-burnished pottery	4
6		Hwasun	Daesinri	No Lab no.		2500	80	-776	-523	-794	-412		4
7		Yeosu	Hwajangdong	No Lab no.		2770	40	-974	-845	-1009	-828		4
8		Yeosu	Hwajangdong	No Lab no.		2744	60	-971	-824	-1025	-800		4
9		Yeosu	Hwajangdong	No Lab no.		2630	40	-831	-787	-896	-675		4
10		Changwon	Deokcheonri	No Lab no.		2650	50	-893	-789	-917	-674		4

Reference

1. Park, Hee-hyeon. 1984. The study of Korean dolmen culture. The study of Korean history (Hanguksa yeongu) No. 46.

2. Kim, Jae-won and Moo-byeong Yun. 1967. A Study of Korean Dolmens Burials. Seoul: National Museum of Korea Publications (in Korean).

3. Pak, Chan-kirl and Tyung-rin Yand, 1974. Kaeri Radiocarbon Measurement III. Radiocarbon. Vol. 16. No. 2. p.192-197

4. Lee, Yeong-moon, 2002. *A study of Dolmen Society in Korea*. Seoul: Hakyeon Munhwasa. (In Korean) p.258

Appendix 9

^{14}C DETERMINATIONS ON CHARCOAL FROM THE SETTLEMENTS IN GYEONGGI PROVINCE (STUDY AREA). CALIBRATED IN OXCAL 4.1

No.	Site_Code	Site_Name		Lab code	Material	^{14}C BP	±	cal BC (68%)		cal BC (95%)		Location
1	3	Paju	Okseokri	GX-0554	Charcoal	2590	105	-891	-540	-967	-408	Settlement under BI dolmen
2	8	Bucheon	Gogangdong	KCP462	Charcoal	2690	50	-896	-806	-971	-791	No.10 settlement
3	8	Bucheon	Gogangdong	KCP463	Charcoal	2910	70	-1252	-1008	-1367	-916	No.12 settlement
4	9	Siheung	Gyesudong	SNU02-042	Charcoal	2830	30	-1017	-927	-1111	-906	No.2 settlement
5	9	Siheung	Gyesudong	SNU02-041	Charcoal	2410	40	-700	-404	-751	-396	No.1 Settlement
6	9	Siheung	Gyesudong	SNU02-043	Charcoal	2580	40	-809	-669	-821	-549	No.3 settlement
7	11	Anyang	Gwanyangdong	SNU01-470	Charcoal	2580	40	-809	-669	-821	-549	No.7 settlement
8	11	Anyang	Gwanyangdong	SNU01-471	Charcoal	2490	40	-763	-541	-781	-417	No.7 settlement
9	11	Anyang	Gwanyangdong	SNU01-356	Charcoal	2680	60	-896	-801	-976	-771	No.3 settlement
10	11	Anyang	Gwanyangdong	SNU01-358	Charcoal	2870	50	-1124	-948	-1213	-912	No.5 settlement
11	11	Anyang	Gwanyangdong	SNU01-472	Charcoal	2440	60	-746	-410	-762	-403	No.8 Settlement
12	11	Anyang	Gwanyangdong	SNU01-354	Charcoal	2950	60	-1262	-1056	-1379	-1001	No.1 settlement
13	11	Anyang	Gwanyangdong	SNU01-469	Charcoal	2740	40	-917	-834	-976	-810	No.6 settlement
14	11	Anyang	Gwanyangdong	SNU01-357	Charcoal	2740	40	-917	-834	-976	-810	No.4 settlement
15	11	Anyang	Gwanyangdong	SNU01-355	Charcoal	2370	90	-748	-374	-771	-209	No.2 Settlement
16	12	Hwaseong	Gogeumsan	SNU00-360	Charcoal	2940	60	-1259	-1052	-1373	-979	No.1 settlement
17	12	Hwaseong	Gogeumsan	SNU00-359	Charcoal	2880	60	-1189	-943	-1261	-910	No.1 settlement
18	13	Hwaseong	Cheoncheonri	HS-5	Charcoal	2900	60	-1208	-1005	-1289	-920	No.7 settlement
19	13	Hwaseong	Cheoncheonri	HS-7	Charcoal	2850	60	-1114	-928	-1251	-848	No.7 settlement
20	13	Hwaseong	Cheoncheonri	HS-8	Charcoal	2800	60	-1022	-848	-1121	-824	same material HS-7
21	13	Hwaseong	Cheoncheonri	HS-6	Charcoal	2770	40	-974	-845	-1009	-828	same material HS-5
22	13	Hwaseong	Cheoncheonri	HS-4	Charcoal	2980	60	-1313	-1121	-1391	-1027	No.6 settlement
23	13	Hwaseong	Cheoncheonri	HS-3	Charcoal	2900	40	-1188	-1012	-1257	-948	same material HS-4
24	13	Hwaseong	Cheoncheonri	HS-2	Charcoal	2890	40	-1129	-1005	-1251	-938	No.6 settlement

No.	Site_Code	Site_Name		Lab code	Material	^{14}C BP	±	cal BC (68%)		cal BC (95%)		Location
25	13	Hwaseong	Cheoncheonri	HS-1	Charcoal	2800	40	-1004	-907	-1051	-839	same material HS-2
26	13	Hwaseong	Cheoncheonri	HS-11	Charcoal	3140	80	-1500	-1313	-1613	-1211	No.11 settlement
27	13	Hwaseong	Cheoncheonri	HS-12	Charcoal	2350	60	-702	-369	-752	-211	Cairn
28	13	Hwaseong	Cheoncheonri	HS-10	Charcoal	2560	80	-809	-544	-837	-413	No.9-2 settlement
29	13	Hwaseong	Cheoncheonri	HS-9	Charcoal	2480	60	-761	-520	-775	-413	No.9-2 settlement
30	15	Suwon	Yuljeondong	SNU03-212	Charcoal	3160	60	-1503	-1386	-1606	-1271	No.3 settlement-1
31	15	Suwon	Yuljeondong	SNU03-213	Charcoal	2990	40	-1302	-1132	-1386	-1059	No.3 settlement-2
32	15	Suwon	Yuljeondong	SNU03-216	Charcoal	2780	40	-997	-860	-1019	-829	No.2 pit
33	15	Suwon	Yuljeondong	SNU03-210	Charcoal	3020	40	-1377	-1213	-1396	-1129	No.1 settlement-2
34	15	Suwon	Yuljeondong	SNU03-209	Charcoal	2780	40	-997	-860	-1019	-829	No.1 settlement-1
35	15	Suwon	Yuljeondong	SNU03-211	Charcoal	2730	40	-907	-831	-975	-806	No.1 settlement-3
36	15	Suwon	Yuljeondong	SNU03-216	Charcoal	2520	40	-781	-552	-797	-517	No.4 pit
37	15	Suwon	Yuljeon II	SNU03-465	Charcoal	2510	50	-776	-544	-796	-417	No.3 pit-2
38	15	Suwon	Yuljeon II	SNU03-464	Charcoal	2470	40	-753	-519	-765	-414	No.3 pit-1
39	15	Suwon	Yuljeon II	SNU03-466	Charcoal	2410	80	-746	-398	-780	-381	No.3 pit-3
40	15	Suwon	Yuljeon II	SNU03-467	Charcoal	2450	50	-747	-414	-761	-407	No.4 pit
41	18	Pyeongtaek	Hyeonhwari	GX-21692	Charcoal	3110	130	-1522	-1134	-1681	-1013	No.2 settlement
42	18	Pyeongtaek	Hyeonhwari	GX-21694	Charcoal	2910	130	-1290	-932	-1414	-831	No.4 settlement
43	18	Pyeongtaek	Hyeonhwari	GX-21693	Charcoal	2830	140	-1193	-836	-1408	-781	No.3 settlement
44	18	Pyeongtaek	Hyeonhwari	GX-21691	Charcoal	2715	130	-1111	-768	-1262	-518	No.1 settlement
45	18	Pyeongtaek	Hyeonhwari	GX-22017	Charcoal	2560	370	-1191	-207	-1636	208	peat layer
46	18	Pyeongtaek	Hyeonhwari	GX-21695	Charcoal	2525	150	-802	-417	-1007	-232	No.5 settlement
47	27	Hanam	Misadong	GX-28885	Charcoal	2560	130	-829	-428	-978	-392	고상건물
48	27	Hanam	Misadong	GX-28883	Charcoal	2540	70	-799	-544	-811	-415	settlement
49	27	Hanam	Misadong	GX-28881	Charcoal	2510	120	-795	-426	-898	-387	settlement

No.	Site_Code	Site_Name		Lab code	Material	^{14}C BP	±	cal BC (68%)		cal BC (95%)		Location
50	27	Hanam	Misadong	GX-28886-AMS	Charcoal	3010	40	-1371	-1211	-1387	-1129	The site of a fire
51	28	Yeoju	Heunamri	KAERI	Charcoal	2145	60	-352	-93	-369	-45	No.14 Settlement
52	28	Yeoju	Heunamri	KAERI	Charcoal	2089	60	-196	-42	-354	52	No.14 Settlement
53	28	Yeoju	Heunamri	KAERI 154-1	Charcoal	2696	160	-1115	-571	-1261	-411	No.8 Settlement
54	28	Yeoju	Heunamri	KAERI 154-2	Charcoal	2666	160	-1025	-544	-1254	-403	No.8 Settlement
55	28	Yeoju	Heunamri	KAERI 153	Charcoal	2541	150	-811	-417	-1026	-234	No.8 Settlement
56	28	Yeoju	Heunamri	KAERI-70	Charcoal	3210	70	-1605	-1412	-1668	-1317	No.12 Settlement
57	28	Yeoju	Heunamri	RIKEN	Charcoal	2980	70	-1370	-1116	-1400	-1014	No.12 Settlement
58	28	Yeoju	Heunamri	RIKEN	Charcoal	2920	70	-1255	-1015	-1370	-924	No.12 Settlement
59	28	Yeoju	Heunamri	KAERI	Charcoal	2620	100	-906	-552	-996	-416	No.12 Settlement
60	28	Yeoju	Heunamri	KAERI	Charcoal	2290	60	-405	-211	-515	-196	No.13 Settlement
61	28	Yeoju	Heunamri	KAERI	Charcoal	2110	60	-336	-46	-359	17	No.13 Settlement
62	28	Yeoju	Heunamri	KAERI-121	Charcoal	2520	120	-799	-511	-901	-391	No.7 Settlement
63	28	Yeoju	Heunamri	KAERI	Charcoal	1810	90	86	332	18	417	No.7 settlement
64	45	Hanam	Mangwoldong	No Lab no.	Charcoal	2960	70	-1292	-1056	-1395	-997	
65	45	Hanam	Mangwoldong	No lab no.	Charcoal	2870	40	-1121	-980	-1193	-922	
66	45	Hanam	Mangwoldong	No lab no.	Charcoal	2860	40	-1112	-946	-1191	-914	
67	45	Hanam	Mangwoldong	No lab no.	Charcoal	2820	50	-1041	-910	-1123	-843	
68	45	Hanam	Mangwoldong	No lab no.	Charcoal	2770	40	-974	-845	-1009	-828	
69	45	Hanam	Mangwoldong	No lab no.	Charcoal	2720	30	-896	-833	-918	-811	
70	48	Hanam	Deokpungdong	HD-6	Charcoal	2800	60	-1022	-848	-1121	-824	No.1 settlement
71	48	Hanam	Deokpungdong	HD-7	Charcoal	2760	60	-976	-833	-1049	-805	No.1 settlement
72	48	Hanam	Deokpungdong	HD-5	Charcoal	2750	60	-973	-828	-1041	-802	No.1 settlement
73	48	Hanam	Deokpungdong	HD-1	Charcoal	2880	60	-1189	-943	-1261	-910	Outdoor hearth-1
74	48	Hanam	Deokpungdong	HD-3	Charcoal	2760	60	-976	-833	-1049	-805	Outdoor hearth-3

No.	Site_Code	Site_Name		Lab code	Material	^{14}C BP	±	cal BC (68%)		cal BC (95%)		Location
75	48	Hanam	Deokpungdong	HD-2	Charcoal	2750	60	-973	-828	-1041	-802	Outdoor hearth-2
76	54	Uiwang	Idong	SNU07-214	Charcoal	2750	50	-970	-831	-1006	-810	No.10 settlement
77	54	Uiwang	Idong	SNU07-211	Charcoal	2710	50	-900	-816	-976	-797	No.10 settlement
78	54	Uiwang	Idong	SNU07-216	Charcoal	2820	50	-1041	-910	-1123	-843	No.1 settlement
79	54	Uiwang	Idong	SNU07-217	Charcoal	2820	50	-1041	-910	-1123	-843	No.1 settlement
80	54	Uiwang	Idong	SNU07-215	Charcoal	2690	50	-896	-806	-971	-791	No.1 settlement
81	54	Uiwang	Idong	SNU07-212	Charcoal	2740	50	-926	-826	-999	-808	No.11 settlement
82	54	Uiwang	Idong	SNU07-213	Charcoal	2690	60	-896	-806	-995	-781	No.11 settlement
83	60	Hwaseong	Banwolri	PRI-53	Charcoal	2500	40	-767	-544	-791	-418	Songgukri type settlement
84	61	Hwaseong	Bansongri	HS-33	Charcoal	2730	40	-907	-831	-975	-806	No.14 settlement
85	61	Hwaseong	Bansongri	HS-32	Charcoal	2690	40	-895	-807	-914	-798	No.14 settlement
86	61	Hwaseong	Bansongri	HS-29	Charcoal	2890	40	-1129	-1005	-1251	-938	No.9 settlement
87	61	Hwaseong	Bansongri	HS-30	Charcoal	2700	50	-896	-812	-973	-795	No.9 settlement
88	61	Hwaseong	Bansongri	HS-31	Charcoal	2480	40	-758	-538	-770	-416	No.9 settlement
89	61	Hwaseong	Bansongri	HS-27	Charcoal	2530	40	-790	-558	-799	-524	No.8 settlement
90	61	Hwaseong	Bansongri	HS-28	Charcoal	2490	50	-765	-540	-783	-416	No.8 settlement
91	61	Hwaseong	Bansongri	HS-23	Charcoal	2460	40	-752	-419	-760	-411	No.5 settlement
92	61	Hwaseong	Bansongri	HS-20	Charcoal	2500	40	-767	-544	-791	-418	No.2 settlement
93	61	Hwaseong	Bansongri	HS-22	Charcoal	2480	40	-758	-538	-770	-416	No.2 settlement
94	61	Hwaseong	Bansongri	HS-21	Charcoal	2430	60	-742	-406	-761	-400	No.2 settlement
95	68	Pyeongtaek	Bangchukri	SNU02-279	Charcoal	2720	40	-902	-827	-971	-804	No.1 settlement
96	68	Pyeongtaek	Bangchukri	SNU02-280	Charcoal	2700	40	-896	-812	-920	-800	No.1 settlement
97	68	Pyeongtaek	Bangchukri	SNU02-284	Charcoal	2630	50	-841	-771	-911	-594	No.4 settlement
98	68	Pyeongtaek	Bangchukri	SNU02-282	Charcoal	2890	40	-1129	-1005	-1251	-938	No.3 settlement
99	68	Pyeongtaek	Bangchukri	SNU02-283	Charcoal	2720	40	-902	-827	-971	-804	No.3 settlement
100	68	Pyeongtaek	Bangchukri	SNU02-281	Charcoal	2750	40	-926	-835	-997	-816	No.2 settlement

Appendix 10

R_combined (combines radiocarbon dates in OxCal 4.1 prior to calibration: (Ward and Wilson, 1978)) ^{14}C determinations on charcoal from the settlements in the study area). Calibrated in OxCal 4.1 (The ratio of length and width of house shape are included)

No.	Site_Code	Site_Name		Lab No.	Material	Date BP	±	+1 σ cal BC	- 1 σ cal BC	+2σ cal BC	-2σ Cal BC		Length	Width	L:W
1	3	Paju	Okseokri	GX-0554	Charcoal	2590	105	-891	-540	-967	-408	settlement	1570	370	4.2
2	8	Bucheon	Gogangdong	KCP462	Charcoal	2690	50	-896	-806	-971	-791	No.10 settlement	1500	360	4.2
3	8	Bucheon	Gogangdong	KCP463	Charcoal	2910	70	-1252	-1008	-1367	-916	No.12 settlement	910	220	4.1
4	9	Siheung	Gyesudong	SNU02-042	Charcoal	2830	30	-1017	-927	-1111	-906	No.2 settlement	220	180	1.2
5	9	Siheung	Gyesudong	SNU02-041	Charcoal	2410	40	-700	-404	-751	-396	No.1 Settlement	270	305	0.9
6	9	Siheung	Gyesudong	SNU02-043	Charcoal	2580	40	-809	-669	-821	-549	No.3 settlement	290	100	2.9
7	11	Anyang	Gwanyangdong	SNU01-358	Charcoal	2870	50	-1124	-948	-1213	-912	No.5 settlement	1075	375	2.9
8	11	Anyang	Gwanyangdong	SNU01-472	Charcoal	2440	60	-746	-410	-762	-403	No.8 Settlement	1546	346	4.5
9	11	Anyang	Gwanyangdong	SNU01-355	Charcoal	2370	90	-748	-374	-771	-209	No.2 Settlement	1080	280	3.9
10	11	Anyang	Gwanyangdong	R_combine: SNU01-470,471		2535	29	-791	-593	-797	-544	No.7 settlement	409	364	1.1
11	11	Anyang	Gwanyangdong	SNU01-356	Charcoal	2680	60	-896	-801	-976	-771	No.3 settlement	855	340	2.5
12	11	Anyang	Gwanyangdong	SNU01-354	Charcoal	2950	60	-1262	-1056	-1379	-1001	No.1 settlement	525	285	1.8
13	11	Anyang	Gwanyangdong	SNU01-357	Charcoal	2740	40	-917	-834	-976	-810	No.4 settlement	640	350	1.8
14	11	Anyang	Gwanyangdong	SNU01-469	Charcoal	2740	40	-917	-834	-976	-810	No.6 settlement	485	225	2.2
15	12	Hwaseong	Gogeumsan	SNU00-360	Charcoal	2940	60	-1259	-1052	-1373	-979	No.1 settlement	964	430	2.2
16	12	Hwaseong	Gogeumsan	SNU00-359	Charcoal	2880	60	-1189	-943	-1261	-910	No.1 settlement			
17	13	Hwaseong	Cheoncheonri	R_combine: HS-5,6	Charcoal	2811	34	-1004	-921	-1055	-846	No.7 settlement	2910	400	7.3
18	13	Hwaseong	Cheoncheonri	R_combine: HS-7,8	Charcoal	2825	43	-1038	-917	-1122	-851	No.7 settlement	2910	400	7.3
19	13	Hwaseong	Cheoncheonri	R_combine: HS-1,2	Charcoal	2845	29	-1047	-940	-1114	-921	No.6 settlement	680	380	1.8
20	13	Hwaseong	Cheoncheonri	R_combine: HS-3,4	Charcoal	2925	34	-1194	-1054	-1259	-1014	No.6 settlement	680	380	1.8
21	13	Hwaseong	Cheoncheonri	HS-11	Charcoal	3140	80	-1500	-1313	-1613	-1211	No.11 settlement	510	300	1.7
22	13	Hwaseong	Cheoncheonri	R_combine: HS-9,10	Charcoal	2509	49	-775	-544	-795	-417	No.9-2 settlement	440	350	1.3
23	15	Suwon	Yuljeondong	SNU03-212	Charcoal	3160	60	-1503	-1386	-1606	-1271	No.3 settlement-1	625	170	3.7
24	15	Suwon	Yuljeondong	SNU03-213	Charcoal	2990	40	-1302	-1132	-1386	-1059	No.3 settlement-2	625	170	3.7
25	15	Suwon	Yuljeondong	SNU03-209	Charcoal	2780	40	-997	-860	-1019	-829	No.1 settlement-1	930	160	5.8
26	15	Suwon	Yuljeondong	SNU03-210	Charcoal	3020	40	-1377	-1213	-1396	-1129	No.1 settlement-2	930	160	5.8
27	15	Suwon	Yuljeondong	SNU03-211	Charcoal	2730	40	-907	-831	-975	-806	No.1 settlement-3	930	160	5.8

No.	Site_Code	Site_Name		Lab No.	Material	Date BP	±	+1 σ cal BC	- 1 σ cal BC	+2σ cal BC	-2σ Cal BC		Length	Width	L:W
28	18	Pyeongtaek	Hyeonhwari	GX-21692	Charcoal	3110	130	-1522	-1134	-1681	-1013	No.2 settlement			
29	18	Pyeongtaek	Hyeonhwari	GX-21691	Charcoal	2715	130	-1111	-768	-1262	-518	No.1 settlement			
30	18	Pyeongtaek	Hyeonhwari	GX-21693	Charcoal	2830	140	-1193	-836	-1408	-781	No.3 settlement			
31	18	Pyeongtaek	Hyeonhwari	GX-21694	Charcoal	2910	130	-1290	-932	-1414	-831	No.4 settlement			
32	18	Pyeongtaek	Hyeonhwari	GX-21695	Charcoal	2525	150	-802	-417	-1007	-232	No.5 settlement			
33	18	Pyeongtaek	Hyeonhwari	GX-22017	Charcoal	2560	370	-1191	-207	-1636	208	peat layer			
34	27	Hanam	Misadong	GX-28885	Charcoal	2560	130	-829	-428	-978	-392	고상건물			
35	27	Hanam	Misadong	GX-28886-AMS	Charcoal	3010	40	-1371	-1211	-1387	-1129	The site of a fire			
36	28	Yeoju	Heunamri	R_combine: KAERI, KAERI	Charcoal	2202	43	-358	-204	-386	-171	No.13 Settlement	700	280	2.5
37	28	Yeoju	Heunamri	R_combine: KAERI-70, RIKEN	Charcoal	3069	50	-1410	-1273	-1443	-1134	No.12 Settlement	970	360	2.7
38	28	Yeoju	Heunamri	R_combine: KAERI, RIKEN	Charcoal	2867	58	-1127	-937	-1258	-902	No.12 Settlement	970	360	2.7
39	28	Yeoju	Heunamri	KAERI 154-1	Charcoal	2696	160	-1115	-571	-1261	-411	No.8 Settlement	745	300	2.5
40	28	Yeoju	Heunamri	KAERI 154-2	Charcoal	2666	160	-1025	-544	-1254	-403	No.8 Settlement	745	300	2.5
41	28	Yeoju	Heunamri	KAERI 153	Charcoal	2541	150	-811	-417	-1026	-234	No.8 Settlement	745	300	2.5
42	28	Yeoju	Heunamri	KAERI	Charcoal	2145	60	-352	-93	-369	-45	No.14 Settlement	1000	420	2.9
43	28	Yeoju	Heunamri	KAERI	Charcoal	2089	60	-196	-42	-354	52	No.14 Settlement	1000	420	2.9
44	28	Yeoju	Heunamri	KAERI-121	Charcoal	2520	120	-799	-511	-901	-391	No.7 Settlement	960	280	3.4
45	45	Hanam	Mangwoldong		Charcoal	2960	70	-1292	-1056	-1395	-997				
46	45	Hanam	Mangwoldong		Charcoal	2870	40	-1121	-980	-1193	-922				
47	45	Hanam	Mangwoldong		Charcoal	2860	40	-1112	-946	-1191	-914				
48	45	Hanam	Mangwoldong		Charcoal	2820	50	-1041	-910	-1123	-843				
49	45	Hanam	Mangwoldong		Charcoal	2770	40	-974	-845	-1009	-828				
50	45	Hanam	Mangwoldong		Charcoal	2720	30	-896	-833	-918	-811				
51	48	Hanam	Deokpungdong	HD-6	Charcoal	2800	60	-1022	-848	-1121	-824	No.1 settlement	690	310	2.2
52	48	Hanam	Deokpungdong	HD-7	Charcoal	2760	60	-976	-833	-1049	-805	No.1 settlement	690	310	2.2
53	48	Hanam	Deokpungdong	HD-5	Charcoal	2750	60	-973	-828	-1041	-802	No.1 settlement	690	310	2.2
54	48	Hanam	Deokpungdong	HD-1	Charcoal	2880	60	-1189	-943	-1261	-910	Outdoor hearth-1			
55	48	Hanam	Deokpungdong	HD-2	Charcoal	2750	60	-973	-828	-1041	-802	Outdoor hearth-2			

No.	Site_Code	Site_Name		Lab No.	Material	Date BP	±	+1 σ cal BC	- 1 σ cal BC	+2σ cal BC	-2σ Cal BC		Length	Width	L:W
56	48	Hanam	Deokpungdong	HD-3	Charcoal	2760	60	-976	-833	-1049	-805	Outdoor hearth-3			
57	54	Uiwang	Idong	R_combine: SNU07-214,211		2730	36	-906	-832	-972	-809	No.10 settlement	710	300	2.4
58	54	Uiwang	Idong	SNU07-216	Charcoal	2820	50	-1041	-910	-1123	-843	No.1 settlement	745	360	2.1
59	54	Uiwang	Idong	SNU07-217	Charcoal	2820	50	-1041	-910	-1123	-843	No.1 settlement	745	360	2.1
60	54	Uiwang	Idong	SNU07-215	Charcoal	2690	50	-896	-806	-971	-791	No.1 settlement	745	360	2.1
61	54	Uiwang	Idong	R_combine: SNU07-212,213		2720	39	-901	-827	-971	-804	No.11 settlement	720	340	2.1
62	60	Hwaseong	Banwolri	PRI-53	Charcoal	2500	40	-767	-544	-791	-418	Songgukri type settlement			
63	61	Hwaseong	Bansongri	HS-23	Charcoal	2460	40	-752	-419	-760	-411	No.5 settlement	350	250	1.4
64	61	Hwaseong	Bansongri	R_combine: HS-20,21,22	Charcoal	2478	26	-755	-540	-768	-418	No.2 settlement	418	312	1.3
65	61	Hwaseong	Bansongri	HS-33	Charcoal	2730	40	-907	-831	-975	-806	No.14 settlement	560	410	1.4
66	61	Hwaseong	Bansongri	HS-32	Charcoal	2690	40	-895	-807	-914	-798	No.14 settlement	560	410	1.4
67	61	Hwaseong	Bansongri	R_combine: HS-27,28	Charcoal	2514	32	-772	-553	-791	-538	No.8 settlement	630	460	1.4
68	61	Hwaseong	Bansongri	HS-29	Charcoal	2890	40	-1129	-1005	-1251	-938	No.9 settlement	490	370	1.3
69	61	Hwaseong	Bansongri	HS-30	Charcoal	2700	50	-896	-812	-973	-795	No.9 settlement	490	370	1.3
70	61	Hwaseong	Bansongri	HS-31	Charcoal	2480	40	-758	-538	-770	-416	No.9 settlement	490	370	1.3
71	68	Pyeongtaek	Bangchukri	R_combine: SNU02-279,280	Charcoal	2710	29	-896	-823	-909	-809	No.1 settlement	314	300	1
72	68	Pyeongtaek	Bangchukri	SNU02-281	Charcoal	2750	40	-926	-835	-997	-816	No.2 settlement	360	320	1.1
73	68	Pyeongtaek	Bangchukri	SNU02-284	Charcoal	2630	50	-841	-771	-911	-594	No.4 settlement	620	360	1.7
74	68	Pyeongtaek	Bangchukri	SNU02-282	Charcoal	2890	40	-1129	-1005	-1251	-938	No.3 settlement	380	330	1.2
75	68	Pyeongtaek	Bangchukri	SNU02-283	Charcoal	2720	40	-902	-827	-971	-804	No.3 settlement	380	330	1.2

Appendix 11-a

R_COMBINED ^{14}C DETERMINATIONS OF DOUBLED-RIM WITH SLANT LINE POTTERY (THIS CATEGORY INCLUDES DOUBLED-RIM WITH SLANT LINES, DOUBLED-RIM ONLY, AND SLANT LINES ONLY ON THE RIM)

Site_Code	Site_Name		Lab No.	Date BP	±	+1σ cal BC'	-1σ cal BC'	+2σ cal BC'	-2σ cal BC'	Material		House No.
18	Pyeongtaek	Hyeonhwari	GX-21692	3110	130	-1522	-1134	-1681	-1013	Charcoal	III district	No.2 settlement
28	Yeoju	Heunamri	R_combine: KAERI-70, RIKEN	3069	50	-1410	-1273	-1443	-1134			No.12 Settlement
18	Pyeongtaek	Hyeonhwari	GX-21694	2910	130	-1290	-932	-1414	-831	Charcoal	III district	No.4 settlement
61	Hwaseong	Bansongri	HS-29	2890	40	-1129	-1005	-1251	-938	Charcoal		No.9 settlement
28	Yeoju	Heunamri	R_combine: KAERI, RIKEN	2867	58	-1127	-937	-1258	-902			No.12 Settlement
18	Pyeongtaek	Hyeonhwari	GX-21693	2830	140	-1193	-836	-1408	-781	Charcoal	III district	No.3 settlement
61	Hwaseong	Bansongri	HS-33	2730	40	-907	-831	-975	-806	Charcoal		No.14 settlement
18	Pyeongtaek	Hyeonhwari	GX-21691	2715	130	-1111	-768	-1262	-518	Charcoal	III district	No.1 settlement
61	Hwaseong	Bansongri	HS-30	2700	50	-896	-812	-973	-795	Charcoal		No.9 settlement
61	Hwaseong	Bansongri	HS-32	2690	40	-895	-807	-914	-798	Charcoal		No.14 settlement
28	Yeoju	Heunamri	KAERI 153	2541	150	-811	-417	-1026	-234	Charcoal		No.8 Settlement
18	Pyeongtaek	Hyeonhwari	GX-21695	2525	150	-802	-417	-1007	-232	Charcoal	III district	No.5 settlement
28	Yeoju	Heunamri	KAERI-121	2520	120	-799	-511	-901	-391	Charcoal		No.7 Settlement
61	Hwaseong	Bansongri	R_combine: HS-27,28	2514	32	-772	-553	-791	-538			No.8 settlement
61	Hwaseong	Bansongri	HS-31	2480	40	-758	-538	-770	-416	Charcoal		No.9 settlement
61	Hwaseong	Bansongri	R_combine: HS-20,21,22	2478	26	-755	-540	-768	-418			No.2 settlement
61	Hwaseong	Bansongri	HS-23	2460	40	-752	-419	-760	-411	Charcoal		No.5 settlement
28	Yeoju	Heunamri	R_combine: KAERI, KAERI	2202	43	-358	-204	-386	-171			No.13 Settlement
28	Yeoju	Heunamri	KAERI	2145	60	-352	-93	-369	-45	Charcoal		No.14 Settlement
28	Yeoju	Heunamri	KAERI	2089	60	-196	-42	-354	52	Charcoal		No.14 Settlement

Appendix 11-b

R_COMBINED ^{14}C DETERMINATIONS OF PERFORATED RIM POTTERY

Site_Code	Site_Name		Lab No.	Date BP	±	+1 σ cal BC'	-1σ cal BC'	+2σ cal BC'	-2σ cal BC'	Material	House No.
15	Suwon	Yuljeondong	SNU03-212	3160	60	-1503	-1386	-1606	-1271	Charcoal	No.3 settlement-1
13	Hwaseong	Cheoncheonri	HS-11	3140	80	-1500	-1313	-1613	-1211	Charcoal	No.11 settlement
15	Suwon	Yuljeondong	SNU03-213	2990	40	-1302	-1132	-1386	-1059	Charcoal	No.3 settlement-2
11	Anyang	Gwanyangdong	SNU01-354	2950	60	-1262	-1056	-1379	-1001	Charcoal	No.1 settlement
12	Hwaseong	Gogeumsan	SNU00-360	2940	60	-1259	-1052	-1373	-979	Charcoal	No.1 settlement
13	Hwaseong	Cheoncheonri	R_combine: HS-3,4	2925	34	-1194	-1054	-1259	-1014		No.6 settlement
68	Pyeongtaek	Bangchukri	SNU02-282	2890	40	-1129	-1005	-1251	-938	Charcoal	No.3 settlement
11	Anyang	Gwanyangdong	SNU01-358	2870	50	-1124	-948	-1213	-912	Charcoal	No.5 settlement
13	Hwaseong	Cheoncheonri	R_combine: HS-1,2	2845	29	-1047	-940	-1114	-921		No.6 settlement
13	Hwaseong	Cheoncheonri	R_combine: HS-7,8	2825	43	-1038	-917	-1122	-851		No.7 settlement
54	Uiwang	Idong	SNU07-216	2820	50	-1041	-910	-1123	-843	Charcoal	No.1 settlement
54	Uiwang	Idong	SNU07-217	2820	50	-1041	-910	-1123	-843	Charcoal	No.1 settlement
13	Hwaseong	Cheoncheonri	R_combine: HS-5,6	2811	34	-1004	-921	-1055	-846		No.7 settlement
48	Hanam	Deokpungdong	HD-6	2800	60	-1022	-848	-1121	-824	Charcoal	No.1 settlement
48	Hanam	Deokpungdong	HD-7	2760	60	-976	-833	-1049	-805	Charcoal	No.1 settlement
48	Hanam	Deokpungdong	HD-5	2750	60	-973	-828	-1041	-802	Charcoal	No.1 settlement
11	Anyang	Gwanyangdong	SNU01-357	2740	40	-917	-834	-976	-810	Charcoal	No.4 settlement
61	Hwaseong	Bansongri	HS-33	2730	40	-907	-831	-975	-806	Charcoal	No.14 settlement
54	Uiwang	Idong	R_combine: SNU07-214,211	2730	36	-906	-832	-972	-809		No.10 settlement
68	Pyeongtaek	Bangchukri	SNU02-283	2720	40	-902	-827	-971	-804	Charcoal	No.3 settlement
54	Uiwang	Idong	R_combine: SNU07-212,213	2720	39	-901	-827	-971	-804		No.11 settlement
68	Pyeongtaek	Bangchukri	R_combine: SNU02-279,280	2710	29	-896	-823	-909	-809		No.1 settlement

Site_Code	Site_Name		Lab No.	Date BP	±	+1 σ cal BC'	-1σ cal BC'	+2σ cal BC'	-2σ cal BC'	Material	House No.
8	Bucheon	Gogangdong	KCP462	2690	50	-896	-806	-971	-791	Charcoal	No.10 settlement
61	Hwaseong	Bansongri	HS-32	2690	40	-895	-807	-914	-798	Charcoal	No.14 settlement
54	Uiwang	Idong	SNU07-215	2690	50	-896	-806	-971	-791	Charcoal	No.1 settlement
11	Anyang	Gwanyangdong	SNU01-356	2680	60	-896	-801	-976	-771	Charcoal	No.3 settlement
68	Pyeongtaek	Bangchukri	SNU02-284	2630	50	-841	-771	-911	-594	Charcoal	No.4 settlement
3	Paju	Okseokri	GX-0554	2590	105	-891	-540	-967	-408	Charcoal	settlement
11	Anyang	Gwanyangdong	R_combine: SNU01-470,471	2535	29	-791	-593	-797	-544		No.7 settlement
61	Hwaseong	Bansongri	R_combine: HS-27,28	2514	32	-772	-553	-791	-538		No.8 settlement
13	Hwaseong	Cheoncheonri	R_combine: HS-9,10	2509	49	-775	-544	-795	-417		No.9-2 settlement
11	Anyang	Gwanyangdong	SNU01-472	2440	60	-746	-410	-762	-403	Charcoal	No.8 Settlement
28	Yeoju	Heunamri	KAERI	2145	60	-352	-93	-369	-45	Charcoal	No.14 Settlement

Appendix 11-c

R_COMBINED ^{14}C DETERMINATIONS OF NOTCHED RIM POTTERY

Site_Code	Site_Name		Lab No.	Date BP	±	+1 σ cal BC'	-1σ cal BC'	+2σ cal BC'	-2σ cal BC'	Material	House No.
15	Suwon	Yuljeondong	SNU03-212	3160	60	-1503	-1386	-1606	-1271	Charcoal	No.3 settlement-1
13	Hwaseong	Cheoncheonri	HS-11	3140	80	-1500	-1313	-1613	-1211	Charcoal	No.11 settlement
15	Suwon	Yuljeondong	SNU03-213	2990	40	-1302	-1132	-1386	-1059	Charcoal	No.3 settlement-2
13	Hwaseong	Cheoncheonri	R_combine: HS-3,4	2925	34	-1194	-1054	-1259	-1014		No.6 settlement
61	Hwaseong	Bansongri	HS-29	2890	40	-1129	-1005	-1251	-938	Charcoal	No.9 settlement
11	Anyang	Gwanyangdong	SNU01-358	2870	50	-1124	-948	-1213	-912	Charcoal	No.5 settlement
13	Hwaseong	Cheoncheonri	R_combine: HS-1,2	2845	29	-1047	-940	-1114	-921		No.6 settlement
9	Siheung	Gyesudong	SNU02-042	2830	30	-1017	-927	-1111	-906	Charcoal	No.2 settlement
13	Hwaseong	Cheoncheonri	R_combine: HS-7,8	2825	43	-1038	-917	-1122	-851		No.7 settlement

Site_Code	Site_Name		Lab No.	Date BP	±	+1 σ cal BC'	-1σ cal BC'	+2σ cal BC'	-2σ cal BC'	Material	House No.
54	Uiwang	Idong	SNU07-216	2820	50	-1041	-910	-1123	-843	Charcoal	No.1 settlement
54	Uiwang	Idong	SNU07-217	2820	50	-1041	-910	-1123	-843	Charcoal	No.1 settlement
13	Hwaseong	Cheoncheonri	R_combine: HS-5,6	2811	34	-1004	-921	-1055	-846		No.7 settlement
48	Hanam	Deokpungdong	HD-6	2800	60	-1022	-848	-1121	-824	Charcoal	No.1 settlement
48	Hanam	Deokpungdong	HD-7	2760	60	-976	-833	-1049	-805	Charcoal	No.1 settlement
48	Hanam	Deokpungdong	HD-5	2750	60	-973	-828	-1041	-802	Charcoal	No.1 settlement
11	Anyang	Gwanyangdong	SNU01-469	2740	40	-917	-834	-976	-810	Charcoal	No.6 settlement
11	Anyang	Gwanyangdong	SNU01-357	2740	40	-917	-834	-976	-810	Charcoal	No.4 settlement
54	Uiwang	Idong	R_combine: SNU07-214,211	2730	36	-906	-832	-972	-809		No.10 settlement
54	Uiwang	Idong	R_combine: SNU07-212,213	2720	39	-901	-827	-971	-804		No.11 settlement
61	Hwaseong	Bansongri	HS-30	2700	50	-896	-812	-973	-795	Charcoal	No.9 settlement
8	Bucheon	Gogangdong	KCP462	2690	50	-896	-806	-971	-791	Charcoal	No.10 settlement
54	Uiwang	Idong	SNU07-215	2690	50	-896	-806	-971	-791	Charcoal	No.1 settlement
11	Anyang	Gwanyangdong	SNU01-356	2680	60	-896	-801	-976	-771	Charcoal	No.3 settlement
61	Hwaseong	Bansongri	R_combine: HS-27,28	2514	32	-772	-553	-791	-538		No.8 settlement
13	Hwaseong	Cheoncheonri	R_combine: HS-9,10	2509	49	-775	-544	-795	-417		No.9-2 settlement
61	Hwaseong	Bansongri	HS-31	2480	40	-758	-538	-770	-416	Charcoal	No.9 settlement
11	Anyang	Gwanyangdong	SNU01-472	2440	60	-746	-410	-762	-403	Charcoal	No.8 Settlement
28	Yeoju	Heunamri	KAERI	2145	60	-352	-93	-369	-45	Charcoal	No.14 Settlement
28	Yeoju	Heunamri	KAERI	2089	60	-196	-42	-354	52	Charcoal	No.14 Settlement

Appendix 11-d

R_COMBINED ^{14}C DETERMINATIONS OF HEUNAMRI POTTERY

Site_Code	Site_Name		Lab No.	Date BP	±	+1σ cal BC'	-1σ cal BC'	+2σ cal BC'	-2σ cal BC'	Material	House No.
28	Yeoju	Heunamri	R_combine: KAERI-70, RIKEN	3069	50	-1410	-1273	-1443	-1134		No.12 Settlement
28	Yeoju	Heunamri	R_combine: KAERI, RIKEN	2867	58	-1127	-937	-1258	-902		No.12 Settlement
48	Hanam	Deokpungdong	HD-6	2800	60	-1022	-848	-1121	-824	Charcoal	No.1 settlement
48	Hanam	Deokpungdong	HD-7	2760	60	-976	-833	-1049	-805	Charcoal	No.1 settlement
48	Hanam	Deokpungdong	HD-5	2750	60	-973	-828	-1041	-802	Charcoal	No.1 settlement
28	Yeoju	Heunamri	KAERI 153	2541	150	-811	-417	-1026	-234	Charcoal	No.8 Settlement
28	Yeoju	Heunamri	KAERI-121	2520	120	-799	-511	-901	-391	Charcoal	No.7 Settlement
28	Yeoju	Heunamri	R_combine: KAERI, KAERI	2202	43	-358	-204	-386	-171		No.13 Settlement
28	Yeoju	Heunamri	KAERI	2145	60	-352	-93	-369	-45	Charcoal	No.14 Settlement
28	Yeoju	Heunamri	KAERI	2089	60	-196	-42	-354	52	Charcoal	No.14 Settlement

Appendix 11-e

R_COMBINED ^{14}C DETERMINATIONS OF RED-BURNISHED POTTERY

Site_Code	Site_Name		Lab No.	Date BP	±	+1 σ cal BC’	-1σ cal BC’	+2σ cal BC’	-2σ cal BC’	Material	House No.
12	Hwaseong	Gogeumsan	SNU00-360	2940	60	-1259	-1052	-1373	-979	Charcoal	No.1 settlement
68	Pyeongtaek	Bangchukri	SNU02-282	2890	40	-1129	-1005	-1251	-938	Charcoal	No.3 settlement
61	Hwaseong	Bansongri	HS-29	2890	40	-1129	-1005	-1251	-938	Charcoal	No.9 settlement
13	Hwaseong	Cheoncheonri	R_combine: HS-7,8	2825	43	-1038	-917	-1122	-851		No.7 settlement
13	Hwaseong	Cheoncheonri	R_combine: HS-5,6	2811	34	-1004	-921	-1055	-846		No.7 settlement
48	Hanam	Deokpungdong	HD-6	2800	60	-1022	-848	-1121	-824	Charcoal	No.1 settlement
48	Hanam	Deokpungdong	HD-7	2760	60	-976	-833	-1049	-805	Charcoal	No.1 settlement
68	Pyeongtaek	Bangchukri	SNU02-281	2750	40	-926	-835	-997	-816	Charcoal	No.2 settlement

Site_Code	Site_Name		Lab No.	Date BP	±	+1 σ cal BC’	-1σ cal BC’	+2σ cal BC’	-2σ cal BC’	Material	House No.
48	Hanam	Deokpungdong	HD-5	2750	60	-973	-828	-1041	-802	Charcoal	No.1 settlement
61	Hwaseong	Bansongri	HS-33	2730	40	-907	-831	-975	-806	Charcoal	No.14 settlement
68	Pyeongtaek	Bangchukri	SNU02-283	2720	40	-902	-827	-971	-804	Charcoal	No.3 settlement
61	Hwaseong	Bansongri	HS-30	2700	50	-896	-812	-973	-795	Charcoal	No.9 settlement
61	Hwaseong	Bansongri	HS-32	2690	40	-895	-807	-914	-798	Charcoal	No.14 settlement
61	Hwaseong	Bansongri	R_combine: HS-27,28	2514	32	-772	-553	-791	-538		No.8 settlement
61	Hwaseong	Bansongri	HS-31	2480	40	-758	-538	-770	-416	Charcoal	No.9 settlement
61	Hwaseong	Bansongri	R_combine: HS-20,21,22	2478	26	-755	-540	-768	-418		No.2 settlement
61	Hwaseong	Bansongri	HS-23	2460	40	-752	-419	-760	-411	Charcoal	No.5 settlement
11	Anyang	Gwanyangdong	SNU01-472	2440	60	-746	-410	-762	-403	Charcoal	No.8 Settlement
28	Yeoju	Heunamri	R_combine: KAERI, KAERI	2202	43	-358	-204	-386	-171		No.13 Settlement
28	Yeoju	Heunamri	KAERI	2145	60	-352	-93	-369	-45	Charcoal	No.14 Settlement
28	Yeoju	Heunamri	KAERI	2089	60	-196	-42	-354	52	Charcoal	No.14 Settlement

Appendix 12-a

R_COMBINED ^{14}C DETERMINATIONS OF THE THIN-RECTANGULAR SHAPE HOUSES

Site_Code	Site_Name		Lab No.	Date BP	±	+1 σ cal BC'	-1σ cal BC'	+2σ cal BC'	-2σ cal BC'	Material	House No.	
3	Paju	Okseokri	GX-0554	2590	105	-891	-540	-967	-408	Charcoal	settlement	under BI dolmen
8	Bucheon	Gogangdong	KCP463	2910	70	-1252	-1008	-1367	-916	Charcoal	No.12 house	
8	Bucheon	Gogangdong	KCP462	2690	50	-896	-806	-971	-791	Charcoal	No.10 house	
9	Siheung	Gyesudong	SNU02-043	2580	40	-809	-669	-821	-549	Charcoal	No.3 house	
11	Anyang	Gwanyangdong	SNU01-358	2870	50	-1124	-948	-1213	-912	Charcoal	No.5 house	
11	Anyang	Gwanyangdong	SNU01-472	2440	60	-746	-410	-762	-403	Charcoal	No.8 house	
11	Anyang	Gwanyangdong	SNU01-355	2370	90	-748	-374	-771	-209	Charcoal	No.2 house	
13	Hwaseong	Cheoncheonri	R_combine: HS-7,8	2825	43	-1038	-917	-1122	-851	Charcoal	No.7 settlement	
13	Hwaseong	Cheoncheonri	R_combine: HS-5,6	2811	34	-1004	-921	-1055	-846	Charcoal	No.7 settlement	
15	Suwon	Yuljeondong	SNU03-212	3160	60	-1503	-1386	-1606	-1271	Charcoal	No.3 house-1	
15	Suwon	Yuljeondong	SNU03-210	3020	40	-1377	-1213	-1396	-1129	Charcoal	No.1 house-2	
15	Suwon	Yuljeondong	SNU03-213	2990	40	-1302	-1132	-1386	-1059	Charcoal	No.3 house-2	
15	Suwon	Yuljeondong	SNU03-209	2780	40	-997	-860	-1019	-829	Charcoal	No.1 house-1	
15	Suwon	Yuljeondong	SNU03-211	2730	40	-907	-831	-975	-806	Charcoal	No.1 house-3	
28	Yeoju	Heunamri	R_combine: KAERI-70, RIKEN	3069	50	-1410	-1273	-1443	-1134	Charcoal	No.12 house	West floor
28	Yeoju	Heunamri	R_combine: KAERI, RIKEN	2867	58	-1127	-937	-1258	-902	Charcoal	No.12 house	West floor
28	Yeoju	Heunamri	KAERI-121	2520	120	-799	-511	-901	-391	Charcoal	No.7 house	floor
28	Yeoju	Heunamri	KAERI	2145	60	-352	-93	-369	-45	Charcoal	No.14 house	B spot floor
28	Yeoju	Heunamri	KAERI	2089	60	-196	-42	-354	52	Charcoal	No.14 house	B spot floor

Appendix 12-b

R_COMBINED ^{14}C DETERMINATIONS OF THE RECTANGULAR SHAPE HOUSES

Site_Code	Site_Name		Lab No.	Date BP	±	+1 σ cal BC'	-1σ cal BC'	+2σ cal BC'	-2σ cal BC'	Material	House No.	
11	Anyang	Gwanyangdong	SNU01-354	2950	60	-1262	-1056	-1379	-1001	Charcoal	No.1 house	
11	Anyang	Gwanyangdong	SNU01-469	2740	40	-917	-834	-976	-810	Charcoal	No.6 house	
11	Anyang	Gwanyangdong	SNU01-357	2740	40	-917	-834	-976	-810	Charcoal	No.4 house	
11	Anyang	Gwanyangdong	SNU01-356	2680	60	-896	-801	-976	-771	Charcoal	No.3 house	
12	Hwaseong	Gogeumsan	SNU00-360	2940	60	-1259	-1052	-1373	-979	Charcoal	No.1 house	
13	Hwaseong	Cheoncheonri	HS-11	3140	80	-1500	-1313	-1613	-1211	Charcoal	No.11 house	
13	Hwaseong	Cheoncheonri	R_combine: HS-3,4	2925	34	-1194	-1054	-1259	-1014		No.6 house	
13	Hwaseong	Cheoncheonri	R_combine: HS-1,2	2845	29	-1047	-940	-1114	-921		No.6 house	
28	Yeoju	Heunamri	KAERI 153	2541	150	-811	-417	-1026	-234	Charcoal	No.8 house	near the hearth
28	Yeoju	Heunamri	R_combine: KAERI, KAERI	2202	43	-358	-204	-386	-171		No.13 house	B spot floor
48	Hanam	Deokpungdong	HD-6	2800	60	-1022	-848	-1121	-824	Charcoal	No.1 house	
48	Hanam	Deokpungdong	HD-7	2760	60	-976	-833	-1049	-805	Charcoal	No.1 house	
48	Hanam	Deokpungdong	HD-5	2750	60	-973	-828	-1041	-802	Charcoal	No.1 house	
54	Uiwang	Idong	SNU07-216	2820	50	-1041	-910	-1123	-843	Charcoal	No.1 house	
54	Uiwang	Idong	SNU07-217	2820	50	-1041	-910	-1123	-843	Charcoal	No.1 house	
54	Uiwang	Idong	R_combine: SNU07-214,211	2730	36	-906	-832	-972	-809		No.10 house	
54	Uiwang	Idong	R_combine: SNU07-212,213	2720	39	-901	-827	-971	-804		No.11 house	
54	Uiwang	Idong	SNU07-215	2690	50	-896	-806	-971	-791	Charcoal	No.1 house	
68	Pyeongtaek	Bangchukri	SNU02-284	2630	50	-841	-771	-911	-594	Charcoal	No.4 house	

Appendix 12-c

R_COMBINED ^{14}C DETERMINATIONS OF THE SQUARE SHAPE HOUSES

Site_Code	Site_Name		Lab No.	Date BP	±	+1 σ cal BC'	-1σ cal BC'	+2σ cal BC'	-2σ cal BC'	Material	House No.	
9	Siheung	Gyesudong	SNU02-042	2830	30	-1017	-927	-1111	-906	Charcoal	No.2 house	
9	Siheung	Gyesudong	SNU02-041	2410	40	-700	-404	-751	-396	Charcoal	No.1 house	
11	Anyang	Gwanyangdong	R_combine: SNU01-470,471	2535	29	-791	-593	-797	-544		No.7 house	
13	Hwaseong	Cheoncheonri	R_combine: HS-9,10	2509	49	-775	-544	-795	-417		No.9-2 house	
61	Hwaseong	Bansongri	HS-29	2890	40	-1129	-1005	-1251	-938	Charcoal	No.9 house	sedimentary L 2
61	Hwaseong	Bansongri	HS-33	2730	40	-907	-831	-975	-806	Charcoal	No.14 house	sedimentary L
61	Hwaseong	Bansongri	HS-30	2700	50	-896	-812	-973	-795	Charcoal	No.9 house	sedimentary L 3
61	Hwaseong	Bansongri	HS-32	2690	40	-895	-807	-914	-798	Charcoal	No.14 house	interior pit
61	Hwaseong	Bansongri	R_combine: HS-27,28	2514	32	-772	-553	-791	-538		No.8 house	sedimentary Layer 2
61	Hwaseong	Bansongri	HS-31	2480	40	-758	-538	-770	-416	Charcoal	No.9 house	sedimentary L 3
61	Hwaseong	Bansongri	R_combine: HS-20,21,22	2478	26	-755	-540	-768	-418		No.2 house	sedimentary Layer
61	Hwaseong	Bansongri	HS-23	2460	40	-752	-419	-760	-411	Charcoal	No.5 house	sedimentary Layer
68	Pyeongtaek	Bangchukri	SNU02-282	2890	40	-1129	-1005	-1251	-938	Charcoal	No.3 house	
68	Pyeongtaek	Bangchukri	SNU02-281	2750	40	-926	-835	-997	-816	Charcoal	No.2 house	
68	Pyeongtaek	Bangchukri	SNU02-283	2720	40	-902	-827	-971	-804	Charcoal	No.3 house	
68	Pyeongtaek	Bangchukri	R_combine: SNU02-279,280	2710	29	-896	-823	-909	-809		No.1 house	

Appendix 13

THE NUMBER OF MONUMENT SITES AND MONUMENTS WITHIN 1 KM AND 5 KM RADII FROM EACH SETTLEMENT AND HOUSE NUMBERS

Site_Code	Town	Village	House_No.	Enclosure	Monu_ sites_1km	Monument_ No_1km	Monu_ sites_5km	Monument_ No_5km
1	Yeoncheon	Samgeori	3		1	1	5	6
2	Paju	Dayulri	1		2	40	4	45
3	Paju	Okseokri	1		2	24	5	30
4	Paju	Gyohari	2		1	38	4	45
5	Ganghwa	Samgeori	1		2	3	6	56
6	Incheon	Geumdandong	1		0	0	8	34
7	Incheon	Wondangdong	1		0	0	5	5
8	Bucheon	Gogangdong	21	Y	0	0	1	1
9	Siheung	Gyesudong	4		0	0	1	11
10	Gunpo	Daemiyadong	1		1	2	6	18
11	Anyang	Gwanyangdong	8		0	0	4	29
12	Hwaseong	Gogeumsan	2		0	0	5	14
13	Hwaseong	Cheoncheonri	13		0	0	3	5
14	Hwaseong	Donghaksan	32	Y	0	0	6	24
15	Suwon	Yuljeondong	8	Y	0	0	7	9
16	Suwon	Imokdong	2		0	0	5	12
17	Pyeongtaek	Jijedong	5		0	0	3	6
18	Pyeongtaek	Hyeonhwari	6		0	0	1	2
19	Pyeongtaek	Hyeongokri	34		0	0	1	2
20	Yongin	Bongmyeongri	1		0	0	1	1
21	Yongin	Jukjeon	5		0	0	3	3
22	Seoul	Garakdong	1		0	0	2	5
23	Seoul	Yeoksamdong	1		0	0	4	7
24	Seoul	Myeongildong	1		0	2	6	20
25	Seoul	Ilwondong	1		0	0	5	8
26	Namyangju	Suseokri	6		1	1	5	15
27	Hanam	Misari	38		0	0	1	3
28	Yeoju	Heunamri	14		0	0	0	0
29	Gapyeong	Daljeonri	42		0	0	1	1
30	Gapyeong	Daeseongri	2		0	0	1	6
31	Yangpyeong	Yangsuri	2		1	2	2	5
44	Incheon	Donyangdong	3		0	0	0	0
45	Hanam	Mangwoldong	4		0	0	2	10

Site_Code	Town	Village	House_No.	Enclosure	Monu_ sites_1km	Monument_ No_1km	Monu_ sites_5km	Monument_ No_5km
46	Hanam	Mangwoldong Gusan	1		0	0	3	10
47	Hanam	Deokpungdong Surigol	2		0	0	3	17
48	Hanam	Deokpungdong Ritual site	1	Ritual site	0	0	3	17
54	Uiwang	Idong	13		2	3	11	48
60	Hwaseong	Banwoldong	1		0	0	3	11
61	Hwaseong	Bansongdong	14		0	0	7	26
64	Hwaseong	Gajaeri	2		0	0	4	11
68	Pyeongtaek	Bangchukri	4		0	0	0	0
72	Anseong	Banjeri	9	Y	0	0	4	6
75	Paju	Sikhyeonri	1		0	0	1	1
76	Osan	Gajangdong	2	Y	0	0	12	31
77	Gwangmeong	Gahakdong	1		1	3	7	23

Appendix 14

THE RELATIONSHIP BETWEEN THE NUMBER OF HOUSES AND THE DISTANCE FROM WATER

Site_Code	Town	Village	Period	Enclosure	House_No.	sps_sh_1000 _Tributaries	sps_sh_1000_17 _Main rivers	sps_sh_100 _Tributaries	sps_sh_100_75 _Main rivers
29	Gapyeong	Daljeonri	Early to Late		42	148.9	1,850.8	160.1	1,591.4
24	Seoul	Myeongildong	Late		1	251.1	1,633.0	502.2	502.2
31	Yangpyeong	Yangsuri	Early to Middle		2	297.8	297.8	178.9	11,034.5
16	Suwon	Imokdong	Middle		2	367.4	23,552.9	437.2	5,936.0
23	Seoul	Yeoksamdong	Early		1	372.1	3,819.2	251.1	1,588.2
26	Namyangju	Suseokri	Late		6	376.7	554.9	222.0	480.2
14	Hwaseong	Donghaksan	Early to Middle	Y	32	421.7	14,293.7	773.0	15,515.7
27	Hanam	Misari	Early to Late		38	480.2	480.2	297.8	297.8
30	Gapyeong	Daeseongri	Middle to Late		2	529.4	529.4	779.7	4,564.5
17	Pyeongtaek	Jijedong	Early to Middle		5	532.7	5,091.7	421.7	7,762.3
1	Yeoncheon	Samgeori	Early to Middle (red burnish)		3	577.1	6,486.3	577.1	787.2
45	Hanam	Mangwoldong	Early to Middle		4	621.5	621.5	621.5	621.5
28	Yeoju	Heunamri	Early to Late		14	627.8	627.8	596.4	596.4
20	Yongin	Bongmyeongri	Early		1	628.2	10,878.0	599.7	3,685.1
7	Incheon	Wondangdong	Early to Late (pottery)		1	646.3	4,154.6	1,032.5	4,266.2
64	Hwaseong	Gajaeri	Middle		2	662.2	9,983.6	572.8	6,769.6
11	Anyang	Gwanyangdong	Early to Middle		8	710.3	11,719.2	933.5	3,738.6
21	Yongin	Jukjeon	Early to Late		5	784.4	20,116.6	779.4	5,106.4
4	Paju	Gyohari	Early		2	894.7	6,325.7	338.1	1,533.3
75	Paju	Sikhyeonri	Middle		1	903.5	903.5	741.8	903.5
47	Hanam	Deokpungdong Surigol	Early		2	969.0	2,432.7	872.7	2,432.7
19	Pyeongtaek	Hyeongokri	Early to Middle		34	989.9	3,685.1	532.7	2,472.6
3	Paju	Okseokri	Early		1	1,010.8	4,319.0	744.5	894.7
77	Gwangmeong	Gahakdong	Early to Late		1	1,032.7	14,361.9	534.5	10,634.3

Site_Code	Town	Village	Period	Enclosure	House_No.	sps_sh_1000 _Tributaries	sps_sh_1000_17 _Main rivers	sps_sh_100 _Tributaries	sps_sh_100_75 _Main rivers
48	Hanam	Deokpungdong Ritual site	Middle (Radiocarbon dates)	Ritual site	1	1,137.0	3,358.6	737.8	3,358.6
46	Hanam	Mangwoldong Gusan	Early to Late		1	1,201.8	1,201.8	400.1	1,203.7
60	Hwaseong	Banwoldong	Middle		1	1,203.7	16,829.6	140.4	8,448.0
2	Paju	Dayulri	Early		1	1,243.0	6,680.9	785.4	4,317.9
68	Pyeongtaek	Bangchukri	Middle		4	1,381.1	2,280.1	887.8	2,280.1
25	Seoul	Ilwondong	Late (pottery)		1	1,398.5	6,114.1	388.3	554.9
22	Seoul	Garakdong	Middle		1	1,422.2	1,925.8	188.3	1,726.7
13	Hwaseong	Cheoncheonri	Early to Middle		13	1,429.5	15,230.2	366.1	14,170.6
54	Uiwang	Idong	Early to Middle		13	1,459.0	19,181.1	639.1	18,679.4
12	Hwaseong	Gogeumsan	Early to Late		2	1,492.2	14,003.5	400.1	17,452.0
61	Hwaseong	Bansongdong	Middle		14	1,531.5	14,641.2	548.2	7,309.4
5	Ganghwa	Samgeori	Early to Late		1	1,583.5	11,034.5	532.7	7,517.7
44	Incheon	Donyangdong	Early to Middle		3	1,640.8	6,552.0	480.2	6,552.0
6	Incheon	Geumdandong	Late		1	1,851.3	7,517.7	443.9	4,154.6
10	Gunpo	Daemiyadong	Early		1	1,871.3	21,468.3	372.1	2,640.9
9	Siheung	Gyesudong	Early to Middle		4	2,009.2	13,781.1	280.8	11,719.2
15	Suwon	Yuljeondong	Middle to Late	Y	8	2,027.6	22,217.7	475.0	13,230.7
18	Pyeongtaek	Hyeonhwari	Early to Middle		6	2,294.3	5,101.8	313.9	1,299.0
72	Anseong	Banjeri	Middle to Late	Y	9	2,825.0	7,783.0	1,139.8	6,213.8
76	Osan	Gajangdong	Middle to Late	Y	2	2,938.3	7,814.8	732.8	2,982.0
8	Bucheon	Gogangdong	Middle to Late	Y	21	3,111.5	6,549.5	188.3	8,833.0

Appendix 15

The viewshed range and elevation of settlements (From the highest to the lowest visible cell numbers)

Site_ Code	Town	Village	Revised_2	Visible cell numbers	Elevation	Feature_11	Enclosure	House_No.	Aspect	Slope	Soil_type
25	Seoul	Ilwondong	Late	47594	255	4		1	NW	6.4	Limited_Upland
8	Bucheon	Gogangdong	Middle to Late	33469	119	4	Y	21	SE	2.1	Limited_Upland
19	Pyeongtaek	Hyeongokri	Early to Middle	31852	66	4		34	NE	1.8	Unranked_Upland
68	Pyeongtaek	Bangchukri	Middle	31553	55	5		4	N	0.4	Upland_Poor
76	Osan	Gajangdong	Middle to Late	30060	111	4	Y	2	E	1.4	Limited_Upland
12	Hwaseong	Gogeumsan	Early to Late	23603	123	5		2	NW	0.9	Unranked_Upland
21	Yongin	Jukjeon	Early to Late	18967	164	4		5	W	2.3	Limited_Upland
16	Suwon	Imokdong	Middle	18120	142	4		2	S	3.2	Forest
24	Seoul	Myeongildong	Late	17675	56	6		1	E	1.4	Related_Water
28	Yeoju	Heunamri	Early to Late	17377	115	4		14	NE	2.6	Limited_Upland
48	Hanam	Deokpungdong Ritual site	Middle	15911	116	4	Ritual site	1	E	1.6	Limited_Upland
3	Paju	Okseokri	Early	15430	98	4		1	SE	2.5	Limited_Upland
26	Namyangju	Suseokri	Late	14858	76	5		6	NW	0.6	Limited_Upland
22	Seoul	Garakdong	Middle	14776	37	4		1	NW	0.6	Upland_Good
18	Pyeongtaek	Hyeonhwari	Early to Middle	14412	43	4		6	S	0.2	Rice_Good
23	Seoul	Yeoksamdong	Early	14284	70	4		1	SW	1.5	Upland_Good
4	Paju	Gyohari	Early	12876	51	4		2	NE	2.2	Upland_Good
14	Hwaseong	Donghaksan	Early to Middle	11812	106	4	Y	32	NE	3.0	Rice_Good
27	Hanam	Misari	Early to Late	10412	23	4		38	SW	0.6	Upland_Good
75	Paju	Sikhyeonri	Middle	10301	103	6		1	NW	3.5	Limited_Upland
72	Anseong	Banjeri	Middle to Late	10044	137	3	Y	9	S	0.1	Forest
15	Suwon	Yuljeondong	Middle to Late	9654	111	4	Y	8	S	2.8	Limited_Upland
45	Hanam	Mangwoldong	Early to Middle	9337	42	5		4	SE	0.3	Related_Water
44	Incheon	Donyangdong	Early to Middle	9328	26	6		3	SE	1.9	Limited_Upland
7	Incheon	Wondangdong	Early to Late	9283	33	4		1	S	1.4	Rice_Good
47	Hanam	Deokpungdong Surigol	Early	8605	56	6		2	W	1.2	Limited_Upland
46	Hanam	Mangwoldong Gusan	Early to Late	8605	24	6		1	NW	0.3	Both
6	Incheon	Geumdandong	Late	8357	47	4		1	W	1.1	Upland_Poor
60	Hwaseong	Banwoldong	Middle	8090	62	4		1	N	0.9	Rice_Good
10	Gunpo	Daemiyadong	Early	6927	88	4		1	SE	0.3	Upland_Good
54	Uiwang	Idong	Early to Middle	6643	106	4		13	NW	5.0	Limited_Upland

Site_ Code	Town	Village	Revised_2	Visible cell numbers	Elevation	Feature_11	Enclosure	House_No.	Aspect	Slope	Soil_type
17	Pyeongtaek	Jijedong	Early to Middle	6637	35	6		5	E	2.6	Limited_Upland
31	Yangpyeong	Yangsuri	Early to Middle	6097	35	6		2	N	0.2	Upland_Good
20	Yongin	Bongmyeongri	Early	4608	65	4		1	W	1.5	Rice_Poor
64	Hwaseong	Gajaeri	Middle	4517	80	6		2	SE	2.9	Upland_Good
61	Hwaseong	Bansongdong	Middle	4019	73	4		14	SW	1.1	Limited_Upland
11	Anyang	Gwanyangdong	Early to Middle	3785	69	6		8	E	2.4	Limited_Upland
5	Ganghwa	Samgeori	Early to Late	3317	66	4		1	NW	4.2	Rice_Poor
30	Gapyeong	Daeseongri	Middle to Late	2261	63	6		2	SE	8.9	Limited_Upland
2	Paju	Dayulri	Early	2210	35	4		1	N	1.4	Upland_Good
9	Siheung	Gyesudong	Early to Middle	1908	40	4		4	SE	0.9	Rice_Poor
13	Hwaseong	Cheoncheonri	Early to Middle	1837	57	4		13	S	2.8	Limited_Upland
29	Gapyeong	Daljeonri	Early to Late	1236	80	6		42	N	3.5	Related_Water
77	Gwangmeong	Gahakdong	Early to Late	1126	54	3		1	N	0.8	Rice_Poor
1	Yeoncheon	Samgeori	Early to Middle	667	39	6		3	NW	4.2	Unranked_Upland
	Average			12099	77						
	Standard deviation			10054.51018	44						
	Median			9337	66						
	Mode			8605	35						

Appendix 16

The house number of enclosure and non-enclosure sites

Site_Code	Town	Village	Revised_2	Visible cell numbers	Elevation	Feature_11	Enclosure	River vs. Inland	House_No.	Aspect	Slope	Soil_type
14	Hwaseong	Donghaksan	Early to Middle	11812	106	4	Y		32	NE	3.0	Rice_Good
72	Anseong	Banjeri	Middle to Late	10044	137	3	Y		9	S	0.1	Forest
8	Bucheon	Gogangdong	Middle to Late	33469	119	4	Y		21	SE	2.1	Limited_Upland
76	Osan	Gajangdong	Middle to Late	30060	111	4	Y		2	E	1.4	Limited_Upland
15	Suwon	Yuljeondong	Middle to Late	9654	111	4	Y		8	S	2.8	Limited_Upland
								Average	10			
								standard deviation	8			
								Median	9			
								Interquatile range	13			
54	Uiwang	Idong	Early to Middle	6643	106	4			13	NW	5.0	Limited_Upland
12	Hwaseong	Gogeumsan	Early to Late	23603	123	5			2	NW	0.9	Unranked_Upland
21	Yongin	Jukjeon	Early to Late	18967	164	4			5	W	2.3	Limited_Upland
28	Yeoju	Heunamri	Early to Late	17377	115	4			14	NE	2.6	Limited_Upland
16	Suwon	Imokdong	Middle	18120	142	4			2	S	3.2	Forest
48	Hanam	Deokpungdong Ritual site	Middle	15911	116	4	Ritual site	Han river	1	E	1.6	Limited_Upland
75	Paju	Sikhyeonri	Middle	10301	103	6		Imjin river	1	NW	3.5	Limited_Upland
25	Seoul	Ilwondong	Late	47594	255	4			1	NW	6.4	Limited_Upland
								Average	5			
								standard deviation	5.5			
								Median	2			
								Interquatile range	6			

Appendix 17

The long term change data of Settlements

Site_Code	Town	Village	Period	Soil types	Visible cell numbers	House_No.	Enclosure	elevation	sps_sh_100	sps_sh_100_75	River vs. Inland
2	Paju	Dayulri	Early	Upland_Good	2210	1		35.0	785.36	4,317.87	Han river
3	Paju	Okseokri	Early	Limited_Upland	15430	1		98.0	744.46	894.73	Han river
4	Paju	Gyohari	Early	Upland_Good	12876	2		51.0	338.07	1,533.26	Han river
10	Gunpo	Daemiyadong	Early	Upland_Good	6927	1		88.0	372.07	2,640.90	
20	Yongin	Bongmyongri	Early	Rice_Poor	4608	1		65.0	599.69	3,685.06	Anseong river
23	Seoul	Yeoksamdong	Early	Upland_Good	14284	1		70.0	251.11	1,588.18	Han river
47	Hanam	Deokpungdong	Early	Limited_Upland	8605	2		56.0	872.71	2,432.72	Han river
				Average	9277.1	1.3		66.1	566.2	2441.8	
				Standard deviation	5059.6	0.5		21.6	246.3	1228.3	
				Median	8605.0	1.0		65.0	599.7	2432.7	
				Interquartile range	7812.5	0.5		25.5	409.84	1,602.26	

Site_Code	Town	Village	Period	Soil types	Visible cell numbers	House_No.	Enclosure	elevation	sps_sh_100	sps_sh_100_75	River vs. Inland
1	Yeoncheon	Samgeori	Early to Middle	Unranked_Upland	667	3		39.0	577.08	787.24	Injin river
9	Siheung	Gyesudong	Early to Middle	Rice_Poor	1908	4		40.0	280.75	11,719.25	
11	Anyang	Guanyangdong	Early to Middle	Limited_Upland	3785	8		69.0	933.53	3,738.61	
13	Hwaseong	Cheonjeonri	Early to Middle	Limited_Upland	1837	13		57.0	366.06	14,170.58	
14	Hwaseong	Donghaksan	Early to Middle	Rice_Good	11812	32	Y	106.0	773.03	15,515.70	
17	Pyeongtaek	Jijedong	Early to Middle	Limited_Upland	6637	5		35.0	421.72	7,762.25	Anseong river
18	Pyeongtaek	Hyeonhwari	Early to Middle	Rice_Good	14412	6		43.0	313.89	1,298.96	
19	Pyeongtaek	Hyeongokri	Early to Middle	Unranked_Upland	31852	34		66.0	532.69	2,472.59	Anseong river
31	Yangpeong	Yangsuri	Early to Middle	Upland_Good	6097	2		35.0	178.95	11,034.46	Han river
44	Incheon	Dongyangdong	Early to Middle	Limited_Upland	9328	3		26.0	480.16	6,552.01	Han river
45	Hanam	Mangwoldong	Early to Middle	Related_Water	9337	4		42.0	621.48	621.48	Han river
54	Uiwang	Idong	Early to Middle	Limited_Upland	6643	13		106.0	639.06	18,679.44	
				Average	9422.5	11.3		56.8	503.8	8505.9	
				Standard deviation	8402.6	11.4		27.7	225.3	6156.7	
				Median	6643.0	6.0		43.0	480.2	7762.3	
				Interquartile range	6640.0	9.0		28.8	272.9	10152.9	

Site_Code	Town	Village	Period	Soil types	Visible cell numbers	House_No.	Enclosure	elevation	sps_sh_100	sps_sh_100_75	River vs. Inland
5	Ganghwa	Samgeori	Early to Late	Rice_Poor	3317	1		66.0	532.69	7,517.74	
7	Incheon	Wondangdong	Early to Late	Rice_Good	9283	1		33.0	1,032.51	4,266.17	Han river
12	Hwaseong	Gogeumsan	Early to Late	Unranked_Upland	23603	2		123.0	400.14	17,452.03	
21	Yongin	Jukjeon	Early to Late	Limited_Upland	18967	5		164.0	779.38	5,106.37	
27	Hanam	Misari	Early to Late	Upland_Good	10412	38		23.0	297.78	297.78	Han river
28	Yeoju	Heunamri	Early to Late	Limited_Upland	17377	14		115.0	596.40	596.40	
29	Gapyeong	Daljeonri	Early to Late	Related_Water	1236	42		80.0	160.05	1,591.44	
46	Hanam	Mangwoldong	Early to Late	Both	8605	1		24.0	400.14	1,203.69	Han river
77	Gwangmyeong	Gahakdong	Early to Late	Rice_Poor	1126	1		54.0	534.54	10,634.28	
				Average	10436.2	11.7		75.8	526.0	5407.3	
				Standard deviation	8070.0	16.6		49.3	260.7	5697.9	
				Median	9283.0	2.0		66.0	532.7	4266.2	
				Interquartile range	14060.0	13.0		82.0	196.3	6314.1	

Site_Code	Town	Village	Period	Soil types	Visible cell numbers	House_No.	Enclosure	elevation	sps_sh_100	sps_sh_100_75	River vs. Inland
16	Suwon	Imokdong	Middle	Forest	18120	2		142.0	437.20	5,936.01	
22	Seoul	Garakdong	Middle	Upland_Good	14776	1		37.0	188.34	1,726.69	Han river
48	Hanam	Deokpungdong	Middle	Limited_Upland	15911	1	Ritual site	116.0	737.81	3,358.65	Han river
60	Hwaseong	Banwoldong	Middle	Rice_Good	8090	1		62.0	140.38	8,447.99	
61	Hwaseong	Bansongdong	Middle	Limited_Upland	4019	14		73.0	548.19	7,309.38	
64	Hwaseong	Gajaeri	Middle	Upland_Good	4517	2		80.0	572.80	6,769.64	
68	Pyeongtaek	Bangchukri	Middle	Upland_Poor	31553	4		55.0	887.82	2,280.10	Anseong river
75	Paju	Sikhyeonri	Middle	Limited_Upland	10301	1		103.0	741.81	903.50	Imjin river
				Average	13410.9	3.3		83.5	531.8	4591.5	
				Standard deviation	8981.9	4.5		34.7	266.0	2865.6	
				Median	12538.5	1.5		76.5	560.5	4647.3	
				Interquartile range	9266.5	1.5		46.0	363.8	4762.8	

Site_Code	Town	Village	Period	Soil types	Visible cell numbers	House_No.	Enclosure	elevation	sps_sh_100	sps_sh_100_75	River vs. Inland
8	Bucheon	Gogangdong	Middle to Late	Limited_Upland	33469	21	Y	119.0	188.34	8,832.96	
15	Suwon	Yuljeondong	Middle to Late	Limited_Upland	9654	8	Y	111.0	475.01	13,230.66	
30	Gapyeong	Daeseongri	Middle to Late	Limited_Upland	2261	2		63.0	779.69	4,564.52	Han river
72	Anseong	Banjaeri	Middle to Late	Forest	10044	9	Y	137.0	1,139.78	6,213.80	
76	Osan	Gajangdong	Middle to Late	Limited_Upland	30060	3	Y	111.0	732.79	2,981.98	
				Average	14121.7	4.7		103.7	884.1	4586.8	
				Standard deviation	14341.1	3.8		37.5	222.7	1616.0	
				Median	10044.0	3.0		111.0	779.7	4564.5	
				Interquartile range	20406.0	6.0		8.0	304.7	4268.4	

Site_Code	Town	Village	Period	Soil types	Visible cell numbers	House_No.	Enclosure	elevation	sps_sh_100	sps_sh_100_75	River vs. Inland
6	Incheon	Geumdandong	Late	Upland_Poor	8357	1		47.0	443.91	4,154.60	
24	Seoul	Myongildong	Late	Related_Water	17675	1		56.0	502.23	502.23	Han river
25	Seoul	Ilwondong	Late	Limited_Upland	47594	1		255.0	388.26	554.89	
26	Namyangju	Suseokri	Late	Limited_Upland	14858	6		76.0	221.96	480.16	Han river
				Average	22121.0	2.3		108.5	389.1	1423.0	
				Standard deviation	17424.5	2.5		98.4	120.7	1821.4	
				Median	16266.5	1.0		66.0	416.1	528.6	
				Interquartile range	11922.0	1.0		67.0	111.8	958.1	

Viewshed	Visible cell numbers	Early	Middle	Late
Settlements	Average	9277.1	13410.9	22121.0
	Standard deviation	5059.6	8981.9	17424.5
	Median	8605.0	12538.5	16266.5
	Interquartile range	7812.5	9266.5	11922.0
Monuments	Average	4316.9	5830.5	5991.3
	Standard deviation	3553.1	5071.2	4101.4
	Median	2947.0	5369.0	5877.0
	Interquartile range	4760.0	8489.0	6721.8

Elevation		Early	Middle	Late
Settlements	Average	66.1	83.5	108.5
	Standard deviation	21.6	34.7	98.4
	Median	65.0	76.5	66.0
	Interquartile range	25.5	46.0	67.0
Monuments	Average	51.1	63.6	34.5
	Standard deviation	30.8	24.0	4.7
	Median	44.5	64.0	33.5
	Interquartile range	19.8	36.0	3.5

Distance from tributaries		Early	Middle	Late
Settlements	Average	566.2	531.8	389.1
	Standard deviation	246.3	266.0	120.7
	Median	599.7	560.5	416.1
	Interquartile range	409.8	363.8	111.8
Monuments	Average	423.7	380.4	236.2
	Standard deviation	256.6	240.8	123.7
	Median	393.0	377.3	272.6
	Interquartile range	268.9	349.7	142.5

Distance from main rivers		Early	Middle	Late
Settlements	Average	2,441.8	4,591.5	1,423.0
	Standard deviation	1,228.3	2,865.6	1,821.4
	Median	2,432.7	4,647.3	528.6
	Interquartile range	1,602.3	4,762.8	958.1
Monuments	Average	7,499.2	6,667.0	1,226.3
	Standard deviation	6,746.7	4,630.0	444.8
	Median	4,758.2	4,535.9	1,096.5
	Interquartile range	12,883.2	7,439.1	310.4

Appendix 18

MONUMENTS DATA ON THE BASIS OF EARLY, MIDDLE AND LATE PERIODS

Site_Code	Do_Site_ID	Town	Village	Period	Class_2	Visible	Table	Capstone	Menhir	Monument Total	elevation	Distance from tributaries	Distance from main rivers
15	35	Paju	Bongam-ri	Early	Limited_Upland	465		3		3	39.0	795.64	5,165.46
16	38	Paju	Deokeun-ri 1	Early	Limited_Upland	12346	7	2		14	98.0	776.84	4,347.66
17	52	Paju	Deokeun-ri 2	Early	Limited_Upland	1911		8		10	54.0	619.09	4,512.25
22	110	Paju	Dangha-ri 2	Early	Limited_Upland	9289				2	41.0	500.75	1,628.16
95	312	Anyang	Pyeongchon-dong 1	Early	Limited_Upland	6671		10		12	73.0	357.89	14,992.97
98	335	Gunpo	Bugok-dong	Early	Limited_Upland	923				2	49.0	44.39	17,224.45
102	354	Uiwang	Gocheon-dong	Early	Limited_Upland	6807				1	132.0	938.80	18,623.38
190	118	Paju	Munji-ri	Early	Limited_Upland	739			2	2	20.0	289.39	2,796.64
23	112	Paju	Sangjiseok-ri	Early	Rice_Good	2347	1			1	9.0	393.31	1,401.13
24	113	Paju	Yadang-ri	Early	Rice_Good	10057		4		4	36.0	439.45	1,850.23
104	356	Uiwang	I-dong	Early	Rice_Poor	2693	1	1		2	67.0	387.63	18,660.43
127	423	Pyeongtaek	Dongcheon-ri	Early	Rice_Poor	2947		1		1	55.0	177.56	1,290.40
199	495	Yongin	Chang-ri	Early	Rice_Poor	1080			1	1	42.0	119.53	6,587.89
18	62	Paju	Deokeun-ri 3	Early	Upland_Good	4920		1		1	44.0	392.68	5,004.20
21	72	Paju	Dayul-ri•Dangha-ri	Early	Upland_Good	3973	4	19		38	14.0	119.53	1,328.21
96	311	Anyang	Pyeongchon-dong 2	Early	Upland_Good	3781				1	45.0	426.94	14,572.85
					Average	4434.3					51.1	423.7	7499.2
					Standard deviation	3635.4					30.8	256.6	6746.7
					Median	3364.0					44.5	393.0	4758.2
					Interquartile range	5001.8					19.8	268.9	12883.2

Site_ Code	Do_ Site_ID	Town	Village	Period	Class_2	Visible	Table	Capstone	Menhir	Do_Site_ No_2	elevation	mpf_sc_ sh_100	mpf_sc_ sh_100_75
106	359	Suwon	Iui-dong	Middle	Limited_Upland	3952		2		5	97.0	733.80	13,098.10
107	364	Suwon	Woncheon-dong	Middle	Limited_Upland	9913		1		1	100.0	421.72	12,641.91
109	366	Suwon	Gyo-dong	Middle	Limited_Upland	16434		1		4	101.0	487.29	10,968.19
111	372	Hwaseong	Sugi-ri	Middle	Limited_Upland	7552		1		2	73.0	600.92	3,529.09
113	381	Hwaseong	Bansong-ri 1	Middle	Limited_Upland	5369		1		1	67.0	887.82	6,264.37
115	383	Hwaseong	Gwanhang-ri	Middle	Limited_Upland	60				4	64.0	662.16	3,989.40
117	389	Hwaseong	Dongo-ri	Middle	Limited_Upland	9763				4	85.0	377.32	4,415.07
147	476	Yongin	Sangha-dong	Middle	Limited_Upland	481	1			1	68.0	31.39	14,714.97
195	401	Hwaseong	Dongo-ri	Middle	Limited_Upland	8489			1	1	88.0	268.19	4,535.93
215	683	Suwon	Imok-dong	Middle	Limited_Upland	306				1	69.0	80.03	15,901.63
123	406	Osan	Geumam-dong	Middle	Rice_Good	91		10		11	62.0	523.83	3,085.90
157	508	Anseong	Manjeong-ri 1	Middle	Rice_Good	17122		1		1	52.0	183.03	3,373.72
110	370	Hwaseong	Songsan-dong	Middle	Rice_Poor	5922				2	35.0	178.95	4,219.78
121	403	Osan	Oesammi-dong	Middle	Rice_Poor	3654		1		2	49.0	221.96	5,102.66
158	509	Anseong	Manjeong-ri 2	Middle	Rice_Poor	6079		1		1	23.0	210.57	2,900.92
112	374	Hwaseong	Byeongjeom-ri	Middle	Unranked_Upland	9279		3		7	58.0	548.19	5,060.63
114	382	Hwaseong	Bansong-ri 2	Middle	Unranked_Upland	790		1		1	51.0	603.78	6,690.58
116	387	Hwaseong	Dongo-ri	Middle	Upland_Good	9836				2	97.0	503.21	3,626.03
213	679	Yeoncheon	Wondang 3 ri	Middle	Upland_Good	2037				1	19.0	66.59	440.57
216	684	Suwon	Ha-dong	Middle	Upland_Good	373				1	43.0	199.76	13,073.00
156	507	Anseong	Seungdu-ri	Middle	Upland_Poor	4939		1		1	34.0	198.52	2,374.92
					Average	5830.5					63.6	380.4	6,667.0
					Standard deviation	5071.2					25.0	240.8	4630.0
					Median	5369.0					64.0	377.3	4,535.9
					Interquartile range	8489.0					36.0	349.7	7439.1

Site_Code	Do_Site_ID	Town	Village	Period	Class_2	Visible	Table	Capstone	Menhir	Do_Site_No_2	elevation	mpf_sc_sh_100	mpf_sc_sh_100_75
52	173	Guri	Inchang-dong 1	Late	Upland_Poor	9984		1		7	34.0	323.17	1,060.05
53	180	Guri	Inchang-dong 2	Late	Rice_Poor	9065		1		2	33.0	221.96	844.60
54	182	Guri	Gyomun-dong	Late	Limited_Upland	2227		1		3	41.0	66.59	1,867.73
56	188	Namyangju	Gaun-dong 1	Late	Limited_Upland	2689				1	30.0	332.93	1,132.84
					Average	5991.3					34.5	236.16	1,226.3
					Standard deviation	4101.4					4.7	123.7	444.8
					Median	5877.0					33.5	272.6	1,096.5
					Interquartile range	6721.8					3.5	142.5	310.4

Appendix 19

SETTLEMENT LOCATIONS (RIVER VS. INLAND) AND MONUMENT NUMBERS WITHIN A 1 KM AND A 5 KM EUCLIDEAN BUFFERS AND SITE CATCHMENT ADJUSTED FOR ENERGY EXPENDITURE

Site_Code	Town	Village	Period	River vs. Inland	Monu_sc_No_1km_Buffer	1km_Site catchment_mpf_sc_No	Monu_sc_No_5km_Buffer	5km_Site catchment_mpf_sc_No
2	Paju	Dayulri	Early	Han river	2	4	4	27
3	Paju	Okseokri	Early	Han river	2	2	5	17
4	Paju	Gyohari	Early	Han river	1	1	4	36
10	Gunpo	Daemiyadong	Early		1	2	6	5
20	Yongin	Bongmyongri	Early	Anseong river	0	0	1	9
23	Seoul	Yeoksamdong	Early	Han river	0	0	4	24
47	Hanam	Deokpungdong	Early	Han river	0	1	3	56

Site_Code	Town	Village	Period	River vs. Inland	Monu_sc_No_1km_Buffer	1km_Site catchment_mpf_sc_No	Monu_sc_No_5km_Buffer	5km_Site catchment_mpf_sc_No
1	Yeoncheon	Samgeori	Early to Middle	Injin river	1	2	5	2
9	Siheung	Gyesudong	Early to Middle		0	0	1	2
11	Anyang	Guanyangdong	Early to Middle		0	1	4	5
13	Hwaseong	Cheonjeonri	Early to Middle		0	0	3	13
14	Hwaseong	Donghaksan	Early to Middle		0	0	6	6
17	Pyeongtaek	Jijedong	Early to Middle	Anseong river	0	0	3	12
18	Pyeongtaek	Hyeonhwari	Early to Middle		0	0	1	1
19	Pyeongtaek	Hyeongokri	Early to Middle	Anseong river	0	0	1	7
31	Yangpeong	Yangsuri	Early to Middle	Han river	1	12	2	38
44	Incheon	Dongyangdong	Early to Middle	Han river	0	1	0	40
45	Hanam	Mangwoldong	Early to Middle	Han river	0	11	2	60
54	Uiwang	Idong	Early to Middle		2	2	11	9

Site_Code	Town	Village	Period	River vs. Inland	Monu_sc_No_1km_Buffer	1km_Site catchment_mpf_sc_No	Monu_sc_No_5km_Buffer	5km_Site catchment_mpf_sc_No
5	Ganghwa	Samgeori	Early to Late		0	0	6	4
7	Incheon	Wondangdong	Early to Late	Han river	0	0	5	48
12	Hwaseong	Gogeumsan	Early to Late		0	0	5	6
21	Yongin	Jukjeon	Early to Late		0	0	3	1
27	Hanam	Misari	Early to Late	Han river	0	18	1	56
28	Yeoju	Heunamri	Early to Late		0	0	0	2
29	Gapyeong	Daljeonri	Early to Late		0	0	1	2
46	Hanam	Mangwoldong	Early to Late	Han river	0	17	3	55
77	Gwangmyeong	Gahakdong	Early to Late		1	4	7	5

Site_Code	Town	Village	Period	River vs. Inland	Monu_sc_No_1km_Buffer	1km_Site catchment_mpf_sc_No	Monu_sc_No_5km_Buffer	5km_Site catchment_mpf_sc_No
16	Suwon	Imokdong	Middle		0	0	5	4
22	Seoul	Garakdong	Middle	Han river	0	6	2	64
48	Hanam	Deokpungdong	Middle	Han river	0	0	3	27
60	Hwaseong	Banwoldong	Middle		0	0	3	15
61	Hwaseong	Bansongdong	Middle		0	0	7	11
64	Hwaseong	Gajaeri	Middle		0	0	4	0
68	Pyeongtaek	Bangchukri	Middle	Anseong river	0	0	0	8
75	Paju	Sikhyeonri	Middle	Imjin river	0	0	1	1

Site_Code	Town	Village	Period	River vs. Inland	Monu_sc_No_1km_Buffer	1km_Site catchment_mpf_sc_No	Monu_sc_No_5km_Buffer	5km_Site catchment_mpf_sc_No
8	Bucheon	Gogangdong	Middle to late		0	0	1	1
15	Suwon	Yuljeondong	Middle to late		0	0	7	4
30	Gapyeong	Daeseongri	Middle to late	Han river	0	3	1	21
72	Anseong	Banjaeri	Middle to late		0	0	4	2
76	Osan	Gajangdong	Middle to late		0	0	12	8

Site_Code	Town	Village	Period	River vs. Inland	Monu_sc_No_1km_Buffer	1km_Site catchment_mpf_sc_No	Monu_sc_No_5km_Buffer	5km_Site catchment_mpf_sc_No
6	Incheon	Geumdandong	Late		0	0	8	2
24	Seoul	Myongildong	Late	Han river	0	2	6	62
25	Seoul	Ilwondong	Late		0	0	5	0
26	Namyangju	Suseokri	Late	Han river	1	2	5	54

Appendix 20

House shape numbers in settlement sites

Site_ Code	Town	Village	Site_ District	Period	Thin -rectangular	Rectangular	Square	Oval	Circle	Irregular	Unknown	Total	House_ No.	Enclosure
2	Paju	Dayulri		Early	1							1	1	
3	Paju	Okseokri		Early	1							1	1	
4	Paju	Gyohari		Early	1						1	2	2	
10	Gunpo	Daemiyadong		Early	1								1	
20	Yongin	Bongmyongri		Early	1							1	1	
23	Seoul	Yeoksamdong		Early	1							1	1	
47	Hanam	Deokpungdong	Surigol	Early		1					1	2	2	
1	Yeoncheon	Samgeori		Early to Middle	1	1	0				1	3	3	
9	Siheung	Gyesudong		Early to Middle	1		2				1	4	4	
11	Anyang	Guanyangdong		Early to Middle	3	4					1	8	8	
13	Hwaseong	Cheonjeonri	I	Early to Middle	4	3					6	13	13	
14	Hwaseong	Donghaksan		Early to Middle	10	6	3				13	32	32	Y
17	Pyeongtaek	Jijedong		Early to Middle		1	2				3	6	5	
18	Pyeongtaek	Hyeonhwari		Early to Middle	1	3	1					5	6	
19	Pyeongtaek	Hyeongokri	I	Early to Middle	14	5	10		2	1	2	34	34	
31	Yangpeong	Yangsuri		Early to Middle	1		1					2	2	
44	Incheon	Dongyangdong		Early to Middle		1	1				1		3	
45	Hanam	Mangwoldong		Early to Middle	1							1	4	
54	Uiwang	Idong		Early to Middle	1	7	1					9	13	
5	Ganghwa	Samgeori		Early to Late							1	1	1	
7	Incheon	Wondangdong		Early to Late	1							1	1	
12	Hwaseong	Gogeumsan		Early to Late	1						1	2	2	
21	Yongin	Jukjeon		Early to Late	3	1					1	5	5	
27	Hanam	Misari		Early to Late	9	15	12				2	35	38	
28	Yeoju	Heunamri		Early to Late	3	9	2						14	

Site_ Code	Town	Village	Site_ District	Period	Thin -rectangular	Rectangular	Square	Oval	Circle	Irregular	Unknown	Total	House_ No.	Enclosure
29	Gapyeong	Daljeonri		Early to Late	2	10	21	1	1		7	42	42	
46	Hanam	Mangwoldong	Gusan	Early to Late									1	
77	Gwangmyeong	Gahakdong		Early to Late									1	
16	Suwon	Imokdong		Middle			1				1	2	2	
22	Seoul	Garakdong		Middle			1					1	1	
48	Hanam	Deokpungdong	Ritual site	Middle		1						1	1	Ritual site
60	Hwaseong	Banwoldong		Middle			1						1	
61	Hwaseong	Bansongdong		Middle		1	12				1	14	14	
64	Hwaseong	Gajaeri		Middle			2					2	2	
68	Pyeongtaek	Bangchukri		Middle		1	3					4	4	
75	Paju	Sikhyeonri		Middle			1						1	
8	Bucheon	Gogangdong		Middle to Late	9	7					5	21	21	Y
15	Suwon	Yuljeondong		Middle to Late	1 (Round corner)						2	3	8	Y
30	Gapyeong	Daeseongri		Middle to Late		2 (1-Round corner)						2	2	
72	Anseong	Banjaeri		Middle to Late									9	Y
76	Osan	Gajangdong		Middle to Late		1	1				1	3	3	Y
6	Incheon	Geumdandong		Late							1	1	1	
24	Seoul	Myongildong		Late							1	1	1	
25	Seoul	Ilwondong		Late		1						1	1	
26	Namyangju	Suseokri		Late			4 (Round corner)				2	6	6	

Appendix 21

Volumes of table and capstone type dolmens Early Bronze Age

Site_Code	Do_Site_ID	Do_Site_No	Aspect	Aspect_num	Monu_Type	Capstone_L	Capstone_W	Capstone_D	Volume
16	38	1	Southeast	4	Table	180	120	25	5400
16	39	2	Southeast	4	Table	170	120	40	8160
16	41	4	Southeast	4	Table	330	120	50	19800
16	43	6	Southeast	4	Table	210	160	30	10080
16	46	9	Southeast	4	Table	260	180	30	14040
16	48	11	Southeast	4	Table	220	160	40	14080
16	49	12	Southeast	4	Table	180	160	45	12960
21	86	15	Southeast	4	Table	230	220	50	25300
21	90	19	Southeast	4	Table	298	268	36	28751.04
21	93	22	Southeast	4	Table	160	150		
21	96	25	Southeast	4	Table	237	187	60	26591.4
23	112	1	Northeast	2	Table	270			
104	357	2	South	5	Table	245	200	50	24500
								Average	17242.0
								Standard deviation	8103.2
								Median	14080
								Interquartile range	13380

Site_Code	Do_Site_ID	Do_Site_No	Aspect	Aspect_num	Monu_Type	Capstone_L	Capstone_W	Capstone_D	Volume
15	35	1	South	5	Capstone	220	120	40	10560
15	36	2	South	5	Capstone	220	150	60	19800
15	37	3	South	5	Capstone	180	80	50	7200
16	45	8	Southeast	4	Capstone	210	160	40	13440
16	47	10	Southeast	4	Capstone	200	110	40	8800
17	52	1	Northeast	2	Capstone	170	120	15	3060

Site_Code	Do_Site_ID	Do_Site_No	Aspect	Aspect_num	Monu_Type	Capstone_L	Capstone_W	Capstone_D	Volume
17	53	2	Northeast	2	Capstone	225	220	60	29700
17	54	3	Northeast	2	Capstone	270	180	70	34020
17	55	4	Northeast	2	Capstone	220	150	80	26400
17	58	7	Northeast	2	Capstone	180	106	27	5151.6
17	59	8	Northeast	2	Capstone	237	120	24	6825.6
17	60	9	Northeast	2	Capstone	230	120	35	9660
17	61	10	Northeast	2	Capstone	260	170	60	26520
18	62	1	East	3	Capstone	278	164	13	5926.96
21	97	26	Southeast	4	Capstone	241	189	46	20952.54
21	82	11	Southeast	4	Capstone	190	159	48	14500.8
21	72	1	Southeast	4	Capstone	380	276	60	62928
21	73	2	Southeast	4	Capstone	207	165	40	13662
21	74	3	Southeast	4	Capstone	210	110	48	11088
21	75	4	Southeast	4	Capstone	289	117	60	20287.8
17	58	7	Northeast	2	Capstone	180	106	27	5151.6
17	59	8	Northeast	2	Capstone	237	120	24	6825.6
17	60	9	Northeast	2	Capstone	230	120	35	9660
17	61	10	Northeast	2	Capstone	260	170	60	26520
18	62	1	East	3	Capstone	278	164	13	5926.96
21	97	26	Southeast	4	Capstone	241	189	46	20952.54
21	82	11	Southeast	4	Capstone	190	159	48	14500.8
21	72	1	Southeast	4	Capstone	380	276	60	62928
21	73	2	Southeast	4	Capstone	207	165	40	13662
21	74	3	Southeast	4	Capstone	210	110	48	11088
21	75	4	Southeast	4	Capstone	289	117	60	20287.8
21	78	7	Southeast	4	Capstone	193	104	47	9433.84
21	79	8	Southeast	4	Capstone	250	130	43	13975

Site_Code	Do_Site_ID	Do_Site_No	Aspect	Aspect_num	Monu_Type	Capstone_L	Capstone_W	Capstone_D	Volume
21	80	9	Southeast	4	Capstone	220	170	50	18700
21	81	10	Southeast	4	Capstone	180	135	42	10206
21	84	13	Southeast	4	Capstone	231	182	41	17237.22
21	85	14	Southeast	4	Capstone	263	229	22	13249.94
21	87	16	Southeast	4	Capstone	151	112	24	4058.88
21	88	17	Southeast	4	Capstone	206	141	24	6971.04
21	89	18	Southeast	4	Capstone	285	218	49	30443.7
21	91	20	Southeast	4	Capstone	385	294	52	58858.8
21	92	21	Southeast	4	Capstone	180	125	24	5400
21	94	23	Southeast	4	Capstone	330	250		
24	113	1	Northeast	2	Capstone	250	190	40	19000
24	114	2	Northeast	2	Capstone	170	105	50	8925
24	115	3	Northeast	2	Capstone	210	90	90	17010
24	116	4	Northeast	2	Capstone	160	145	92	21344
79	238	1	North	1	Capstone	220	150	85	28050
79	239	2	North	1	Capstone	200	100	50	10000
95	315	4	West	7	Capstone	185	155	25	7168.75
95	318	7	West	7	Capstone	150	85	35	4462.5
95	312	1	West	7	Capstone	200	105	27.5	5775
95	313	2	West	7	Capstone	340	250	35	29750
95	314	3	West	7	Capstone	174	110	35	6699
95	316	5	West	7	Capstone	205	190	25	9737.5
95	317	6	West	7	Capstone	180	130	35	8190
95	320	9	West	7	Capstone	170	110	32.5	6077.5
95	321	10	West	7	Capstone	370	290	45	48285
95	322	11	West	7	Capstone	75	50	17.5	656.25

Site_Code	Do_Site_ID	Do_Site_No	Aspect	Aspect_num	Monu_Type	Capstone_L	Capstone_W	Capstone_D	Volume
104	356	1	South	5	Capstone	640	430	220	605440
127	423	1	South	5	Capstone	305	200	65	39650
								Average	26879.0
								Standard deviation	77256.4
								Median	13345.0
								Interquartile range	13931.1

Site_Code	Do_Site_ID	Do_Site_No	Aspect	Aspect_num	Monu_Type	Capstone_L	Capstone_W	Capstone_D	Volume
147	476	1	West	7	Table	326	235	105	80440.5

MIDDLE BRONZE AGE

Site_Code	Do_Site_ID	Do_Site_No	Aspect	Aspect_num	Monu_Type	Capstone_L	Capstone_W	Capstone_D	Volume
106	362	4	Southwest	6	Capstone	280	260	70	50960
106	360	2	Southwest	6	Capstone	250	180		
107	364	1	West	7	Capstone	150	130	60	11700
109	369	4	South	5	Capstone	115	100	65	7475
111	373	2	Southwest	6	Capstone	256	148	66	25006.08
112	376	3	Southwest	6	Capstone	270	220	70	41580
112	377	4	Southwest	6	Capstone	160	150	40	9600
113	381	1	North	1	Capstone	293	148	40	17345.6
114	382	1	South	5	Capstone	160	113	40	7232
121	404	2	North	1	Capstone	170	140	46	10948
123	407	2	Southwest	6	Capstone	240	230	70	38640
123	406	1	Southwest	6	Capstone	420	300	127.5	160650
123	408	3	Southwest	6	Capstone	590	290	100	171100
123	409	4	Southwest	6	Capstone	210	140	40	11760

Site_Code	Do_Site_ID	Do_Site_No	Aspect	Aspect_num	Monu_Type	Capstone_L	Capstone_W	Capstone_D	Volume
123	411	6	Southwest	6	Capstone	194	150	20	5820
123	412	7	Southwest	6	Capstone	350	340	110	130900
123	413	8	Southwest	6	Capstone	480	370	100	177600
123	414	9	Southwest	6	Capstone	600	304	100	182400
123	415	10	Southwest	6	Capstone	305	255	92	71553
123	416	11	Southwest	6	Capstone	500	370	125	231250
156	507	1	Northeast	2	Capstone	480	120	90	51840
157	508	1	Southeast	4	Capstone	260	130	105	35490
158	509	1	South	5	Capstone	290	220	30	19140
								Average	66817.7
								Standard deviation	72075.5
								Median	37065.0
								Interquartile range	104348.3

LATE BRONZE AGE

Site_Code	Do_Site_ID	Do_Site_No	Aspect	Aspect_num	Monu_Type	Capstone_L	Capstone_W	Capstone_D	Volume
52	173	1	Southeast	4	Capstone	137	130	25	4452.5
52	175	3	Southeast	4	Capstone	170	170	80	23120
52	176	4	Southeast	4	Capstone	140	105	24	3528
52	177	5	Southeast	4	Capstone	194	130	26	6557.2
52	178	6	Southeast	4	Capstone	126	123	24	3719.52
52	179	7	Southeast	4	Capstone	164	110	40	7216
53	181	2	East	3	Capstone	255	110	80	22440
54	182	1	North	1	Capstone	130	123	30	4797
54	183	2	North	1	Capstone	184	107	52	10237.76
								Average	9563.1
								Standard deviation	7778.2
								Median	6557.2
								Interquartile range	5785.3

Capstone volume	m³	Early	Middle	Late
Table type	Average	17242.0	80440.5	
	Standard deviation	8103.2		
	Median	14080.0		
	Interquartile range	13380		
Capstone type	Average	26879.0	66817.7	9563.1
	Standard deviation	77256.4	72075.6	7778.2
	Median	13345.0	37065.0	6557.2
	Interquartile range	13931.1	104348.3	5785.3

Appendix 22

Settlement and monument sites in the 'Late' Bronze Age

Site_Code	Town	Village	Radiocarbon dating+Pottery	Class_2	Visible cell numbers	elevation	sps_sh_100	sps_sh_100_75	House_No.	Enclosure
6	Incheon	Geumdandong	Late	Upland_Poor	8357	47.0	443.91	4,154.60	1	
24	Seoul	Myongildong	Late	Related_Water	17675	56.0	502.23	502.23	1	
25	Seoul	Ilwondong	Late	Limited_Upland	47594	255.0	388.26	554.89	1	
26	Namyangju	Suseokri	Late	Limited_Upland	14858	76.0	221.96	480.16	6	
				Average	22121	108.5	389.09	1,422.97	2	
				Standard deviation	17424.5	98.4	120.7	1821.4	2.5	
				Median	16266.5	66.0	416.09	528.56	1	
				Interquartile range	11922.0	67.0	111.8	958.1	1	

Site_Code	Town	Village	Period	Class_2	Visible cell numbers	elevation	mpf_sc_sh_1000	mpf_sc_ sh_1000_17	Table	Capstone
52	Guri	Inchang-dong 1	Late	Upland_Poor	9984	34.0	323.17	1,060.05		1
53	Guri	Inchang-dong 2	Late	Rice_Poor	9065	33.0	221.96	844.60		1
54	Guri	Gyomun-dong	Late	Limited_Upland	2227	41.0	66.59	1,867.73		1
56	Namyangju	Gaun-dong 1	Late	Limited_Upland	2689	30.0	332.93	1,132.84		
				Average	5991.25	34.5	236.16	1,226.31		
				Standard deviation	4101.4	4.7	123.7	444.8		
				Median	5877.0	33.5	272.6	1,096.5		
				Interquartile range	6721.3	3.5	142.5	310.4		

IM, H. J. 2005. Development of Korean Neolithic Culture, Seoul: Hakyeon Publications (In Korean),.
WARD, G. K. & WILSON, S. R. 1978. Procedures for comparing and combining radiocarbon age determinations: a critique. Archaeometry, 20, 19-31.
YOUN, M., SONG, Y. M., KANG, J., KIM, J. C. & CHEOUN, M. K. 2007a. Seoul National University Accelerator Mass Spectrometry (SNU-AMS) Radiocarbon date list III. Radiocarbon, 49, 1387-1394.
YOUN, M., SONG, Y. M., KANG, J., KIM, J. C. & CHEOUN, M. K. 2007b. Seoul National University Accelerator Mass Spectrometry (SNU-AMS) Radiocarbon date list IV. Radiocarbon, 49, 1395-1402.

Lightning Source UK Ltd.
Milton Keynes UK
UKOW07f1559130617
303242UK00007B/28/P

9 781407 313511